Weaving the Threads of Life

René Devisch

Weaving the Threads of Life

The *Khita*
Gyn-Eco-Logical
Healing Cult
Among the
Yaka

The University
of Chicago Press
Chicago and London

René Devisch is professor of social anthropology at the Catholic Universities of Leuven and Louvain.

The University of Chicago Press, Chicago 60637
The University of Chicago Press, Ltd, London
© 1993 by The University of Chicago
All rights reserved. Published 1993
Printed in the United States of America
02 01 00 99 98 97 96 95 94 93   5 4 3 2 1

ISBN (cloth): 0-226-14361-9
ISBN (paper): 0-226-14362-7

Library of Congress Cataloging-in-Publication Data

Devisch, René, 1944–
  Weaving the threads of life : the Khita gyn-eco-logical healing cult among the Yaka / René Devisch
    p. cm.
  Based on the author's Se recréer femme. Chapters 2–3 and 1–7 have been expanded, and chapters 1, 4, and 8, the prologue, and epilogue are completely new.
  Includes bibliographical references and index.
  ISBN 0-226-14361-9. — ISBN 0-226-14362-7 (pbk.)
  1. Yaka (African people)—Medicine.—2. Yaka (African people)—Rites and ceremonies.—3. Cults—Zaire—Kinshasa.—4. Traditional medicine—Zaire—Kinshasa. 5. Infertility, Female—Zaire—Kinshasa. I. Devisch, René, 1944– Se recréer femme. II. Title.
DT650.B38D475   1993

⊚ The paper used in this publication meets the minimum requirements of the American National Standard for Infomation Sciences—Permanence of Paper for Printed Library Materials, ANSI Z39.48-1984.

*For 'Maama Maria'
Oswald, Jeroen, and Elisabeth
co-creators of this work*

Contents

	Acknowledgments	ix
	Prologue	1
1	**Field and Method**	**11**
	1.1 The Yaka People 11	
	1.2 Fieldwork 20	
	1.3 Bantu Cults of Affliction 23	
	1.4 Healers in the Town 25	
	1.5 Healing as a Social and Theatrical Drama: A Critique 33	
	1.6 Body and Weave: A Semantic-Praxilogical Approach 37	
2	**The Cosmology of Gender Arrangements and Life Transmission**	**53**
	2.1 Horizontal and Vertical Space 54	
	2.2 Cosmological Portrayal of Gender 60	
	2.3 Animals and Plants 74	
	2.4 Capturing and 'Cooking' Untamed Forces 86	
3	**The Social Formation of Life Transmission**	**92**
	3.1 Life-bearing and Nurturing in the Homestead 93	
	3.2 Marriage as a Transfer "Along the Path to the Village" 101	
	3.3 The Reproductive Cell 106	
	3.4 The Two-forked Tree of Agnatic Descent and Uterine Filiation 115	
	3.5 Hunting versus Sorcery, and the Fabric of Kin 122	
4	**Body, Group, and Life-world: Between Maze and Weave**	**132**
	4.1 Physical and Sensory Modes of Contact 134	
	4.2 The Relational Body 139	

Contents

4.3 The Body and Its Afflictions 146
4.4 Cults of Affliction and Communal Sodalities 147

5 Impediments to Life Transmission **161**
5.1 Masculinist Views on Human Agencies in Infertility 164
5.2 Divinatory Etiology and the Work of Cults 169
5.3 Etiology as an Indication of Therapy 173

6 The *Khita* Fertility Cult: Reversing the Evil **179**
6.1 *Khita* and Similar Cults 180
6.2 The First Stage: Reversing the Persecution into Uterine Bonds of Life Transmission 183
6.3 The Second Stage: The Decay and Cooking of Generative Forces 196

7 The *Khita* Fertility Cult: Reorigination of the Fabric of Body, Kin, and Life-world **213**
7.1 The Third Stage: Seclusion in the Uterus of the World 214
7.2 The Fourth Stage: Emancipating Forest Forces into Social Fecundity 224
7.3 Relapse of Illness 244
7.4 Fertility Rituals and Analyses Compared: A Look at Victor Turner 245

8 The Body as the Weaving Loom of Healing and Life **255**
8.1 The Role of Music and Dance in Healing 259
8.2 The Source of Healing 264
8.3 Paradox, Transgression, and Homeopathic Healing 267
8.4 A Ternary Logic of Mediation and Effusion in Self-healing 276

Epilogue 282
Appendix A: A Case of Infertility 285
Appendix B: Herbarium 293
Maps 296
Notes 299
References 315
Index 325

Plates follow page 160

Acknowledgments

The present study stems from communal enthusiasm and shared exploration, notwithstanding my many disconcerting departures from the family, the hardships of the field, and the apparent paradoxes of a commitment to genuine encounter across boundaries in the wake of cultural decolonization.

My graduate studies at the University of Kinshasa in the late 1960s and early 1970s awakened in me a sense of effective solidarity. My research in Kinshasa and the southwestern part of the country was made possible by the support of the Institut de Recherche Scientifique en Afrique centrale and the Belgian National Fund for Scientific Research, in my capacity as Research Assistant and senior Research Assistant (1972–80), and, since 1987, through research funds of the last-named institution and the Commission of the European Communities DGXII/G4 STD2. A former French version of this study was completed in 1984 but has since been entirely revised and considerably expanded. I most cordially thank Peter Crossman for his translation of the expanded chapters 2, 3, 5, 6, and 7 from the French. Chapters 1, 4, and 8, as well as the prologue and epilogue, are completely new. My thanks to Richard Allen who has carefully edited the whole manuscript. In 1991–92, while enjoying a fellowship-in-residence at NIAS (the National Institute for Advanced Study in the Humanities and Social Sciences, Royal Netherlands Academy of Arts and Sciences, at Wassenaar), staff members and colleagues offered me the optimal 'rite of passage' conditions for my book's rebirth. I must explicitly express my cordial gratitude to Bruce Kapferer—a critical reader of the manuscript—and to Saskia Kersenboom, who have been most generous in amicably offering me many critical and very inspiring comments at a point when I was enmeshed in the data. I have profited from the help of colleagues at the Catholic University of Louvain (K.U. Leuven), Filip De Boeck, Wauthier de Mahieu, Karel Dobbelaere, and Eugeen Roosens. I have also valued the encouragement, remarks, or information supplied by numerous friends including Geert Achten, David Apter, Gilles Bibeau, Wim van Binsbergen, Claude Brodeur, Bumbakini Ekwalama, Jean Comaroff, Ellen Corin, Clémentine Faïk-Nzuji Madiya, John Janzen, Kasaamba Ulenguluka, Jaak Le Roy, Muyika Musungu, N-Soko Swa-Kabamba, Nzala Kianza, Piindi Bintumba, Jan Vansina, Bonno Thoden van Velzen, Jos Van de Loo, and Bart Vervaeck.

Many friends in Kinshasa—whose memories I cherish but all of whom I could not possibly name here—have generously extended their hospitality to me in their homes or parishes and have given the invaluable assistance of their institutions. My greatest debt, however, must be to the Elders, Diviners, Initiates, and Healers, and to the men and women, in Kinshasa and in the areas of Yitaanda and Yibwaati of northern Yaka land, who have honored me as their would-be son, René (the 'Re-born'), into their art of living and healing. I gained a very liberal access to Yaka healing skills and initiatory traditions from many, many elders, among whom I became very familiar with Kha Boondu, Kha Khuundzi, Maa Khiindzi, Maa Kubulu, Maa Kyuulu, Kha Leemba, Maa Lusuungu, Kha Mabisi, Kha Mahata, Kha Mahuungu, Maa M-mweela, Kha Mpaani, Kha Muzikita, Maa N-huumbu, Maa N-hwaadi, Kha N-koongu, Kha N-kiindzi, Kha N-loongi, Kha N-luma, Kha N-saka, Maa N-seenga, Kha Taanda, Kha Tsakala, Maa Tseembu, Kha Yaambvu, Maa Yihoonda, Maa Yikalala, Kha Yikoomba, Maa Yilaanda, Maa Yilandana, Kha Yileenda, Maa Yimbaandzya, and Maa Yiphandulu. I thank them all profoundly. I endeavor to open up the deep dialogue I am engaged in with Yaka elders to a wider authority. It is my hope that the use of a language alien to them does not preclude our joint venture and locus of exchange that, paradoxically, cannot be defined in space and should not dissipate through my engagement in a more fundamental level of discourse. May we continue to apprentice ourselves in the productive weave and folds that embrace and empower us all together, hence driving us to surpass the limits of our webs.

The present book on life-giving is the complement to a former one on death and funeral (1979). *The Oracle of Maama Tseembu,* a film produced in collaboration with Dirk Dumon (1992), is a vital adjunct to this book.

Prologue

Il n'y a pas un lieu que le pouvoir ne s'applique à gagner, mais il n'est pas un lieu qui définitivement lui soit acquis. . . . Là où la vie vient, là où elle donne, du côté du rire et de la peine, de la ferveur et de la colère, du côté des hommes qui s'aiment d'être ensemble, du côté de la joie et de l'intelligence, le pouvoir n'est pas. . . . La jouissance n'est pas transgression de la loi, ou complice du pouvoir, elle est affirmation insolente de vivre . . . du fond de l'obscure matrice où le pouvoir n'est pas entré.
                                    Annie Leclerc, Epousailles (1976:7–12)

Healing cults in Yaka society in the southwest of Zaire, performed as they are at the margins of established order, unveil and grasp forces and signs very much beyond the level of the spoken word and representational thought. The healing performance is a sensuous praxis in which the body opens itself up to the uterine and basic source of life. Healing awakens and frees the primordial virtualities of things and beings: it is essentially a rhythm and a vitalizing resonance in and between the body, family, and life-world, that is, the surrounding world as fashioned in daily, and culturally conditioned, practice. It is the rhythm that aids the senses in their quest to unfold things and beings into their origin-al shape and force, and into a multilayered interweave of forces and issues. Healing cults—there are some twenty of them—reshape and revivify the social and cultural order by tapping a source beyond the coercive order of tradition. The latter is represented by the elders, who through rhetoric and authoritative speech, in council and judicial assembly, reassert relations of power and pursue the continuity of tradition.

Yaka culture, oral and nonliterate, has not been drawn into the "grands récits" of modernity (Lyotard 1979). Here, interaction with the world is not one of representation through the imposition of detached vision and reason, of technological mastery and emancipatory progress. The cults of affliction, held at the fringe of public life, are concerned with the passionate presencing and regeneration of the life-world and social order. In contrast, communal cults and the councils of elders, in the center of the public domain, tend to grasp the world in a production of the word, in legitimating discourse, which however is not as yet a project of a totalizing representation and a capturing objectification by the gaze.

While studying in particular the *khita* healing cult, my focus is on 'gyn-ecology' in a broad sense, that is, on the life-bearing functions pertaining to the woman, the house, and the inhabited world. It is not on the experiencing subject in 'obstetrical care'—how could I know?—but on the cultural constitution and modalities of the role of sickness, of feeling ill and of healing, in particular as these are at play in the *khita* healing cult among rural and urban Yaka. For major treatment, townsmen return to their village of origin to renew the 'weave of life,' namely, their umbilical ties with their maternal forebears and with the uterine source of life. It is only in this natal ecological niche that they tap from *ngoongu:* the earthly, primal source of all life-bearing. My method of writing about this reality will try to embrace the form of the healing practice and to unravel the very alchemy of healing. It is my feeling that in order to outgrow an all too western scholarly credo and masculine field of vision, my anthropological writings and audiovisual productions ought somehow to render the sensuous styles of producing and sharing experience and of empowerment among the people who adopted me. In tune with this I favor an ethnography that "urges a moral and aesthetic practice. . . , one that gets you closer to those you study at the risk of going native and never returning; it is hoped, at least, that you will not again embrace the received assumptions with which you, inheriting your academic texts, methods, and corporate academic culture, began" (Rose 1990:12).

Indeed, my experience with Yaka people has led me away from current postmodern trends that aim at a self-conscious, narrative account of a dialogical or bargained reality. Fundamentally, my perspective does not involve a rendition of a dialogical encounter as such with Yaka people, nor of their experience—I am not speaking for them—but aims more radically at disclosing the 'bodily' ways in which people create and engage in a culture from within its own genuine sources. Yet surely, since I write at some physical and cultural remove from them, I portray processed visions of their world. Indeed, while my assumptions and questions in the field may sometimes be at odds with those of my hosts, we both firmly believe in the reality and probity of our affective and intellectual ventures (cf. Boddy 1989:356ff.). I do consider my ethnographic endeavor very much as an esthetic and moral experience, grounded in participant observation or rather observational participation, and reciprocal sympathy, friendship. To overcome the traps of prejudiced interactions of a colonial and missionary type I opted for an intensive participation in the daily life scene and activities of the Yaka. In the village setting, my attempt was to adopt a status of full membership, not that of a visitor or a guest. Most of my contacts and information dealt with the worlds of oral lore, kinship, hunting, the councils of elders, divinatory seances, the initiatory and healing dramas, and the cosmology. These have increasingly become the scenes of our joint ventures, of both a passionate, affective, and intellectual nature. My very presence and particular interests undoubtedly have changed or obscured parts of reality, but as yet I am unable to systematically sort out these biases either in the field or in my writing.

I take generous friendship and self-critical participation, and more importantly my commitment to mediating between worlds, to be the legitimation for my somehow intrusive presence in Yaka society and my unfamiliar questions. I see respect, genuine sympathy, participation, and associative dialogue as the golden means to acquaintance from inside the culture, that is, to "knowledge through transcendence of the self in the other," as Janice Boddy (1989:358) has put it. Indeed, this kind of gnosis or search and inquiry through acquaintance with someone (cf. Mudimbe 1988:ix) includes also a very Yaka perspective on knowledge gained and shared through sociality. I should not like to give undue stress to my biasing influence on their information and reality, except of course in view of the fact that my questions and perspectives are to a large extent dictated by my concerns, not theirs. As a man, I had no unbiased entry to the female life-world, but I might have a sense of it through the experience that my wife Maria conveyed to me, as we shared the last four months of field work, as well as through my acquaintance with the healing cults. Yet I venture to say that I am making major dimensions of Yaka culture accessible within the framework of its own arrangements, within the terms of its own epistemological locus (cf. Mudimbe 1988:x). In early 1991, I returned for the first time after seventeen years to the village of Yitaanda, where I had lived for more than two and a half years in the early 1970s. It was a gratifying experience that I still had the same very familiar place in the group and a privileged status of great confidence.

Indeed, I use the word *culture* with hope (cf. Frankenberg 1988). By stressing the creative work of culture and the healing capacity of the cults, I do not, however, wish to overestimate their therapeutic efficacy or to embellish the picture, knowing full well that Yaka people are in desperate medical need with regard to a number of infectious diseases and incapacitating dysfunctions. In the 1970s, people in Yitaanda and the surrounding area, like most people today in the entire Kwaango basin, had almost no access to doctors, dispensaries, or drugs in proper dosages, except in one mission hospital and a few mission dispensaries. Nonetheless, my focus is to recognize the important therapeutic resources in the culture. In these small, lineage-based communities, contact with a cash economy—principally through migrant labor—does not deeply affect body symbolism or uproot the core institutions regarding gender roles, descent, filiation, political hierarchy, mediumistic divination, and a number of healing cults. Family elders, who are eager to have their share in the produce of the younger generation, may manipulate and hence vitiate ritual practices and rhetorics as an arena of mere mystification and imposition. In the domain of healing, however, culture acts as a highly embodied resource of creativity. The human body, cosmos, and kin are the keen partners in people's world construction, which is not of writing or co-operating in a technology of curing.

My focus is not primarily on public diurnal life, but on healing at the fringe of established order. Elders, diviners, and healers have forcefully initiated me in their world of intensive, esthetic and moral exploration into the opaque layers of the imaginary register and into the multilayered fabric of symbols and acknowledged intersubjective structures.[1] They have conveyed to me an eagerness to capture its often elusive signs and forces in the daily encounter and the life-world, offering ever new and renewed virtualities of meaning and empowering. Symbolic (re)production and the concomitant recycling of forces constitute the crux of senior men's almost daily endeavor. For example, on opening a council of elders, a pair of senior men solemnly proclaim, dancing all the while to the rhythm of their clapping hands: *Thuna ha muyidika maambu,* "We are here to generate things." Their rhetorics are mostly of a metaphoric kind, and may culminate in a melodious song. Ritual drama is even more creative and body-centered. Healing ritual develops a bodily, sensuous, motoric, affective, and musical approach to the life-world. It is not a deciphering of a message, nor a recollection or commemoration. Healing ritual aims at emancipating the initiate's destiny, that is, at clearing and enhancing lines of force in the wider weave of family and life-world of his or her genuine history. Such experiences led me away from regarding culture as a mere text or program. I became acquainted with the Yaka view of culture as a fabric, a patterning of continual (re)generation: culture is present in its creation rather than in its statics—a very postmodern position with which I am in agreement. It inspires or molds the healing drama as a womb-like regeneration of meaning and forces in the patient, therapy managing group, and the life-world. The healing drama is the texture that engenders new meaning, new relationships, renewed contact with the life source to reinforce the patient, while reasserting the basic rule of exchange (matrimonial, avuncular, and so on) that transmits life and sustains ritual rebirth.

My participant endeavor nevertheless has its due limits, as I am a man, educated in a literate, Christian, and technological culture, and as my research was funded within the controlling articulation of the North with peoples of the South. Moreover, the interplay between ethnographic practice and the present text has been molded by recent methodological and theoretical developments in anthropology and semiotics (see 1.6.1). Further, since I am not writing in my mother tongue, Flemish, I lack the habitus to render my experience genuinely and affectionately. I therefore accept Crapanzano's (1990:307) somewhat overstated point that "the ethnographer is both in—implicated in—the reality he describes and out of that reality. His position in the text is perhaps isomorphic with his position in the field. It is moralized. An appropriate distance must be maintained—in the field (no sex, no leading questions, no arguments, no condescension) and in the text (no exoticizing, no eroticizing, no irony, no contestations, no constructions). And yet . . ."

I contend that my allegiance to the Yaka people makes my swirling field experience into a centered practice and effort committed to acquaintance and comprehension from within, in which no particular creation of social science or western medical understanding is taken as prior or determining, or as the principle to which all else must be reduced. Inasmuch as the interpretive method has grown out of the field experience and of the very nature of the healing practice, I consider it an internal approach with an emphasis on production of meaning and regeneration of forces: I have therefore coined it *semantic-praxiological*. My internal approach and emphasis on metaphoric, hence metamorphic production is meant to render the healer's and patient's genuine presence at, and presencing of, the heart and womb of Yaka culture. The healing culture does not consist so much of a body of knowledge and practices, but of an ongoing, basically self-generative practice. My account is meant to decipher the texture or intricate but vital weave of healing at a level that is self-generative and that reaches beyond its mere reproduction in the authoritative speech and institutions in the center of diurnal village life. Healing rituals divine a most original, wonderful, and practical insight into human reality and the world. While opening himself up to this source of culture, and 'transcribing' the metaphoric and imaginary fabric of healing, and transposing that deep level of Yaka culture, the anthropologist cannot avoid putting his assumptions at risk.

The anthropological endeavor I am engaged in moreover reaches beyond mere participant observation, beyond the neutral stance of the scientist. While working with the younger generation in the city of Kinshasa or in the rural area, the anthropologist may at times be caught up in the perverse effects of entrenched colonial European stereotypes of Black Africa. We may ask ourselves how to think about African people in terms which will not reduce them to otherness, to adversarial alterity. On the one hand, the anthropologist from the West may be trapped in the highly imaginary play of identity and alterity as polar images. Africanist anthropology may serve someone's search of his very imaginary complement—as it is created by the West's 'Invention of Africa' (Mudimbe 1988, Vansina 1985), of the exotic other (Corbey 1959, Fanon 1952, Miller 1985, Nederveen Pieterse 1990). A number of divergent strands in philosophy, religion, politics, economic theory, and in technology depict the West, within the narrative construct of evolutionary time, as a self-appointed vanguard of higher rationality and leadership in the adventure of progress. The

West presents itself with the book—both of linear writing and of the legacy of a salvational faith—that helps to imagine a higher future, yet a future made 'white.' Mass-media, in particular magazines, video clips, and hedonist tourist imagery, depict fantasy qualities which are the inverse of either an idealized or a problematic bourgeois self (see Jewsiewicki 1991).

On the other hand, these imaginary creations are thrown back at the field anthropologist from the ancient Metropole when he comes to participate in Kinshasa, and they may trap him in the position of estranged stranger. At times, he is paradoxically identified with the position of the adversarial other. He may be seen as a descendant of the former colonizer, and a representative of the hegemonic West, as a figure of both adversity and identification. And yet, the field anthropologist himself intends to study an authentic culture and, nostalgic as he may be to reproduce a tale of tradition, he is tempted to treat the colonial past as a parenthesis (Jewsiewicki 1991). In lines with Fanon (1952), or Jeddi and Harazallah (1985), the anthropologist may try to disentangle the very estranging strangeness that he or she is experiencing within a group of those who have assimilated the antinomic or alienating marks from the former colonizer and tried to integrate modernity, inasmuch as this is imagined as the world of higher power, higher life. The field anthropologist feels estranged by these fantasies to the extent that his hosts have introjected the imaginary 'Invention of Africa': these images seem to double the ideals regarding city life and higher school education with a feeling of alienness vis-à-vis the originary space. It is the 'village realm' as associated with the introjected missionary and colonial fantasies regarding paganism, sorcery in fact, the reverse side of the 'white' world. The ancestor, instead of being a source of filiation and identity, is perceived as persecutor, preventing the descendants inscription into the space of the other. Does the anthropologist, in reaction to this alienating mirroring, bring a nostalgic tale of tradition over against the defiled colonial portrayal? Is the anthropologist to heal the wounds of the colonial endeavor, or is he working from a sense of loss or nostalgia regarding a more authentic culture? Or does the anthropologist situate himself within a transitional or intermediate space between cultures that cannot be localized or monopolized, rather than reproducing the West's antinomic paradigms regarding we and the other, good and evil, high and low, pure and defiled, objective and subjective, science and romanticism, world religion and paganism, evolution and tradition?

Because the ethnographic encounter is highly moralized, the anthropologist offers a somewhat estheticized version of partial worlds. While seeking to remain open to another people's own rhythm, way, and sense of fellow feeling, the field anthropologist is often drawn into a dynamic of conflict and anger when initiated into life histories of division and suffering. Some of his dear friends from among various families or generations may be on opposing sides in the conflict. The anthropologist then witnesses the extent to which there may be a vicious recourse to parts of the rituals that he knows to be the very heart of the culture and people's life. Indeed, people may abuse tradition in order to subjugate it and produce mere oppression and subordination. As it may happen anywhere, the anthropologist is of course witness to double talk, to much greed and persecution, and to the selfish search for power and pleasure. All of these aspects are not dwelt on in this book. When, for a few years, in his anthropological endeavor he has shared the intimacy of the life in a village homestead and in suburbs of Kinshasa, attending councils and divinatory oracles, joining in dancing and communal drinking, resonant to passion and enthusiasm, witnessing offense and violence, he is forced to search beyond the obvious, to shift from what is happening to how and why, from event and what is told to process and to the deeper logic and forces underneath. Genuine involvement with elders, diviners, and healers forces him to reach beyond human motives and 'socio-logic,' and to discover, little by little, a more fundamental level of practice: the complex, ongoing, and subtle weave of culture, stemming from the wealth of the senses, the emotions, the body, in and between people and their life-world.

My immersion into Yaka life and its living world of symbols and vitalizations did not leave me untouched. It took me a decade to 'come back home' following my first extended sojourn among the Yaka people. I was able to reintegrate my own Flemish roots only when, fascinated by them, I applied myself to studying medieval Flemish culture and its later developments. A—so-called didactic—psychoanalysis enabled me to work through my ethnographic endeavor and to appropriate the influences that have changed me, thus reweaving my own inner world. Such a belonging to both the Flemish and Yaka cultures and its dynamics fosters insights and questions of a sort that are as yet still refractory to the discursive anthropological writing of the sort this book is engaged in. At this stage, I am not yet ready to self-critically disclose my participatory endeavor in the Yaka village of Yitaanda, my interplay with people, my involvement in everyday life—"part of the goings on in the village, immersed in its sights and smells and sounds" (Jackson 1989:7). The present study is aimed more at unraveling ongoing ritual praxis and the structural constituents of social life, rather than at narrating or 'in-scribing' contextual and initiatory experience and journeys of specific individuals, including myself.

Chapter 1 offers some general background on the Yaka people and on the research itself. I show how the Yaka healing cults are part of the widespread Bantu civilizational traditions, and how they evolve in the urban setting and in contact with biomedicine. Here, I define my approach in a confrontation with Victor Turner's view on Ndembu ritual, since the Yaka culture, with a similar history of Luunda hegemony, shares much in common with the Ndembu. The central argument of the chapter—and indeed of the book—is that the body is the generative source of symbolic, yet morphogenetic healing. It is followed by an outline of the semantic approach which has been adopted and my view of culture as a fabric in continual (re)generation.

From there I move, in chapter 2, to unraveling how the Yaka cosmology or worldview offers a complex matrix of core symbols and space-time arrangements that are constituent elements in the culture-bound experience of body, gender, and life transmission.

Chapter 3 describes how life transmission is a function of social reproduction in the realms of marriage, residence, agnatic descent, and uterine filiation.

Chapter 4 traces the process by which a resonance is brought about—and attuned, through the senses and on the level of boundaries and transactions—between the fields of body, family, and life-world. The concepts of the masculine and feminine person are not so much self-representational as procedural and embodied. From a sketchy outline of various Yaka perspectives on affliction, I move onto a presentation of the various Yaka cults of affliction and healing as distinct from the communal cults or sodalities.

Chapter 5 examines the divinatory etiology of chronic illnesses and incapacitating dysfunctions, gynecological illness in particular, and how patterns of illness prefigure the appropriate ritual treatment. Through interpreting the outcome of the divinatory consultation, the family makes crucial decisions on the type of healing to be organized and the healer to be invited.

Chapters 6 and 7 offer a sequential analysis of the *khita* 'gyn-eco-logical' cult healing. There is first the redressive intervention. It is dealt with in chapter 6. Having firmly reasserted the patient's position in the family web of matrimonial alliance and transmission of life through the line of mothers, the family elders invite the healer with gifts that acknowledge the fundamental assumptions of the cult and install him in full avuncular power over the patient. In his initial intervention, the healer frees the patient from the ill by reversing the persecutive forces at work in the kin group. Just before seclusion, the intense group celebration leads the patient through a cathartic trance in which she jointly and vividly experiences assault, mortal agony, and self-fecundation or autogeneration of a new identity. Chapter 7, then, focuses on the emancipatory action. The seclusion, that may last several weeks, develops a cosmogenetic drama of rebirth of the patient and her life-world. The analysis follows the patient and therapy managing group through a highly dramatized and sequential transformation of a set of affects, states, and meanings. The patient is led to embody these affects and bodily states inasmuch as she is merging with the cult-specific evocations of overlapping experiences regarding fermentation, self-fecundation (incubation), cooking, gestation (laying an egg), emergence from the water, and delivery (hatching out). Finally, the argument is hung on a confrontation with Victor Turner's analysis of the *nkula* and *nkang'a* female fertility cults among the Ndembu.

Chapter 8 examines a series of intricate questions regarding the subject or author in the ritual healing drama, the interplay of senses, forces, and speech, and regarding the source of and cultural inducements to self-healing.

1 Field and Method

1.1 The Yaka People

The Yaka form a dominant cultural presence in the southwestern part of the country on the southern savanna belt bordering Angola. Their culture and society have been forged out of a sustained interplay over many centuries of the Koongo, Luunda, and Tsaamba traditions (Plancquaert 1971; Piazza 1978; Vansina 1966:145–59; Yelengi 1986). They are widely known for their rich wooden artwork (Biebuyck 1985; Bourgeois 1984, 1985). Roosens (1971) provides an overview of their major political institutions and kinship organization. There are, however, few publications providing data from the last two decades.

Population estimates, for lack of censuses, are most tentative. The Yaka number half a million in the Kwaango area[1] and perhaps some 300,000 in the capital, Kinshasa.[2] Their relatively small villages, averaging from 50 to 200 inhabitants in separate hamlets, are dispersed across a very long plateau, between the parallel Kwaango and Waamba rivers, that reaches an altitude varying from 800 meters towards the north to 1,100 meters in the south. In most areas the population density does not exceed six persons per square kilometer. Hunting is the men's main productive activity, alongside of which they may be occupied in clearing parts of the forest to allow the women to grow staple foods, namely cassava, maize, sweet potatoes, and peanuts. There is little production for commerce.

In their social arrangements and cultural practices at the level of village life, the Yaka follow proper traditions that continue to exist within the framework of the Luunda hierarchical political system. On the village level, daily practices, beliefs, and healing traditions are relatively uniform or equivalent throughout the entire region and across political affiliations. All layers of society share a common language and modes of thought, core values, and rituals. Regarding their domestic traditions, in particular the Northern Yaka show moreover some influences from their Koongo neighbours to the northwest, while all owe the centralizing political hierarchy to the Luunda. Three centuries ago, Luunda conquerors imposed a unifying 'feudal' political structure throughout Kwaango land onto the segmentary lineages of the Yaka and the other so-called autochthonous groups. At the base of political hierarchy, the *kalaamba* or *bweeni* titleholders from the autochthonous enclaves of Hungana, Mbuundu, Ngoongu, Phiindi and Tsaamba have continued to exercise ownership of the land as they have done from the dawn of time. Several villages together constitute small, traditionally recognized, territories headed by a local chief. Above him stands a subregional vassal, and/or one of among a dozen Luunda paramount chiefs or dynasts in principalities extending over an area with a radius of some 50 kilometers. The most important of them is the sovereign Kyaambvu of Kasongo Luunda, who stands as primus inter pares. The Kyaambvu and the other paramount rulers head the dynastic lineages founded by those Luunda who, in the late seventeenth century (Plancquaert 1971:103–9; Reefe 1981; Struyf 1948; Vansina 1965:71–75), migrated from Koola, the Luunda nucleus of Nkalaanyi in the Shaba region in the southeast. The paramount chiefs define themselves to be the only direct descendants from Koola: *baana ba Koola*. This site is the cradle of the Luunda empire with the court of Mwaant Yaaf, the paramount Luunda dynast still in power (Hoover 1976). The reference to Koola is foundational, but for the people in Kwaango there is no direct practical contact.

Thus the Luunda have been politically dominant for the past three centuries. According to Van Roy's information (1988), obtained at the court of the former and present Kyaambvu, the Luunda conquerors were able to form a stable political center headed by the Kyaambvu in Middle Kwaango, and to subjugate the Yaka groups of the surrounding area as well as the even more autochthonous enclaves. The Luunda thereby founded a 'kingdom' on the higher reaches of the Kwaango river in Angola which is quite independent from the Luunda cradle in Shaba. The Kyaambvu, however, owes allegiance to the paramount Luunda chief, Mwaant Nzav, in the Kahemba zone of Southern Kwaango.[3] Before his installment, the Kyaambvu candidate awaits the consent and authentification of his dynastic filiation by Mwaant Nzav. Besides the Kyaambvu and the other regional dynasts, there are subregional governors who also claim Luunda descent from Koola, but through lines collateral to the dynastic lineages. They form a category of vassals, *biloola* or *tusyaala*, who set up tributary networks. The rapid territorial expansion and stability of Luunda rule has been based on the generalized use of perpetual kinship for the titleholders, as well as on dynastic families' policy of incorporating newly colonized villages through matrimonial alliances. Moreover, Luunda rulers do no dispossess local notables and traditional landowners; they are, rather, feared for their masterful and powerful use of words and superhuman power.

My study deals first and foremost with the Taanda territory and neighboring area in northern Kwaango land. Politically speaking, the local Yaka chief, Swa Taanda, exercises authority over a territory *(tsi, n-laambu)* of thirteen villages, and is himself subject to two different authorities: the Luunda regional dynast

Swa N-nene and, for the past decades, the Luunda vassal Swa N-saka as well. Chief Taanda is considered to be the most direct descendant, in the collateral lines of agnatic descent, from the founder of the dynasty, Swa Taanda Khapeela.

At the domestic level, the Taanda lineages display strong pre-Luunda traditions. The most senior descendant of Swa Khapeela, founder of the settlement of Yitaanda, honors his Yaka ancestors by building the *ndzo makhulu:* a miniature house sheltering forked stakes representing his ancestors of Yaka descent. Each stake 're-presents' the 'bone' of solidified seminal life force, *ngolu,* that the ancestor, from the time he has begotten his offspring, has transmitted to his descendants. But as a political titleholder in the Luunda hierarchy, during his reign chief Taanda exhibits the traditional Luunda emblems of rulership—such as the anvils, the copper and iron arm ring and ankle ring, and the double-edged and palm tree shaped sword of rulership (Devisch 1988)—and placates his ruling ancestors near the *bindzanda* shrine. This is a roofless rectangular enclosure of poles and dry leaves (signifying the chief's territory) around the ancestral *n-yoombu* trees planted at his enthronement. Not more than some seven to ten names of ruling ancestors are commemorated; that is, as many as define the genealogical ramification of the ruler's direct predecessors and heirs. Chief Taanda ritually controls the success of the collective hunt by propitiating his ancestors so that they bestow plenty of game upon their descendants, collects tribute from the hunt, and authorizes setting fire to the plains for the collective hunts during the dry season.

The relationships of opposition between lineage head and the centralizing Luunda power, or between the autochthonous and matrilineal landowning groups over against the Luunda(nized) ruler, are part of a much broader constellation of assumptions with regard to the origins of physical life versus social identity, blood ties via the mothers versus lineage relations based in agnatic descent of social identity. These presuppositions underpin the relationship of land *(n-totu)* versus territory or rule *(tsi),* which is analogous to that of the uterine life source and vital flow *(mooyi)* versus agnatic life force and social prestige *(ngolu),* or of the vital, soft or fleshy parts of the body that do not resist decay over against the hard bony parts that give the body erectile strength.

A chief is only a sovereign ruler in diurnal time and the village space by virtue of his counterpoising the nightly realms of sorcery and forest. And his own power is kept in balance too: the *lukhaanga* priest who initiates the ruler in the cult of paramount power impersonates a contraposition to the ruler. In the occurence of repeated cases of mortal disease and lasting misfortune in the chiefdom, the priest will be summoned to intervene. During the enthronement, while acting as the maternal uncle of the ruler-to-be, the priest exhorts the enthroned to respect the rules of 'alliance' that he now has established with this subjects and territory. It is believed that the *lukhaanga* priest can counter the chief's nighttime violence. In his turn the mediumistic diviner (see ch. 5) is another and yet even more effective counterpole of the chief, keeping the political and patriarchal order in some balance. In trance, in the clairvoyant sensing out and etiological divining of problems in the uterine life transmission, the mediumistic diviner's body witnesses to a deep ontological understanding and linkage of all with the uterine life source. The diviner does not enact the authoritative speech of tradition and power, but opens himself up to the body's and life's innermost way of being with others and in the world. To witness to the diviner's having completed his nine month of initiation, the chief should carry the diviner on his shoulders from the bush into the village.

Kwaangolese people are very much aware that order, health, and life stem from uniting or balancing out polar elements or values. Health and prosperity derive from the very branching out of the uterine line of life, on the one hand, and agnatic ties on the other. To bring out an asymmetry in this doubly unilineal descent, I am using the terms uterine filiation and agnatic descent.

Uterine filiation of physical life is reckoned within the span of at least two and more commonly four generations. As I will show in chapter 4, the Yaka hold that health, blood, vitality, and inborn capacities are passed on to the individual through maternity from a primal source of life via the mediation of mother, maternal grandmother, and great-grandmother. According to Roosens (1971:194–95), the Yaka of Middle Kwaango tend to merge uterine ascent with the agnatic forebears of one's mother's mother. Even more than mothers, brothers—namely, the maternal uncles—may channel this 'life source and lifeblood' to their sisters' children just as they may choke it off. To keep oneself in touch with this flow of vital blood from the uterine life source, a married man in particular should share the product of his work with his maternal uncles during any of the major moments of transition in the life-cycle: when children are born, undergo circumcision or marry, when returning home from Kinshasa or marrying, as well as when becoming a title-holder or undergoing a major initiation. The uterine life flow is also further manifested and transmitted through various natural elements that feed, restore, or signify vitality, such as cassava, some herbal medicines, and white kaolin clay.

Agnatic descent transmits social identity and membership in segmentary patrilineages: the 'house' is the basic social unit of kinship organization and patri-virilocal residence. Each corporate local patrilineage group makes up a relatively autonomous hamlet in a village. One's name and position in the kin group, in short the individual's social identity, are passed on through the agnatic line. Moreover, the patrilineal ancestors fructify the soil with their rains and populate the savanna and forest with game. It is the main duty of fathers and ritual elders to maintain the flow of sacrifices with their forebears, so that the latter may continuously reinvigorate the life force or potency in their descendants. Junior members in the patrilineage must show their respect toward family heads. By offering them valuables (European imports, such as belts, cloth, guns, gunpowder, salt, domestic animals, or armchairs), the juniors acknowledge how much the elders exercise full control over the life force in man and environment. The words of elders are empowering when they reenact tradition, that is, when words spoken long ago by the ancestors are reawakened to once again interweave ascendants and descendants, humans and their lifeworld. These words of power thereby establish order and link up with the agnatic life force. Only when elders have received the necessary gifts serving to arouse their own bodily strength are they willing to reaffirm the bonds linking the juniors with the ancestral life force: palm wine, the booty of the hunt, and cola nuts are all highly valued items in their exchange.

Colonial rule, in place from about 1910, weakened Luunda control by imposing alien masters on the Yaka people. The literature on the colonial and missionary endeavor and conquest in Kwaango land is not to be summarized here (see Bailleul 1959; Lamal 1965:297–306; Piazza 1978; Roosens 1971:19–29; Ruttenberg et al. 1967; Willame 1966, 1973). Colonialism as a threat to the survival of some groups and the culture, particularly the missionaries' attempt to undermine the healing cults and authority of the diviners, has not been dealt with in that literature. On their side, people recall the forced military recruitments for collective work, as well as the trade, the taxes, the benefits of school and medical—preventive and curative—care; the colonial repartitioning of the chiefdoms has led to disputes that are not all yet settled. People recall the names of those expatriate doctors, agronomists, missionaries, teachers, traders, and entrepreneurs who made common cause with villagers or chiefs. It is a most complex picture. And in lines with Vaughan (1991), I suspect that an in-depth study of the colonial period in Kwaango land would reveal as much about the collective fantasies of colonizer and missionaries as about the dynamics of Kwaangolese society and cultures.

Kwaango land has remained in the margins of techno-economic development, as motorized access from Kinshasa across the sandy plateaux, particularly in northern Kwaango, is difficult. The activities of colonial government, schools, and the medical and Christian institutions have not produced lasting or deep changes in Yaka kinship patterns, political institutions, and healing cults beyond the administrative, educational, or commercial centers in Kwaango. Most commercial and medical services have disappeared due to nationalization in 1970s and to disastrous inflation in the late 1980s. In large parts of Kwaango land, secondary school education, reliable medical care, and the elementary consumer imports (such as salt, sugar, tinned or dried fish, rice, soap, and paraffin) are now unavailable.

Migrations to town and back to the village are part of the life of young men. From about 1930 on many of the young men have been migrating from the Kwaango area to Kinshasa in order to procure consumer goods and accumulate the bride-wealth—at least for their first marriage—through casual wage labor and petty commerce. People conceive of their ties to and movements between city and village through the related categories of male and female, husband and wife, young and elder, individual and communal interest, forest and village, insubordinate and subordinate. In village talks among men, Kinshasa represents the male realm of individual freedom and abundance, achieved through ingenuity or good fortune, comparable to that of the forest of which the hunter and trapper is so immensely fond. However, in the conversations of Yaka urbanites, town and village seem to complement each other, as do husbands and wives. Indeed, for the Yaka, life without a marriage partner is unbearable, and in the many overcrowded houses in the suburbs, conjugal intimacy is almost impossible. A man's first wife, that is, the mother of his heirs, should ideally come from and remain in the village (Kalambay 1986–87). However, since the 1970s, an increasing number of young people prefer to settle in Kinshasa—although housing in the suburban towns often imposes living conditions below those of the village. The few senior men who migrate to Kinshasa maintain their first spouse with the younger children in the village while they found a second household in town. Yaka townsmen, like most other people in Kinshasa, tend to adopt the outlook, and to some extent the lifestyle, of the younger generations.

For Yaka townspeople, 'the village' of their origins in Kwaango land represents the world of the elders and of cults, and as such provides a topological framework for the idealized foundations of their existence and a unique base for Yaka identity in town. Notwithstanding the fears they feel towards the village realm, many young people do consider it as the ontological space where life, meaning, replenishment, and healing, but also life-threatening illness or misfortune, principally originate. Particularly in discourse related to marriage, descent, and the search for health and good luck, the village and especially the healing cults figure as a nurturing source from which people may draw time and again in order to refresh and reinvigorate all who tap it. In political and etiological discourse, the village represents the world of the elders. The village, not so much as a colonial invention but as a moral realm, unfolds the ancestral space-time order *(mu yitsi khulu)*, the legitimate order of moral values, empowerment, gender differences, gerontocratic social organization, coercion, and persecution. As such, 'the village of the elders' entails the coercive, both life-enhancing and -threatening use of charms and interaction with the ancestral shades and cult spirits. In the mind of the Kwaango immigrants in Kinshasa, the village also stands for lineage privileges, territorial affiliation, and ethnic identity: the reference to one's village of origin helps to define allegiances within the urban neighborhood. Moreover, in the present catastrophic recession and implosion of wage-earning, most townspeople are very much dependent on their good relationships with the village of origin for their economic, social, and psychological security. Young men purchase cassava in their villages of origin; they then hire their part in a truck that may come along once in two months. Back in Kinshasa, they sell the produce to women of their kin or region. Political titleholders, family heads, and many cult leaders do stay in the village, but their delegate—often an oldest son—moves back and forth between village and town for marriage arrangements, mortuary and purificatory rituals, collecting the elders' part from the junior descendants' income in town, and the like. In search of vigorous healing or cleansing from bad luck, townsmen will ultimately turn to their maternal uncles and a reputed healer "in the village," inasmuch as it evokes *ngoongu:* the "primal womb or source of life" ceaselessly renewing itself and reenergizing from the center of the earth, where rivers spring up along with all that grows and lives on the soil. The pregnant mother, the maternal uncle, and the healer may all tap from this source and uterine space for the benefit of family or client.

The ways in which the individual acquires both a social identity and individuality or uniqueness in Yaka society reflect the contrasts between public or diurnal village life and life at the interstices where one connects with *ngoongu*, the source of life (see 3.4 below). Social identity is acquired or bestowed on the individual in the center of diurnal and public village life, in particular through name-giving and the mastery both of language and of household or production skills, as well as through the ceremonies of marriage, chiefly enthronement, and funerals. Social identity may also be conferred through circumcision and initiation rites for the pubescent boys of a village, or negotiated in the competitive collective hunts, as well as through the acquisition of rhetorical skills in councils and judicial deliberations. All of these procedures mobilize social roles, publicly shared knowledge, the discourse of authority, and finally the sovereign 'super-vision' and control by the ruler. They are all means to empower (cf. *ngolu*) the subjects, the group, and their life-world.

Insofar as personal identity is concerned, the many healing cults (see 4.4) concentrate on the afflicted individual and in particular on his or her physical and uterine ties (cf. *mooyi*) with the life source. Illness is considered not so much as a mere process in the body alone but as stemming from a disturbance in the relationship between persons and their life-world. Illness is not in the last instance considered to reside within the individual, but derives from some disturbance in the relationship between persons themselves and/or between them and the life-world. Healing cults reshape the various bodily and sensorial ways in which an individual has contact with others, the life-world, the world of dreams, and with spirits and ancestral shades. At the edge of society and of public space—that is, in uterine space and a concentric space-time order of transition and cyclical renewal—healing cults lead the initiate through the motions of death, self-fecundation, and rebirth, simultaneously both on the corporeal level and on that of personal bonds with the kin group and life-world.

Ensorcellment and cursing are reckoned as the major source of illness and misfortune (see 3.5). Night and the gloom of the deep forest inspire popular imagination with images of the 'other world' of sorcery, licentious sexuality, and metamorphosis, where all conventional values and partitions mix or invert. The sorcerer is thought to be able to enhance his own life force through secretly intruding upon his close kin by means of clairvoyance. He then feeds himself by "eating" from his victim's life source. The intrusion leads to death only when the victim's maternal uncle is complicit. There are dozens of different types of ritual experts for the manufacture and manipulation of medicines and powerful objects *(n-kisi)* to protect, cure, and secure the unity of the house, or to enhance success in hunting, love, fertility, and hence to inflict misfortune and protect the sorcerer.

More pervasively, in the collective imagination the world of sorcery figures as an encompassing realm of heterogeneity, that is, of forces and signs which are beyond conventional order and control, and which can both reinvigorate and overthrow social allegiances and diurnal village life (see 2.4). Particularly at night in the period of the new moon, in the gloomy and luxuriating realm of the deep forest, or through the hunting of ferocious animals like the buffalo, the entire local society and life-world enter into a state of excitement and tap and gain power from the free-floating or imaginary registers of forces and potent signs. Through the medium of clairvoyance and the mixing of registers, sorcery seems to arouse and feed upon a totalizing and encompassing imaginary mode of apprehending people and the world. Its greed *(ndzala, kheni, yiphala)* must be continually tempered through the conventional rules of village daytime, kinship, and political allegiances.

In Kinshasa, Yaka divinatory and healing protocol tends to become simpler, less ritualized, and less kin-oriented; Yaka therapy is also requested by many non-Yaka clients. Healers are also solicited for problems that relate more directly to the cash economy, urban employment, and school education. The practice of Yaka divination and healing in the urban context tends to involve more speech—which may be very colloquial when the Lingala, the lingua franca, is employed—and ritual therefore loses much of its multilayered metaphorical resonance. In town, the herbalists engage increasingly in a trading relationship with their clients, giving in more easily than initiated healers to what I would term bricolage: they readily offer potions and instruments of luck intended to provide the consumer-client with sexual or economic success and social standing. In any case, traditional healers in the Yaka neighborhoods of Kinshasa share the same lifestyle and standard of living with their fellow people. The support of local community elders and the rapport among healers and in the cult groups seem to guarantee the initiated healers' professional ethics. In search of vital kinship support and treatment, particularly for reproductive and mental affliction, townspeople may return to the village. The patient will try to settle in a supportive domestic group, either in his or her village of birth or marriage, or in one of the uncles'. Weakened by the emigration of many active people, some households may be unable to offer care. Yet, lasting incapacitating dysfunctions like disability, barrenness, and insanity may leave the sick stranded without proper care.

In seeking by one means or another to withdraw or protect themselves from gerontocratic control, the younger generations may at times provocatively reject traditional healing cults and other customary practices and proclaim their allegiance to Christianity or to an independent spiritualist healing church. Many adherents openly say that the faith healing and empowerment obtained in the church and the watchful protection expected of the Holy Spirit act as a safeguard against the elders' sorcery and their demands for a share in the income. In some areas, these churches start as a prophetic witch-hunt movement whose aim it is to cleanse the village of all ritual paraphernalia and sorcery, or, as in Kinshasa, to purify the prayer group from all of Satan's machinations. Some of the charismatic leaders of these movements are genuine spiritual healers. They attract followers largely because of the urban traumas of social breakdown, psychopathological crisis, and vacuousness that come with the breaking of the roots of tradition or ties of family solidarity to support oneself, or with an inability to adapt oneself to a new social role and lifestyle. Escape from gerontocracy, unemployment, marital problems, disease, or some other misfortune may lead people to join a church, or even to adopt the lifestyle of the 'converted,' whether in the congregation or in the familial and public world. Converts acquire new identities by shedding something of themselves in favor of a new source of personal strength; conversion entails leaving behind a state of illness, misfortune, servility, error, or emptiness to enter a world of truth and light, a fraternal and protective community, in a word, a new world of positive metamorphosis. A great many of these churches are rooted in the Christian, Pentecostal, and particularly Kimbanguist traditions (MacGaffey 1983), or are inspired by the precepts and appeal of contemporary prophets (Devisch 1979:160–61; Roosens 1971:90–91). At the same time, they borrow heavily on the traditional images of evil drawn from sorcery, both employing the traditional forms of bodily expression and integrating trance and its abreaction patterns.

In the present context of severe socio-economic crisis and general breakdown of state institutions—called the villagization of town— and their disruptive effects on kinship solidarity and on gender and seniority relations, many prophets and healing churches act as purveyors of new forms of moral accountability. In their preaching and etiological assessment of ills and societal disorder, prophets suggest that the destiny of the individual is linked to the state of sin or of grace of all of God's people. Moreover, elders, diviners, healers, prophets in healing churches, and popular songs speak of the "disease of money" *(yimbeefu kya mboongu)*: they refer to the frustrations of contact with capitalism and the vices of possessive individualism when condemning the schools of privileged minorities, joblessness, great income inequality, inadequate housing, and hunger. Additionally, chaotic public affairs, displaced persons, the breakdown of family solidarity, the insubordination of youth, as well as AIDS—in sum, the experience of the contradictory social realities of capitalism and urbanization—are labelled "the diseases of the city, or the whites" *(malaadi maville, malaadi mamindedi)*. In late September 1991 and January 1992, I witnessed how, in widespread civil unrest and looting, people seemed to have aimed at cleansing the major cities from the grim ensorcellment of 'imperialist' technology from the North. In a kind of Jacquerie or Luddite eruption, many industrial complexes, enterprises, dispensaries, and businesses and houses of expatriates and notables were emptied or dismantled within a couple of days. People sought thereby to rid themselves of the grim social costs of economic growth, and hoped to unleash the conditions of self-determination and the cosmic power of regeneration. Sadly, for these people in despair, the whole impetus and source for revitalizing the diurnal order of urban society seems to stem from an imaginary order of "night and sorcery" (see 2.4).

1.2 Fieldwork

The ethnographic data dealt with in this study stem first from field research carried out between January 1972 and October 1974 among the Yaka of northern Kwaango. My sojourns of at least some six weeks annually, since 1986, among the Yaka population in Kinshasa (in Masina, Camp Luka-Ngaliema in particular, as well as in Kintambo, Ngaba, and Yolo) and, since 1991, in northern Kwaango land, mainly in the localities of Yitaanda and Yibwaati—a region of some 60 kilometers radius—have allowed me to complement and update my information.

In 1972, after a few weeks of progressively mixing with the people of the Yitaanda territory, I was given a double identity. I came to be considered as a reborn chief Taanda, namely N-leengi, who, in 1939, had been led into exile. Moreover, I appeared to them to be a good omen as I often reciprocated hospitality with the offer of first-aid medical treatment, an activity which throughout my stay took up an average of two hours a day. Perhaps reassured by this aid, my hosts came to domesticate somewhat the unprecedented and intrusive nature of my presence by ascribing to me a capacity to divert evil or danger. They first had perceived me as a sauf-conduit during a fatal thunderstorm one evening in late January 1972, when lightning set fire to the house of chief Taanda Kapata's successor, N-noongu. Kapata was alleged to have sent the lightning—it was the night preceding his death—in an attempt to kill his successor. Upon my arrival in the area at the beginning of January, chief Kapata had been in mortal agony, and I was solicited for medical help. Because of my association with Swa Kapata, people believed that he had reached his exceptionally old age in anticipation of my arrival. During a council following his burial, I became in some way assimilated with Kapata's predecessor. Surely unaware of the etymology of my first name—'René,' literally 'the reborn'—a delegate from the regional chief N-nene associated me in a kind of mythic narration with "Taanda N-leengi, reborn from death." The Belgian colonial administration had taken N-leengi into exile at Oshwe far away in the Kwilu region, some five days' walk eastward, where he had died upon arrival in 1939. He was accused of having participated in the anticolonial revolt of the *Bamvungi* prophetic movement. Somehow this position made my anthropological interest in the ancestral past of the Yaka appear as something genuine to the tradition. As I experienced things, this event initially added to my confusion in the field, and only later did it make sense when I discovered how one's biographical and genealogical pedigree can be redefined to conform to a consensus with regard to one's succession as titleholder.

The Taanda group of villages is situated some 160 kilometers by road to the southwest of Kenge and about 450 kilometers to the southeast of Kinshasa. A dispensary and some cash goods are at times available at the nearest parish centers of Kasiindzi, 70 kilometers to the northwest, or Yimbeela, some 60 kilometers to the south. Yimbeela boasts a school for training primary school teachers. The Taanda area is separated by the Waamba river from Mosaamba, some 40 kilometers to the east, which is the local and lowest level administrative center serving some hundred villages comprising the Taanda cluster. Several such centers together make up the zone of Kenge. The Taanda group includes thirteen villages totaling some 1,500 inhabitants. I had more or less frequent contacts with thirty-four other villages, which I could reach in less than one day's walk. As I lived most of the time in Yitaanda, the locality around chief Taanda's court, I quickly acquired an insight into daily life and at the same time learned the language by sharing as best I could in daily activities. The first months were spent establishing contacts and recording some 260 folktales, 35 songs, about 600 proverbs, the complex fields of kinship and genealogies, agricultural activities, flora and fauna. Unfamiliar as people were with photography, which they considered as "capturing their shadowy double," I delayed it till the end of my stay. I combined participant observation with lengthy conversations with the elders responsible for the preservation of the essential traditions. I had the opportunity to be present at diagnostic oracles—noting extensively more than 200 oracles—and to attend some fifty judicial councils. I repeatedly held lengthy conversations, at times using a grid of prepared questions and tape-recorder, with twenty-seven therapists individually during the first period, and with eight more in Kinshasa, later in the 1980s. I maintained intense contacts with five therapists in the village, and three of them in town, and witnessed the healing seclusion of some fifteen patients. I also collected information on disease classification, on illness career seen in the light of family histories, as well as on the curative powers attributed to a variety of plants and animals and specific medicinal recipes. Moreover, I asked the therapists to theorize about their art and core concepts. Further, I took care to check my observations and some of my tentative interpretations with some senior men and women with whom I became very familiar on an almost daily basis.

The data I have been able to gather on the various rites of circumcision (1972), mourning and funeral (1979), sorcery (1986), paramount rulership (1988), divination (1991a), and the healing (1991a, b) as well as the hunting cults, and the familial and judicial councils seem to me largely representative of the entire Northern Kwaango. Because all the data I am reporting stem from my own fieldwork, yet concur in fairly great detail with the observations of Huber (1956), Vorbichler (1957), and particularly with the abundant information of De Beir (1975a, b), it would be rather self-serving to cite the findings of these authors throughout my study. It was in the regional chiefdom of N-nene comprising the Taanda territory that Father De Beir and his catechists, between 1938 and 1945, collected the data published only thirty years later. I myself chose the Taanda area as the group I wanted to live with upon his advice, and because his writings could serve as a precious source for some diachronic comparison. When I met De Beir in October 1971, he portrayed the area as one in which the traditional healing cults had been very much kept alive and, politically speaking, as a fascinating in-between zone where the regional dynast N-nene and the subregional vassal N-saka were competing for control over chief Taanda. From accounts by Eugeen Roosens (1971) and Father Alain van der Beken (1978),[4] as well as from my own research in Kinshasa with Yaka emigrants from Middle Kwaango, I could gather much evidence of a profound cultural continuity between the Northern and Middle Kwaango peoples. Luunda titleholders are more prominent in Southern Kwaango, particularly in the area of Yiteenda, as are the accompanying cults (Plancquaert 1971). My recent sojourns in Kinshasa and Northern Kwaango allow me to say that traditional political structure and authority as well as divination and the major healing cults remain popular among Kwaangolese people.

My special interest in symbol and rite in fact derives from my perplexity regarding the strong hold of Yaka traditions: why have fifty years of 'development' efforts in the fields of trade, agriculture, medicine, education, and religion not brought about, as expected, more important changes in the principal sociocultural institutions of the Yaka? More specifically—and here I am indebted to the research of Eugeen Roosens (1965, 1971)—at the onset of my research I asked why cash crop production, animal husbandry, and petty trade all seemed to have disappeared within a few years of the departure of western technicians. Instead of accepting the moralizing and economic explanations provided by outsiders, I sought to investigate this problem of development from inside the core values of Yaka culture and society. This approach of course assumes a knowledge of the conceptions of the individual, society, and time, and of the social division of labor and its benefits, which govern the Yaka response to development initiatives.

Fieldwork allowed me to observe how, through ritual means, the senior men and elders, the holders of power and authority, confront and absorb the effects of contact with the technological and Christian world. They see to it that at least the meaning of the various practices in the fields of kinship, seniority, sharing, and etiology over which they preside remains linked to tradition, that is, grounded in the basic moral values. In the face of such resistance, the influences of western schooling, health care, missions, trade, and government have only been able to introduce very superficial and material changes into the customary milieu.

Because of the key role of ritual activity in the cognitive and moral issues of a group confronted with foreign technology and new material needs, I gradually focused my research on the ritual domain (*khita* therapy had as yet not been identified as the primary theme of my fieldwork). Indeed, ritual activity constitutes a single drama putting into question individual and group, past and present, tradition and innovation. This is why a knowledge of the hold exercised by rite on its participants appeared to me as a first step towards an internal approach to the modes of intercultural contact among the Yaka. It goes without saying that, because of its limits, such an investigation would not alone be able to furnish a valid explanation of the problem of technological development. But it should allow an insight into the ethnocentric, masculinist, energetic, and functionalist presuppositions which generally govern many a current approach to the question.

1.3 Bantu Cults of Affliction

To appreciate the importance of the gynecological *khita* healing cult, let me first sketch the wider African civilizational traditions (Janzen's expression: 1989) and Bantu cults of affliction of which the *khita* cult forms an integral part, only then raising some questions about its place in the modern urban setting.

Traditional medicine forms an important part of these civilizational traditions. In its attempts to revalorize traditional health practices, the World Health Organization (1976:3) has defined traditional medicine as "the sum total of all knowledge and practices, whether explicable or not, used in diagnosis, prevention and elimination of physical, mental or social imbalance and relying exclusively on practical experience and observation handed down from generation to generation." The term 'traditional' thus refers to a rootedness in civilizational traditions as well as to the predominantly oral means of transmitting *(tradere)* information, practices, and imagery in seeking or improving health within family or initiation group circuits. These traditions are nevertheless characterized by their capacity to invent, adapt, and incorporate elements from other cultures, despite their allochthonous nature. There are, moreover, the questions of the professionalization of healing and of controlling the issues affecting health and illness (Feierman 1985:114ff.).

African health and healing traditions, also called African medicine, are less ethnically based and fragmentary than has been alleged by colonial discourse. For their survival vis-à-vis the biomedicine[5] introduced by colonial power paired with the negative attitude toward popular healing by missionaries, healers cultivate secretness. Anthropologists and historians such as Chavunduka (1978), Feierman (1981), Janzen (1982, 1989, 1991), Janzen and Prins (1981), M'Bokolo (1984), Prins (1979, 1989), Turner (1975), Vansina (1990), and Werbner (1975) have begun to offer thoroughgoing historical and comparative analyses of the major healing cults in the societies of central and southern Africa. These societies, from the equator down to the Cape of Good Hope, are grouped by linguists as speakers of interrelated Bantu languages. This region displays extensive linguistic and symbolic homogeneity alongside the somewhat more evident institutional variations. The Bantu traditions have evolved through a diffusion not so much of populations but of cultural traditions or civilizational forms, of technologies (pastoral, agricultural, and perhaps also metallurgical), and of health and healing traditions. There is a common and robust core of basic assumptions and institutionalized behaviors in the fields of etiology, diagnostics, and therapy, which are often invoked and displayed in the context of elaborate ceremonies or cults. *Ngoma*—in southern Bantu regions spelled *isangoma,* for example—is a healing cult known throughout the Bantu area (Janzen 1991). This cult focuses on reproduction—of persons, game, herds, and harvests—and is therefore also invoked in cases of sterility and drought. It organizes group therapy around the large *ngoma* drums that rhythm dance and song, and it weaves together interregional networks of patients and therapists. In the decentralized societies of southern Africa (particularly the Xhosa, Zulu, Nguni, Sotho, and Tswana), *isangoma* comprises a web of pluricultural networks: initiates may participate in parallel fashion in several *isangoma* beyond the ethnic borders that the so-called Zionist healing churches and homelands have enforced. Other cults or therapies, such as *khita,* have spread only within more restricted areas.

Civilizational forms, for centuries ingrained in people's culture, shape the ways in which the therapeutic notions from the Islamic East, western science, and Christianity are being received. They determine specific reactions towards the forces of European colonialism and industrialization and its attendant social forms, like the new modes of urbanization, the state, wage and migrant labor, and mass production and consumerist needs. Particularly in the domain of therapeutics, the classical African health cultures or civilizational traditions continue in the urban areas alongside scientific-industrial health systems. The interpenetration is often rather superficial, and biomedical health services tend to become the privilege of an increasingly smaller part of society. At least in the popular suburban milieux, where wage labor remains subordinate to kinship and community co-operation, cults of affliction survive violent attacks from Christianity and prophetic or spiritualist healing churches; here, divination is in no way threatened by laboratory tests and science, and people consider pills to be more efficacious when paired with a kind of client-healer interaction (Van der Geest and Whyte 1988).

Janzen (1989) offers a broad outline of classical Bantu ideas about well-being and affliction in relation to worldview, divinatory diagnostic techniques, and therapeutic traditions. In the towns of western and central Africa it appears that, like the healing traditions, many curative practices also lose their ties with the traditional cosmology of healing and healing sites, or come to partly ignore the practical knowledge and cosmological understanding of flora, fauna, and other curative substances and devices.

1.4 Healers in the Town

1.4.1 *Healing arts have recently been revalorized on the national and international scene.* The forecasts with regard to the disappearance of traditional therapy have proven inaccurate (Bibeau et al. 1979; Feierman 1979; Good 1979; Janzen 1978). In previous decades western modernist thinking about development placed far too much stress on the socio-economic discontinuity with the past and on a decline of tradition and its alleged magical or irrational pursuits. Things traditional were considered to be prescientific, inefficient, or even 'primitive.' In other words, in this view development had to do with the transfer of money, technology, and other means for change and implied the spread of western knowledge. Development meant secularization, an increase in the chances of survival, and the arrival of prosperity and higher standards of living. The rationalistic optimism of the 1960s fueled the belief that the traditional healing arts would disappear in the African context as western-style biomedical practice became more accessible to health seekers (Janzen 1978). As a consequence, stress has been laid on the planning and implementation of Primary and Preventive Health Care Programs and the managerial organization of campaigns to combat diseases such as acute respiratory illnesses, malaria, malnutrition, measles, smallpox, leprosy, dysentery, skin and venereal infections (Foster 1982). Neither the colonial and missionary hospital approach nor the Primary Health Care Program favor or support traditional healing, but the first is not incompatible while the second is. Nowadays, in view of the dramatic economic crisis, effective biomedical programs are becoming far too expensive for a growing number of African countries, owing principally to the cost of training, infrastructure, and drugs. Moreover, the problem is far from being only an economic one. Given its numerous failures, the strictly technological model of (health) development is clearly in crisis. Very often the major causes of failure of development programs are not only managerial but also sociocultural: the root of any health problem and any conceptualization and implementation of healing is cultural.

The end of the 1970s saw a rediscovery and revaluation of African healing arts on the international African scene (WHO, UNESCO, OAU, international colloquia and publications; cf. also Ademuwagun et al. 1979; Janzen and Prins 1979; Last and Chavunduka 1986; Maclean and Fyfe 1986). This recognition goes hand in hand with an increasing cultural emancipation. Attention is being paid to the potential role of the different categories of healers who live and work in the rural or popular urban milieux (Aryee 1983; Bannerman 1983; Bibeau 1979, 1981; Corin 1979; Fassin 1992; Good C. 1987; Lapika 1980; Last and Chavunduka 1986; Pillsbury 1982; Sofuluwe and Bennett 1985). More and more it is recognized that the African art of healing, because it is to do with meaning and forces, constitutes the regenerative heart of a people's culture (Comaroff 1985a, b). Collaboration between major African civilizational traditions of health care, more local folk traditions of self-help, and biomedical health care programs is one of the major options enunciated by WHO's African Committee at Kampala in its discussion of traditional medicine's role in the development of health services in Africa (WHO 1976). It was restated with an even broader scope, some time later (WHO 1978:13):

> Since Traditional Medicine has been shown to have intrinsic utility, it should be promoted and its potential developed for the wider use and benefit of mankind. It needs to be evaluated, given due recognition and developed so as to improve its efficacy, safety, availability and wider application at low cost. It is already the people's own health care system and is well accepted by them. It has certain advantages over imported systems of medicine in any setting, because, as an integral part of the people's culture, it is particularly effective in solving certain cultural health problems. It can and does freely contribute to scientific and universal medicine. Its recognition, promotion and development would secure due respect for people's culture and heritage.

Recent WHO reports (Akerele 1984) show that a growing number of African governments subscribe to the position taken by the WHO. However, and despite enthusiastic official proposals and recommendations, actual attempts at collaboration between medical services and traditional healers, except in midwifery, are facing difficult problems almost everywhere, and research on traditional healing is by and large restricted to the study of herbal knowledge. Some imaginative forms of modest co-operation seem possible (Feierman 1985:126; Warren et al. 1982). Recently, the promoting of useful health care skills has been targeted on women and their participation in health and development initiatives (McCormack 1988).

In Kinshasa there is now a growing awareness among administrators of the national health services, as well as at the 1992 Sovereign National Conference, that the functioning of a country-wide health plan cannot rely on 'modern' medicine alone. This system requires an all too costly infrastructure and intensive training. It must therefore revalorize the positive contributions of classical African health and healing traditions. However, the government has so far supported only one exploratory research project among healers, in 1974–76. This research was conceptualized along the lines propagated by the WHO in view of restoring the image of and hence promoting traditional medicine as a complement to biomedicine (cf. Bibeau 1979, 1981). However, because of a lack of means this programme was prematurely called off and never led to a practical implementation. Today we are still in the starting phase: traditional healers are excluded from the national health policy which continues to support only the very classical (para)medical training and the use of patented pharmaceutical goods. If these research programs were not that productive in research output, or in adequate legal recognition of the healers' status, at least they undeniably helped the healers to recover their dignity, emerge from semi-hiding, and receive broad de facto recognition. Biomedical health care facilities in Kinshasa and the country nowadays tend to offer services that either are of poor quality or are too expensive for the average individual or family to afford. Moreover, the demand of health-seekers largely surpasses the supply of health care. In the recent years the existing official community health care infrastructure has almost completely collapsed. This situation has contributed to a reinforcement of the position of traditional healers and healing cults, which are increasingly becoming the sole recourse for many health-seekers.

Past failures with regard to the promotion of traditional healing within public community health care were often due to the fact that the political decision makers themselves had an inadequate knowledge of the specific nature of these therapeutic forms. They ignore the cultural dimension and multilevel interweave in the culture-bound syndromes, and in the therapeutic skills and forms of cult healing with regard to these syndromes. There is, moreover, a considerable gap in the knowledge concerning the daily health-related behavior and practices of health-seekers, as well as of the major healing cults in the ever-expanding urban milieux. One often ignores how the ritualized gestures of daily life (blessings and curses, invocations of peace, visits of uncles, purifications, and so on) continue to have much impact on the health or mental balance of individuals in both town and village. Self-treatment with more or less well-known folk remedies is also rather commonplace, if not frequent. Sellers of medicinal plants and recipes can be found at most marketplaces and on the fringes of bus stations, while the number of pharmacies and small privately run 'medical centers' along the major urban thoroughfares continues to rise.

The function and prestige of traditional diviners and healers are growing steadily in the towns (Lapika 1983; Mahaniah 1982). Mass media and popular songs both praise and criticize the role of the traditional healers (Tshonga-Onyumbe 1982). In turn, many town-based healers maintain hopes of providing their services within the context of recognized health centers, or of collaborating with the national "Health For All" program.[6]

1.4.2 *African healing arts are more than herbal medicine.* Many traditional healers have sought, particularly in the 1970s, to reidentify themselves as herbalists. They might thus be able to divest themselves of the negative image regarding healers—an inheritance from colonialism and Christianization, which identified traditional healing with magic and the occult or with prescientific, inefficient, primitive, and even satanic practices.

Many African countries are now founding centers for the promotion of traditional healing—in most cases with the help of pharmaceutical firms. Although biomedicine is the most recent of developments in this field, the 'lastborn,' it nevertheless plays the role of 'senior brother,' often with the support of political and international institutions. In order not to deprive themselves of international financial resources, these centers often comply with their sponsors' wishes and exclusively study chemical-therapeutic qualities in plants or animal and mineral products. A pattern of neglect and disregard for psychological and socio-anthropological dimensions, or for the clinical evaluation of the healer's total performance, has thus become apparent (cf. Corin and Bibeau 1975; Kaba 1981).

The major healing rites became more and more widely practiced in the towns in the 1970s, in coexistence with the biomedical services. In Kinshasa, the major healing rites are performed in the language and style of the culture of origin, and are thus adapted to the kinship allegiances and cosmology of the given group. Nevertheless, as many as fifty percent of the clients who turn to these healing cults belong to a different culture. Prospective patients easily cross cultural boundaries because the cults possess a common cultural substratum, especially with regard to therapeutic strategies and to the metaphors related to the body and to other preverbal symbols at play in the therapeutic setting: dances, mimes, bodily decorations, ritual objects, massages, fumigation, medicinal substances, and, above all, possession trances. Who are these healers? Depending on whether they use medicinal plants, diagnosis through divination, and/or healing rituals, they are known as herbalists, diviners, or specialists of the major healing rites. The patients, for their part, do not resort indiscriminately to the various types of treatment available, but ultimately choose a healer on the basis of his effectiveness. The 1974–78 national survey guided and reported by Bibeau (1979, 1984; this study is unparalleled, and has not yet been updated) suggests that women, half of them between the ages of 21 and 30, account for a clear majority of those seeking the help of the main healing rites. The study was conducted by some thirty investigators who interviewed almost 5,000 patients and about 500 healers. It revealed that in the towns most of the healers' clients turn first to the biomedical health care system, contrary to what has been commonly held. This was at least true at the time of the investigation; since then the economic crisis has made biomedical care unaffordable for most of the population. The most frequently cited reasons for resorting to traditional medicine were as follows (Bibeau 1979:15–16): the desire to know the underlying cause of the disorder (for example sorcery, ancestral wrath); the presence of particular symptoms that threaten social functioning, for example, because they hamper orificial functions, or entail a lasting humoral disbalance; referral to traditional health care by a member of the biomedical institutions because the symptom or the patient's great anxiety seems to suggest the need for closer group support and ritual treatment; the inaccessibility in the area of Western type medicine.

Life in the Kinshasa suburbs is hard. As it appears from my own observations among the Kwaangolese population in Kinshasa, the degradation in nutrition, housing, and environment that occurred in the late 1980s is increasingly threatening ever larger parts of the capital city. Correspondingly, Yaka people abandon the jerry-built type of self-proclaimed healers whose curative techniques and commoditized practices are divorced from Yaka culture. They tend to spend their little available spare cash only in cases of serious misfortune, and then turn rather to the classical traditions and the reputed and fully initiated healers in the centuries-old cults (see plate 1).

1.4.3 *Traditional therapy is a total phenomenon and differs qualitatively from biomedicine.* Much of the skill, method, and meaning displayed in traditional healing practices escapes the biomedical understanding of physical well-being (cf. Good and DelVecchio Good 1981; Lock and Gordon 1988). Many a project envisaging a revaluation of traditional healing methods has failed when healers have been invited to work in a hospital setting and under the supervision of medical doctors. Such a relationship between healer and medical doctor remains from the start a one-sided one. In this situation healers are never able to acquire an independent or full status. The setting alienates their method, which heavily relies on cosmology and group dynamics. Furthermore, they tend to feel that biomedicine is not only a critical judge of their activities but also that it empties their identity of meaning: in the eyes of the clients healers no longer have control over the total therapeutic process and therefore appear to lack proper ancestral legitimation (Dozon 1987:16).

The traditional healer—at least in the Yaka and related cultures—works from a broad definition of health pertaining to the interactive spheres of physical, social, and spiritual life. In other words, his etiology involves at least three fields of parallel investigation. The interpretation of the cause of the sickness begins with the hypothesis that there exists a meaningful resonance between the three fields, namely, of the body *(luutu)*, of interacting persons *(muutu)* or group *(tsi)*, and of the life-world *(n-totu)*. Symptoms and illness are read as markers of socio-moral lesions, as a disruption both of the life of the individual sufferer and of the physical, social, moral, and cosmological contexts which embrace him or her. The traditional healer attempts to throw out the sickness, that is, to expel the conflict to which the patient's symptom is a witness. In this way the therapist seeks to rehabilitate the patient within the group. At the same time, however, he is also concerned with the illness; in a holistic, symbolic, and multifaceted way he tries to counter the cause, or rather to master the origin of the illness and turn it against itself. Illness concerns the subjectively and culturally informed experience of the ailing person and the way it is given shape and interpreted in the terms of the meaning and core values of that culture. The cult objects and medicinal preparations, the use of cupping horns, scarification, and ointments, and the regulation of cooking and food are all part of an encompassing ritual drama that works on corporeal processes by using metaphorical equivalents of bodily processes. For example, a woman suffering from amenorrhea may be invited to self-administer lukewarm enemas at sundown while crouching in the doorway between the sleeping chamber and the cooking hearth. The particular potion she employs, one made from buds of some tree or shrub, associates her with the transformative process of ripening. The healer's attention is in the first place directed neither towards the disease nor the somatic trouble.

In order to understand and value the spectrum of Bantu healing practices in their own right, it is necessary to study their group ethics, religion, and cosmology (see chs. 2 and 3). Only when the underlying conceptual framework and the logic of their symbolism with regard to solidarity and the coherence between body, group, and cosmos have been brought to the fore (see ch. 4) do the healing practices and symbolic imagery no longer appear as irrational acts and beliefs. At that moment one also begins to understand why or how the solidarity built up between healers, or between healers and patients in cult groups, forms part of and is informed by a more encompassing cosmic and cultural order. Healing practices then appear as condensed expressions of beliefs and etiologies concerning man, descent, life, good and evil, and the resonance between the various fields of experience (see ch. 5). Insofar as the cults are founded on these elements, they often act as strongholds against capitalism and bureaucracy. Their coherence and totality are partly generated in the conditions of imposed totalizing bureaucratic systems, particularly of colonial health care and missionary activities, as well as of the hegemonic ideology conveyed by the modern state (cf. Comaroff 1985a, b).

Illness and healing are multilayered realities. Contrary to current biomedical notions that view health merely as the absence of organic dysfunction, the members of Yaka cult and self-help groups in Kinshasa and the villages appear to interpret health and individual well-being as resulting from specific relations seen in a much broader context. To be in good health depends on the relations between people—or between the individual, the group, and the environment or life-world—and results from the vital integration of elements which also determine the fertility of the social group, success at school or work, and the moral and material well-being or continuity of the family group. Being in good health therefore means being whole, that is, being integrated in a meaningful way into the relational fields of body, group, and life-world.

Notions of sickness, illness, and misfortune are related to this integrative notion of personhood and health. The interpretation of the meaning of illness can only be understood within the wider context of the forces at work in the social context and life-world. Like health, illness situates itself between people, or in the relation of the individual to the social group and the life-world. Illness, disintegrative acts such as sorcery, or the transgression of the vital boundaries (of the individual body, household space, marital relationships, and so on) are viewed as a "binding" of the victim, a "tying up" or "blocking" of vital connections and junctions. The pathological condition thereby consists of an entanglement of those ties which should ideally form legitimate bonds connecting body, group, and life-world into one single vital unity. In other words: illness obstructs, disconnects, or deflates. It isolates individuals and groups, and hems them in. It "ties the victim with cords" into a disintegrative bond that counters vital integration.

Biomedicine, conversely, is chiefly and intensively concerned with physical disease and pathogens rather than with illness and sickness. Through biomedicine's preoccupation with the signs of physical health and disease, illness is naturalized and transformed from a cultural into a natural fact: it is defined in terms of a predominantly biological and functional view of the body. The medical doctor fights the disease allopathically and approaches the patient as an isolated instance and in a dyadic relation that is characterized by unequal authority and one-sided responsibility. Inasmuch as he works as a scientist, the doctor neither shares in the patient's network nor wants to influence it. Medical doctors and paramedical staff belong to a formal, bureaucratic medical organization which exists in virtue of the written word and is characterized by its particular conceptions of authority, rational and equivocal allocation of tasks, impersonal rules, strict segregation between persons and roles, and its quantitative conception of linear, progressive time. In biomedicine, power and dependence are generated and concentrated on a so-called scientific basis and in the name of therapeutic service.

Healing arts, as a major civilizational tradition, are at pains to recover from undue marginalization. Alongside education, jurisdiction, church, public security, and commerce in modern technology and consumer goods, public biomedical health care forms part of a set of formal organizations that force the more traditional institutions into the informal or private sector: one might think of kinship relations of solidarity and authority, or of production, exchange, and consumption, as well as marriage relations, health practices, and cult associations. However, the more the formal sector has become bankrupt or out of reach for the majority of those living in shanty towns, whose incomes are rendered worthless by the extreme rates of inflation (Houyoux et al. 1986), the more strongly does economic, social, and psychological security become dependent on the maintenance of good relations with one's village of origin.

The clash between healing, urban life, and biomedicine is replete with paradoxes and bewildering issues. In *The Professionalisation of African Medicine* (Last and Chavunduka 1986), the contributors show how the co-operation between traditional healers and biomedicine in various African countries creates the risk of a deprofessionalization of healers and a degeneration in their practices. Moreover, there exist many healers, as well as scientific and political authorities, who wish to avoid an adventurous or makeshift approach to public health. On the one hand, public health care policy makers must increasingly address the following questions with regard to the health care system imported from the West:

(1) Is biomedical health care really capable of solving the country's health problems or responding to the expectations it has raised, given the absence of economic growth and spectacular demographic expansion?

(2) What must be done about the concentration of hospitals, biomedical staff, and curative health care in the cities (more than 80 percent), thus "leaving poor rural populations woefully short of elementary health services, immunizations, pure water and proper sanitation" (Morley 1976; cf. also Buschkens 1990).

(3) How must one come to terms with the uncontrolled trading of pharmaceutical products (often very expensive) and the fact that multinationals use cities such as Kinshasa to dump medicines which are often taken off the markets in the West (cf. Gereffi 1983). What can be done about the conception that a medicine derives its power and effect from the person who administers it (cf. the placebo effect)?

(4) Can one continue to ignore the existence of a plural approach to health care, and the fact that most people, at least in chronic cases, systematically consult both health care systems at the same time?

On the other hand, there are questions concerning the 'scientific' validity, practical efficacy, acceptability, and legality of the therapeutic and curative action of healers. Last and Chavunduka—the latter being an anthropologist, president of the Zimbabwe National Traditional Healers Association, and chairman of the Zimbabwe Government Traditional Medical Council—rightly conclude their important study of these problems as follows:

> The most obvious difficulty lies in the formal training and certification of healers in the future, and in particular what the content of that training will be.... There is an inherent danger that traditional medical knowledge will be defined simply in terms of its technical herbal expertise, that this experience will in turn be recognised only for its empirical pharmagnosy, without reference to the symbolic and ritual matrix within which it is used—still less, the social matrix in which those rituals and symbols have meaning at any particular time or place.... Traditional medical knowledge, however, is much broader and more subtle than technical herbal expertise. Indeed, the very nature of this knowledge may militate against its formal structuring in the way professionalisation might seemingly require with its objective examinations and tests of efficacy. (Last and Chavunduka 1986:267–68)

Development, in my opinion, must occur to a large extent in unison with the structure, logic, and finality of the culture of the involved group, with its particular concepts of time, space, causality, solidarity, need, utility, efficacy, productivity, and so on, or with its own views on fauna, flora, and cosmos. In particular, women's associations, often linked to one or another church, act as self-help groups that sustain health, fertility, and sanitation programs. They offer a forum where traditional healers as well as medical care are exposed to social critique. In-depth understanding of women's curative skills and resources, as well as their therapy management in Kinshasa, is out of reach of a male anthropologist. In the following chapters, I will be concerned with analyzing the cultural bedrock of the Yaka, the core of assumptions and institutionalized behaviors in Yaka culture, and the fundamental metaphors that seem to persist over time and shape health behavior both in the countryside and in the city.

1.5 Healing as Social and Theatrical Drama: A Critique

Traditional healing arts among the Yaka have much in common with those of the Ndembu in northwestern Zambia, who have become so well known through the carefully detailed and insightful analyses by Victor Turner. Both the Ndembu in Zambia, southwestern Zaire, and northeastern Angola and the Yaka in southwestern Zaire have for more than three centuries been exposed to the Luunda sphere of influence. However, my experience in the context of Yaka culture prevents me from fully adopting Turner's view on Ndembu ritual as a pragmatics of social transformation, hence as a theatrical drama. Since I consider Turner's position as antithetical to the perspective that I attempt to outline here, I will first briefly sketch his approach. I would claim that Turner's ritual analysis is the product of what remains an external, though tender, look, "a staring through the window" (to paraphrase Edith and Frederick Turner 1985). The narrative voices of ritual specialists and privileged informants bespeak social and cultural reality, and establish a go-between the Ndembu and his ethnographic text.

The fine-tuned description and analysis of meaning that Turner offers of Ndembu ritual has elicited widespread admiration (Deflem 1991), and has inspired new approaches to ritual action, variously called situational analysis, symbolic action theory, comparative symbology, processual symbolic analysis, or the transactionalist approach of symbolic interaction. The central focus of his work, in which he develops a processual-dialectic perspective, is on microsocial drama, a ritual resolution of social and emotional conflict, and a strengthening of community values. In this ongoing social drama, Turner has us see social structure in action: conflict, contradiction, breach, crisis, redress, or recognition whether of reconciliation or of irremediable split are unveiled as a process. Conflict is cast in a dramatistic mode in which conscious choice (Turner 1957:230) and accidental circumstance are as significant as structural principles in the creation of social life. Life-crisis rituals like initiation and funeral mark the transition from one phase of an individual's development to another. Biological metaphors give way to a terminology of growth, maturation, conflict, adaptation—that is, of both cyclical movement and historical production—and we come to see Ndembu villagers as producers of the history they are at the same time living out.

Turner's processual view (1967:7ff., 1974:35ff.) deals both with the dialectics of social process as well as with ritual performance and process created out of the group's effort to resolve the tension between reproductive social structure and anti-structure, inasmuch as the latter is conducive to creative communitas and liminality. In other terms, symbols are part and parcel of social action and dynamics: they sustain a given social structure. Through their polysemy or multivocality, ritual symbols may in a similar manner bring out and seek to overcome this tension. The interchange between the sensory, affective, and/or normative poles in the symbols allows them to function as operators in the various phases of the social process, inasmuch as these phases are reenacted in the ritual. Symbols move actors, correct deflections and deviations, resolve social contradictions, and wed actors to the categories and norms of their society. Rituals store crucial symbols and deal authoritatively with social and religious values of the community. By virtue of their reference to the supernatural, they are also transformative with regard to human attitudes and behavior. Turner is religiously committed and convinced that symbols may have a load or effect that outreaches their meaning.

Symbols, in Turner's approach, are above all to be observed when ritually performed. Concerned with the efficacy of symbols, he analyzes how ritual works, what it does, and how people handle symbols. Symbols are thus primarily studied for their action-meaning in their significant social or action field, and/or their cultural field of beliefs, rituals, and religion. According to Turner (1967:45, for example), ritual symbols are as much a material locus in a universe of forces—a materialization of a moment or a politicized unity in social reality—as they are a captation point in the network of signifiers. Symbols are representatives of the political structure just as they are reiterations of the virtues of kin in the language of physiology. Ritual symbols and indeed affliction and communal cults are seen as strong means of maintaining group unity, and of mitigating tendencies of Ndembu social life. In Turner's perspective, social process, religious beliefs, ritual, and symbols are essentially interrelated. Ritual is "a stereotyped sequence of activities involving gestures, words, and objects, performed in a sequestered place, and designed to influence preternatural entities or forces on behalf of the actors' goals and interests" (1977:183). Turner focuses on the individual as the very agent or locus in the social drama. He is innovative in reenacting the 'speaking subject'—a phenomenological dimension of his approach that builds up an ethnography from what participants say about what they do in the ritual, why, and what this all represents to them. Turner relies heavily on the views and exegesis of master-healer Muchona, his best informant. While acknowledging his intellectual indebtedness to Monica Wilson, Turner is, however, unable to accept Wilson's principle of going no further in explaining symbolic meaning than the informants' own statements permit. In Turner's view: "The anthropologist who has previously made a structural analysis of Ndembu society . . . can observe the real interconnections and conflicts between groups and persons, in so far as these receive ritual representation. What is meaningless for an actor playing a specific role may well be highly significant for an observer and analyst of the total system" (1967:27). Turner later adds an important qualification to this particular statement. At least in the case of the Ndembu, with their paucity of myths, knowledge of "the total system" is to be obtained "atomistically and piecemeal" through patient analysis of ritual symbols. There are, according to Turner, "no short cuts, through myth and cosmology, to the structure of Ndembu religion" (1969:20).

However, Turner has great difficulty considering ritual in its own right. His concept of metaphor is imprecise. In his studies of the Ndembu, he confuses metaphor and symbol inasmuch as they are assumed to assign meaning to social behavior and conduct. At times, he considers metaphor as an englobing structuring principle, as an archetype, or a root paradigm. Turner basically adopts the interactive sense of metaphor: it is metamorphic or transformative, it effects an instantaneous fusion of two separated realms of experience into one illuminating, iconic, encapsulating image. Metaphor is understood as the "intercourse of thoughts, a transition between contexts" (1975:156). It effects an "instantaneous fusion" (1974:25) that provides "new perspectives" (1974:31). In short, the transformative interaction—intercourse or transaction—that is brought about by metaphor between the various realms explains, in Turner's view, the efficacy of symbols. The ritual action in gestures, music, chanting, dress, or celebration brings about a very concrete interchange of qualities between the "normative or eidetic pole" (norms, behavioral patterns, values) and the "orectic pole" (taste, feeling, pleasure, desire) (1974:55). In the interactive forms, norms and values become saturated with emotion, while gross and basic emotions become ennobled through contact with social values: the emotional norm becomes a 'norm-alized' emotion. Turner's views on liminoid experiences and his approach to communitas are influenced by Csikszentmihalyi's study (1977) of liminoid activities—sports, arts, and the like—that are autotelic. In ecstatic states, the body stands in a direct relation of immediate feedback with itself: it is centered on itself in a flow of action that passes beyond reflection or self-awareness.

I contend that Turner's viewpoint does not fully capture the autoproductivity of metaphorization, since it seems to presuppose an intention and goal that is somehow programmed and only accessible through the voice of an individual author or subject. My major criticism of Turner's views on Ndembu ritual concerns his dramaturgical view on ritual and the liminal, and his half-spoken Durkheimian sociological approach to the social organism. If Turner takes into account the creative potential of the liminal, it is in virtue of the fact that it ensures the bonding of man to society, as it is a source both of social order and of change seen as a fundamental reordering. Analysis of the type offered by Turner reduces the emergent or genuinely creative capacity of the ritual to something else: ritual is not regarded as an autogenerative praxis, and the social order is seen as its hidden script. For Turner, contradiction or conflict are the major source of symbolic production, and conflict management is its major function. Turner's more interpretive focus on the webs of significance embodied in symbols represents a shift in his approach and stems from a phase after his major work on Ndembu ritual was completed. Although the later Turner (1974:31–32) credits the religious beliefs of the Ndembu with ontological value, when conveyed by ritual their religious content appears merely as a surplus-value over and above the social value of ritual action and thought. In identifying the sensory and ideological poles of symbols, Turner has contributed to reconciling sociological and psychological interpretations of ritual symbols. Social organization and ideological meaning, as well as normative or moral values, are the very program for the staging of a ritual: symbols are storage units filled with information, capable of instruction and rearrangement in view of their staging this very program in their own terms, infused as they are with bodily or psychic energy. A ritual represents a storehouse of traditional knowledge, of meaningful symbols by which information is revealed and axiomatic social values are reempowered (1968:2). Turner analyses the properties of multivocality and unification within a single dominant symbol, but he fails to investigate the interrelation between symbols.

Against Turner's substantivist views, I hold that metaphorical production in drama is a structural innovation, and only to be understood in its very elaboration. As I will argue more fully (see 1.6), metaphor transforms various domains by transferring, for example, spatio-temporal principles or potent images on to previously unrelated domains. This unprecedented linking receives tangible form in metonymical elaborations. The basis and locus of this creativity is to be sought not in liminality (Turner 1969) or inchoateness (Fernandez 1974), but in the body seen as a surface upon which the group and the life-world are inscribed, and as a model for these, that is, in the body's liminal capacities. I will argue that the body is a genuine source of transformational symbolic creativity, of true praxis or action capable of intervening effectively on the world. My perspective gives actual primacy to the body and develops an inside perspective on ritual as a transformational, hence self-generative process.

Exegesis, in my view, is not explanation, and ritual is neither liturgy nor theatre. Although I have had the opportunity to work with very reflective healers, I do not believe that their own exegesis has laid bare the heart of the healing drama. And yet my more fundamental criticism of the works of Turner is that the interpretation they offer of Ndembu healing relies heavily on representation and interactional plot and yet does not lay bare the proper ways in which cult healing deals with the human body and draws on its genuine resources: as I will more fully argue in 7.4, Turner overlooks the genuine and creative significance of the human body.

1.6 Body and Weave: A Semantic-Praxiological Approach

Healing cults in Yaka culture develop a transformative, synesthetic, multivalent, and multiscenic drama. They produce a multilayered and comprehensive interweave between the flow of affects, motivational forces, images, and bodily states, on the one hand, and the various processes governing the behavior of the group, on the other. Body and group are interwoven with the life-world, that is, the lived, partially shared and encompassing worlds of images, meanings, values, and strategies in which the participants are immersed. At play in these cuits are a 'shape of life' and habitus, that is, a tradition and skills that develop and manifest themselves without referring to a script. Patterns may be made to emerge through a comparative and sequential analysis of the different cults, or of the various performances of a same cult by different cult leaders. A comparison, for example, regarding the theme of death and rebirth in the healing cults and in circumcision or enthronement rituals not only lays bare patterns of acts, relations, images, symbols, meanings and entitlements, but also demonstrates how these patterns echo one another, even in the various transformations they undergo. Observation may uncover how each interweave and flow of action anticipates or calls for other interweaves and engagements as well. Therapy is not concerned with historiography, nor with trying to unravel and reweave the very contingent life and family-history of the patient. Instead, the healing ritual projects the body experience and life-history of the patient onto the space-time weave formed by the seclusion house and the intervention of healer and family. Expressed in general terms, the patient moves from a state of being tied in, closed up, or emptied out, towards a remolding of the body's shell and content, while simultaneously being gradually reinserted in the complex interweave of body, group, and world. The therapeutic drama develops a space-time weave into which metaphoric correspondents of organs, affects, energies, and bodily functions are constituted and manipulated. The cult spirits that are invoked are associated with basically ambivalent forces which may be both life-threatening and life-giving. In the rite, the patient's body merges with the significance of the ritual house, itself a metaphor of macrocosmic life-bearing processes. Both the trance and the seclusion are a libidinal engenderment or birth-giving to meaning that surpasses or precedes conventional speech and that may recast a very deep bodily reminiscence of childhood experiences and a set of imaginary and mythical themes concerning society's beginnings. Moreover, the various members of the therapy managing group, with their multiple roles in connection with life transmission as organized by kin and alliance, all offer a projective space for the patient who is thereby invited to relate herself or himself to these roles and positions, or at least to endorse one or several among them.

1.6.1 *Adopting a semantic-praxiological approach, I investigate how healing cults among the Yaka develop a transformative drama.* The approach is selectively in line with some of the perspectives taken in Merleau-Ponty's phenomenology (1945, 1964), Lévi-Straussian structuralism (1958, 1962), Julia Kristéva's structuralist semiotics (1969), the poststructuralist praxeology of Pierre Bourdieu (1980) and Jean Comaroff (1985a), as well as with the processual performance study of Bruce Kapferer (1991). Healing cults enact a condensed version of daily life—but as it is apprehended from the edge and interstices of social order. In the cults, life is reimmersed in and reenergized in contact with the unconscious imaginary world of potent forces (Castoriadis 1975:ch. 3). It is a very sensuous and bodily enactment. Healing drama, in Yaka culture at least, draws on transformative transpositions of sensory qualities and forces from one realm to another: it aims at bridging between body, group, and world, between tangible and immaterial realms. Ritual drama is a sort of play for the large part beyond the grasp of verbal discourse and conceptual representation: there is no full transparency of the ritual creativity in the rite to ritual wording or to elucidating comments supplied by experts or participants. I therefore advocate an approach that reaches beyond a logocentric view and a model derived from linguistics, literary criticism, or (linear) writing. In the cults proper to this oral culture, traditions and skills develop and manifest themselves without reference to a script or foundational myth. Cult healing does not proceed in a deliberate manner, from one realm to another, or from one meaning to another: healing does not develop as a theatrical play. Its very performance points only to itself, its structuring and display here-and-now, that is, to the ways in which it unconceals and inventively intertwines diverse fields and aspects of life. The flexibility and inventiveness of the bricolage and creative achievement-in-context proper to the healing rite exclude any possibility that it might be comprehended according to a theatrical or liturgical model governed by a script and strict rules. Ritual activity in its most genuine characteristic is therefore not conceived here as a 're-presented' narrative, as a reproduction of a myth, or as a reflection or replay of a social reality.

The concept of 'rite' is alien to Yaka culture. What I label, for lack of a more fit notion, as rite pertains to a basic 'technē.' I will show how much rite entails a phatic contact with life, a highly bodily dramatized presencing of forces and signs. In particular, healing rite involves a rejoicing in the group and aims at 'resting' in the life-world in an expanded aliveness and sharing.

It seems best to approach rite as a work of art, a happening within whose framework the actors may improvise a part of the drama. Sharing as they do a number of themes and objectives, they are able to reveal themselves to each other and to the outside world as a group. It is appropriate to analyze the ritual drama from an interior perspective, a little like following the development in a speech, not from the point of view of the speaker or listener, but from that of the compelling argument and esthetic form that come about through particular devices and transformative processes. My fieldwork is very much a kind of esthetic experience, and my task in writing could be compared to that of a specialist in art engaged in the unveiling of the creative and esthetic dimensions of a work of art. My objective is to grasp the autogenerative development of the therapy whose signification and healing effects coincide with its forms—I witness to the moral aspect of my task in the Prologue and Epilogue. I focus on how ritual 'works,' not so much in the sense of its achieving something, but rather in the sense of how it works in and of itself, having no author other than itself. The act through which the healing drama forms itself is the same one that presents itself to us. My comprehension of the drama should have no other focus than the process of its formation. Ritual practice, for example, is no longer primarily studied as communication, as the theatrical expression of a myth or tradition, or as a reflection of social process. More precisely, the object of this approach is to discover how people constantly bring about meaning and empowerment from out of themselves—their dreams, fantasies, bodies, gestures, and actions, their social, spatial, and historical contexts—by relating these forces, significative phenomena, and webs of relations to one another. By virtue of this very fabric they are able to produce new relations in order to overcome tensions, contradictions, or disconnections in which they had become inextricably entwined. I attempt to follow this weave or articulate process of drama, whose very *autogenerative production may be seen as the actor and author,* from within. In a similar way, artistic creation could be viewed as a highly original patterning and interweaving of forms, colors, rhythms, and intensities which embrace one another, rather than as the fulfillment of some project of the artist, his patron, or the spectator.

As for the semantic-praxiological analysis of ritual production, I distinguish three partly overlapping steps. They do not constitute successive moments either in the research or in the presentation, but offer distinct angles of approach.

(a) There is first that of the internal structure of the ritual activity, namely the patterning of the devices into a ritual process. I situate myself, in terms of perspective, at the interior of the whole ritual process. To the extent that the process informs and links together a set of diverse activities that arise in connection with a death, therapy, or divinatory vocation, it is my task to highlight the internal configuration. I thereby concentrate on the way in which an institutional set of activities is structured into a whole.

A number of elements, procedures, and devices are in focus at this level. The first is the ritual vocabulary, revealing as much continuity as it does semantic disruptions. For example, the notion of *-kaya* evokes a self-destructive reversal of evil or of the onset of illness; that notion underlies also the view that the booty of the hunt has to undergo a decay similar to fermentation that transforms palm sap in wine, or to the trance that authenticates the patient's vocation to initiation in a spirit cult. That very notion thus opens up a whole work of transferences of meaning (6.3.3). This explains how the healer also acts as hunter. The transformation proper to fermentation is not only mastered in view of a healing, but it is also one of the many sources of inspiration for transformative metaphors, that is, for metamorphic transpositions from one network of meaning and vital web onto another. Another procedure involves the recurrences and shifts in the composition of the participants in the rite inasmuch as they are impersonating certain social or kinship roles, or representing stitches in the vital webs of life transmission. This is the case, for example, with regard to the intervention of the maternal uncle and the family responsible for the cult (6.2). Change and recurrence referring to time and space—as, for example, the vigils playing on the threshold between night and day, or the transitions between village and forest—all are constitutive elements in the production of the drama. The various afflictions in a kin-group that lead to convening a family council or consulting a diviner, or the social dynamics that are brought to light in the oracle itself or come into play at the reception of the oracle by the afflicted family, constitute yet another category of elements. Further, there are all the recurrent and interactive constituents of the meaningful drama, be they of a sensible, gestural, verbal, interactional, or quasi-intentional nature.

(b) The second angle of analysis consists of discovering the lateral or connotative references which often occur—also in a latent fashion—in the production of the drama. It is assumed that ritual practice comes about by interweaving significant elements that evoke or stem from various paradigmatic contexts, that is, from various semantic structures and classifications. This is to say that the analysis examines all the elements, acts, objects, devices, instruments, or skills in the rite and compares them with analogous phenomena in oral lore, other rites, or daily life. The component elements, in other words, are figured out. Drawing on the connotations or latent references to other contexts, I retrace the conventional sociocultural classifications, procedures, and systems which the elements of the rite stem from, conform to, or are at variance with. I thus try to delineate the positions the participants either hold or withdraw from in the systems of kinship, hierarchy, gender and age categories, and so on. But, the perspective is also to be reversed: if the kinship positions may inform the ritual drama, conversely, the very ritual dynamics may as well uncover or shape other and very genuine, perhaps less masculinist, perspectives on the kinship or on reproduction, gender, and the like.

Moreover, while unraveling the various paradigmatic contexts that are made present in the ritual, I examine how they coexist and interact: how, for example, gestures or scenes of eating, childbirth, or taking an enema may call forth or even make present the weave of commensality and conjugality—and the analogous processes in the life-world involving growth, flowering, decay, lunar or seasonal cycles, and the like. Similarly, I attempt to discover whether and to what extent the acts, objects, colors, ornaments, and arrangements of space and time in the ritual drama are in consonance or dissonance with conventional classifications regarding space and time, cosmological phenomena, female and male attributes, and similar categories.

For example, the ritual constituents permit one to uncover the relations of signification and empowerment between various activities or phenomena, whether these relations remain latent or otherwise appear only when placed in the appropriate configuration. In this way the analogy between the rainbow, the erect python, and the "river which rises to the sky" allows an interpretation of why the Yaka associate the diurnal and nocturnal movements of the sun as being parallel to the great rivers crossing the Kwaango and vice versa (2.2). It may perhaps be the case that this type of analysis reveals contradictions between some social signification, as hearsay or popular comments would render it, and latent structural meaning. Thus, the healer who appears as a "male mother" at the same time appropriates the behavior of the hunter-trapper. In this indirect way he communicates to the patient that she will meet death the moment she is about to harm the healer or her consanguines.

(c) The third step consists in trying to find how a meaningful and empowering drama is brought about, involving the interactive fields of body, family, and life-world. In other terms, the dynamics, quasi intentionality, and efficacious or transformative nature of the ritual drama become the focus of attention. In order to discover how the healing drama differs from routine practice and mere reproduction, ritual may be studied in itself as a species and a creative totality. The central question might be put this way: how is a given ritual performance more than the nth reproduction of a model, or more than the sum of its parts? The unity, specific meaning, and efficacy of a ritual practice cannot be accounted for by the lateral references of the significative elements alone, that is, by the contexts from which these elements are borrowed, or by the way they were structured or classified in their original, more conventional contexts. Nor can it be accounted for by its lineal development or staging, as if it were a kind of theatrical representation, both thematic and interactional, of a historical sequence or a theory. Nor, further, can it be accounted for by an interpretation based only on its social significance, informants' opinions, collective representations of the group, or ritual terminology. The genuineness, innovative meaning, and effectiveness of a ritual practice come about through the creative metaphoric production of meaningful drama and its metonymic elaborations.

My interest is in ritual creativity. The emphasis in my approach on the formative, transferential, and transformative capacities of ritual metaphor and its grounding in bodily processes contrasts with many theories of metaphor in the fields of linguistics and literary criticism.

Let me, however, start from definitions of tropes and their ever-transforming play proper to langage. Metaphor and metonymy may be said to be in oscillation with one another (Rosolato 1978:52–80; Durham and Fernandez 1991). Metonymy elaborates upon both the 'like' and 'unlike' parts in the metaphor. A metaphor involves an innovative transposition or 'transportation' of meaningful elements from a given semantic field into another with which it had no prior link. It violates conventional meaning by bridging various semantic realms in a transformative way, thus bringing about a symbolic congruence between affective, sensory, corporeal, social, and cosmological fields. The symbolic relationships that develop out of this transposition, but within one and the same semantic field, are metonymical. A metaphor relates elements from separate semantic fields; for example, in the case of the trance of the diviner-to-be, these are the fields of spirits, mortal agony, the water shrew or the hen that lays an egg, and the macrocosmic womb (1991a). A metaphor cuts across fields. The relationship in this case is unprecedented and structurally new: as such it is not fully suggested by natural resemblances or by a prior signification, nor can it be paraphrased or explained without a substantial loss in meaning (Ricoeur 1975: 243–45; Zenoni 1976). A metonymy, however, in an indexical signification that interrelates contiguous elements within the same semantic domain by virtue of relationships that are precodified by language, convention, or use. The relationship is easy to grasp, for example, in terms of part and whole or cause and effect. Metonymy differentiates between the domains or fields that metaphor interconnects in that it 'translates' the metaphorical link in terms of the unique structuring or qualities proper to that field. The metaphorical intertwining of separate fields is thus worked out and made concrete through the use of metonyms that give it sensible form in the very terms of the context or the particular setting, plot, or mood (see Beck 1978).

My praxiological definition of *metaphoric production in ritual* breaks away from linguistic ones which impose a hierarchy between body, senses, and cognition and thereby limit the capacity to generate meaning and empowerment in ritual practice to coding and communication. I contend that ritual metaphors in Yaka culture are not a flickering touch of mind on mind but a blending and empowering of senses, bodies, and world. Here rituals seem to be very careful in using words, always highly styled, because there is a fear that naming the person or his attributes may open the person up to sorcery and deflate him. I define ritual metaphor as a performance that does actually effect the innovative interlinking that it exploratively signifies in a given context and according to a set procedure. This approach differs from what Sandor (1986) calls the transfiguring of an objectively given reality in terms of something else. Ritual metaphor does not primarily aim to impose a grid of meaning or control, but rather aims to disclose and activate one. In the oral culture of the Yaka, where cognition and institutional discipline are not mastered by linear writing, dictionaries, and positive science, or by goals of efficient economic production and progress, the approach to reality is usually a highly sensuous and transactional one. Ritual encourages the senses, emotions, and habitus to be very active and prominent in informing the participants to what is going on in an endeavor in which the physical, social, ethical, and spiritual are interactive or weakly demarcated. Ritual meaning is understood not so much as a text, a predication or an exposé, but primarily as *-disoongidila, -ditaandumuna,* literally, "showing, spelling out something by displaying its ingredients or its motto." Ritual displays the polar side of reality: it is associated with the realm of rest and dream that, like the reverse side of a leaf, reveals the unknown edge or side of diurnal life while recycling the sensuous and imaginary forces. Ritual releases forces and discloses meaning, but does not aim at mere representation. A ritual metaphor is a performance and transaction in a field of meanings and forces. I define ritual metaphor as a productive and metamorphic process grounded in corporeal capabilities and skills that search out and develop beyond linguistic expression. It brings with it sensuous, emotional, physical, cognitive or ideational, and dramatic effects. It is somehow at the very foundation of operative meaning of which ritual vocabulary is a very imperfect voice.

Ritual metaphor is basically a bodily enacted method for the innovative production of synesthetic meaning and empowerment. It makes a ritual into a morphogenetic, hence cosmogenetic art. In its creative move, ritual metaphor does not know beforehand how its ingredients should cohere or commit to one another. It does not point to facts in terms of other facts but rather establishes 'facts of experience' and webs of relationships mostly through confluence, and in some cases through shock or astonishment. Various fields of experience and the plus-values of meanings are intertwined or superposed in ritual metaphors: in many cases the olfactory, visual, tactile, verbal fields of substitutables are familiar, but the junction is innovative, striking, or appealing, and in some cases a shock. Bearing on people's daily life and context, ritual metaphor is the unsettling art of fantasy and wonder for 'mind and body,' bearing on people's daily life and context. All this does not imply that in metaphor people relate to the world in a poetic, dreamy, or subversive way; on the contrary, metaphor entails a multilayered and multisense contact with and deep engagement in the world in its actuality.

Let me give an example to briefly illustrate the metamorphic capacity of ritual metaphor. In the *ngoombu* cult, the diviner-to-be rounds off his initiation to become a clairvoyant medium by metaphorically embodying while in trance the behavior of the water shrew *(lutsokutsoku)*. This small mammal catches fish and eats insects. Its hole has a double entrance, one in the water, the other above. A keen sense of smell makes the water shrew a good night hunter. Similarly, the diviner, in trance and with his bare hands, digs a tunnel under the ground and crawls through, emerging at the far end.[7] This particular metaphor is worked out and concretized through metonyms. The underground journey and reappearance of the 'diviner-water shrew' act as a projective space for the participants' feelings regarding death versus rebirth, and the world of the spirits and ancestral shades versus that of the living. While embodying the water shrew, the entranced diviner goes through the motions of mortal agony and rebirth. He himself is said to acquire the keen sense of smell characteristic of the water shrew that should enable him to track down sorcerers and uncover their nocturnal plots. Through an unbroken feedback process of alternation, metaphors and metonyms thus bring into play the mediating and differentiating connections and transpositions within and between the bodily, social, and cosmological fields of existence. And at the same time, these connections generate or unleash the forces, values, and conditions that are evoked in the expressive acts: the 'diviner-water shrew' is both reborn and a mediator between worlds.

Healing rituals also include, at transitional moments, powerful interstices of anti-structure and baffles to perception. There are irruptions of non-signification, ungrammatical speech, license, and emotional outbursts. These moments may set the conditions for and be followed by a sequence of increasing configurational order and 'co-ordinated' interaction. License, nonsensical behavior, parody, jokes, or laughter bring people to relate to one another in the setting of specific experience and make them receptive for a new message or a transformation.

Metonymic ritual production gives contextual consequence to the metaphoric creation by spelling it out in the terms of more conventional meanings, knowledge, status, skills, devices. Metonymy is the 'crystallization' displayed iconically or in a text. It elaborates on the unsettling metaphoric production by bringing out a practical correlation of partial similarities. There is a familiar filter used for naming or interpreting. Popular understanding identifies a ritual element by relating it to another, more customary meaning, belief, folk concept, gesture, fact, or sensation, as, for example, when someone says that the meat of spotted animals is prohibited to the initiates to preserve them from leprosy. This is also the case when, in an effort to grasp a ritual and esoteric or foreign element, people reduce it to a familiar value or enterprise and give an explanation in social terms. Another example would be people's contention that breaking the rule of silence imposed on the candidate to the throne while in seclusion weakens his health or compromises the prosperity of his reign. This type of exegesis predominates in folk etiology, and, when the ritual behavior is confined to one correlation among many, it may pervert symbolic activity into some fetishistic sacralization or magic. An example would be pretending that the chief imposes self-containment so as not to lose self-control in his contacts with the shades of his precursors. Likewise, initiands are recommended to use a leaf in the shape of a heart as a hanger to bring peace to the heart during circumcision or enthronement; patients may tie to their left wrist a minute copy of a trap which is conjured into ensnaring the illness; or a libation consumed at the ancestral shrine summons the ancestral shades to release the animals where the hunter goes. Popular etiology of an illness, failure, or death is based on similar metonymic and sacralizing interpretations, and attributes responsibility for these evils to ensorcellment, acts of revenge, or ancestral wrath. Sacralizing elaboration tends to predominate among the non-initiates in their popular beliefs, commentaries, sayings, and domestic rituals.

Metaphor predominates in the esoteric ritual vocabulary and the specialized knowledge of ritual experts or senior initiates. Neither healer nor diviner is pretending to hold the keys to the truth. In the context of ritual, the healer, like the diviner, speaks in metaphors. When asked to explain what they do and why, ritual experts spontaneously associate their procedures with similar ones, or offer proverbs, elements of tales, or fragments of divinatory oracles. They may clarify ritual terms by means of homonymy. To assure the transformative, self-generative potential of the healing ritual, the practice has to be prevented from exhaustive exegesis of a vernacular cause-effect type of reasoning. Exegesis may lay bare the ritual's sources of inspiration or its frames of reference—such as uterine links and spatial structuring. The etiology of an ill furnished by the diviner also functions in a metaphoric manner, in that it consists of the creation of an original relation between the realities of the body, familial life, and the world. Metonymic comprehension reduces and impoverishes the ritual sense. Either sacralized or reified, the ritual element no longer denotes anything more than a conventional intention, and conveys but a univocal bit of information.

1.6.2 *The praxiological focus in this study is on the transformational capability of ritual praxis, mainly healing, through the use of the body.* The perspective has aspects in common with Bourdieu (1980), Csordas (1980), Lock and Scheper-Hughes (1987).[8]

Stressing the autogenerative dimension of ritual, my study extends beyond a pragmatic focus on expressing some meaning of things while doing them. A proper understanding of Yaka ritual should take into consideration a number of characteristics of this oral culture and subsistence form of life. The Yaka culture's view of reality is multidimensional. It makes no equation between biology and the pre- or nonsocial, and in practice the boundary between physical and nonphysical is very imprecise; there are but a few physical artifacts—tools and house—which are physical extensions of the human body. There is no dualism of mind and body or of man, animal, and machine. Rituals are a form of technē, but not technologically mediated. There is no notion of progressive time: ritual develops in euchronic time. The senses—smelling, hearing, touching, seeing—are quite equal modalities for comprehension and practice (see ch. 4). Regarding ritual praxis, my question is, how can such a drama produce a healing effect on the physical and lived body and on the emotions and conceptual representations such that it restores the patient to health or creatively forms a new identity for him or her? Unlike Beidelman (1966), however, I do not rely on the perspective of depth psychology regarding libidinal bodily functions. I am concerned here with the ways in which a culture shapes experience that is not only inspired by the body but also lived and mediated by and through it. The body is both source and agent, embodiedness and embodiment. I look at ritual as a praxis that produces meaning and power in and through bodily action enhanced and reinforced with images, metaphors, and forces, all enacted or orchestrated in an unfolding drama. In ritual, corporeal praxis thus shapes, expresses, and reembodies a particular bodily and social order, and a particular view of, and relation with, the lifeworld or cosmos. From this very viewpoint, I intend to show that the *khita* healing of the gynecological patient (see chs. 6 and 7) springs from a specific metaphorical integration of the patient's bodily experience, family life, and life-world. I contend that these metaphorical relationships and alignments are symbolic and performative, yet metamorphic: they explore new forms of drama and produce the conditions and dynamics of innovation or transformation; that is, the participants are bringing about a rich and operative drama that, for them, is innovative and transformative.

The dramatization operates largely beyond the conscious level of representation and explicit discourse: it comes about in the dynamic and culturally structured weave of the fields of body, family or group, and life-world. The very transference of the cosmological space-time order onto bodily experience, or vice versa, through highly dramatized ritual, has a transformative effect inasmuch as it operates metaphorically. I would claim that body, group, and life-world constitute morphogenetic fields that are at times consonant, and at other times dissonant.[9] My account views ritual more as a weave or a musical oeuvre, rather than a narrative or an architectonic structure. This approach is concerned with the ongoing fabric of plurivocal, verbal and subverbal meaning, multidimensional drama, and forces, through the body and the senses, through social interaction and in resonance with the life-world.

Healing is a corporeal method. I will thus analyze the healing cult as a corporeal praxis, a bodily method of interweaving, that relies on transformative and mediatory devices. In the ritual process, these devices at play include a method. The inspiration for the method stems from the human body and consists in interweaving, in a genuine way, the social, cosmological, and corporeal fields. The method of healing basically develops as a rite de passage: the patient is led to symbolically die to his or her former condition of illness and to be conceived and reborn into a new condition. While reinserting the patient into the world and familial context, the life-world itself undergoes a transformation. The antagonistic, illness-causing aspects are expelled or overcome. Ritual form is given to this death and expulsion via cult-specific metaphors and metonymies embedded in the wider cosmology. As I will demonstrate, *khita* healing springs from a transformational process and performative production of encompassing symbolic realms that lead the patient through the very motions of death-agony, self-fecundation, gestation, and rebirth, that revitalize her relationships with the healer, coinitiates, and relevant kin, and that reconnect her with the resources and processes of life-bearing in the life-world. The symbolism of the seclusion house fuses the patient's bodily experience with the signification and forces of the hen that is killed or that lays an egg, doubled by the metaphors of incubation, the cosmic womb, and so on.

The analysis of the *khita* healing cult will be *sequential,* since any praxis only takes shape in its temporal unfolding. I subscribe to the view of Pierre

Smith (1978), who, in his discussion of the Incwala ritual, stresses the need to look at rituals as wholes and to understand them as an organic sequence developing around a cluster of themes central to the culture (just such clusters of major themes regarding Yaka culture will be examined in chapters 2 to 4). Bourdieu (1980:135–65) and Werbner (1988), each in his own way, have shown that one cannot hope to grasp ritual practices by reducing them to theoretical and synoptic schemes, be they structuralist, functionalist, thematic, or any other sort of abstract construction that ignores the particular temporal unfolding of the ritual. By using a sequential analysis, I wish to show that every step in the healing ritual is a step towards a specific integration via a progressive embodiment of the role of life-bearing and of other more comprehensive, transformative, and mediating functions. The healer is referred to as the one who reweaves the patient into a more encompassing tissue in which personal health and well-being are essentially coextensive with the kin-group and the broader life-world. Therapeutic efficacy is generated in an innovative and transformative drama which disentangles the confused knots the patient has been bound in, and which reweaves them into a vital fabric.

1.6.3 *The focus of this study is very much on 'the work of culture' in and through the organization of the sensorium in illness and healing.* The Yaka do not regard the individual as a dichotomous structure of mind and body, and neither do they conceive self and other, male and female, ruler and subject, rational and sensuous as polar opposites. Polar elements in Yaka symbolic order, such as in healing cults, become, however, oppositional in the ideological and political realm under men's control. In healing cults at the edge of public order, culture operates as a predominantly prereflexive set of symbols and as a source of meaningful drama: it acts primarily not through cognition per se but rather through multiple sensory or synesthetic bodily experiences and interactions. Culture sets the scene in which meaningful interaction and transaction take place. In ways that are specific to a given group, culture molds the individual's 'inner' or 'subjective' world of dreams, affects, bodily acts, senses, thoughts, and conscience while connecting these with the 'outside' world. The work of culture is simultaneously a transmitted and an inventive production of drama in and through sensory, corporeal praxis. Culture is conceived of as a fabric or a drama, rather than a text or narrative. Whole layers of culture are unconscious or simply felt or acted out; that is, they are not brought to verbal discourse, and yet participants actively engage in the symbolic practices or drama while drawing on these layers and mobilizing them.

Culture is an "intermediate and potential space" (Winnicot 1971). To study the impact of culture on the patient, and in particular on bodily experience and acts (in healing), it would seem appropriate to conceive of culture as a potential space or interface between, on the one hand, the world of unconscious feeling and understanding, of affects, images, thoughts, and the sensory body, and, on the other hand, the group and life-world. Culture is seen as an intermediate space between a given individual and relevant others, between, say, husband and wife, parent and child, the living and the dead, or between past and present. The intermediate function is constituted and expressed primarily via the body as a surface of both separations and contacts (Anzieu 1981:71–72). As a self-confined space and one of contact, the body allows for the mediation between fusion and separation, corporeality and language, subjective images and shared symbols. Thus, the 'potential space' develops between the infant and its mother on the basis of maternal care, nursing, enveloping sounds and odors, the smile, touch, and embrace, and the alternate presence and absence of the mother. This potentiality gradually becomes the "site of cultural experience" (Winnicot 1971). At this interface between inner and outer, body and enveloping cult house, self and others, the patient participates in the cultural heritage, meanwhile satisfying his own needs while making sense out of his affects and memories.

Culture as an intermediate space will be studied here more specifically from the perspective of bodily mediation. This is the locus of the culture as weave, as well as the very site and focus of the *internal approach* that I am undertaking. As "analogic operator" (Bourdieu 1980:111ff.), the human body institutes homology and communication between the fields of body, group, and life-world. It thereby brings about a kind of resonance between these fields. As I will demonstrate (see ch. 4), the Yaka are very concerned with both respect for and trespassing of bodily boundaries particularly in expressions of intimate fellow-feeling, such as amiable commensality, the intertwining of legs (an expression for conjugal sexuality), the mutual exchange of bodily odor, the sharing of parental affection and intimacy of the home, or in the exchange of speech and sharing of palm wine, and so on. This marking and crossing of bodily boundaries operates within the clearly delineated space of the conjugal home or in the meeting place at the center of the compound, and takes place at set moments of the day or lunar cycle. Yaka culture and in particular the healing cults position the human body as a stage and agent of intertwining, as a fabric and weaving loom: the body shell, orifices (mouth, nose, eyes, ears, etc.), and sensory and communicative functions (smell, touch, hearing and speaking, looking and being seen) are poignant avenues of exchange between initiate and healer, husband and wife, parent and child, between body, group, and world. The ritual house, by way of metaphor, is a hen laying an egg, a human and cosmic womb in gestation.

It is my thesis that, in the *khita* cult, the human body, through the senses, affects, attitudes, intentional stances, gestures, and activities, is the basic locus for and agent of remolding the patient's experience of her body in reproduction, of her relations with the other gender and the kin-group, or with the life-world. As displayed in the healing cults, the human body offers a sensory and practical grasp or understanding of events, a web and weaving loom for it. The measure of such grasp is pragmatic: it is a feeling and yet constitutes a know-how or competence.

Knowledge in ritual is primarily practical rather than declarative. Indeed, in Yaka ritual, speech is either highly esoteric and fixed or performative. In ritual activities, to know or understand something is to sense it and react appropriately. Insofar as research is concerned, it appears very difficult to gain precise and reliable information about a healing ritual outside the context of its performance, or outside a patient-healer relationship. A few weeks after a therapeutic initiation, it is as if the practical and embodied knowledge no longer has the interactional, contextual, and practical stimuli necessary for that knowledge to become the property of public discourse.

Therapy is for a large part preverbal and beyond cognitive or predicative mediation. Inasmuch as it involves affects, therapy operates basically through bodily experience embedded in the very sense of being both bounded and connected with, and yet receptive or tied to, family, ancestors, and life-world, all of these being rendered or transformed through symbolic drama. That sensory and affective responses are primarily bodily experiences or actions that are already lived prior to becoming self-consciously aware of them is even witnessed on the verbal level in expressions commonly heard among the Yaka: "My head feels heavy," "My leg feels malignity," "He made my heart lift up," "My heart feels stiffened," "That man can no longer keep cool," "The gentle look of kinsmen strengthens me" (1990b, 1991c). One is trembling, agitated, feverish, in a state of arousal or trance before becoming aware of it. The cognitive content of sensory perception and emotional states varies greatly from one culture to another (Kirmayer 1984; Middleton 1989). This is to say that bodily manifestations—facial expression, quality of look, rhythm of speech, palpitations of the heart, gestures, posture, and the like—interconnect, in ways proper to the culture, the experiential and communicative facets of emotions: smiling not only communicates but also produces an emotional experience. This means that any social interaction that alters how and when people smile, grimace, or blush can partly change their emotional experience beyond cognitive mediation. The experience brought forth through the body thus also goes beyond verbal discourse and conceptual representation and involves processes that link perception directly to the realm of sensory or bodily experience.

In and through ritual action, the body's creative symbolizing and empowering capacities intertwine, in innovative and multivalent ways, the various levels of experience with group life and life-world. The healing rituals manipulate the body—in particular its surface or boundary and orifices, its inner rhythms and functions—into a meeting point between patient, family, and life-world. The "social(ized) skin" (T. S. Turner 1980) becomes the stage in space and time upon which the drama of body experience and image, (re)socialization and identity formation, is played out and constituted in healing or in life-cyclical development. By taking into consideration the body both as agent and scene of multivalent drama (at the level of tactile, sexual, visual experience) and metaphoric transference between the fields of body, group, and life-world, I favor, and claim to have adopted, a genuine Yaka approach that ignores much of the divide between mind and body, emotion and idea, subjective and objective, irrational and rational, lower part and upper part of the body, individual and social, action and thought.

My approach has its due limits. The choice of a point of view should necessarily prevent me from attending to all dimensions of ritual, and at the same time limits the number of topics envisaged. Indeed, even if I seek to situate myself on the side of the actors, or more precisely in line or in tune with the ongoing ritual drama being enacted, my method urges me to go beyond the participants' experience, views, or declarations. In my search for the underlying logic and very fabric of healing, I do have in mind the subjective accounts given by various participants, or the contingent interactions and concrete context, but I cannot possibly report all these data. Insofar as the topics are concerned, my analysis focuses on the therapeutic dimension of the *khita* cult rather than on its initiatory aspect. I am not thoroughly unraveling the ideological role of healing, though I assume—in line with Feierman (1985)—that therapy shapes ideology by interpreting the patient's experience (see ch. 5). I will show how much the cult healing proper develops at the edge of the public and masculinist order of control.

Ritual healing, I contend, unfolds a corporeal, maternal, and cosmological space-time order: in relating only by way of metaphor to the social management of the sickness by the elders, the cult aims at a metamorphosis of the social fabric. It is also not my intention to consider the cults as a sociological device through which Yaka society would defuse the supposedly numerous latent structural conflicts between its rules of agnatic descent and uterine filiation. If this last analysis attracts little attention, I may recall that it is also because the subject of Yaka kinship has already been amply treated by Roosens (1971). Moreover, the cult healing proper gives neither privileged weight nor straightforward attention to the social dimension or the conflicts exacerbated by the occurrence of a serious illness. The formal procedures for ordering the fabric of social relations pertain to men's councils in the center of diurnal village life. Healing cults, however, develop at the edge of public space and political strategies. The divinatory oracle does not primarily aim at moral accusation; instead, it lays bare shortcomings in the social fabric for which family members who hold major positions in the kin group are responsible. By means of metaphor, the ritual drama reweaves the familial tissue basically, albeit indirectly, through its cosmological referents and a resonance attained between the corporeal, familial, and cosmological. Rather than acting in concert with power-holders or being social reformers, healers tend to be genuine 'artists of life' and innovators of culture via its basic sources of inspiration: the human body or corporeality inspiring and informing a situational interplay or interweave between micro- and macrocosm, and itself informed by the resonance between bodily states and processes in the group and the life-world. They aim at healing the body, the kin group, and life-world as an interweave and rhythmic resonance.

2 The Cosmology of Gender Arrangements and Life Transmission

Yaka oral lore, cults, and ritual activities depict the seasonal, lunar, and life-cyclical changes in the cosmos and in the plant and animal worlds as fundamentally processes of life transmission. To the Yaka it is self-evident that the processes of conception, flowering, fruit-bearing or birth, ripening or maturation, decay, death, and rebirth are never ending and bring together both the sexes and the successive generations. Because the cosmic world order is less tangible than the social patterns of gender, descent, marriage, and labor division, there is, in healing cults, a pervasive transvaluation (see Flax 1990) of the social and corporeal onto the cosmic. It is not so much 'representation' that orders the life-world and gender relations, but an intertwining of forces and meaning pertaining to the realms of gender, kin, and life transmission with the cosmological fields of regenerative forces. This indirect cosmological portrayal of gender and life transmission, since it is so encompassing and very much acted out in an unspoken way in daily practice, gains the quasi-autonomous status of a self-evident world order. Space is not so much shaped by a visual journey or by a will to power that would gradually turn the life-world into a man-made layout of located forces to subjugate, of pathways and divisions to impose, or of predefined goals to achieve. Space is differentiated through awareness of and participation in various centers and vectors of forces, events, and movements. In discussing these spatial layouts, I mainly render the perspective of men in both their discourse and daily activities. However, the homestead and the home, as well as the cults, display a more maternal sensing and reembodying of space (see ch. 5).

In this chapter I argue the following points: First, concerning public daily life, the social categories of maleness, patrilineal descent, and seniority are correlated with lineal order, uprightness, and verticality, while femaleness, uterine filiation, and mediatory roles are correlated with a cyclical and concentric space-time order. The asymmetric attributions of gender reflect and also act as a paradigm for the cosmological field: they undergird the interplay between the agnatic life force and the uterine vital flow, and also between the life-bearing processes of bloodshed in the hunt and of cooking in the home. Gender arrangements and categories are associated with one or another of the various processes of plant growth—rising of sap, flowering, bearing and ripening of fruit. There are, moreover, appropriate foods and medications for men as distinct from the ones for women. Second, particular space-time aspects that are related to the various habitats of fauna or flora, to the lunar and female cycles, or to colors are imbued with motifs of death, (re)generation, (re)birth, and sexual maturation. The same motifs are the core of the transition rituals of boyhood, political enthronement, and funeral. And third, the 'collective unconscious' conveyed in folktales and uncensored speech portrays the hunter, sorcerer, and paramount ruler as culture heros. The hunter and sorcerer in particular engage in a capacity for 'imaginary' world-making that blends together key symbolic themes in an indistinct realm, a wilderness, which nonetheless acts as a catalyst for capturing untamed forces and for 'cooking them outdoors.'

2.1 Horizontal and Vertical Space

Movements through horizontal and vertical space offer a weave, rather than a map, for gender differences and their mediation. Culturally encoded meanings and values related to such pairs as upstream/downstream, present/past, dry/wet, cold/hot, bitter/sweet, open/closed, accessible/concealed, raw/cooked, propitious/ominous, right/left, light/darkness, day/night, visible/invisible, and life/death are all components or conceptual underpinnings of this spatial ordering and of the gender-appropriate activities that are associated with the various spatial domains.

2.1.1 *The cardinal points of cosmological space originate in a specific and practical interaction with the surrounding life-world.* They are not fixed in reference to some objective, 'universally' valid, criteria. For example, when standing, Yaka men indicate the direction of the rising sun with the right arm and the setting sun with the left. In such a position the individual will have a horizon (*ndilu*, "border, limit") both in front and behind. The courses of the great rivers in Kwaango land—the Waamba, Twaana, and Kwaango—offer the Yaka specific points of orientation. Needless to say, these orientations do not necessarily correspond to a set of objective geographical directions established mechanically in relation to abstract points—as with the aid of a compass, for example. North, south, east, and west are a terminology alien to Yaka culture. In practice the Yaka define the directions of the rivers with reference to the heavenly course of the sun from dawn to dusk. Folktales (*yitsimbwa*) and ritual texts, like the elders, explain that the sun rises upstream of the great rivers and sets downstream. The sun emerges from the earth in the morning after having traversed its breadth by following a subterranean watercourse. It exits the earth at the source of the large rivers. Upstream and rising sun—

situated toward the east—all acquire in this manner a significative value relative to diurnal origin as well as to masculine rule. Political traditions hold that the Luunda arrived in the Yaka region at a point not far from the sources of the Kwaango river: these spots are sometimes associated with Nzofu, in the area of Kahemba, the cradle of the Luunda dynast Nzav. Kaolin clay destined for the enthronement of the paramount chiefs is said to come from Koola by way of the Luunda dynast at Nzofu. During the accession to power of a political chief at the local or regional levels, the handing over of white clay or kaolin coming from this Luunda cradle to the chief, followed by his anointment with it, contributes to his ritual 'birth' into power. The anointment confers on him the status of sovereign ruler and supreme mediator of animal and human fertility (see Devisch 1988). Just as upstream and river source connote, in the male view, the masculine origin of life, conversely the water flowing downstream connotes the law of exogamy and the succession of generations, as expressed in the proverb: "As water does not flow upwards to its source, so the man does not marry his mother." In other words, the descendant does not spill his lifegiving capacity into the ascendant. The sorcerer who takes the lives of his descendants by withdrawing the life which he himself had previously transmitted to them is furthermore likened to an incestuous person. A proverb applied to both the sorcerer and the committer of incest declares that for such persons "the source and mouth of the stream are situated at the same point on the Yingubu plains."

In folktales, the notions downstream (*kubaanda,* "below") and setting sun— as does also west—signify a decline or end, but one pregnant with a new beginning; the male perspective associates this world with the onset of motherhood. In the evening the sun appears to submerge into the tributary of the great rivers. Some oral lore associates this tributary with the Zaire river, more than six days' walk from the northern border of Yaka land, or with the 'river of salt' (the Atlantic Ocean). Folktales report that, with the exception of paramount chiefs and powerful ritual specialists, commoners may be stricken with blindness when reaching the place where the sun sets. For ritual purposes, this location is assimilated with the confluence of great rivers like the Waamba and Mbaamba situated at the edges of the Taanda district and flanked by forest galleries. Here also, it is thought, life is extinguished, and from this site come death and its agent, evil sorcery. According to popular narratives, the forests of the river valleys are, by extension, populated by nonancestral spirits *(m-fu)* and monstrous dwarfs *(yitsuutsu)* roaming around to molest *(-tsuutsa)* the wayward individual or drag him down to the underworld where he will visit with the ancestral shades. According to the Luunda traditions, at the time of their arrival in Kwaango land the Luunda drove back the autochthonous Tsaamba and Hungana populations into these forests. The flow of the water signifies to the Yaka that every ordeal comes to an end, as in the expression:

N-koku kesi naana, kiima kyatwaala yibeti, "Water does not run for no reason at all, it is the slope which sweeps it along."

Every act that has no further bearing on the present situation is carried downstream, as is every stain from which the newly circumcised, the initiate, the patient, or the bereaved ritually rids him- or herself by bathing in the stream or wading upstream towards its source. The corpse is likewise buried with its gaze fixed in the direction of the water's descent. Tradition recommends that one lie in the same direction when retiring at night; ideally, one faces the north when getting up in the morning, so that the rising sun is on the right hand.

Front and back, left and right offer the cardinal points. Within the frame of reference I have been describing, the left bank of the Waamba river is situated 'in front of' the Taanda population. This location serves as a horizon 'in front' (that is, to the north) of the familiar universe, as it is evoked by oral lore, while the right banks of the Twaana and Kwaango rivers function as horizons 'behind,' that is, the southern boundary. This south is opposed to the north as is behind to front, the shadow to that which is clearly perceived, and as strange or dreaded phenomena are contrasted to that which is known and controllable. The oral lore describing the great migrations relates that the Kwaango river was crossed from the left bank. It is striking, furthermore, that the Yaka groups tend to consider people living to the left bank of the great river of reference to be backward; its inhabitants are dubbed "the people who eat dogs"—in other words, those who do not practice exogamy, held to be the distinctive human trait.

These lineal directions and flows in the cosmological order, as they are depicted in the folktales, display a concentric and cyclical pattern in the female realms of the conjugal home and of the house of seclusion in the healing cults. Source and mouth, high and low, upstream and downstream, left and right meet in the initiand couched in fetal position on her bed: the positions of ascendant and descendant, male and female intertwine in the androgynous identity of the initiand in a process of self-gestation. In Yaka symbolism, the same positions fuse in the couple in conjugal union.

2.1.2 *Village, forest, and savanna, day and night, and origin and end are key polar concepts that differentiate between the realms of inhabited and noninhabited space.* The distinction between "village" *(hata)* and "forest" *(n-situ)* is primarily of an ontological rather than a geographical or sociological order. (An analysis of gender and kin-related partitions and activities in the village realm figures in 3.1 below.) Village corresponds to the realm of life, day, the known, organized, and licit, in opposition to forest, the realm of the dead, night, the obscure, unknown, uncommon, where the ancestral shades, spirits, and forces that deflate or empower mix, where toxic and edible plants grow side by side, and both illness and healing find their sources. In other words village designates the space of the *societas,* the organization of life for the good of all, the relations of subordination, familiarity, and of mutual aid within a particular group, that is, their recognized activities and social bonds. Those persons forming a community or hamlet in a village aid each other in working the fields, gather at the well to steep manioc, launder clothes or draw water at the stream, and may well travel together or attempt to resettle in the same neighborhood when migrating to the capital city of Kinshasa. Domestic animals belong to that same village realm: chickens, pigeons, goats (approximately three to every household), and pigs (a third again the number of goats). They serve especially as means of exchange and symbolization.

The category 'forest,' in contrast, is applied either to the fantasy or imaginary realm including people and spirits one has no relation with—the foreigner and all monstrous spirits—or to the domain of the wild, including the predatory animals, the evil sorcerers, and the revengeful deceased who are kept out of the ancestral world. In the eyes of the Yaka, any individual who does not figure among one's acquaintances and who lives in a distant region—that is, far enough away such that one does not go there to contract a marriage or exchange goods or services—is considered *n-ndzeendza,* literally, "the separate." It is, however, especially the deviant (this notion will be defined later on; see 5.3) plotting in secret who is counted as a forest dweller: such include the sorcerer, thief, or individual who violates the rights of another, in particular matrimonial rights. When an illness or a disorder in the village life is held to stem from some illicit act, it is understood that the forest has taken hold of or encroached upon the dominion of the village. Popular fantasies hold that shades, sorcerers, and monstrous figures live in the twilight of the forest. Night and forest are opposed to the social visibility of the *societas* and infringe on the inhabitable space: one presses close to companions on the dark moonless evenings. A solitary stroller at night draws suspicion. For this reason the Christian missionary, for example, in the habit of taking the air at twilight, became suspect of seeking to draw the deceased into his service.

Only men may enter the forested areas and marshlands. The forest galleries are situated in the humid valleys of the great rivers and shelter the majority of the larger game animals (greater herbivores); hunting them is a highly valued activity restricted to the men. Similarly, only men may penetrate the marshlands bordering the streams. Braving snakes, they there cultivate bananas and tap palm sap for wine. Secondary forests are to be found on the plateau bordering the forest galleries. It is on this plateau and on the hillsides flanking the valleys that each family unit engages in subsistence agriculture (see 2.3.7). The cultivation of crops *(sodi)* on burnt-off land makes it constantly necessary to relocate the fields and consequently renders impossible any demarcation *(ndilu)* of the field being worked *(yilanga),* other than the name of the valley or forest where it is found.

The sandy savanna plateau *(tseki)* covered with herbaceous vegetation is recognized as a feminine milieu. The women engage in various sorts of gathering on these steppes and savannas. The men do not venture onto the plains except for the collective hunts carried out during the dry season when the grasslands are burned. As the savanna gives way to denser vegetation, it is usual to distinguish between the wooded steppes or secondary forest *(mabwaati)* and the more lightly wooded savanna *(bikwaati)*, where grasses are more abundant. Vegetation thus readily serves as an indicator of seasonal differences.[1]

2.1.3 *Certain zones and activities assure the transition or mediation between the realms of village and forest.* Inasmuch as they allow transition, they are propitious. Thus the outskirts of the village serve as a meeting place in the evening for youth where recreational sex and in particular joking relations have free reign. Again, it is at the periphery of the village, or at the stream where the villagers bathe, that the numerous healing and purification rites, as well as the phases of seclusion and reintegration belonging to the rites of passage, are held, frequently at twilight or at dawn. In these transitional realms men and women mix freely, in contrast with gender and age arrangements observed at diurnal assemblies held in the center of the village.

Menstruation is associated with the transitional zone at the edge of the village, where in former times women had their little houses for menstruation; it is there that garbage is disposed. Unprocessed goods from the bush—firewood or plants—are brought in, although not on the regular paths, and left at the edge. Once disassembled, they may be brought into the homestead.

Beyond the village itself, arrangements of space become more and more unmarked. The zone in which the inhabitants live and carry out their activities is called *n-totu*, "land that yields food." The category is distinct from that of the "chiefdom or territory" *(tsi)*, which groups a particular population under the same traditional political authority. Referring to the tributary relations *(-laambula)* of that population to the ruling chief to whom they should pay a tribute *(n-laambu)*, the territory is also called *n-laambu*. *Yikoolu* designates the familiar region that extends in concentric waves around one's village and within whose limits the adult might move about, or at least not hesitate to do so, in order to engage in matrimonial relations, or to exchange goods or services. Any distance within this familiar region appears to its inhabitants to be significantly shorter than an equivalent distance beyond its bounds. The point of reference here is not one's own domestic space but may depend on any of several possible orientations: the positions of the sun corresponding to the traveller's points of departure and arrival, the number of nights one must spend on the journey, and precise spatial landmarks including related households, chiefly residences, or the homes of diviners or ritual specialists. The rites of puberty, by which pubescent boys prefigure their marital condition, allow them access to the *yikoolu*. The newly circumcised are permitted to organize dances involving several dozens of the villages in the region during which they strike up ludic relations with girls of similar age.

In the *yikoolu,* plains and forests are divided into named sections with imprecise and partially overlapping boundaries; the region's rivers and the watercourse serve as the main reference points for locating them. Their partitioning reflects the activities that take place there—hunting, collecting, agriculture—activities which themselves are especially determined by the ecology and types of vegetation to be found in the region.[2] Lineage groups may relate to one another in terms of geographical landscape: rivers, hills, forests, savannas, graves mark the routes of migration and give a stability to the past. The land bears the signs of the sequentiality of the journey and helps to fix the order of successive migrations: the most prestigious group, by referring its deeds to the source of a river or to hills "up high," earns primacy in time. The landscape becomes a cultural one. Lineage names may recall such located deeds. The land tells a story of lineage hierarchy and sustains relations of co-operation, for example, in the seasonal collective battues.

Any area beyond the *yikoolu* is foreign land: it is usually out of reach for childrearing women and their children. Young marriageable and married men may venture into this area in search of school education or paid labor. Sometimes senior men and women will enter this unknown region to meet with a renowned diviner. On a journey into the foreign land, men walk ahead and women follow. Indeed, the world is open far wider for men than women. The young men who travel to Kinshasa outnumber by far their female peers.

The noninhabited land within one's region, in particular the savanna area, figures as a benevolent transitional zone between related locales as well as between the genders. An in-married woman is referred to as one who has followed the path through the savanna. Recreational sex or any seductive demonstration on the part of a married woman evoke this in-between zone. Popular imagery situates extramarital relations on the edges of the fields *(n-teetwa sodi);* in folktales or palavers, a woman's lover is indicated with the expression: "he from the top end of her field." Popular judgment thereby practically excuses the woman for her behavior; however, the offended party tends to situate the extramarital affair in the conjugal home.

The crossing of paths *(phaambwandzila)* forms the junction point for all the partitions and directions of the horizontal space, especially when it is found in proximity to a village: it links upstream and downstream, the village with forest, savanna, stream, and fields, hunting tracts and the inhabited space, different locales with each other, the homestead and the lineage quarter. Intersections located at some distance from the village, near a spring or stream, are sites where the solitary wanderer is likely to be whisked underground by ghosts, or where he may reach or reemerge from the underworld. The ground of such crossings is tread by all inhabitants of the village without distinction; it is here that the footprints are superposed *(-dyaatasana)*[3] and that misfortune may settle itself upon the individual, or may be chased away. The numerous rites of purification and incorporation intentionally make use of these points in order to exclude the participants from the inhabited space as it was before and to reintegrate them into it after cleansing. It will also be seen that a crossing of footpaths constitutes a junction in the vertical spatial ordering between high and low, surface and underground, and between the living and the dead. It is at a crossroads, at the outskirts of the village space, that foreign merchants set up their business: it is here that cassava and peanuts are compiled and packed for trading, when about every two months a truck comes along.

2.2 Cosmological Portrayal of Gender

Certain mythic statements or ritual activities depict reproductive union between sun, moon, and earth, or between fire and water. Transposed onto the human domain, this macrocosmical union sets the scene for depicting both gender differences and their surpassing in the transmission of life. The rainbow palm, parasol, and banana trees, the he-goat, the earthen jar set in the fork of a three-pronged stick, the cock crowing at dawn, the laying hen, and the termite mound all serve as cosmological icons of life-bearing sexuality.

2.2.1 *Palm tree and earthen jar are metaphors of the world.* The oil *(mbati* or *tsaamba)* and the raffia *(yiimba)* palms, which grow both in the village and the forest, are rich in cosmological and sexual symbolism. When the tree has reached an age of approximately fourteen years, its trunk may attain a height of eight meters or more: it becomes smooth, except at the base and immediately under its sphere-shaped crown of abundant leaves. The buds of the crown successively engender female and then male inflorescences; by bearing these simultaneously, the palm tree fecundates itself. The clusters of palm nuts require six months to mature. As soon as the whitish sap of the raffia palm seeps from the trunk and is collected in a calabash, it begins to ferment and produces palm wine, a drink highly prized by the men. This sap is gathered either by making an incision in the stem of a male cluster or by cutting the trunk at the base of a leaf.[4] In certain narratives the cluster of red nuts nested in the center of the leafy crown symbolizes the sun placed in the center of the firmament, as well as the paramount Luunda ruler, regional dynasts, and vassals. The trunk of the palm tree denotes the junction between the earth, where one stands, and the firmament. The azimuth, the vertical link between the sun at its zenith (which bears male connotations) and the earth's surface (which bears female connotations), is signified by the long, smooth trunk of the parasol tree that grows on fallow land. It is also represented by the trunk of the palm tree as well as of the banana plant which produces a lengthy inflorescence curved down towards the ground and strikingly colored with violet and reddish-brown shades.

The palm tree is first an icon of the diurnal life-bearing journey of the sun. The sap rising up within the trunk and oozing from the male inflorescence is associated with the rising sun. The sun itself is considered as a body of water emerging from the spring which is the source of the great rivers of Yaka land. Both the sun's trajectory and the rainbow's arch are said to outline or demarcate the heavens. At the height of its heavenly course, the sun may sometimes "boil over" and flood the earth with a downpour, especially when it appears in its rainbow form, *khongolu,* as the rainbow-serpent *n-kongolu.* At the moment of flowering the palm tree fertilizes the inflorescence with its white sap. The Yaka believe that through fermentation *(fula),* the whitish inflorescence is transformed. This is their way of saying that the male flower-cluster is changed into the female inflorescence, thus producing the growth of a bunch of red palm nuts. The rising of sap is seen as a kind of fermentation which results in the bearing of the red fruits at the top of the trunk. Once ripened, the reddish palm oil may be extracted from the nuts through a laborious process of cooking done by men. Thus the sun, which at its height seems to boil over onto the earth, is metaphorically associated with the maturation of the palm tree, its flowering, and the effusion of sap.

The palm tree, moreover, metaphorically depicts how much the genitor and genitrix—like the initiate—tap from a maternal source of all life. The emergence of the palm nuts and the movement of the sap downwards in the palm tree and back into the earth for cooking or gestation serve as metaphors of pregnancy. In the rites enthroning the political titleholder and in the healing cults, the macrocosmic significance of the palm tree is transferred to the seclusion house and to the initiate's body. The *khita* or *ngoombu* initiate, for example, is returned to "the egg-like womb of the world" by being confined in the ritual house. Through seclusion, the initiate relives the foetal condition, experiencing both gestation and self-generation, *ngoongu,* by sponsoring in his or her body the cross-fertilization of the white (palm) sap and the red life-giving fluid (extracted from palm nut). *Ngoongu* includes the cosmogonic images of 'arche,' the 'arch-mother' or 'arch-womb,' the primal and ever-renewed generation of life from the egg- or palm tree-like 'macrocosmic womb' suspended between the heavenly and subterranean trajectories of sun and moon. In the Yaka worldview, this womb is bounded by the trajectory of the sun, which is thought to be parallel to the great Kwaango river that drains the whole Kwaango basin, a major part of Yaka land. The palm tree thus evokes the unceasing emergence of life when male fecundation 'ferments' into maternal potency.

The double-edged sword of the ruler is an icon of the palm tree whose form is depicted in the shape of sword and scabbard. Itself a macrocosmic metaphor for life regenerating itself, the palm tree may well display a 'ternary' logic, that is, one of mediation overcoming the separation between the realms of heaven and earth, upstream and downstream, white (of the blossom) and red (of the palm nuts, the sun), male and female, polity and autochthony (see Devisch 1988). This symbolism receives an iconic embodiment in the chief's sword of rulership, called "the sword of life and death." As commonly interpreted, the sword, wrapped in a leopard pelt or brandished in the Luunda war dance, recalls the bloody Luunda invasion. It is a long, double-edged sword, with two parallel lines engraved in the middle and over its whole length and with a pointed, spherical metal hilt. The blade and hilt thus evoke the mythical and virile *kyandzangoombi* python inhabiting the trunk of the palm; the parallel lines represent the palm sap that first rises within and then, after fermentation, oozes down the trunk. The sword's scabbard is indeed shaped like a palm tree; it depicts a vagina-cum-uterus. Male and female connotations are thus joined in sword and scabbard. As such, the sword stands for the chief's mediating (ternary) function: he combines male and female attributes and metaphorically represents both himself and his offspring; that is, he is his own life source. His sword is a political weapon and a symbol of his chiefly power over continuity and rebirth, life and death. The act of enthronement, like the chief's sword, transfers the basic metaphor of the palm tree to the Yaka nation. The region under the direct control of the paramount ruler in Yaka land, *Kyaambvu*, can be figuratively depicted as that cluster of palm nuts that is the most central and the closest to the trunk and its original blossom. Other clusters gravitate around this central cluster, and this serves as a metaphor for the various regions and subregions in Yaka land. Like palm nuts, the clusters of villages are axially situated on the stalks that stand for the autochthonous landowners.

The palm tree, in particular its rising sap, symbolizes the backbone of the agnatic social organization in doubly unilineal Yaka society. The parasol tree *(n-seenga)* that grows on fallow land acts in the *khita* 'gyn-eco-logical' healing cult as the substitute of the palm tree and contributes to the symbolism of self-fecundation (see 6.3.2). The palm tree and in particular the parasol tree, through its association with suffering and the overcoming of death, are the polar opposite of the *mudyi* "milk tree" among the Ndembu (Turner 1967:20–25, 52–58). (The *n-seenga* parasol tree in Kwaango is however not to be confused with the *museng'u* tree in Ndembu land.) In Yaka culture, the palm tree testifies to men's erectile stance of authority, and palm wine sustains their word of power: both the men's stance and word aim at regenerating social ties, masculine values, and hierarchy. Among the Yaka *ngoongu* seems to bear much of the values of *mudyi* in Ndembu culture, as a female or maternal principle pervading society and nature.

The earthen jar *(loondu)* is an icon of the cosmos. Pottery is made exclusively by women who are widowed or whose husbands have left home for a time as migrant workers. In molding a jar from clay, the widowed or celibate potter anticipates a new pregnancy (see plate 2). She forms it in the image of the macrocosm, the universe formed like an egg; she also fashions a neck that depicts the male principle of life transmission. She then allows the jar to dry in the sun and fires it, preferably on an evening when the (male) sun tints the (female) moon with a blood-red hue as it rises above the horizon at the beginning of the lunar cycle.

Another example of the cosmic iconography of pottery is the *yisuungu* shrine. The property of a chief or patriarch, the *yisuungu* can be activated by way of a proper indictment to protect the courtyard from an alleged threat of sorcerous abuse of lightning and thunderstorm. A three-pronged stick, esoterically termed the *lungundzyala*, is placed in a hole filled with water drawn from the confluence of two rivers—a site which stands for the set sun. (Since it represents the parturient with bent legs—a position known as *n-kuunda*—the three-pronged fork evokes the mother and the house.) The bottom portion of a jar, also containing water, is placed in this fork. The region to be protected from the lightning and thunderstorm is figured by the bottom of this jar in which a cowrie, with vagina-like connotations, is thrown. In some varieties of *yisuungu,* the bottom portion of the jar does not contain water and is surmounted by a conical structure of woven lianas covered with linen, almost like the neck of a jar, or like the top half of the masks used by the newly circumcised. The shrine is topped with feathers of those birds of prey that from heaven stoop on their prey in a movement compared to lightning. Onto the conical top are hung two flat round baskets *(kolu)* believed to bear, respectively, the sun and the moon as well as their fields of light. The firmament *(lufuumba)* "across which the light of the sun pierces" is figured by the top of the masks or by the linen cone of the *yisuungu* shrine: as it is told, the white spots evoke the rain and the light of the stars. I speculate that the crown of geometric shapes engraved on the neck of many jars is also meant to signify the firmament.

2.2.2 *The hen about to lay and the cock crowing at dawn are core symbols in the cosmology and healing cults.* They introduce the particular ability to surpass the conventional arrangements of vertical and horizontal space. The hen and the cock ensure not only the transition between the forest and the village or between the various familial and domestic spaces—these fowl peck about in all the dwellings without distinction—but also between earth and sky, low and high, and day and night. As a two-legged creature of the domestic realm that cuts across core spatial and temporal divisions, the hen is the optimal symbolic substitute of the human being in mutation. The hen about to lay as well as the crowing cock inspire core metaphors underlying the emergence of clairvoyance in a mediumistic diviner-to-be (see 5.2).

The crowing cock *(khokwa khookula)*, and in particular the white-feathered cock with a blood-red comb *(buluundu)*, that announces sunrise while standing on one leg is an icon of the rising sun (see plate 13). By substitution the cock also depicts the seminal hearts of the palm tree, the parasol tree, and the banana plant. Like diviners, renowned healers are buried with the inflorescence of the palm or parasol tree placed on their head. In ritual context, the crest of the cock and the one claw on which it postures itself metonymically trace the vertical line stretching from the point on which one stands to the firmament above. The pose struck by the cock is named *kataku* and depicts the virile and fecundating erection. At sunrise and sunset while in seclusion, the young newly-circumcised initiates, naked and chanting songs of their role in life transmission, are required to hold themselves erect on one leg; the other leg is bent with the sole of the foot resting on the inside of the other knee. Family elders adopt this virile stance when they address the agnatic cult spirits (see plate 4). Just as the *kataku* position implies virility, a fractured leg instead expresses impotence. The guardian and healer of masculine fertility (the *yisidika*) who presides over the numerous rites of puberty proper to the *yikubu* cult, also called *n-khanda*, and who is meant to foster the boys potency during the circumcision ceremonies, is the same person who practices the ritual art of healing bone fractures. There is another position considered equivalent to the *kataku* posture which consists of pressing the legs against each other and crossing the toes. This gesture, called *-lama,* refers rather to sexual union, to the "union or intertwining of the legs" *(-biindasana maalu),* and to taking possession of the conjugal space.[5]

Like birds of prey, cocks crowing at dawn may also evoke the realm of night and sorcery. The Yaka say of sorcerers that in giving a white hen over to a renowned master-sorcerer they actually kill one of their kinsmen and hand over that life to their initiator in order to acquire the occult power of sorcery. This occult initiation is the reverse of that of the clairvoyant diviner who tracks down the sorcerous plots. In a secret and perverse way, the apprentice-sorcerer seeks to appropriate some of the auspicious forces bundled in the chiefly *yisuungu* shrine or embodied by the diviner-to-be. On such occasions the apprentice-sorcerer is invited to bite off the head of a cock with his teeth and to place it in the base of a broken jar set into the fork of a three-pronged stick. This event is held at dawn and at a river source. Malignant sorcery is compared to death-giving virile sexuality that causes bleeding instead of fertility. It has the power of lightning *(ndzasi);* this last is pictured as a cock which, head thrown back, swoops down from the sky toward the earth to sow his sperm there in the form of glazed sand *(ndiingyandzasi).* The sexual symbolism of malignant sorcery is further evoked by some small carnivores and birds of prey. Small predators *(phuku)* such as the weasel *(lumbongi)* creep into the village at night in order to steal hens, chicks, and eggs. Pregnant women and initiates—the initiate is associated with the fetus—are forbidden to eat, touch, or even name them (see Devisch 1979:181-85). Animals whose skins are spotted *(matona)* may also depict a sorcerer; they also are forbidden to initiates and pregnant women.

2.2.3 *The trope of color displays gender and moral properties.* By virtue of their capacity to reflect the successive phases of day and night, of heat and coldness, from one sunrise to another and in the various stages of the lunar cycle, the colors red, white, and black serve to symbolize the complementary arrangements of the genders; they also frame the definition and handling of illness, healing, and health. Combined with spatial polarizations, they denote the boundary-trespassing value of fecundation, gestation, and delivery, and the links between generations crossing over death.

Blue *(buundi)* signifies the sun at rest. The sun as it is about to rise is associated with the subterranean world and with what is not erect, with whatever is considered low on the vertical axis, with the river source from whence the sun emerges, or with cold. In this phase it is thought to have a bluish hue, that of water in the shade or of "blackened wood, pulled from the hearth" *(bundyambaawu)*. When used in fertility rituals, the *bundyambaawu* connotes the virile member at rest. For curing masculine impotence, it is a piece of a trunk of the banana tree blackened by the fire which serves as a *bundyambaawu*. For circumcision, it is a log extracted from the fire lit near the house of *yifiika,* 'mother' of the circumcised, around which the initiates and the whole community have danced through the preceding night. At dawn, the *bundyambaawu* is placed on a path which leads away from the village to the circumcision camp located on the periphery. The most senior of the circumcision candidates is seated straddling the log before undergoing the operation. Shortly before the ceremony and dressed in a red loin-cloth, he would have executed a chiefly dance on the roof of the house while displaying the chiefly sword.

Just as red may evolve from being pure color *(tona)* to fire red *(mbaawu)*, it is said that pubescent boys and girls have the inner capacity to grow to full ardor and fertility. The rising sun is associated with the vertical 'high up' and with the sky. It is emphasized that the rising sun "feeds or strengthens itself" *(taangwa buditsaatsa),* in that it constitutes its own vital source. That vigor *(khoondzu)* incarnated by the rising sun is what men wish each other when, in the morning, they exchange the cola nut *(kaasu),* a stimulant. Circumcision or rites of reintegration that conclude an initiation, healing, or mourning period also take place at sunrise. A final step in the reintegration may be arranged for on the roof of the conjugal home, or if necessary on an elevated platform erected in the middle of the village for the occasion. There, initiate and partner are invited to exchange pepper and to "entwine the legs" *(-biindasana maalu)* in a gesture signifying the lifting of the conjugal prohibition. In line with this, ritual vocabulary designates defloration and the first experiences of orgasm with the term *-yoka tona*, that is, "to make the color incandescent," with reference to the sun. According to ritual symbolism, the sun at zenith maintains itself in a constant state of ebullition *(taangwa budifusukidi)*: to it are attributed the characteristics of fire *(mbaawu*, a term designating anything that gives off heat or light), and, consequently, it is associated with blood *(meenga)*. Fire red is equally identified with upstream—the 'above' of the horizontal axis and the east, and further may evolve into an icon of the androgynous principle of autogeneration, after the manner of the crowing cock and the hen about to lay. In line with this, the sun is assimilated to an origin and a source of heat and force *(ngolu)*. Oral lore, in evoking the sun which rises and approaches its zenith *(nyaangu)*, describes the ardor *(ndzuundza)* of the conquerors, the great hunters, or those who legitimately seek revenge. One also turns to this metaphor in order to depict high fever, inebriety, or liminal experiences such as parturition, mortal agony, or trance. In situations such as these in which certain limits are exceeded, the color red, considered as self-sustaining, connotes existential completeness. The red of the morning sun, depicted as *tona*, pure color, is the harmonious blending of colors and of spaces. This red similarly indicates a fulfilled and mature human condition. Once news of her pregnancy has been made public, the young wife is adorned with a belt of red pearls, after she has been spat upon with water on her womb. Paramount chiefs monopolize red garments.

Dark reddish brown, *khula*, also labelled *ngula* or *luundu*, evokes longing and readiness for fertility, pregnancy, and the setting sun. The setting sun is also associated with ravines and the downstream direction of rivers, where it enters the earth for its nocturnal subterranean journey. Red takes on a ambivalent value when it is mingled with the white of the moon at the onset of the lunar cycle. During initiatory seclusion the small brownish termitary *(mbaambakhuku)* is suspended from a branch or fastened in a treetop with a liana; the object thus carries, to put it in metaphoric terms, the fetal signification of the setting sun and first moon. The moment the darkening sun disappears over the horizon is in ordinary language expressed with the terms *budisika khula*, "when the sun prepares *khula*." This phrase also applies to the novice preparing a paste by rubbing a section of the red wood of the *n-kula* tree against a wet stone. Mixing it with palm oil, he oints his body with this paste. Identified with the fetus bathing in its mother's blood, the novice is therefore required to avoid the sunshine of broad daylight and never leaves the ritual dwelling except at evening. Other prohibitions see to it that values of the setting and rising suns should not contaminate the novice. He must avoid any allusion to spotted animals, for their skins may combine different shades of red or mix red with white. It is also forbidden to have anything which might resemble lightning in the initiate's presence, hence the prohibitions against bringing fire into the cult house, throwing water or allowing a piece of firewood to fall nearby, offering the novice some manioc which during preparation has spilled over into the fire *(luku lwatyaamuki)*, or any reference to birds of prey who dive out of the sky, or birds whose plumage or legs are red in color. The setting sun, as well as the night and red clay that are associated with it, connote concealment, subjacency, latency, rest, or gestation. Ritual practices and some folktales allow a glimpse of the following cosmological scheme through their layers of metaphorical transpositions. At twilight the sun descends into the waters downstream and disappears into the earth by way of the ravines *(mbeengi)* to which the sun has conferred its reddish color *(kabeenga)*, or by way of the caves *(yitadi)* situated along the water's edge. During the night the sun returns to the upstream side by way of a subterranean river. The reddish clay *(luundu)* collected in the ravines and that which one might find in discarded snail shells or in hollows inside the caves *(muundu)* thus come to depict the earth as a place of gestation.[6]

White is basically associated with kaolin clay. Since kaolin is collected at marshy spots that evoke the cradle from whence the full moon emerges, it carries the life source in emergence. It is believed that the moon retires in or rises up from one or another marshy spot near the main river Kwaango. Kaolin is primarily the privilege of the maternal uncle, who uses it to link up his sister's child with the uterine source of life (see 3.4). In the agnatic line of political titleholders and sodalities, the agnatic role is passed down through the male line, but it needs to be vitalized by the uterine life flow to gain a capacity to regenerate itself. When a patriarch, a political chief, or the initiate of an agnatic sodality (as, for example, the blacksmith) is close to death, the ancestral kaolin *(pheemba yibati* or *pheemba ya yitsi khulu)* must be applied for at least one night to the erectile muscle behind the scrotum of the dying man. Popular exegesis has it that the hereditary kaolin put near the scrotum of the patriarch in mortal agony absorbs the vital flow or life source which is in the process of escaping the person near death. The kaolin of rulership is transmitted to the successor when he is ritually 'born' into his function. It is brought into the home of the new owner at dusk, and, like other ancestral objects *(bisiimba)*, it must be protected from the light of day. These ritual items and the kaolin may, however, be found outdoors at the full moon in the case of their owner's illness or of repeated failures in the hunt. White clay is then painted on the cult objects and around the eyes of the ritual figurines, thus repeating one of the gestures that the initiate himself was exposed to during initiation. It is said to "wash" or "distemper" the cult objects: *-kusa pheemba*, or *-yebala pheemba*. As the different names used for it imply, kaolin represents that which revivifies health *(pheemba yakolala baatu)* and sustains longevity *(pheemba yiziingu; pheemba yiziingisa baatu)*. The ancestral kaolin further insures an abundance of game *(pheemba yabambisi)*. It unifies members of the same homestead or lineage quarter and demarcates them from outsiders. After a family reconciliation or rite of passage in the community, certain patriarchs will spray the kaolin in all directions before kindling the fire and distributing it to all the members. The uncle, or the healer who has confirmed avuncular links with his client, whitewashes the left arm of his 'uterine descendants' or the left-hand side of the cult objects with his kaolin in order to enhance the transmission of life from its uterine source. This practice takes place on the occasion of an initiation or its commemoration. Kaolin may also be utilized along with the red *muundu* clay in similar transitional contexts. These two types of earth are different yet complementary, as are the full moon and the setting sun with regard to one another.

Pitch black, *kaphiinda,* is associated with the moonless night: it is a quality associated with charcoal *(holu),* black ashes, or the darkish-red pearl referred to as *ndiimba,* literally, "stain" (Devisch 1979:132–35). The latter refers to bloodshed or the violent and bloody work of an abusive sorcerer. Red shades off into the value of black when high and low intersect in one of its symbols, as, for example, in the case of lightning, birds of prey, or bloodshed. Charcoal and *ndiimba,* like dark night, and in particular the black of midnight *(katankolu)* during which the villagers are in deep sleep and incapable of self-defense, are the marks of the violent and bloody work of abusive sorcery. Ensorcellment that belongs to the black of night is one of illicit violence, inasmuch as the selfish sorcerer appropriates the life of another, bringing the victim to an immutable death of never-ending darkness. Black may be associated with low, cold, the inanimate, and with the darkness of night during the new moon. Articles of kitchen refuse (such as corn cobs, banana peels, pressed palm nuts, and so on) that have been blackened over the fire denote "that which can no longer reproduce." These blackened waste elements can be placed alongside the corpse of someone who has succumbed to his own mischievous deeds or to a mysterious disease, or also alongside the corpse of a deformed or sterile individual, in order to prevent the unfortunate being or its defect from ever reappearing among the descendants. The black of night as a trope of degradation, impurity, negative death is a basic constituent of the "ritual arms of war" *(mateenda).* These arms contain charcoal, gun powder *(thuya,* black in color), dark-colored feces whose appearance connotes the decomposition of lost blood, and the blackish and poisonous *loombi* ashes that are obtained by charring a mixture of toxic ingredients in a casserole over the fire. For the popular imagination a sorcerer may appear at the receiving end of his own wrongdoings and thereby kill himself with these *mateenda*: in death-agony his body swells up, discharges black blood, and vomits a substance similar to charcoal. Such a 'black death' (my expression) with no after-life—the latter being associated with a white condition—strikes culprits undergoing the poison ordeal. The black of night contrasts with the positive values of white and red. A blood sacrifice in rituals of family reunification and of healing aims at compensating for blood shed illegitimately. Then black becomes red, thus recovering its positive qualities of height and heat. The subsequent application of kaolin clay has the capacity to "whitewash, whiten" *(-seemasa)* the stain or defilement *(mbviindu)*, to make it 'blank.' On the ontological level the black/white antinomy, associated with the perversion of red and with the rising sun, serves to designate certain vices. By manipulating this antinomy the group may succeed, for example, in expressing its rejection of the sterile individual when at the death of this person the community seeks to definitively disassociate him or her from society: a banana peel, a corncob, and a piece of sugarcane—all whitish in color—are blackened in the fire, wrapped up, and placed on the buried corpse. This practice expresses the wish that the individual disappear forever.

White and red are in a kind of balance. White, *kaseema,* may positively be associated with lowness, coolness, with fluid or animate life, and with cold and the full moon. It may denote *mooyi,* the uterine life flow that connects each individual through the blood ties with his mother, mother's mother, and maternal great-grandmother, with the uterine source of life. As *kaseema* is the polar complement of positive red proper to *buundi* and *mbaawu, mooyi* is the uterine complement of agnatic life force, *ngolu,* when the heat has hardened the bone. Medicines obtained through boiling but administered cool are powerful *(ngolu).* When in denoting the full moon white mixes with the red of the sun— which also means that it is associated with vertical height—it acquires an ambivalent or transitory value. The kaolin clay *(pheemba)* which serves to mediate between high/low, hot/cold, day/night, daylight/darkness, and red/black neutralizes this ambivalence. Kaolin is used at ritualized moments of transition in the life of an individual, a family or a community. Finally, white is charged with a negative value, and is defiled or degraded to black, when its connotes the last quarter of the moon, that is, when vanishing moonlight and rising sun, day and night, high and low, are conflated.

The smithery manipulates the colors black, red, and white: it is an instance of both violation and foundation of cosmic order. The forge *(luufu)* is situated on the outskirts of the village. The smith dispenses both life and death, for he fashions agricultural and artisanal tools, on the one hand, and weapons, on the other. The smith is regarded as capable of reanimating the bodies of the dead or of treating anemia. In times past the forge had been transformed on occasion into a sort of tribunal where conflicts of interests between competing brothers, that is, of conflict between the realm of diurnal village and nocturnal forest, were adjudicated through the ordeals of poison or fire: "Is not my brother at the source of my lasting failure in the hunt? Is he not the one who causes my wife's repeated abortions by intruding upon her in nightmares?" The smith has earned the name of *ngaangula:* literally, "the artisan who is able to undo someone's secret arts."

2.2.4 *Lunar and female cycles parallel one another.* The lunar cycle at full moon enlivens the night as "a threshold to a new beginning" *(-kyeela),* and it may also chill it into the fallow state of the new moon. Night, inasmuch as it is a time category, is portrayed in the oral lore as that which separates one day from another and which leads to the dawning of the new day. The duration of a journey or of some exceptional activity is normally measured in terms of the number of nights involved. Some narratives deal with the mediative role exercised by the moon on behalf of the sun, in order that the latter may reappear. The idea of gradual progress towards the dawn of a new day is otherwise expressed by the term *-kyeela;* it designates the collective celebration by means of which the community, in dancing the whole night through, celebrates the social rebirth and newly acquired status of one of its members.

The new moon, in particular its total obscurity, connotes coldness: it evokes negative feelings and keeps the villagers indoors and self-absorbed, making them more anxious and, they think, more vulnerable to sorcery. Oral lore marks it as an intrusion of the forest realm into the order of the village. The passage from the new moon or moonless nights to the crescent moon connotes the end of menstruation. The crescent moon is associated with the state of fallow land ready to be cleared for a new cycle of agricultural production. It evokes menarche and the bride after joining the groom. Partners may then resume conjugal communion. It is moreover associated with the sap that starts rising in the palm tree. When the moon appears before the sun has set—in tropical Yaka land, sunset and sunrise occur at almost the same time throughout the year—it may signify how much the moon takes over the role of the sun to warm the coldness of the dark nights. The explanation given to this speaks of the crescent moon as a renewal equivalent to that which marks the new year. A cryptic formula in songs—that are said to date back to ancient ancestral lore—surnames the crescent moon as *kyan-ziinga mateesa:* "a struggle waged in order to remove an obstacle." The same notion reoccurs in an archaic formula which is pronounced on the occasion of the rite of the crescent moon:

1   Kutukedi kungoondyakhulu
2   taangwa tsiindza
3   ngoondi bilalu.
4   Leelu kabalukidi. (a)
5   Tukola khoondzu, tukola ngolu.

1   When the moon reappeared,
2   the sun had its course obstructed
3   while the moon crawled along like a log in the water.
4   The moon has just turned a new phase.
5   May our health be restored.

Comment:

(a) The term *-baluka* (to change states or condition) is often employed in designating the onset of pregnancy.

In this expression, just as in the therapy used in curing masculine impotency, the crescent moon is figured by a gourd—an object that in certain contexts signifies the uterus—which is hung next to a cluster of ripe red nuts in order to collect the whitish sap oozing from the incision in the inflorescence of the palm. One thinks here of the folktale that adults tell to children in which the tortoise wagers with man as to who is best capable of reaching the sun. Each time the tortoise attempts to climb up into the sky the lightning takes the gourd from the animal and throws the tortoise back to earth. The tortoise then hides itself in the gourd and is thus successful in reaching the heavens. The archaic formula implicitly points to the appearance of the crescent moon as the moment when the palm sap rises and is about to spill over, a sign of life attempting to regenerate itself. According to popular accounts, the young bride should wait for the crescent moon before moving into the conjugal home. It is always at the crescent moon that cult initiates behave as if they have come back to life. Once the period of seclusion has been completed, they prepare themselves to once again face the light of day by eating of the tonifying cola nut, usually in the morning. At crescent moon, the household of a chief may temporarily suspend the means of union within the familial and domestic unit by dampening the hearth, abstaining from cooked food and sexual intercourse, and avoiding contact with knives. In order to do this each person will "administer himself an aphrodisiac" *(-diseengula)* while "pronouncing his motto" *(-ditaandumuna)* evoking the origin and role of the institution or cult that each represents. The following day familial union may be restored: the hearth is rekindled, the family shares a cooked meal, and conjugal communion may be resumed. The confusion between day and night brought on by the crescent moon is thus resolved.

At the time of the full moon, joyful dancing and singing, in celebration of rhythm and desire, revivify and interweave the flow of life in and between people and their life-world. Mostly only women join in the dance at full moon to celebrate the never-ending fluctuation between life and death. These dances are most vivid at the onset of the seasons of seedtime and harvest, or to anticipate and celebrate collective hunting during the long dry season. According to the Yaka, the succession of lunar cycles and of the seasons, like the passing on of life and the succession of generations, are all an outflow of rhythm. Transmission of life, growth, and healing are rhythm. In singing and dancing, in particular at full moon, women, children, boys and a few married men usually celebrate a collective arousal and sharing of the life source and libidinal forces. Songs may voice libidinal desire, themes of love and loss, but indirectly in the imagery of forest spirits, of popular animals, or of cooking. Women's dancing possesses mediating and ordering functions. In rural Yaka areas, women always dance in groups. Women's dancing seems to arouse the effervescent vital flow in themselves, the community, and their life-world, while superimposing a weaving movement onto the group and their world. An oblong wooden cylindrical drum *(ngoma)* with a single leather membrane is usually accompanied by one or two shorter but larger drums *(yimbandu)*, each of which has a different tonality, along with shakers *(sakila, bisaangwa)*. Keeping time with the rhythm of the drum and chants, each woman swings her hips and belly in a kind of wheeling involving a skilful circular rotation, while slightly undulating her upper body. The women interrupt each rotation by extending their left hips in a powerful rolling wave. While dancing they remain fixed to one spot. Within the bonds of conjugal intimacy, the wife may dance in a similar way as a prelude to conjugal intercourse, during which she is expected to make similar movements with her belly; *-niingasana n-ti myathaangi,* "rhythmically shaking the sticks of the bed" is an expression for conjugal communion. Underlying all these dances is a sense of collective celebration that enhances the life source or vital flow. Dance reinforces the Yaka ideal of the female form: a round belly, generous hips and breasts that suggest nurturing, fullness and ripeness—*maasi kuthulu, kuvumu kaanda dyabaatu,* "breasts filled with grease, and the womb with offspring." The dancer's movements evoke the mysterious transmission of life through the act of insemination and childbirth. Maintaining a tense *(ngaandzi)*, erectile *(khoondzu)* posture, the male drummer grasps the phallic-shaped cylindrical dance drum between his legs; some songs, particularly those employed in the context of circumcision rituals, make the association between the drum's appealing rhythm and the erect penis's movement.

By dancing at transitions in the group and seasonal calendar, the community engages in a rather lustful celebration of the vital flow. The success of the transition in the life of an individual, the group, or the life-world is anticipated by a night of celebration *(-kyeela)* at full moon, involving an all-night vigil of nonstop dancing by women, children, and young men. The themes and style of the mourning dance in which both men and women participate are not very different from the women's normal dancing at full moon. It is as if the libidinal affects in women's undulating movements and in their singing intensely mediate between life and death, sorrow and vital flow, chaos and order. The women seem to share and express their affects through their bodies. Moreover, in the chants that accompany the dances the women are offered a unique opportunity to voice their feelings, especially towards the men's group.

Dancing is a form of weaving and a reenactment of the universe's birth. Weaving, like dancing, seeks to symbolically regenerate, re-empower, and reorder the life-world. Weaving raffia palm fibers requires the co-ordinated manipulation of the weaving-hook *(n-noongu)* and the fibers. The hook's movements are determined by the progression of the weaving itself: from top to bottom (high to low), left to right, back to front. The raffia cloth connotes the effervescent, sexual, and cosmological symbolism of the raffia palm, and the ascending and descending flow of its sap. The weaving-hook bears a virile sexual connotation and is shaped in the form of the palm tree's inflorescence that later develops into a cluster of palm nuts— itself a metaphor for both the sun and offspring. Women's dancing—in particular in the undulating movement of the hips, as the dancing movement in sexual union—links weaving to the celebration or act of life transmission. As a metaphoric form of weaving, the women's dancing from sunset to sunrise reactualizes the cosmogenetic significance of *ngoongu,* the earthly womb, that is, the pristine cosmic emergence of (re)generative forces in the universe which ceaselessly renew themselves at their point of origin. By mimicking the flow of life in the palm tree, both dancing and weaving reenact the birth of the universe and the individual by celebrating the constitutive imbrication of the polar principles that characterize beings and things: east and west, up and down, front and back, heaven and earth, decomposition and rebirth, sowing and flowering, ascendance and descendance, genitors and offspring, masculine and feminine. Like sexual intercourse, the dance aims at weaving the vital flow. It is stimulated by and fed from the dancer's most interior source, connected to her most interior rhythm, respiration, fantasies, and affects, and to her interaction with others and the world. Dance produces a reorganization of synergies, channelling the vital flow from body to world and vice versa.

2.2.5 *The rainbow snake transcends both spatial and color divisions.* It is in fact likened to the appearance all at once of the total diurnal course of the sun. Popular narratives employ the esoteric name *n-kongolu* for the terrestrial or aquatic rainbow snake and describe the rainbow, *khongolu,* as an immense liana or as a giant being, perhaps a crocodile, or python. It takes on the *kyandzangoombi* form when it arches its back across the sky and brings about abundant rains; it is considered a serpent with its arched form stretched across the sky, its head and mouth at each extremity.[7] It comes to rest in a ravine that has been eroded by a heavy rainstorm or "retires into the trunk of a raffia palm" to fertilize it by channeling through it the unceasing emergence of life. The narratives hold that, once the storm is over and the leviathan bedded down, the ravine where it abandoned its skin is further deepened, or variously, that a giant palm tree develops in proximity to a spring. These valleys are therefore seen as the points where the setting sun enters into the earth and transfers its fetal signification to the red clay *(luundu)* that is used in the healing cults and rites of initiation. Fragmentary mythic lore associates *kyandzangoombi* and the subterranean journey of the sun at night. Oral lore reports that a large conical termite mound of red clay *(luundu)* will emerge like an eruption of the earth towards the sky on the tomb of the so-called *kyandzangoombi* healer of masculine fertility. He is buried in a seated (that is, fetal) position, with a bract and inflorescence of the palm or parasol tree placed on his head, "in order that he may be soon reborn." The termitary of course shelters a queen ant whose extraordinary fecundity enchants people's imagination.

2.3 Animals and Plants

In their attitudes toward animals and plants, Yaka people very much display the genius of the *yiphiti* gazelle, which is one of their most popular and cherished figures in folktales and is characterized both by ardor and by lighthearted cleverness in relation to chance. The hunter, trapper, collector, fisher, or planter takes his or her chance. Animals and plants are suitable for human consumption or use, not only because of some utility, but also because they are "good to think with"—to paraphrase Lévi-Strauss (1962). Some offer very distinct qualities, while others display mixed ones. As such they may serve as markers for gender differences and for the transitional states of gestation and initiation, and more generally for social belonging. What one eats or does not eat, what one uses for therapy or not, helps to posit boundaries between what can be internal and what should remain external to oneself and one's groups. Dietary differences express gender, age, or other social differences. (See 4.4 for discussion of herbalistic and phytotherapeutic practices.) The outline classification proposed here is founded on linguistic criteria, insofar as it refers to generic Yaka terms, as well as on information gleaned from oral lore and ritual activities.

2.3.1 *Most big game animals make for the hunter's good fortune, and are the choicest food to strengthen the life force of senior men.* Hunting is the men's most idealized productive activity in Kwaango land, not only because it yields rich food and materials for symbolic or practical use, but because it links men's virility and life transmission (see 3.5.1) with the deeds of the founding ancestors and the ancestral life force (see 2.4.1). Hunting stirs up the ebullient life resources *(fula)* in the life-world just as the genitor arouses the life flow in the genitrix. The savanna forests, open grasslands, and valley forests support a rich variety of fauna. Extensive use of firearms, however, has nearly decimated the large mammals. The prestige accorded to hunting game derives more directly from what it signifies than from what it produces. Such esteem is a throwback to the mythic narratives regarding the foundation of Yaka society, which elevated the first hunter to the status of founder. Luunda settlers prized the use of firearms. The significative value of the hunt is extended to all the rewarded activities of men, reflecting and even ratifying them, and invokes a number of complex ritual practices. Hunting is associated both with virility, as reproductive and foundational to some cosmic order and to social life, as well as with the life-bearing dimension in violence and sorcery. The hunt is compared to an oneiric journey and is therefore associated with clairvoyance. Oneiromancy in this context is deemed particularly significant: a man's dreams about a fight, a tearful woman, dancing, or seduction are held to be auspicious, while dreams involving menstrual blood or feces are inauspicious. In the forest the hunter forms a type of alliance with the game and the spirits guiding it. Meat from the hunt is a basic constituent in the establishment of the matrimonial alliance. A successful hunt enhances the hunter's sexual appetite, and therefore the desire for marital union. Inasmuch as a man should not abuse or waste his reproductive powers or semen, he should not kill more than his family strictly needs.

Trapping—but also fishing—is the means for boys to explore and prove for themselves their own talents. In folktales, children and youth are highly praised for their inventiveness and courage to explore the many life forms in the savanna and purvey their share for the family meal. Men experience vivid emotions and take much pride in hunting, and important imagery and folktales derive from it. Each hamlet reserves for itself certain hunting zones, staked out by footpaths, in the forest and savanna. The men may set traps in these areas at any time of the year. During the rainy seasons—from October to December and from February to June—the men, armed with rifles, individually track and hunt *(ndzoomba, -zoomba)* game within the tract. Hunters originating from different villages organize collective beats *(-ta busuungu)* in the forest galleries and steppes during these same periods; on such occasions bows and arrows are used as well as guns. The major beat, in contrast, takes place in the dry season in the months of June and July. The vast plains are lit with fires *(-yoka miila)* in a bow formation in order to better flush out the game. This type of hunting rarely produces more than one to three large animals per hamlet and per season, however. The shrubs and plants that survive the annual fires take on, following the context in which they are found, a significant value of misfortune to the agent of evil or exceptional resistance to one who suffers an affliction. It is also in the forest and savanna that the Yaka gather different species of wood, lianas, plants, and minerals used for dwellings, wickerware, curative practice, and ritual activities.

The category *mbisi* principally covers the vertebrates whose meat or skins are highly valued. This category includes, in addition to the python and crocodile, the nonrodent quadrupeds that live in horizontal space, that is, on the surface of the land. Capture of big game animals *(mbisyakyaama, mbisyanhaku)* is reserved to men, probably because it involves the spilling of blood. The meat of these animals is prized and is the only meat to be found in the exchange circuit or to be designated by the same term as that for the animal category: *mbisi.* Further, hunts for *mbisi* are used to test the pronouncements of divinatory oracles, and a successful hunt is taken as verification of the truth of an oracle or, in some situations, as a sign that conjugal communion may be reestablished after a period of ritual abstinence. Similarly, cases of repeated failure to bring home *mbisi* are themselves submitted to examination by divinatory oracle. The rarity, ferociousness, and size of the *mbisi* animal make it a prestigious catch. The leopard *(ngo)*, the crocodile *(ngaandu)*, and the python *(mboma)*, all animals capable of killing men, are "animals of paramount power" *(mbisyayiluwa)*: they are not suitable for human consumption, and the hunter is obliged to hand over the skin to the paramount chief of the region who, in turn, offers the latter his ceremonial protection. For the other so-called ancestral animals, the patriarch presides over the "sharing of the meat" (*-bukwasana mbisi*, an expression evoking the communality of the family meal: *-diisasana*). He offers a morsel of liver to the ancestral shrine caring for the hunter. Animals with spotted or striped hides *(mbisyatona)*, such as ocelots and zebras, combine colors which are held to be incompatible in that they represent distinct spatial categories and may evoke the world of sorcery; these creatures are therefore subject to numerous prohibitions. They are strictly forbidden food to pregnant women, bereaved persons, novices, initiates, and initiators, but their pelt is used in paraphernalia to induce or sustain the liminal state of these persons. Except for anomalous *mbisi* such as apes and monkeys, tortoises, crocodiles, pythons, cocks, and hens, most *mbisi* are categorized according to the shape of the foot or tail or according to their feeding habits.

The *mbisyakhoodya* (hoofed animal) group of ungulates comprise the bovine ruminants including the domestic goat, of which the larger part are uniparous. It also includes the *ngulwan-situ* (literally, "the forest pig," a nonruminant swine), with which is associated the domestic pig, *hyooka*, because of its snout.

Mbisyakaandzu (clawed animals) designates those *mbisi* which prey on other vertebrates or insects, sometimes complementing their diet with plants. Carnivores such as the cheetah *(ngo, khooyi)* and the civet *(ndzima)* are considered among those animals with spotted hides *(mbisyatona)*. The insectivorous giant Kivu shrew *(pfweengi*, Soricidae), whose bite is mortal for the rats it attacks, can be associated with this category. The uniparous anteater *(ndziimba)* with clawed front legs and hoofed hind legs tunnels into the ground. All these predators are thought of as ornery and aggressive beasts *(mbisyakhemena)*. The fact that they cover their excrement also gives them a negative reputation. Because of their individualism, diet, hide, nocturnal customs, and ability to climb or dig, they incarnate modes of inverted life, and are thus strictly forbidden to any persons undergoing ritual phases of transition. They symbolize wild spirits of the bush. By adding bits of pelt, a tooth or a claw in his paraphernalia, the hunter seeks to turn his art of good luck into a battue or foray. In other words, a hunter is not a brutal killer of game, but should await his chance; however, some may transform the 'art' into a food-getting enterprise.

2.3.2 *Small mammals are seen as products of the earth.* They are a prized food for women and children, but prohibited for pregnant women, novices, and initiates. The category of *phuku* comprises the small quadruped mammals (including rodents) of whom the majority are considered *kaandzu*, "clawed."[8] Since they do not live on the ground, the *phuku* represent a confusion of the categories of vertical and horizontal space: they comprise burrowing, arboreal, or amphibious creatures (*Mustelidae,* as well as the water shrew, *Potamogalidae* and the Kivu shrew, *Soricidae*), some of whom, the bats, are capable of flying despite the fact that they share no other characteristics with birds. Like the weasel, the water shrew lives in the water and on the ground, and feeds itself at night on fish or insects; it is symbolically interchangeable with the anteater. Rats and weasels are known to leave the forest in order to steal food, hens, and eggs from village homes. Because of the animals' gregarious instincts, men stereotypically associate them with young women. The fact that they find shelter themselves or nest their young in burrows, cavities, hollow trunks, or between the roots of trees suggests the process of gestation; because they may be forced to emerge from a burrow by prodding it with a hand or stick or even with the help of a dog has made them a sign of miscarriage. Many of them are nocturnal, have a spotted skin *(phukwatona)*, and pass for aggressive creatures *(phukwakhemena)*. These characteristics mean that most *phuku* are forbidden food to novices and cult initiates; they may not pronounce their names or hear them spoken.

The most prominent attribute of the majority of species in this group is without doubt their prehensile tail, for it represents a disconcerting anomaly. This characteristic seems to place them in the same family as serpents *(nyoka,* "creepers"), or even as fish without scales like the catfish. The most striking examples are the genet *(mbala)*, which sleeps with its tail curled around a branch, and the arboreal pangolin *(khaka)*, which does the same. But the pangolin also rolls itself in a ball to protect itself, and its upper side is covered with scales. The tail of many of these animals is covered with fur whose ringed pattern resembles certain snakes, or with small scales *(yiheyi)*, sometimes covered with hairs. However, it is not clear to me why the tail and the whole of the dorsal portion, called *n-kila* (whether for *phuku* or *mbisi* captured in the hunt), are meat reserved for wives. Again, if one is to judge from the oral lore and the rites, certain *phuku* supply a greater proportion of food than *mbisi,* despite the fact that the former are not at all considered a prize catch. The little cultural value that men assign to the meat of *phuku* is evidenced by the fact that only women and children hunt them. The meat of *mbisi* is a prestigious and most invigorating food for men, and as such contrasts with the soft and fatty flesh of the *phuku;* it is similarly supposed that man, strong and firm like bone, is contrasted with woman, whose flesh is more tender (this comparison involves a generalized conceptual homology between man versus woman and bone versus flesh).

2.3.3 *Insects, as well as the large category of worms, most reptiles, and a number of aquatic animals are considered inauspicious and unedible.* The Yaka will say of a foreign group considered inferior to themselves that it eats snake meat. When a serpent, even a nonvenomous variety, is encountered or observed just after it has shed its skin within the domestic area or on the path, the event is understood to forecast an ominous curse or a threat on the individual or on his family.

Aquatic animals are not prized food, and only the catfish has any symbolic significance. *Ndzoondzi* (small fish with whiskers and dorsal fins), *ngola* (eels), *n-tsuka* (catfish), and *n-kosu* (crustaceans) are considered edible. Eels pass for relatives of the serpent as they have no skeleton and lack a hard head; besides, the eel-like catfish (*ngaandzi, leembwa*) is able to move from water to land. Eels and catfish are prohibited animals for persons in a state of initiatory transition. Like food collecting, fishing is considered the prerogative of the women and children who, according to the season, might employ a basket trap, dam the stream, or catch the fish bare-handed. Boys also utilize imported hooks and lines. The men mix the ichtyotoxic plants in damned-up streams and use bows and arrows, as if in the hunt, to catch the stupefied fish.

2.3.4 *Birds are a prized catch.* The category of *nuni*, birds, comprises animals with feathers *(lusala)* capable of flight. Subcategories draw in no exclusive way on particular physical configurations or behavior. First, there is the category of birds with spotted plumage *(nunyatona)*, including the black partridge *(khaanga)* and the Numidian guinea fowl *(kheledi)*, whose dark plumage dotted with white evokes the starry sky. Second, there are the birds attracting attention because of their red plumage (the *nduwa*, a turaco) or the reddish tint of the tarsus and foot (the *nguumbi, ngwaadi*, and *yikwaaki* partridges); similarly, the grey parrot *(khusu)* is distinguished by its red tail feathers and the fact that its first and fourth claws are directed backward. Both categories of birds are held to pair incompatible colors—such as red with black, or black with white—and are therefore prohibited to individuals in the throes of ritual transition. Third, there are the fowl that nest on the ground or on the water, or seek food in the village: guinea fowl starlings *(ngoongu)* and nighthawks *(kabwaabwa)*—a nocturnal species—nest on the ground, and geese *(yikoongi)* nest in rocky places; pigeons *(yeembi)* feed in the village; wrens *(yityeetya* and *tseetsyamaamba)* confine themselves to the dense brush bordering marshes and streams. Fourth, there is the category of birds classified according to their song or cry. The shriek of the waxwing *(thoyi)* in flight over the village presages a sorcerous act, a death, or announces an animal caught in a trap. The loud call of the turaco or of the crested hoopoe *(mbudikhoku)* may be compared to the cackle of a hen. The cry of the honeybird *(tseyi)* signals to the alert hunter the presence of a snake or other animal. Fifth, there are the birds of prey. Because of the forward position of its eyes and the unique development of its external ear, the owl shows similarities with the caracal *(ngaayi: Felis lybica)*. Though a nocturnal bird of prey, it is still classed with its diurnal cousins: the buzzard *(mbaandzya)*, African kite *(mbeembu)*, eagle *(yisyo)*, and the renowned vultures of the plains *(ngosolu)* and of the forests *(mbaandzya-mbvwooki)*, which are widely held to be subject to the sorcerer's *(nunyabaloki)* beck and call.

2.3.5 *The freestanding tree is an epitome of descent.* Plants are closely associated with man, as food, force, tool, material for fire or housing, and as a 'forest of symbols.' Plants may also symbolize complementary gender differences or the life cycle of a group by virtue of their ecological, morphological, and cyclical characteristics. As they do for the animal kingdom, the Yaka employ several distinct registers for the classification of plants, in line with people's use of them: hunting, collecting, agriculture, construction of houses, crafts, therapeutic and ritual practices, and so on. The density and layering of the forest vegetation obstruct a clear view of the treetops, make fruit gathering difficult, and render agricultural production in the forest quite impossible. These factors clearly influence the types of different registers brought into play. It may explain, for example, why the Yaka, in order to identify a plant, do not primarily examine its form or size but crush the leaf between their fingers and sniff its odor, chew a piece of the wood, scrape away the outer layer of the root, tear a piece of bark from the trunk, break a twig in order to see the sap, or observe its fruit and the birds that feed on it.

N-ti is the generic term used to designate the ligneous plants (trees, bushes, arborescents, and their foliage) that grow upright and stand by themselves. It is this verticality of *n-ti* which assumes a cosmological dimension in relation to the human beings. The peak of the tree *(n-taandu,* the "up high") is also indicated by the term *kuzulu,* "in the sky," or by *ha thandan-ti,* "in the top of the tree." The entire space covered by its umbrage constitutes the base of the tree: *hatsi,* "on the ground," or *tsyaandi n-ti,* "the ground surface under the tree." More specifically, *n-ti* refers to the central vertical part of the plant (this may equally be the bore of a forest tree and the pseudo-trunk of species related to the palm or banana plants), whether they be crowned with leafage or simply a section cut off and replanted: the term can therefore indicate a cutting of manioc *(n-ti myan-toombu)* as well as a shaft of the parasol tree *(n-seenga)* or of the "life tree of the village" *(n-saanda)*. A derivative of this word, *n-tya biloongu,* designates any curative plant. The term thus covers any element of a plant—bark, shoot, twig, root, or even fruit—that may be collected for therapeutic or symbolic designs. *Sina* denotes the foot of a plant, that is, the whole of the root and stem (or trunk) structure supporting it in a vertical position. The term is also applied to any plant species, including grasses and herbs, that fixes itself in the ground at a specific point. *Sodi,* a name also given to rhizomes, denotes the central root which, in contrast with the peripheral roots called *n-zeembu,* is considered as the subterranean inverse of the stem or trunk.

The larger tree, because of its branching and its upright and freestanding position, is an icon of the continuity of generations and descent. The side and branches to the right are distinct from those to the left, as agnatic descent differs from uterine filiation. The foot *(sina)* designates distant patrilineal ancestry—or even the origin of the lineage, order, and tradition. The summit *(kuzulu, n-taandu)* points to the living descendants, and the branching—especially the left-hand side—refers to alliance and uterine kin. Any parts of the tree which have fallen to earth—branches, leaves, bark, or fruit—and rot on the ground represent the evil that kinsmen may inflict on each other. To place a twig that has fallen from a tree onto the roof of an elder's dwelling is to accuse the elder or another inhabitant of a sorcerous plot. It is said that a *yibalu,* a dried leaf caught in the upper reaches of a tree, is sought after by sorcerers plotting an attack. In order to deny co-responsibility or the duty to share with another, for example, one pronounces the words *yuzeeyi n-taanduku,* "I can't imagine what relation at the treetop could link us." The tall straight bore of some forest trees, like the denuded rachis *(lukawu)* of the rotin palm, symbolizes how much the vitality of a lineage rests on strong ties between the successive generations that are able to overcome the risks of segmentation caused by succession or sorcerous acts. Trees with a similarly erect appearance may symbolize virility or domination in particular ritual contexts. Certain of these trees in fact serve as ridge poles *(m-baangu,* also bearing a virile connotation) in the construction of the seclusion house. The statuette representing the *yifiika hathandan-ti,* that is, the "mother of the young circumcised initiates perched in a tree," is called by this very name and signifies as much. It is exhibited to the public during the dances which mark the close of the rites of puberty. Certain forest trees are inauspicious, namely those "devoured by lightning" *(n-ti wadyandzasi),* those in which birds of prey roost *(yikuundinuni,* "where a lone bird sits"), or those "whose slippery trunk defy" the climber *(n-tyandelumuka).* The parts of valleys that are cleared for manioc gardens acquire a female quality. However, where the high forest giants abound, the valley denotes verticality and virility, in contrast to the flatness of the savannas.

2.3.6 *Tangled vines and lianas symbolize ligature as well as entanglement. N-zeembu* designates vines, lianas, or projecting root buttresses that abound in humid forest as well as the peripheral subsurface roots of a large number of plants, whether ligneous or nonligneous. These lianas usually exhibit a distinct foot *(sina)* and a central root *(sodi).* Like the plants that support them, the *n-zeembu* also point to the vertical dimension. During the rites of political investiture, a liana is looped around the newly instituted authorities in order to affirm the bonds of solidarity and mutual dependence that now link them together. Sometimes these vines may be so heavy that they break loose and fall back to earth; for this reason they may also bear an ambivalent value. Popular exegesis holds that the liana used in ceremonies of investiture or in the event of a family reunification may be transformed into a serpent that strikes or bites an imposter, that is, someone who is ritually united to the family yet later betrays it. On the other hand, vines *(n-zeembu)* that grow and thrive on the forest floor, perhaps after the tree to which they had been attached is cut down or has been pulled down by their very weight, are called *fwaangi*, literally, "that which rests on the ground." In certain ritual contexts tangled vines *(n-zeembu)* may stand for illness, negative forces, or ensorcellment. The tangled vines are properly called *m-bindusi*. It might be added that the tendrils *(maziingu)* and thorns *(makoongi)* of climbing flora *(Cucurbitaceae)* bear a signification equivalent to that of *m-bindusi*.

2.3.7 *The year circle, and men's and women's work.* Mboongu denotes offspring and other forms of resourcefulness, such as the abundance of plants, crops, animals, and humans, as well as money. The emphasis is on abundance, not on needs. The association suggests a kind of connivance or mutual solidarity between these various manifestations of fructification. Podded legumes (a group including beans and groundnuts, for example) serve to indicate fertility of the kin rather than of a singular individual. Peanuts are part of family reunification rituals. In the same way, the preparation of a meal from different agricultural produce over the same fire is a major step in the family rituals striving for the fertility of one of the members.

Seasons and the months are named after changes in the ground vegetation of the savannas and woodlands, but not in reference to a numerical calendar of moon phases. Several of the generic terms covering nonligneous flora therefore indicate both the season and a seasonal characteristic of the vegetation, or an agricultural activity. The seasonal calendar begins around the middle or end of September, with the first rains *(mbvula zamateti):* this is the period of the *mutseengwa nguba,* the "time of the hoe," that is, for planting peanuts. At this point the men rush to burn off the debris from fields they have cleared in the forest; these mild rains allow them to better control the brush fires. The suffrutex *yiyeembi*—a very low plant with a woody base and a herbaceous growth above—is the first of the greens to appear on the plains which have been fired in anticipation of the major game beat; this is also the time at which the women collect termites. The suffrutex and the savanna termitary *(yikuku)* act as symbols that mark the secluded initiate's return to life. In the months of October and November, during the "season of germination and of new savanna vegetation" *(mwaanga ndeendi),* the women first sow their fields, which also bear the name of this season, *bimwaanga,* and then later occupy themselves with fishing and honey-gathering. *Mwaanga kubidi* is the "time at which the savanna vegetation achieves maturity." Following the peanut harvest, the women clean the fields of weeds, some of which have thorns (designated by the generic terms *tsaaka, khamu),* before planting the manioc. Tied in a bundle, these particular weeds are used as a tuft to splash water for purification *(boondzu)* in rituals of healing, mourning, and cleansing. At this time the women may spend time gathering caterpillars and mushrooms; these latter are given the generic name *luhwa.* According to the Yaka, certain spongy whitish mushrooms that tend to grow from decomposing vegetation evoke the flesh of a very weak and anemic person; they are prohibited food for the sick, initiates, and nursing mothers. In March and April, a period called *yisoki,* "the time when plants produce seeds," heavy rains flatten the higher grasses *(n-zaanga,* again a generic term) in such a way that the narrow paths *(n-soku)* that cross the plains are obstructed with *matootwala,* "grasses which one crushes beneath the feet." The men rarely hunt in the forest during this period of frequent rains; moreover, supplies of manioc flour are usually in short supply and belts are tightened. *Kyangaanga,* "the short season in preparation of the longer," occurs in May and is a half-length dry season. The women may begin to harvest the yams (the generic term is *yisadi)* while the men once again take up game beats in the forest and tap the first palm wine. Finally, the onset of the dry season, *mbaangala,* is announced by the *tsoki,* "the rains which bury the seeds," and by other events: some plants and trees flower, certain birds appear in the vicinity of human settlements, and some species of trees lose their leaves. The great game beat on the plains may now take place. In preparation for the occasion, the Tsaamba landowners deposit some manioc and palm wine on the ancestral burial ground, while the patriarchs and elders weed the familial burial grounds. The firing of the savanna is then organized by zones. Once cloudy days return, the men begin to clear the areas chosen for the new fields. From time to time game beats on the burnt plains and on the edges of the forest may be repeated. Hunting in the forest is made impracticable because the dry underbrush of the forest betrays the hunter's presence, and only trapping can be carried out.

Savanna and steppes stand to the fields as menarche to motherhood, or menstruation to gestation. Menstrual periods convert the conjugal dwelling into a *ndzo tseki,* literally, a house of the savanna. During this period women of childbearing age, as it is said, must sleep on the ground at the site of the deadened hearth. It may be recalled that this is the same period in which the husband forgoes hunting and may not wield a knife. Blood shed during circumcision is symbolically associated with the blood of defloration and menstruation (one term, *-lweeka,* "to make blood flow," is used in all three instances), and the suffrutex *yiyeembi,* the first greenery to emerge from the blackened grasslands, is ritually applied to the circumcised's wound. If one wishes to invoke the ominous significance attached to these savanna bushes, it is explained, a piece of the bark or root of this plant is cut off with a knife and grated *(-kulula)*. If, on the other hand, it is the meaning of renascent life which is desired, the use of a knife is prohibited and a club is used to detach *(-teembula)* a piece of the woody base which is crushed in a mortar.

In July, the men collectively invade the feminine space of savanna and steppes and set fire to the plains and organize a major beat: this intrusion is inauspicious and is compared to menarche, menstruation, and the new moon. The blackened brush which slowly returns to life is called *n-tyambeembi*, "shrubs stricken by misfortune." The term *mbeembi,* in the various nuances of common usage, indicates what hampers fecundity or constitutes a threatening intrusion of conjugal intimacy.[9]

During the day, women are always involved in some productive manual work (cf. Roosens 1965, 1971:296–97, for Central Kwaango). During the three or four hours in the hottest part of the day, while sitting, they are busy with the children, husking cereals, hulling peanuts and beans, hair-styling, making pottery, or preparing some *khula* paste for ointment. Their hands find rest with the gloom of the night. Men are hunters. They clear parts of the forest to allow the women to grow staple foods. Men grow maize. Women cultivate both sweet and bitter manioc or cassava, yams, gourds, and sesame. Peanuts are preferably grown on the sites of former villages, where the plots are more easily protected from goats. Once the husband has cleared the area marked off for cultivation of trees and brush, and burned it, the wife, alone or with the aid of the maidens in the household, is left with the remaining tasks of weeding—leaving stumps and roots in place, sowing or planting the cuttings, maintenance of the field, and finally the harvesting and conservation of seed. The field and the pool where manioc is steeped are both considered preeminently feminine spaces, and the women are expected to defecate close to the entrances to their fields. A woman develops a mother-child relationship with her field and the cash crops grown on it, particularly the manioc and yams whose suckers may be considered vegetal offspring. She should nurture her manioc patch with almost the same fervor she bestows on her young children. Her movements in hoeing are very similar to those of dancing: she advances from spot to spot, each time making several strokes of the hoe while rotating in a semicircle.

In the savanna and steppes, and depending on the season, women and children catch locusts, caterpillars, termites, and crickets, collect mushrooms, pick fruits and edible leaves, and dig for certain tubers. They also trap rats and mice by destroying their holes with hoes. The boys set snares for birds and chase bats.

There has been little cash crop production in the last decade, and the colonial or missionary incentives for cattle herding failed because such activity proved irreconcilable with the mindset of hunters. Men build the houses. The more men gain seniority, the more they adopt a position of rest, stability, that is, the less they move around or use their hands for production. They no longer go out hunting and rely on juniors for clearing the fields. Most men spend half the day "generating things with words" *(-yidika maambu)*, as they say, in meetings, councils, rituals, palm wine parties, while some attendants are busy with wickerwork and the carving of tools. Salaried work is valued in as much as it "produces new resources" *(-sala mboongu)* for the group.

2.3.8 *Some plants and animals blend the habitats of water, soil, and heaven.* When upright green plants are found on the ground, they take on an ambivalent or mediative value. The *yiludi* is a vine, surface root, or bush which has been felled and, barring a path, forces the traveler to step over it. The ritual specialist may shoot an arrow into the vine before collecting it for ritual purposes. Other *yiludi* are included in the cult objects laid across the entwined legs of spouses in order to seal their reunion after a period of initiatory separation and abstinence. They also belong to the ritual paraphernalia deployed in order to reinforce that fortune which leads game and hunter to each other. The *n-kweengi*, a fragment of bark worn smooth through the rubbing action of two branches swayed by the wind, may replace the *yiludi* on occasion. Similarly, a branch which hangs down into the stream and has been agitated by the flow of water can be employed in making the ritual object used to signal well-being to a troubled person. It may be recalled that the direction of a stream's flow gives a significative value to the water: downstream is the locus of forgetting and of the dissolution of evil. An uprooted *(n-tyakiinduka)* or, a fortiori, a rotting tree or shrub *(n-tyafusa)* may signify either an evil or that same evil turned against itself self-destructively.

Makaya (sing. *lukaya*) is the generic term for the foliage of plants, or living verdure.[10] *Bisaka* denotes the tender part of leaves used in the preparation of condiments, while the harder stem and vein structure of the leaf is called *matiiti*, "plant refuse"; *bisaka* can also designate a leaf freshly picked for use in ritual, curative, or alimentary preparations (each of these preparations also has its own name). In this context, the esoteric term *mbakunumbakunu* indicates a series of plant substances considered as a whole and made up of young shoots of different species of savanna and forest plants deliberately picked at different heights. Such an assortment signifies the various means by which illness, pain, or sorcery may overtake individuals, or the multiple ways in which calamity may manifest itself. The *n-tsumuni*, an offshoot of a species of large forest tree or of a toxic plant, carries a value equivalent to that of *mbakunumbakunu* when it is pulled out of the ground with the root. Again, in similar ritual contexts, *bimbongwala* (leaves which fall from the tree or which are blown into the air by the wind) or *tsatsala* (dried leaves found on the ground) may bear the same signification. Other bearers of good fortune can be employed in like fashion or in conjunction with the vegetal elements mentioned here; these include *lukuunga* (flotsam collected by branches obstructing a stream), *tsatsala zaseenguka* (leaves floating upside-down on the water, lying lazily on their backs), *tungyatungya* (leaves or other matter caught in a spider web), and *phyangu zaphaambu* (footprints at the crossing of paths: they may be represented by vegetal refuse left at such places).

There is no specific term for nonligneous flora as a group. However, the continuously lush greenery of the ferns, mosses, algae, and herbs that thrive in the humid microclimates of stream beds and marshy wooded areas contrasts with the cyclical vegetation of the plains. Such greenery is used to cover the front of the novice and her or his major icons in healing cults, particularly in the *khita*. The significative value of the verdure worn by the novice or of that which goes into the making of the purificatory tuft employed in what is literally labeled the "tuft for gaining weight" *(boondu dya wutooka)* (see Devisch 1979:104) is combined with that of water from the spring; the verdure and flow reflect a return to life of those who have been associated with the dead, namely widows, widowers, and novices.

Sap, resin, and latex exuded *(budiimbu)* by plants display an inside/outside dialectic. In order to signify the disappearance or riddance of an affliction, the sick person is administered a preparation based on this vegetal liquid, in the form of an enema or by drops *(m-mweemwa)* in the eyes, ears, or nose. In order to indicate recovery or return to consciousness following an epileptic crisis, this potion is poured into the ear or on the individual's cranium; this symbolizes a restitution to the body of the "foam" *(fula)* which has escaped from the lips of the epileptic. In order to increase the capacity of the potions to penetrate the whole body, they are mixed with vegetal substances giving off strong odors *(tsudi, fiimbu)* that are supposed to traverse the various partitions of the organism. The individual undergoing this treatment should avoid any form of contact with plants that are off limits: he is forbidden to pronounce the name of the plant or to consume any pithy or viscous *(leendzi)* fruit or any vegetable or squash to which oil has been added or which produces a starchy liquid *(leendzi)* during preparation.

Customs of consumption, prohibition, and ritual use introduce yet other classifications. A few insects are considered delicacies: locusts, winged termites, larvae, and caterpillars. The myriapods, arachnids, and some true insects—especially venomous species, wasps, and dung beetles *(kokotu)*—are of course not fit for consumption. These insects are burned to ashes, so as to signify the destruction of the offender and to form the ingredient *loombi* of ritual weapons, that is, ritual means of defense and attack. These ritual arms also comprise substances which are ambivalent in nature and thus by themselves able to revert the evildoing against the culprit himself. Such substances are derived from amphibians (toads and frogs) and reptiles, with the exception of the iguana *(tseengi)*, which may be eaten.

2.4 Capturing and 'Cooking' Untamed Forces

Young manhood, chieftaincy, the hunt, and sorcery share similar utopian intentions of exploring desire and harnessing mysterious forces beyond the rules and conventions of village life and matrimony in the far off or unknown domains of the forest realm. These domains captivate men's and women's fascination for what reaches beyond the order and limits of their known and domesticated world, that is, for invisible and untamed forces and forms of being, for the mysterious resources of desire or passion, and of sleep or dream. My information mainly stems from men whose fascination for this realm yields a wealth of masculinist metaphors portraying men essentially as predators in the realms of reproduction, that is, of the hunt and life transmission. Conversely, sorcery and healing depict men's fascination for women's generative capacities in gestation and cooking. In other words, men's fascination for the untamed is predicated on a split between male and female gender. Men picture themselves in the profuse flow of folktales as enchanted wanderers and adventurous predators in the realms of forest and darkness. Men's life in the diurnal village realm stands to forest as confinement stands to the realm of desire and affluent forces.

2.4.1 *The healer and paramount ruler, like the hunter, seek to harness, detect, or counteract untamed forces of the forest realm* in view of empowering the individual, the group, and the life-world. Initiation has led them to embody attributes of both virility and motherhood. On the one hand, they are an epitome of virility inasmuch as they engage in ritual activities that, each in their own way, reenact foundations of an ordered cosmos and group life. And on the other hand, it is said that through their clairvoyance they reach beyond the bounds of customary order and the norms of established society in search of potentialities of renewal and life-bearing.

In his virile function, the therapist in the major healing cults—as I will show below—acts as a demiurge and trapper who considers the patient's body and life-world as a hunting ground and a space over which he must gain dominion. The healer traps and tames the wild nature of the evil in a way analogous to the snaring of game. Hunting symbolism offers the healer a method for detecting the disease, catching it, and converting it into its opposite, that is, into something life-bearing. Ensnaring the game moreover initiates in the animal a process of 'cooking in the forest' that draws on its inner heat—the animal's decay being seen as a cooking. It is later completed by the cooking in the house done by the hunter's wife, so that the game can then release all of its vital force in the sharing of the meat in the family meal. In a similar way, the therapist aims at trapping the disease so as to domesticate and appropriate its vital force. Seclusion leads the patient to identify her- or himself with the motions of cooking and gestation.

Hunters bestow on themselves the attributes of their most popular model, the gazelle *(yiphiti)*. In folktales and leisured speech while sharing palm wine or in the evening in the homestead, men praise both the gazelle and the good hunter for their sharp gaze, wanderlust, and ardor *(n-tsuuta)*, for their desire or greed *(ndzala)* and sexual lust *(luhweetu)*, as well as for their light-hearted cleverness *(nduuka)*, which enables them to penetrate into the remotest areas of the forest. Analogously, the hunter's and lover's conduct inspires that of the therapist when he tries to outwit the evil(doer). For example, it is essential for the hunter never to step on the game's imprints. This is the reason why he systematically avoids all places where the walking is easy. In the same way the therapist approaches the village where the treatment will take place at sunrise, unexpectedly and avoiding the paths. One of the therapist's main methods resembles homeopathy: here he seeks primarily to outwit the evil by its own rapacity rather than by sheer force, like the trapper-hunter who seeks to play on the animal's greed in order to attract and catch it. The skilled hunter-trapper can cunningly transform an area unfrequented by game into a crossroads; he creates a source of attraction by urinating on the ground to either side of a trap or pit. Once the animal perceives the smell of ammonia, it seeks out the place where it can lick away the uric acid crystals left by the urine. Odor and the animal's gluttony thus make up the real trap. Likewise, a hunter believes that a good catch will awaken his wife's desire, and hence the meal with meat is a prelude to conjugal union and life transmission.

The chief is both a hunter and a nurturer. The realm of the forest and, in particular, the productive processes associated with the termite mound, the palm tree (see 2.2.1), and the hunt are important sources that provide the chief with paramount power and nurturing capacity. The chief is portrayed as the one who in his capacity of hunter and culture-hero regenerates and nurtures his group, and moreover, yet most importantly, as the one who seals these roles with his capacity for sovereign control over aggression and sorcery. In this, he appears as the virile instance bounding off his territory and land seen as a maternal domain from any noxious intrusion. The route that the newly enthroned chief follows across his territory—literally, in order to "eat his tribute" *(-dya n-laambu)*—defines the boundaries of the territory and completes his taking possession of it: the journey is a way of integrating and enclosing his territory. In his body, regalia, and functions, the chief ties the whole territory up with the "primal maternal life source" *(ngoongu)*. To fully assume this control and nurturing function, the chief takes possession of his sacred enclosure *(ndzo malala)* and behaves as the supreme predator when eating of the product of the first collective beat organized in his territory shortly following his investiture. Before that, he performs his dance with the sword of rulership while entering the enclosure as hunter-warrior: he thereby gives metaphoric expression to the alignment, beyond challenge, of chieftaincy, society, land, and cosmos.

The sacred house is constructed for the chief alone at the outskirts of the village at the back of his house. The structure resembles a small hut and its entrance faces the village. Each of the chief's totems is represented in the hut: the leopard and the crocodile are depicted in one drawing set on a mound next to a hole in the ground where the chief deposits the remains of the meat from the hunt. The rainbow is portrayed by a *n-ngubanguba* liana forming an arch from one wall to the other along the roof. There is also a collection of ritual objects referring to the origins and hero-founders of the Yaka civilization, the first couple evolving out of an androgynous twin figure, the invention of fire, hunting, smithery, and so on. According to skilled informants, the chief, accompanied by Kha Mandzengedi—literally "his counselor in the affairs of the night"—enters the house in the secret of twilight. As supreme predator, he then consumes the raw meat of one of the greater antelope species caught in the hunt, normally an adult female. It is also prescribed that he snatch morsels of the meat from the hands of his companion. The animal, it is said, stands in fact for the flesh of a human victim that should have been sacrificed in order to bestow the new chief with the "reign of the night," that is, the power of and over both the maternal life source and sorcery. The metaphoric cannibalism is a substitute for royal incest, which is another form of extreme violation of the minimal boundaries that exist between consanguines. The act completes the metamorphosis of the chief-to-be into the male ruler's absolute dominion over the maternal domain and uterine life source. Then, keeping a stiff posture, and with the sword of rulership on his knees, he displays a stance of undisputed authority: unflinching, composed, and firm, he maintains order within the bounds of his territory. Data presented in a previous study (Devisch 1988) show that the relation between ruler and people mirrors the one between patriliny and matriliny, between virility and motherhood: it is from the agnatic founder that the ruler inherits his power to rule and use violence, whereas the matrilineal landowners—the Tsaamba autochthons—link him up with the uterine life source fructifying the soil. In his double identity, the chief is the regent who oversees life transmission.

2.4.2 *The sorcerer and hunter explore an imaginary world of the nonsedentary and unsettling over against the familiarity with the enfolding village world and its surroundings:* they feed on a flux of forces that emerge in dream, in fantasy, and the imaginary. Folktales and dream-like or imaginary discourses with respect to the remote nightly forest realm depict a world of sorcery *(buloki, busingi ye buwandi)*—almost like a fairyland—which evades constraints and brings together in a play-like manner animal and man, ancestor and living. In this world, animals act as king and become witty companions of the hunter; they express the far-off utopia of collective fantasies, hopes, and desires that are so much alive with children. There is an imaginary transposition between the fusional and darkened realms of the forest and the utopia of the home where hierarchy and role division dwindle. These discourses materialize in anti-sorcery practices and rituals to assure the hunter's good luck which bring the diurnal village realm of order and distinction face to face with what is not sedentary, with a form of 'extraterritoriality' pregnant with wonder, surprise, bafflement, excitement, fear, instability, or wildness. This imaginary order does not show off but rather conceals the existence of a split into two opposed worlds: the realm of sorcery and forest is not thought of over against the village realm as subversive, 'demonic,' but as the locus of unsettled, vagabond desires, intermixture, and confusion.

The collective images regarding sorcery and hunting seek to capture excitement, liveliness, ebullience, forces, insights, and sensibilities beyond the bounds of diurnal village order, so to speak, in view of energizing *societas*. Both sorcerer and hunter draw on their keen sense of smell and mobility to track down their prey in the density of the forest or the night. Folktales depict fabulous journeys of sorcerers and hunters who fraternize with ghosts and animals, join sorcerous banquets, learn extraordinary skills, or receive forces of clairvoyance and bilocation from deceased kinsfolk whom they meet with at the other side of the river in the remotest forests that lead to the ancestral underworld. At least in folk representations the image of the sorcerer, like that of the hunter, depicts people's longing for surpassing limits: in this, they portray a popular, but very much utopian, version of the culture-hero, a utopian quest for reaching out beyond mere customary order and for tapping unknown potentialities and untamed forces from zones of uncertainty, ambiguity, and mixture. They show how much the Yaka world order is neither fully caught up in polar contraries nor traceable back only to an interplay of contrary entities. Though the imaginary locus of sorcery has very much to do with hybridization, inversion, or reversal, it nevertheless points beyond polar divisions or oppositional elements. Collective fantasies of sorcery do not primarily depict a world turned upside down, a kind of dreamed of *communitas*, but essentially the world turned inside out. Sorcery, as an imaginary construct, is not so much an instance of reversal of or offense against the diurnal and known order of the world. Sorcery is not to be seen as the otherness figured by mere inversion and thereby reduced into sameness—a reduction, for example, that characterizes European fancy fairs since the Renaissance. There is no hierarchy at play here between upper and lower bodily strata, but rather between inside and boundedness, on the one hand, and outside and openness, on the other. Sorcery strives at a form of defamiliarization with the local customary world. It feeds on and displays the forces of the night. And night is not only the inverse of day: it exceeds day since night is considered the source for the regeneration of the diurnal, and day is not born from an inversion of the night. In folk representations, sorcery expresses a longing for a basic source of vitality, empowerment, bafflement, desire, prior to distinctions and divisions. This quest is not in a relationship of inversion to customary order, or of deficiency to the realm of the day. Sorcery is the topos of movement, inclusion, intrusion, looseness, irregularity, or mixing, proper to affects, emotions, and motions, such as desire, affinity, seduction, passion, chance, aspiration, hunger, curiosity, avidity, ardor. It is as if, for the Yaka, the structure of the world, knowledge, classifications, and customary order do not keep all things in their bounds. The realm of sorcery, like that of the hunt, reaches beneath and beyond the compelling—patriarchal—order and obedience. The imaginary realm of sorcery does not entail a political or moralizing discourse that would claim that reality entails but substantive contrariety in all natural, intellectual, and social phenomena. The discourse on sorcery displays people's fundamental resistance to draw down the richness of experience in the world to a categorical ordering in terms of opposition and hierarchy.

2.4.3 *Men's fascination with 'cooking outdoors' celebrates and domesticates men's violence.* Man, the hunter-predator, associates his acts of killing game and tapping palm wine with acts of cooking and feeding. They metaphorically portray man's contribution to life transmission. (This hunting symbolism differs from the complex agricultural metaphors that may inform the erotico-sexual imagery of agriculturalists in the eastern part of the country, as we know of through Remotti 1987.)

The man hunts and harnesses the life forces in the forest realm. The palm sap that he collects in a calabash hanging from the male inflorescence of the palm tree (see 2.2.1) is compared to game caught in a trap. By being caught, both game and sap undergo a process of fermentation—man's method of tapping the life forces in the forest. They imply a similar process of cooking outdoors by stirring up the inner heat or energy of the sap, or the ardors in the animal, and result in a highly valued cultural product for sharing and conviviality.

Smell makes for a basic connection (see 4.1) between the hunt and the use of palm wine, on the one hand, and views regarding the contribution of genitor and genitrix in the gestation and the transmission of the flow of life and life force to descendants. Decay and flowering, fermentation and cooking evoke the maternal realm, and they all inspire metaphors that disclose something of the mysterious reciprocity between the realms of forest and village, or between bride-givers and bride-takers. They are metaphors regarding maturational processes in the couple of genitrix and genitor, in the mother-child dyad, in the relation between kitchen and homestead, as between society and cosmos. They are core metaphors in cult healing.

Folktales and fragmentary discourses on sorcery express a similar masculinist fancy regarding forms of feeding and cooking 'beyond the village realm' that men can induce. They celebrate highly individualist and transgressive intentions for a lifestyle that escapes the demands of *societas* and customary world order. Phantasmagoric discourses on sorcery depict how sorcerers reenergize themselves through abominations in cannibal banquets and promiscuity in the remote forests and the darkness of the night. In these imaginary realms of libertine predation, women figure as those who are victimized and surrender as passive means for sexual gratification and tribute, or who themselves become highly active, reaching the limits of luxury, thereby disbalancing the rule of sorcerous exchange. As such, the fantasies of sorcery glorify men as predators, but the spectacle of inversion that the women undergo at sorcerous banquets brings to light the ambiguity in men's role as predators vis-à-vis women's nurturing role for the community. In the actual division of labor, men also behave as predators, but contrary to the idealized picture, they are quite rarely able to provide the family with a good catch from the hunt, whereas women are responsible for feeding the family on a daily basis and recycling the product of men's violence in the hunt into a means of nurturing. Men's imaginary fascination with the realms of night and forest figure their unease with the concretely existing social order, with what I will portray in the next chapter as the asymmetrical relationships between bride-takers and bride-givers, genitor and genitrix. When bridging worlds—that is, in conjugal sexuality, in the hunt, on a journey, or more generally outdoors and outside formal councils—a man's behavior should be that of the hunter: forceful, explorative, and witty. On the contrary, the female space is depicted in public and masculine discourse as one of confinement and containment in which the male may temporarily enter for meals, life-bearing, and sleep. Women's cooking is to be done in enclosure, indoors, out of sight and any talk; it is a basic and routine task at the very core of the community's reproduction. These maternal tasks are taken as self-evident, and sparsely addressed in folktales, family unions, and rituals. Men portray their ideal marriage partners as mothers for 'their' children, as clever and devoted nurturers in the domestic realm but pleasing and self-contained in the public domain.

The imaginary realm beyond the customary order yields an imagery of forces, and a scene and some empowerment for the symbolic interweaving of the realms of body, group, and life-world. Yet, these forces and symbols are prone to an ideological 'use' in the highly masculinist power game.

3 The Social Formation of Life Transmission

At the center of Yaka social space stands the reproductive family unit and its homestead. In widening concentric waves are the other kin in the domestic quarter and, across the local savanna area, the homesteads of those with whom marriage has been or could be contracted. Infringement upon the boundaries of the homestead connotes "intrusion, assault, rape" *(yidyaata)* into the maternal or commensal domain: this is an even more ominous threat to fertility and the physical health of the offspring than "the breaking of the social, viz. marital rule" *(-hoonda tsiku)*. Marriage is seen as linking up various homesteads across the savanna stretch between the villages of bride-givers and -takers, and the bride is "the one who came along the path to the village" *(weedi mutsekya loongu, weedi mundzila hata)* to join the bridegroom and his homestead. Bridegroom and bride, bride-takers and bride-givers stand to one another as the domesticated village realm *(hata,* literally "the weeded or cleared land") stands to the bush *(tseki)* understood as source of renewal. Agnatic descent stands to uterine filiation as village realm with its founder and history of successive generations and settlements stand to the back-and-forward movements which lead the in-married woman "across the path to the village" from her parental home to the conjugal one, or to the one of her maternal uncle, granduncle, and great-granduncle. Gender, doubly unilineal descent, and roles in the social hierarchy shape and express concepts of selfhood, and sort out appropriate attributes and relations with others. Uterine filiation sustains the large degree of autonomy that in-married women have and share with the women in the neighboring hamlets. Marriage, parenthood, social roles, and life-cycle changes moreover modify the gender relations.

The cosmology of gender arrangements generates and replicates basic gendered values and views of the body. The ability to control and be in control, that is, to stand erect, is a requirement and symbol of virility. Force and vitality *(ngolu),* erect stance and excellence *(khoondzu)* are highly praised qualities of virility. They are at stake in the specialist roles that men monopolize in the social hierarchy, such as hunter, orator in the family council, judge, family head, political titleholder, cult leader, and ritual specialist. Blood relations through the mothers channel the vital flow *(mooyi)* from the uterine life source through the successive generations of mothers and their children.

The social relations of gender and the gendered values and relations of domination help to constitute the very fibers and fabric of experiences of self that a person develops throughout his or her life. These relations and values help to shape feelings, dispositions, and bodily awareness, and they are experienced as self-evident, and as such are not readily accessible to the subject's rational consciousness.

Though cult healing is practiced at the edge of social space, it ties in with the webs of agnatic descent and uterine filiation. It leads the patient to experience anew the ingredients of gendered relations, but in an overtly maternal domain.

3.1 Life-bearing and Nurturing in the Homestead

Inhabited space takes the pattern of a series of successively larger concentric domains. Thus name-giving introduces the newborn into the community of home and village quarter. The rites of boyhood, by inducing the newly circumcised boys to anticipate the conditions of marriage, incite them "to cross the neighboring savanna area as witness to their circumcision" *(bu beedi mutsekya n-khanda)*. It is within that same nearby area that later they will seek marriage partners. Similarly, domestic space is organized according to a concentric pattern. The center is the meeting place for public palavers and councils, and the houses face this center. Next, domestic space extends to neighboring compounds, and it is further expanded by people's movements back and forth to the fields, the nearby river, and the savanna. Rivers and locations in the savanna bear proper names inasmuch as they constitute zones of mutual aid. Finally, the large river or the dark forest at the outer frontier of the familiar region, as well as the capital Kinshasa, are considered as antipodes to the village realm.

3.1.1 *The homestead (ndzo) is relatively autonomous and connotes rest and equal sharing.* Housemates understand that care and empowerment is a shared task. No one works for himself or herself alone. The compound or homestead unites into a common dwelling the elementary family comprising the husband *(yakala),* his wife *(n-kheetu)* or wives, their children (sing. *mwaana,* gender undefined, often called "those who snuggle together, *n-leeki),* and possibly the widowed mother of one of the spouses. These coresidents are referred to as *n-ziika,* literally, "those who share one hearth." The residence is viri-patrilocal as a general rule, but in the case of some dissension it may be either neolocal or avunculocal. The familial space is organized around the kindled hearth *(ziku)* in or in front of the home. Most houses are rectangular and quite small, 3 meters wide and 5 long, with one or two rooms; walls and roof are made of sticks and are usually covered with palm leaves and grass. To mark out the limits of the compound, the husband will sweep the courtyard in the morning or trace a circle around the domestic space at the menace of an approaching thunderstorm. Having constructed or renovated a house, the newlywed husband brings to it his wife, "she who must live in a conjugal home" *(fweeni kundzo)*. This house becomes the conjugal home in reality when, as we shall see, the husband actually invests his wife with her reproductive and domestic functions. The spouses take exclusive possession of the conjugal space through sexual communion.

As a protective shell for mother and nursling, the home is the very icon of motherhood. In and around the house, a mother holds her baby on her lap, carries it on her hip or in a cloth on her back; she keeps it close to her in bed. She nurses the child on demand and comforts it when it cries. She will hand it over to others only for brief periods. Mothers are very playful with their nurslings. Till weaning, the strong mother-child tie isolates the father.

Life in the homestead is one of equal sharing. The sharing of table and of bed, the enduring intimacy of physical and olfactory contact between husband and wife, parents and children elicits affectionate fellow-feeling *(yibuundwa)* and, literally, "a unity of heart" *(mbuundwa mosi)* and confidence: members of the family offer mutual comfort and find protection in the familial dwelling at mealtime, around the hearth, and in the common sleeping place. The range of habitual and stable contacts in the home assures and supports the reciprocal identification of the family members while at the same time forming a boundary and a rampart that separate and protect the family. The maternal body and the family dwelling are one another's icon: here parents and children retire and confide in each other, abandoning themselves to the community of life and to the shared quest for well-being. In this way the home, and particularly its aspects of commensality and the shared sleeping place, acquire a vital completeness and an inviolable integrity similar to that of the mother's body. By offering one another the image of all taking for themselves what comes from the common dish, eating creates togetherness within the family shelter. By its very nature, eating must be shared equally. Eating circumscribes a space of physical co-presence. In the evening parents and children sit cross-legged on the ground in a semicircle around the pots of food. They, literally, "invite and give themselves reciprocally to sharing the meal" *(-diisasana)*, a term composed of the verb *-dya* (to eat) to which is added the causative suffix *-isa* and the suffix *-ana*, indicating reciprocity. The act of sharing a meal becomes a model and a norm for the distribution of goods produced by cultivation, hunting, or salaried work (in Kinshasa) by the family members. Prized or cooked food is by definition required to be shared: the hunter who eats his game all alone would be suspect of maleficent sorcery.

Commensality displays symmetrical reciprocity. Any form of competition or inequality at mealtime is carefully avoided; such would be the deed of a sorcerer who feigns commensality in order to feed on the blood of his own people. Through sharing the meal, the commensals in fact serve as mirrors for each other, that is, each person offers another the possibility to perceive or identify himself or herself as a partner in the meal. One consequence of this mirroring is that it is impossible to maintain a special diet for young children or for a sick person; such would mean excluding them from this basic form of fellow-feeling and the vital protection of the family shell. Like the adults, children eat the solid food of cassava, yams, vegetables, and bits of meat. Although it is unthinkable that a child take its meals alone, children nonetheless experience a large margin of freedom concerning their mealtime behavior, the portions they take, or their desire to be fed by their mother. Following weaning, mothers encourage the child to share food, to offer it to siblings and to accept food in return; adults will often praise a child who makes such gestures.

The homestead is a realm of interiority, and its bounds are like a veil of shame. Husband and wife, fathers and grown children demonstrate affection and physical intimacy only in the interior of this space. Contacts occurring within the home are protected by the veils of night and decency. In such contacts, one does not comment on what one sees. Family members almost do not speak to each other during the meal or in bed, look at each other at mealtime, or comment on what they see while making love. This conjugal or familial intimacy is of course protected from the gaze of any outsider. The integration of the wife in the conjugal home and the familial space grants her a certain autonomy, for the inviolability of the familial space reflects that of marital rights. The familial space is also the space that is trampled by the spouses and their children; members of a household may declare: *thaambi tudyaatasana, mbaawu tudiisasana,* "the tracts in which we walk bring us together, and eating what was prepared at the same hearth unites us." Here one lives in physical intimacy, and here the children until pubescence spend the night snuggled close to one another. When they exit the domestic shell and come into the public arena, diffidence requires that husband and wife, parents and grown children keep their distance from one another unless role relations govern their staying together. In public, they will avoid speaking to each other or allowing their eyes to meet. Such diffidence and restraint *(tsoni, n-kiindzi)* is especially required of the young wife. It prevents turning the wife into an object of another's desire in public, but it also constitutes an important norm of sexual appetite *(luhweetu)* in the conjugal home. Pubescent boys leave the parental home and seek housing with classificatory brothers of the same age group. The father may also construct a new dwelling belonging to him and bearing the name of *kyoota*. The dwelling may later become a conjugal home *(ndzo)* in the event of a second marriage.

The conjugal and parental home *(ndzo)* is like a double or extension of the maternal body: it is an exclusive space. The focus is on the maternal shell and its opening up in sexual communion and childbirth. Likewise, threshold, hearth, commensality, and conjugal bed all refer to life transmission. Thus it is forbidden for the pregnant woman to pause erect on the threshold of the house or to seat herself, legs crossed, in the doorway or on the bed under penalty of miscarriage or a difficult birth. Intrusion on this familial space is perceived as a real encroachment, as is expressed by the terms *yidyaata* (the nominal form of *-dyaata,* "to walk over or trample on") or *n-luta* (nominal form of *-luta,* "to pass over"). The arrival of a cowife or the fact that the husband inordinately favors one of the cowives also constitute cases, literally, "of encroachment on the marriage" *(-dyaata loongu).* Anything that might violate family unity is also seen as an intrusion: abusive commensality, grave insults or curses, and especially extramarital or premarital sex, or even attitudes, gestures, jokes, and touch by a stranger which might be interpreted as an invitation to intercourse. Such intrusions into the familial space, particularly should they occur shortly after the conjugal home has been founded or when the woman is pregnant or nursing, tend to rupture the intimate wholeness of the family and constitute an attack on the shared corporeality of the members by exposing them to illness. The intrusion may entail afflictions with regard to the body and its orifices: the spouse is "shut up" *(-biindama),* that is, incapable of conception, or runs the risk of miscarriage. She or one of the small children might be fatally stricken with *phalu,* that is, vomiting, dysentery, or menorrhagia. Husband and wife may nonetheless prevent any such intrusion on the domestic space by avoiding both physical contact with nonkin (namely, by refusing to shake hands and by making sure that nonkin do not sit on the bed or step over the hearth or one of the fire-logs) and any allusions to extramarital sex; they might also offset the consequences of such offenses in advance by offering a hen or substitute to those under the threat. To show that they avoid intimate contact *(-batika)* with one another and with any outsider to the house, they may tie a loin-cloth between the legs (a dress called *yibati*) as a public sign of abstinence. It is prescribed for the same reasons at moments of family disintegration. When death or a fatal injury in the hunt of one of the members leaves the domestic group open to disintegration, the survivors will wear the *yibati;* additionally, the hearth fire will be quenched, the family members will remove any footwear, uncover their torsos, abstain from cooked meals, and "sleep on the bare earth" *(-niimba hamaafu)* or "live in a closed place" *(-kala kuyikaangu),* in other words, forgo sexual relations. Such behavior, on the one hand, enables the members to avoid having to deny the disunity of the group, and, on the other, prevents them from being overly distressed by the fatal accident or death of the other.

Maternal space offers the great intimacy of the shell and yet hides a dimension of alienness. The status of the in-married woman is ambivalent to the extent that she perpetuates the agnatic group of the husband and at the same time represents the out-group, the alien, namely her group of origin. Depending on whether or not her matrimonial and life-bearing function is emphasized over against her foreignness, the woman may either be perceived positively or negatively. The hearth, bed, cooking pots, and reserves of grain are unambiguously positive. The far side of the house *(m-fungulwandzo)* and the refuse heap *(m-buumbwa n-totu)* both to the edge of the village denote a married woman's double belonging. The stillborn or the deceased nurseling *(mwanandzeemba)* is buried in next to the wall at the far outer side of the house behind the conjugal bed, so that it may "rapidly return to the maternal womb." It is there that the shrine of healing cults of uterine origin is installed. It is at the ambivalent edge of the village that the initiand in the seclusion house goes through the motions of gestation and ritual rebirth. Furthermore, inasmuch as she is alien to the agnatic group of her husband, the in-married wife whose fertility is not yet integrated in the husband's household may evoke the sphere of encroachment, literally, "overstepping" *(n-luta)*. Everything in her that might be opposed to her domestic and life-bearing role in the service of the husband's family can be charged with a negative, hence menacing, signification for her people and for the husband in particular; any such opposition is considered as an encroachment, an irruption of the forest or the sphere of sorcery into the familial space. It is a recurrent motif in folktales, for example, that women who refuse to share the conjugal bed run the danger of becoming barren or dysmenorrheic, by virtue of their supposed intercourse with forest spirits. Similarly, this concept of "overstepping" is applied to adultery, menstruation, miscarriage, barrenness, and rectal piles, the latter being seen as mixing discharge and menstruation, the anal and the genital.

Defilement destroys basic sociality: because it cuts off vital ties, it is close to cursing. The specter of defilement evokes all that the individual must keep away from, it is said, in order to stay alive: impure foods, feces, any excretions, or incest. Bodily stain links the fragility of the corporeal boundary to the fragility of social and cultural norms and limits. At the outer limits of the body, the individual—in particular at childbearing age—seems to control the boundaries of his or her social identity. It is not the absence of cleanliness or of health which degrades, but that which threatens the normalized order and divisions regulated by the cultural norms that may be considered an abomination, an object of disgust and abjection *(mbeembi, -beembula)*. Defilement represents a virtual attack on the person's health. Vomiting, flatulence at mealtime, defecation in the house, genital scents or the odors of excrement while taking a meal, ejaculation outside of coitus, and manual or oral excitation of genital parts are such acts of defilement: they cause consternation in that they evoke particular boundaries and a corporeal topography while negating them. This confusion is all the more anomalous when it occurs within zones of transition. To leave excrement at the entryway to a house or to commit an obscene act (for example, for an adult to show his or her genitals or naked backside: *-bolomana*) in this space signifies an eruption of the social order by a formidable and chaos-causing assault on vision *(mbeembi)*. Such acts are in fact considered those either of an insolent sorcerer or of an unbalanced individual, that is, someone who is ensorcelled or crazy. Erotic dreams augur evil *(ndosyambeembi)* in that they prefigure an encroachment or mixing of conjugal spaces; or they underscore exogamy or incest prohibitions in that men and women may use charms to free themselves from dreams where they are visited in bed by a close relative. If a family would fancy to share a meal outside of the domestic perimeter, in the forest for example, this would not only mean taking a serious risk with regard to their health, but would also connote an act that popular imagination relegates to the sorcerous banquets in forest darkness where consanguines engage in incest and consume raw human flesh.

The symmetric joking relations characterizing the rapport between grandparents and grandchildren are by contrast largely exempt from standards of shame and reveal the lively expression of intimate familiarity. Such relations are designated by the verb *-mokasana,* "to entice one another into joking and making advances." Within the domestic environs, the grandfather may for example apprise the attractive body of the granddaughter, particularly when she is returning from the river or the fields. He may describe or touch, in playful fashion, the erogenous zones of the pubescent granddaughter: the cheek, neck, breasts, hips, or abdomen. The young granddaughter may steal food from the mouth of the grandfather, or both may urinate or defecate side by side. The joking relationships that develop between grandson and grandmother are less intimate and transgressive, tempered as they are by their difference of patrikin.

Marked transitions in the domestic space are paired with transitional moments in time. One does not, for example, prepare or eat meals at night, and one does not have intercourse during the day. Sexual communion may not be practiced during moments which are clearly marked as transitional, such as new or full moon, mourning, rites of passage, and the eve of a collective hunt or trip into a foreign land. Similarly, the space reserved for food preparation, meals, and the conservation of prepared foods is strictly separated from that area reserved for sleep. Any allusion to sex is prohibited during the preparation or eating of meals. While she is getting a meal ready, the married woman—at least the wife of a man with some prestige—must wear "clothing which keeps the breasts covered" *(n-ledya kaanga mayenu).* If a visitor joins the family, the women will retire in order to avoid any allusion to sex during the meal. This rigorous demarcation between alimentary and sexual activity implies that the prohibition of incest is thereby being inscribed in the realm of bodily exchange, insofar as commensality is prevented from becoming an incitement to sexual union. Nourishment manifestly carries a maternal signification, especially since the mother gives up her maternal and nutritional role in favor of the wife of her son the moment the wife first takes up residence in the conjugal home. Such delimitations equally encourage brothers to respect one another's marital rights: in the absence or indisposition of his wife, the husband may no longer join his married brothers at a meal. He also prefers to forego meals rather than be forced to do the cooking, which is strictly a feminine task. If he no longer has a mother or a cowife to prepare the evening meal, he must content himself with food that does not need elaborate cooking (such as yams, maize, or peanuts) or that is imported one (rice, canned meat, or fish—which are no longer available) and which does not connote the context of commensality.

At times, the means of familial unity, in particular hearth and commensality, are ritually rejuvenated. These rituals aid in renewing the transactional qualities of the boundaries, especially after periods of affliction. When a lineage group seeks to purify itself of anything that might bring it misfortune, each homestead renews the bonds of its union with the local lineage group. A purification takes place a few days after a burial (see Devisch 1979:83, 119–20). It is sometimes followed by a powerful cleansing of the whole neighborhood called *-kula hita,* literally, "chasing the specter of death and evil," namely, an individual feared for his prowess in sorcery or one having died following a mysterious illness. It simultaneously aims at a cleansing of the sorcery in the group. The whole compound participates in a carnivalesque night of misrule during which customary forms of language and priorities of status and value undergo a series of inversions. Licentious folly leads to the interchange of gender roles and to simulated combat in which the men, brandishing domestic utensils, and the women, holding bows and arrows, fight each other. Gathering all over the village, men and women mix freely during these periods of deliberate topsy-turvydom. Through dissonant singing, indecent contortions, and derisive imitation, some of the behavior of the deceased is mocked and thereby expelled. It is also the moment that scores are settled against neighbors. At the first crow of the cock, husbands and wives gather up the ashes of the fire put out the preceding evening, in order to "get rid of the old fire" *(-lobula mbwaawakhulu).* They run in the direction of setting sun, beating the packet of ashes with a stick taken from the dismantled conjugal bed, until they reach a fork in the path outside the village. There they abandon the ashes and the stick. On their return, the patriarch "rekindles the new fire" *(-koolala mbwaawapha—* an expression that connotes the man's role in his partner's sexual arousal), employing ancestral instruments *(n-kaamba)* transmitted in the agnatic line; it is then shared in each of the domestic hearths and thereafter exclusively reserved for the family's own use. The patriarch offers a morsel of meat cooked over the same fire to each adult member of the family. The men then go off together on a hunt. The sexual prohibition is not lifted until the termination of a successful hunt, that is, when at least one animal has been killed; the product of the hunt, destined for a communal meal, is in fact held to justify "the rekindling of the fire," according to the expression -*sakwasa mbwaawu.*

3.1.2 *Life-bearing, nurturing, intimate fondling, the growth of food, and cooking are basic tasks in the female space.* Motherhood and the caring for offspring and husband in the latter's residential group assign the inmarried women an ambigous status and confine them to their kitchens—in the front part of the conjugal home or in an abandoned house in the compound—or to the transitional zones of the paths between homestead and fields or between the conjugal home and the parental one. In order to perform her domestic chores in the service of her husband's community, the woman proceeds to the periphery of the village where she dries the sodden manioc or other foodstuffs, to the edge of the dwelling area where her mortar for manioc is kept, and finally to the front or inside of the hut where she prepares the manioc paste and cooks it over the fire. It is in the shade of the dwelling, to the side or back of the conjugal home that one observes the potter at work and other women at rest or busy coiffing each other's hair. The physical act of birth-giving is socially unmarked, relegating the parturient to the margins of society.[1] One custom requires that the woman in labor remove herself to the outskirts of the village. During delivery she must be undressed and seated on the ground, supported by another woman, for the newborn is expected to emerge in an almost upright position. The afterbirth is to buried near the roots of the *n-saanda* lifetree in the compound planted there to connect the eldest branch of the lineage groups in the settlement with the life force originating from their founding ancestor. Some parturients withdraw to the conjugal home and seat themselves at the extinguished hearth. There is no talk of a distinct midwife role, for the assistance brought by some elderly women to the one in labor does not entail a privileged status.

Activities, utensils, and tools are part of this gender-related topology. The mortar, the fish trap, the carrying basket strapped to the back, the cooking pot, and kitchen utensils all signify at least the woman's domestic role, if not her reproductive one. In certain ritual contexts, the pestle and the fire-log in the hearth display an overt masculine significance, while the carrying basket—an overt symbol of the womb—and in particular the fireplace, with its coals and ashes, like the bed, denote the inviolability of the conjugal home and union. Men avoid mixing with the women while they work and would belittle themselves if they handled their utensils. Moreover, there are probably no chores which would mobilize both men and women or which could be performed by either gender indifferently, apart from several tasks related to basic provisions. Even here differentiation is attempted: a man would rather draw water with a demijohn than with an earthenware jar, which is reserved for the woman's use;

the husband gathers and cuts logs for the hearth while the wife gathers dead wood.

3.2 Marriage as a Transfer "Along the Path to the Village"

Contracting a marriage is spoken of in terms of a repeated journey of the bridegroom with goods and valuables to the house of the bride, and of her passage "along the path to the village." She is associated with abundant fecundity, "as the one with breasts replete with grease and a womb with offspring" *(maasi kuthulu, kuvumu kaanda dyabaatu)*. Through their many crossings of the savanna area between their respective households, bridegroom and bride seem to tune their life-bearing capacities to each other. One commonly refers to marital alliance in terms of "the marriage path across the savanna to the village," namely, of a passage leading the bride to the marital home. Any form of casual sex, as well as menarche, menstruation, and delivery are all thought to take place in the savanna near the village or at the edge of village space. It is there that the seclusion house for healing is built, and it is the site for the circumcision camps. The passing of the bridewealth from the groom's household to the bride's socializes conjugal sexuality or introduces it into the social realm and center of the homestead. The typical expressions with regard to wedding used in the palavers, oracles, and rites all refer essentially to the following notion: *tsiidiza mundzo nongonu, bapheka mayenu maloongu,* "I have paid the bridewealth to the house of so-and-so, so that they would return me breasts to marry." The Yaka strictly regulate access to marriage and to the transmission of life, as well as rights over progeny, through a system of reciprocal obligations and rights between households. This handing over of goods validates and makes public the surrender of the bride, called *-kweela loongu,* and the constitution of the couple. A full matrimonial alliance sealing together the lineages of the married couple will not be achieved, however, until after the birth of several children in good health.

The various transactions and wedding ceremonies prefigure and socialize life transmission. According to the themes in songs at circumcision or at wedding dances, crossing the path in the in-between savanna by bride and groom acts as an anticipation and figuration of marital intercourse and reproduction, both human and agricultural. According to circumcision songs, certain wooded and humid strips in the savanna display a genital connotation; it is there that the maternal uncle collects the bouquet of plants which he hands over to his sister's pubescent or newlywed daughter.

The choice of a spouse is subject to certain restrictions. The Yaka, however, do not hold to a preferential primary marriage. Normally, alliances are struck within the confines of the same *yikoolu,* a region specified by the ability to make contact in less than one day's march. Approval of the choice of a spouse falls to those who are responsible for the patrikin. The elders in both the boy's and the girl's patrikin take into account the social origin of the spouse as well as his or her individual qualities. Criteria indicating that a girl will make a good wife include good health, signs of fertility including a well-developed body, particularly the breasts and pelvis, a brownish shade of skin color, deferential speech, lightheartedness, and diffidence with regard to men. The boy should display a sense of respect towards the elders, vigor, endurance, ingeniosity, and an art with words. Two types of prohibitions further limit the choice of a marriage partner. First, there is the rule of exogamy that forbids marriage with a partner of the same patrikin or with an agnatic descendant of one's matrilateral grandmother and great-grandmother; spouses who might be assimilated to the mother, such as a co-spouse to the mother or the widow of an elder brother, are also strictly prohibited. Second, alliances are forbidden where a marriage between members may have been cursed by an ascendant who had been the victim of an unfortunate or tragic alliance. In the collective imagination, these prohibited families are associated with the dark forestland to the north, that is, a nocturnal zone.

The practice of restricted customary polygyny is governed by the same rules concerning the choice of a spouse for a primary marriage. While the more extensive customary polygyny involving more than two or three wives is the privilege of paramount rulers alone, petty polygyny these days is less widely practiced than it has been (Ngondo 1982). A man of an average age of thirty-five years may take a young woman as a second wife to increase his progeny and access to the products of female labor. Nevertheless, polygynous marriage does not imply the monopoly of spouses by elders at the expense of the younger men, because of the differences in age at the time of marriage. A young woman may in fact marry soon after menarche, at about the age of sixteen years, while a man gets married not earlier than the age of twenty-three. At the death of the husband, the youngest of the co-spouses is quite often still of childbearing age and a junior brother of the deceased may inherit her as a marriage partner.

Marriage tends to be delayed among those who have settled in Kinshasa or in the administrative centers of the Kwaango region. In these areas, a woman marries at the age of twenty to twenty-five, a man in his late twenties. While in the 1970s many men in these same milieux hoped to acquire two wives, and that without too great an interval, or cohabited with more than one woman, steadily worsening economic conditions in the 1980s—which seemingly do not affect the birth rate—as well as the threat of AIDS have put a damper on these virile aspirations. Nowadays city dwellers tend to exert their seductive talents and sexual prowess far less than previously: unlike in the 1970s, bars and dance halls are no longer the heart of popular life in the suburbs. Among the adult generation, there is at present a greater and greater tendency to place importance on the education parents can offer their children, often at great sacrifice; it is no longer acceptable for a father to flaunt his involvement in a "second office," a euphemism widely used in Kinshasa for an extramarital companion. Yaka youngsters find it increasingly difficult to produce the bridewealth, and in a growing number of cases (one household on ten, perhaps) the mother's serial cohabitation with the several genitors of her children adds to their economic vulnerability.

The marriage process generally takes shape in the following way. The young man informs his father or the household chief of his intentions to marry and thereby finds out if the latter have already selected a spouse for him. It is in fact rather rare that a father would have arranged a marriage for a son who has been absent from his rural home in order to study in school or engage in paid labor. However, even if he has not chosen a marriage partner for his son, the father reserves himself the right to eventually veto his son's own choice. Having consulted the father or household chief, the young man pays a visit to the village where the girl of his choice lives. He offers, through intermediaries, some palm wine and cola nuts to the chief of the girl's household. This step is understood by those involved as a request for marriage. The following day the household chief advises the suitor to return with palm wine, thereby signaling that he is not opposed to negotiations. The chief then consults with the mother of the girl. The favorable attitude of the chief does not yet constitute a commitment, however, and a negative answer for the young man on his return would not require compensation. On the occasion of the second visit, the young man will also go to greet the girl's mother. The mother will indicate her own agreement to the proposal by declaring: "Go and see the girl yourself." This time the suitor offers the girl a small plate *(loonga)* and a cup *(kawa).* These presents are called *yizaayidila,* "a thing which invites reflection." Popular commentary in fact conveys the same meaning through a homonymous association of terms: *loonga kadiloonga, kawa kawa,* "the plate, in order that she advise herself, and the cup, in order that she listen."[2]

In order to show her readiness for marriage, the girl takes an initial step towards commensality by preparing that evening a first meal of meat for the young man. It is the mother, however, who presents it to him. The suitor is expected to set aside a portion of the meat, which he will take back to his father "in order to break the news to him." Accompanied by a younger sister, the girl will spend the evening in the house that has been made available to the young man. The couple is then together for part of the night. Nevertheless, if the girl is already pregnant when the bridewealth is to be paid, her uncle will demand a *khoombwatsiku,* "a goat for the interdiction." As we shall see, this goat and other valuables are intended to compensate for the ill that offending the rule against premarital pregnancy may have caused the girl or her close family. The suitor and young girl will take turns visiting each other, residing each time for several weeks in the compound of the future partner. They are gradually introduced into the domestic space and the familial environment of one another by taking part in agricultural or household chores. These visits permit the couple to "explore and anticipate marital life" *(-laanga loongu)*. If now the girl's family fails to propose a date when the bridewealth is to be handed over or makes unrealistic demands with regard to its amount, it is because they wish to break the engagement. In this case there is no compensation for exchanged services and goods. However, at this point, if the patriarch agrees on the bridewealth, neither the refusal of the girl nor that of her mother will necessarily pose an obstacle to the marriage.

The bridewealth has a triple function, according to common exegesis. First, it makes official "the news of the alliance" *(n-samwa makweela);* second, it constitutes a "value of exchange" *(ndziimbu)* in that it has a compensatory function; and finally, it legitimates the couple's participation in the transmission of life. Giving birth, *-vweela,* is a reproduction of "stock, goods" *(-vwa)*. The whole of the local community celebrates and is associated with the families as witness to the payment of the most significant part of the matrimonial goods. Particularly the women will join in the collective dancing, in the evenings, to celebrate the wedding. The different moves towards the alliance witness to the rapport husband and wife will have. Their union is a weave of life transmission and not a 'writing together of a common life-script,' for all essential communication between the partners regarding the children's and their own destiny passes through the husband's mother, the wife's brother—that is, the maternal uncle of the children—and, later, through the grown oldest son.

(a) First, the payment of the bridewealth is an all-important procedure which makes the alliance official and acts as a major wedding ceremony. The two families meet together in the village of the girl. As the formula designating this practice, *n-samwa mata,* expresses it, "gunshots announce the news to the surrounding areas." All the elders gather during the morning and the goods to be handed over are placed in the center of the congregation. The bridegroom is seated apart from the assembly, however. He is careful to avoid any behavior or dress which might be considered ostentatious. In contrast, the place of honor which the bride occupies in the assembly suggests that it is through the woman that new bonds are woven between the family groups. The bride is dressed in the beautiful attire that she has received shortly before from the groom as part of the bridewealth. For most women in rural Kwaango, these articles will probably be the finest that they will ever own: wig, kerchief, a luxurious blouse and pagne, underclothing, shoes, and perhaps sunglasses. The bride takes her place next to a classificatory brother who will later be an uncle to her children. The spouses will not approach each other, as decency *(tsoni)* prohibits them from displaying any form of conjugal intimacy outside the home. The household chief or one of the groom's fathers then speaks. He first identifies the new husband by situating him in the genealogical line, either by patrilineal descent or matrilineal filiation. The speaker declines *(-sasa)* the groom's identity: he mentions the different grades the groom has achieved or honors that have been attributed to him, and notes any other important events in his life.[3] Next, he traces the history of the relations the groom's household or patriline has had with the family of the bride. Finally, he expresses wishes for cordial relations between the families and for the fertility of the new couple to the benefit of the home and the whole lineage. The discourse is applauded by the assembly. The girl's patriarch or one of her fathers in turn gives a similar speech. This oral exchange constitutes "a formal announcement of the alliance" *(n-samu makweela).*

(b) Second, the actual transfer of the bridewealth is designated by the expression *-kweela biima* or *-kweela ndziimbu,* "to pair off the goods," in order "to wed the wife" *(-kweela n-kheetu).* The goods are both an anticipation of and compensation for the bride's fertility and work, expressed as *-fiika ndziimbu,* "to furnish plenty of goods and valuables."[4] Today, as in earlier times, besides some commercial items, most goods are rare or highly valued ones, like salt and gunpowder, whose compensatory value with regard to human life probably dates back to the slave trade across the Angolese boarder. There are moreover dyed cloth *(matona),* white woven fabric *(marecani),* rifles, demijohns, cutlasses, machetes, large basins, large pots, and a goat or its equivalent in cash. A part of the cloth goods offered may come from the house of the groom's father, where they were kept in a packing-case; the bride's father may transfer them later to another household on the occasion of the marriage of a son.[5] During the transfer of the marital goods, the whole of the audience acts as witness, and each of the gifts is closely examined by a third party. Additional goods may be claimed *(biloombi)* by the family of the bride if they find the preceding gifts insufficient. Judging from oracles and cases brought before the council of elders, the required goods are often not surrendered quickly but become the pretext for much haggling as each party seeks to maintain the upper hand in these relations of dependence. Thus, when the young husband has finally offered the last of the required goods, the father of the wife can no longer claim any services from the son-in-law. One of the parties may go so far as to invoke the nonpayment of the required goods in order to demand or refuse a divorce, or to place the blame on the partner for infertility or the death of a child.

(c) Finally, the bridewealth places strong expectations of motherhood upon the bride in a continuity with her mother, mother's mother, and mother's mother's mother who connects the bride with the uterine source of life. Therefore, certain goods, called *diwu,* of the bridewealth compensate in advance the uterine forebears for the offspring to be born out of the bride. In other words, the husband's kin do not only 'pay' for the bride, but also—and anticipatively—

for the children that will be born out of her connectedness with the uterine source of life. An initial portion of these goods is due to the one who gave birth to the young wife. The bride's mother receives the *yidiimbu kyangudyamwana,* literally, a mark that she is the bride's mother; it usually consists of two or three colored pagnes and several household utensils. A second part of the *diwu,* including a sow and a she-goat, both pregnant, as well as enough colored cloth to make six to ten pagnes, go to the bride's maternal uncle who in turn gives one or two of the pagnes to both his uncle and granduncle. A popular local tradition demands that the primary uncle then mime, to the great amusement of the audience, the labors of a woman giving birth. When the bride's mother also joins in the mimicry, she is given the remainder of her *yidiimbu kyangudyamwana.* Finally, in order to seal the alliance, the two parties share the palm wine offered by the groom's junior brothers. The transition to permanent cohabitation only takes place a few weeks later, when the elders are satisfied that they have received most of the bridewealth.

There is no actual transfer of bridewealth for a marriage by inheritance, that is when a widow is inherited as a spouse by a junior brother of the deceased husband, or when a widower's untimely deceased wife is replaced by the latter's junior sister. Children born to these latter types of union are in fact dependent on the group guardians who originally offered the bridewealth. One therefore distinguishes between the *genitor* (*taata meenga,* "father by blood") and the *pater* (*taata ndziimbu,* "father by payment of the bridewealth").

3.3 The Reproductive Cell

Begetting and raising up children are inseparable from marital status and alliance, and vice versa: these tasks must be woven into the existing social fabric. In practice as in speech, motherhood is far more valued than the wife's economic productive function. The difference in values here is even more evident when the spouses live apart (in bilocal residence), as in certain secondary marriages.

Marriage is consummated by the partners' sharing of a meal and, literally, by their "intertwinement" in the reproductive act, both of which help to mark off the bounds of the conjugal home within the web of the larger household and lineage quarter. In anticipation of their cohabitation, that is, of their constituting a new hearth in the existing homestead or domestic body, the bridegroom offers a hen to the household chief or the patriarch as well as to the bride. The chief will have the meat prepared over the fire and distributed to the different houses which share the same fire. The bride does the same for her coinitiates if she is a cult initiate. Each of the coinitiates turns over the hen to her own mother's brother. In return, the latter offers bouquets of plants for a lukewarm vaginal or cold anal rinse (a practice described below, 4.2.2). These gifts elicit the community's recognition of the passage to conjugal life.

The transfer of the bride that follows, from her parental home to the conjugal one, is a symbolic rebirth. The bride's father or lineage chief shows the young woman to the door of her parental home and commands her mother to "take her to the marriage" *(-fila kuloongu)*. On the same day her father counsels her to seclude herself in the parental home "three days" *(yitatu)*—in fact till the next morning—before joining her husband. He strengthens her by offering a "hen to conduct her out of the parental home" *(khoku ban-lobwelele kundzaawu)*. When she comes out from the parental shell, the father of the bride then instructs her in the rights that her status as wife confers on her: specifically, her right to the game her husband brings home from the hunt, as an incentive to sharing meals and the conjugal bed. He advises her to apply herself to household work and display an attitude of submission toward her husband and mother-in-law. He spits on her front and authorizes her "to leave from between his legs" *(-lobula mumaalu mayaandi)*. This phrase echoes the name-giving ceremony following birth (as we will see next) as well as the emancipation from the therapeutic relationship (see 7.2). The bride's departure from the parental home is called *-tolula n-loombu*, "to break or divide the loins"—of either father or mother," almost like breaking an off-shoot or twig from the 'treelike' parental body; *n-loombu* being the term for the lower body and its vital flow which are compared to the tree trunk and its rising sap.

The task of introducing the young wife into her nurturing role falls to her mother. For this, the mother will have taken care to put together some stocks of dried meat, manioc flour, and peanut and corn seed so that the bride can be "sent away with a full basket" *(-loongala n-yendi)*. Further, her mother or uncle will provide her with other goods: several pagnes, household utensils, agricultural tools, and a pregnant goat. These goods remain the property of the woman or her uterine kin if the marriage is untimely ended through death or divorce.

The bride's integration into the husband's village and conjugal home is gradual. Given the rule of virilocal residence, only the in-married women are able to introduce the bride into the introverted residential group. The bride's mother and one or more younger sisters escort her to the entrance of her husband's village. But the bride will not enter before several of the women of her conjugal homestead come out to greet her and to offer some fruits of a recent harvest. Her mother-in-law will sit in the middle of the path, barring the way until she receives several pieces of cloth as a mark of recognition. She will repeat this scene the first time that she accompanies her daughter-in-law to the fields or to draw water.

The bridegroom introduces the young bride to her new home for the nuptial event and the creation of a new hearth *(ziku)* in the larger homestead. It is at the same time symbolized as the constitution of a new weave, inasmuch as his gifts are called *m-fiku myaloongu,* literally, "the interlacing of those who rejoin." In front of the women of the homestead escorting the bride, the husband gives her some gifts, mainly dyed cloth, while briefly insisting on his marital rights over her: he expects that "she will be sure to sweep" *(keti kakoomba)* and also to fulfill her other household duties; he hopes to see her "chew and swallow" *(m-minu),* that is, share the meal; and to "see her naked" *(kan-mona khoonga),* and "straddle her in bed" *(kasuumbuka kuthaangi).* (At the death of a spouse, there are gifts, known as *bikookulu* [Devisch 1979:135], that echo the ones at the nuptial retreat, in which the husband pays compensation to the maternal ascendents of his deceased wife for all the household and conjugal services she has rendered.) The partners express their desire for reciprocal belonging and ultimate physical union by "exhorting each other to embrace the other with the legs" *(-biindasana maalu).* They allow one another within their respective bodily intimacy: *-dyaatasana,* "making one another walk and sit in each other's imprints and to hold each other closely." The next morning, as a sign of her new status, the bride dresses in some of the dyed cloth she received the day before and shares some money with her mother-in-law and fellow women in the homestead.[6]

The ritual announcement of the first pregnancy affords the various groups linked through the alliance an occasion to affirm their respective rights—of descent for one, of filiation for the other—with regard to the progeny of the new couple. In the third or fourth month of pregnancy husband and wife select a day on which they will *-tuumbula zimi,* "reveal the pregnancy." The husband or chief of the compound gathers together the presents to be given: a goblet *(kawa)* and a small plate *(loonga).* The husband appoints one of his brother's daughters to hand over the presents to the pregnant woman. The girl joins her at her work place, lifts up her blouse, and pours some of the water contained in the goblet on her belly with the words *dya mbote, zimi dyeetu nyeedya,* "eat well [that is, stay with us and fare well], you carry our child." The girl then offers her the presents. In stating "our child" the emissary speaks in the name of those agnatic ties that link herself both with her own classificatory father, who is the husband concerned, and with the child to be born. As noted above (3.2), the gift of goblet and plate is intended to encourage the wife to "reflect" upon the fact that, socially, the child will belong to the father and the patriliny. If the husband is himself a first son, the girl will offer the pregnant woman, along with the cup and plate, a necklace of pearls *(ndzelwa n-saangu)* belonging to the husband's mother, who would have received the necklace, a generation ago, from her mother-in-law on the occasion of her first pregnancy. On her next return to the parental home, the pregnant woman is expected to turn over the goblet and plate to her father. If she does not do so, her family of origin may disregard the pregnancy and refuse to intervene in the case of any subsequent problems. The transfer of these symbolic gifts also affords the young woman an occasion to stay in the company of her mother for several weeks.

When the pregnant woman prepares to return to her conjugal home, the head of the parental household offers her a hen signifying that he renounces any claim on her and the child she will bear. At the same time and for the benefit of the child, he will entrust his pregnant daughter to her maternal uncle:

> Nge mwana nganya maleemba.
> Taa khoku, nda kola.
> Nda buta batsuki ye ndzala.
>
> You, you are another's child, a child of the uncles. (a)
> Here is a hen; may your health be reinforced.
> Leave now and bear children who have hair and nails. (b)

Comments:
(a) Life is transmitted along the uterine line.
(b) The normal birth of healthy children is wished for.

By offering a hen and bouquets of plants for an anal or vaginal rinse, the uncle protects the expectant mother and her child from any malevolent force that could result from an offense or curse that is being transmitted along the uterine line.

Other practices serve to further convert sexuality into social reproduction so that the flow of life that the woman channels is appropriated for the husband and for the sole benefit of his patrikin. At least ideal culture forbids the married woman any pleasured sex outside the conjugal relation or to the detriment of the reproduction of the husband's patrikin. A few days before the announcement of her first pregnancy, or immediately after, the expectant woman is invited to "reveal the names of her lovers" *(-tuumbula mazina mabatsuutsa)*. She is required to give to her husband or mother-in-law as many small pieces of wood or straw as lovers *(n-tsuutsa)* she has had out of mere "erotic attraction" *(yitsuutsa)*. If the pregnancy is complicated or a difficult birth is indicated, the confession of lover's names is given a new urgency and an even more ritualistic character. In this case, the husband requests the intervention of his wife's uncle, as the latter represents both the line of transmission of physical life as well as of the rules of reciprocity between bride-givers and bride-takers that govern it and whose infringement may choke off the life flow: either the angered uncle may have ensorcelled the young wife, or an ancient curse once put on a extramarital affair in the wife's uterine kin may now again have acted as a trap.

When the uncle arrives, the husband presents him with a *khoombwatsiku,* a "goat for the interdiction" against extraconjugal relations in order that the uncle in turn give his niece a hen, thus neutralizing the offense and foregoing any further hindrance in the uterine transmission of life. The goat offered serves as a compensation for a past wrong and as a scapegoat.

Conjugal sexuality is aimed at achieving reproduction.[7] First, the wife may exhort her husband to regular conjugal communion. If for some reason he refuses, he is exposed, especially if he has more than one conjugal partner, to the wife's public reprimand or to her threats to break the marriage. Since the marriage no longer serves its reproductive function, the woman may declare: *baana bapfuula mukati,* "children are dying in my belly." Second, mother and nursing are very vulnerable to any rupture of the reproductive shell. The postpartum taboo on conjugal intercourse holds as long as mother and nursing form one body in breast-feeding. A new pregnancy is not preferred as long as the last-born is not yet walking and has not been weaned. It is believed that if the mother does not abstain from sexual relations until weaning, her milk will dry up. In practice, and especially in urban milieux, this spacing of births either is not wanted or is not successful.[8] Where adequate spacing of births is not achieved, the infant may suffer; children weaned before the age of twenty months show great difficulty in adapting to the poorly varied diet of the adults. Third, conjugal commitment is asymmetrical and a function of social reproduction: the wife is more coercively than her husband under the threat of social rule or marital prerogatives, *n-tsiku.* Sterility on the part of the husband is overcome by inviting a younger brother to spend several nights with the wife. The husband will nevertheless be considered as the "father by blood" of the children begotten by the brother (see 3.2). In compensation for this mixing of conjugal spaces, some chickens or a minute substitute in cash are exchanged between the younger brother and the husband and between that brother of the husband and the wife, just before or after the period of sharing the bed. Where the wife lacks continence—a woman's adultery is seen as an extreme and ill-fated form of rupture—she may be repudiated for having "gone above the prerogatives of the husband" *(n-tsiku myayakala kasuumbuka).* The wife's refusal to prepare food or share the conjugal bed (the latter behavior being motivated, for example, by jealousy towards a cowife preferred by the husband) could be the occasion for repudiation by the husband. The contrary does not hold after healthy children have consolidated the marriage: a mother with children is not entitled to divorce on the ground that her husband is lazy, does not produce any food from the hunt, favors a cowife, or stays in Kinshasa and leaves his wife empty-handed.

The marital prerogatives are asymmetrical: it is as if the rule imposed on the marriage by the in-laws does not bind the husband as long as there appears no impediment to the transmission of life in his marriage. Neither partner nor tradition can forcefully reprove a man for his extramarital affairs as long as he has ritually and effectively prevented any harm falling on his extraconjugal partner or on his own children. In order to neutralize any harmful effects in advance, the two partners of an extramarital affair perform a ritual exchange of hens. The man may also present his child or first-born son with a hen. Insofar as young mothers and pregnant women more explicitly incarnate the conjugal cell than other women, they carefully resist any seduction. It may be recalled in this context that, according to deep-running convictions, a man's or a wife's extramarital affairs may provoke abortion, dysentery, or fatal hemorrhaging in the wife and fetal dysentery *(n-luta)* in the infant. As gossip would have it, women whose husbands are repeatedly absent a year or more in search of income in Kinshasa might acquire a certain independence in their husband's village and be apt to have a sexual affair. In particular, when she joins her village of origin, or at feasts where people of a same region meet for a whole night of dancing and rejoicing, the unmarried sons of the wife's brothers or husband's sisters may tease their aunt of their age by cracking jokes with a sexual content or attempt to solicit her for sex. These lovers are almost like the physical double of the absent husband whose place they take: their love affair is like a conjugal one and hardly a social offense. It is not brought before a council of elders. In case these affairs lead to pregnancy or to a gynecological problem, the husband will do no more than reproach his wife "for disrespect to her husband" *(wakoonda luzitu lwayakala);* or the betrayed husband may seek to ensorcell the relative with whom his wife was having an affair.

Name-giving marks the social birth of the neonate. It recycles a forebear's name and socializes some of the special circumstances attending the birth. Not parturition—an event which takes place in the margins of public space and attention—but the coming-out rites and the naming assure the infant's social birth into the agnatic group. Mother and infant end their 'three day' seclusion *(yitatu)* following delivery and leave the conjugal home. The child is for the first time exposed to the light of day. At the request of the mother and in the presence of coresidents, the father, in a gesture of spitting, "vomits the name" *(-luka zina)* and covering it with a rag "dresses the child" *(-viika mwaana)* thereby starting to shape its social skin (see T. Turner 1980). The father, a grandfather, or the mother may have dreamed of a forebear, either living or deceased, and interpreted this vision as an invitation "to revive his or her name" *(-tuumbula zina).* The oldest son often receives his father's first name, whereas the oldest daughter is named after her father's or mother's mother. This birth name integrates the child into the genealogy. It is not exceptional that an infant receives two names at birth. The birth name *(zina dyakabutukila)* may otherwise refer to events or persons marking either the birth or the period during which the group awaited the newborn.

Here are a few birth names that illustrate how they may mark the individual child's history. Many of these names emphasize, as much as some folktales do, how reproduction appears as an oft-thwarted enterprise, and how circumstances determine the fate of the couple and the kin groups they belong to.

Tseki, "savanna": a name of a child born on a journey.
N-suunda: a name for infants who have been born feet first.
Luyaalu, "government": a name for a child born to a newly enthroned political titleholder.
Lumeengu, "hate, enmity": a name for a girl whose mother or father is hated by the patrikin or the in-laws.
Batukudidi, "we have been chased away": the birth followed divorce.
Maafu, "earth": the birth came after several still-births.
Kafiikaku, "she was fruitless": the mother's illness postponed the marriage.
N-swa kaluungidiku, "he did not wait for permission": the infant was begotten before the transmission of the bridewealth.
Beenda kwaawu, "may they leave": the parents have been forced to flee the patrilocal homestead.
N-dyaata, "favorite wife": the mother aroused jealousy in the cowives.
Tatameni, "he hesitated a long time": the infant's father did not like the marriage arranged for him.
Yitswandzuka, "talkative girl": the infant's mother is a reputed gossip-monger.
Kyasala bayakala, "whatever the men do gets attention": the mother feels peripheral in the husband's household.
Wubatakana, "to be a neighbor": the father has quarreled with his neighbors.

The name introduces the child into the social space and into nurturing contact with housemates. One custom, which seems more and more neglected, requires that at the name-giving the mother, without a word, carry the infant across the homestead. She will hold it above the threshold of each home, chicken coop, pestle, and manioc rack with the intent of uniting the child to the basic elements of domestic life. Thus the infant, who is referred to as *kadi* (newborn not yet become human) and who up to this point has no ties to any particular space, experiences an initial mark of demarcation or of individuation. A name, clothing, and the integration into a domestic space confer on the infant the first qualifications of a human being: *muutu.* If the newborn should die before the naming ritual, the death will be of no social significance and there will be neither mourning nor public burial. The birth name inscribes on the child's body, as it were, a mark of belonging to the lineage and thus testifies to the claim held by one generation over another and to the expectations arising from that claim. When the child receives its name, the parents may be addressed to by their tecnonym, as "father/mother of..." and the child moreover by its patronym, as "child of . . . ," by adding the name of the father or family head. Because of the individualizing function of the birth name, it is employed only within the domestic circle or among age-mates. The child will bear it until it may select a second or more public name out of a stock of ancestral names at boyhood rituals or marriage for girls, that is, until they leave the maternal shell and search elsewhere for physical affection.

The nursing baby remains almost constantly in close bodily and nurturing contact with its mother and siblings. The father, his parents, and cowives may all fondle the baby, thereby progressively breaking open the mother-child dyad. There is rarely an occasion where a lack of physical contact would inspire the baby to learn to fill the void with an affective and lasting relation with an object—a comforter or toy. A child is breast-fed for two to two-and-a half years. To withdraw the breast from the nursling, a mother may put pepper or bitter substances on her nipples. From then on, the mother may leave the child alone in bed for some moments, or with other siblings, at the time she resumes marital intercourse. Then, when a new baby is born, the young child is left to the care of a young (classificatory) sister, usually one who is very indulgent, and the father may also spend some time with his weaned child during the day. A child is in any case rarely left alone.

When children reach the age of three, games begin to have a mirror function. Children like very much to switch roles in the course of their play or games: a child will then imitate his playmate's gestures or exhibit his own for the on-lookers. In this way the child learns to fashion his gestures for his own and the others' pleasure. Any aggressive move toward a younger sibling on the part of an older brother or sister is reprimanded, whereas the adults encourage the child to stand up to his age-mates. Adults, through their remarks and commentary, gradually tame and thereby socialize the aggressiveness of the boys. A mother will quickly and loudly point to the aggressive act of an older child as cause of her own child's discomfort.

When coming of age as a new generation, boys undergo circumcision, *-tapa*, literally, "to cut," just before or in early adolescence, "when they turn over" *(babalukidi)* from weakness *(n-ndzeendza)* to strength. When the boys reach the age of ten or eleven, parents "hand their boys over" *(-laambula baana)* for circumcision combined with initiation into the *yikubu* male fecundity cult (see 4.4). The circumciser, namely the *tsyaabula* priest, is responsible for the rite, which is carried out in the bush at the outskirts of the village. While a boy "straddles" *(-suumbuka)* a log of a banana tree blackened by the fire or a mortar turned upside down, placed in the middle "of the road to the village," the circumciser pulls forward the foreskin over a little stick. He cuts it off and collects the foreskins of the various boys on the same piece of wood. The boys then withdraw to the seclusion house, where they will remain for four days without a fire or cooked food. Their foreskins will be buried in the seclusion house's backyard, a place they are strictly forbidden to enter.

For the time of seclusion which may last from three to six weeks, the initiands receive initiatory names. Under the responsibility of the circumciser and the *kyandzangoombi* priest who ought to secure the boys potency, three young companions—soon to be or just married—stay with the youngsters during the entire seclusion. They act as identification figures regarding masculine leadership roles and their turnover. Both the young companions and a same number of newly circumcised boys bear the following role names: *Khahyuudi* (Messenger, Consultant), *N-lobu* (Subchief), *Mangoma* (Drummer). In a kind of mirroring relation they stand to one another as two successive generations of major leadership roles in rural society. Throughout the coming weeks, the newly circumcised boys must give their full attention to what is conveyed *(mahoodi)*, and more importantly to cultivating (called *loongwa)* bravery, strength, and potency: they, literally, "learn to keep in step with the elders" *(bakandaandi)*. In the morning and evening they gather in front of the seclusion house. While cherishing the heat of the morning sun and standing upright with their big toes crossed, they call attention to their penis through erotic songs. They sing of the virtues of the gazelle and of hunting it; the boys are led to identify with both the game and the hunter. The ambivalence experienced here directly points to their relationships with their fathers. Circumcision identifies the boys with their fathers—like them, the boys now have virile penises. At the same time however, the hardships oppose boys and fathers since the suffering is somehow mandated by the fathers who pay the circumciser.

One month later the newly circumcised, wearing masks, are paraded around the territory (Devisch 1972). More than an object to be admired, when worn in the dance the mask represents an intermediary space for all of the participants, inviting them to join in the regeneration of the group and of the cosmos. Alternating with or opposing this celebration of social order, some carnivalesque dancers and the *mweelu* mask seek to shock and also to tap from the profuse and untamed forces of the wilderness. Overtly erotic and transgressive dancers seduce *yifiika,* the ritual mother-figure of the initiands, and lead her onto the roof of the seclusion house or onto a stage made for the occasion, where they act out a fantasy of hunting. I interpret this as an expression of men's anxiety regarding the sexual act: facing *yifiika* and standing tight against her, they imitate an animal caught in a trap, called *-yekama,* a term that connotes also the movements of pairing.

Initiation severs the strong ties of dependence boys have with their mothers and sisters and turns them into adult-males-to-be. Initiation teaches them to control females through social and affective distancing from the mothers and their sisters very much through a process of strengthening their relationship with their fathers and maternal uncles and engaging in the gerontocratic authority structure.

A few years later, most adolescent boys will probably find their way to Kinshasa. From there, the young men may return to the village more than once to prospect for a marriage partner. They will reach maturity only when they beget children through marriage some ten or more years after their circumcision. Usually a man reaches the age of marriage when his father retires from begetting children, at about age 40 to 45. With marriage and begetting children, men start to function as co-responsible adults in their father's compound, where they may remain for life.

3.4 The Two-forked Tree of Agnatic Descent and Uterine Filiation

I am principally dealing here with the predominant kinship system in mainstream society in northern Yaka land and thus not with the ruling Luunda clans and those of the landowners. The Yaka individual is led first to develop a sociocentered identity through the vital ties shared with those to whom his or her existence is owed; senior men and cult initiates are stimulated to acquire a self-conscious, cultivated sense of a unique self. In fact, the more one's identity is interwoven with consanguines and allies, the more one develops a strong— that is, highly socialized—sense of personhood. On the public scene, the individual is defined as a knot of familial relations and therefore owes his or her well-being and social value essentially to familial bonds. This heritage represents the intersection of patrilineal descent with its rights and privileges determining social status, on the one hand, and, on the other, the uterine filiation through which the mother transmits life.

3.4.1 *Agnatic descent (yitaata) forms residential kin groups.* Yaka society is organized in segmentary patrilineages within loosely structured patriclans. Each person is socially identified in relation to a line of agnatic ascendants from whom he receives his position in a kin group, his rights, privileges, and ancestral names, in short, his social belonging or identity. Agnatic kin live as corporate groups in homesteads and hamlets. Origin and location of the lineages reflect and legitimate their hierarchy. In urban settings, neighborhoods are usually constituted of kinsmen or at least emigrants from the same territory of the Kwaango region.

A major lineage group or clan *(kaanda* or *yikhanda)* is segmentary, and comprises all those persons who trace their common and distant ascendance *(kaanda)* in the agnatic line to the same mythic founding ancestor. Just as the foliage of a tree covers an assembly with its shade, so this common ascendance coifs its members with the same clanic name: *phu,* literally, "head covering." Even though the clan at present no longer occupies its own or original territory alone, or has a unique chief, members of prestigious clans do consider the territory of the founding ancestor as their civilisational cradle. There, the legitimate successors may still tap the life-giving force of the mythic founder: white kaolin clay "is put to sleep" *(-niimba)* on the ancestor's grave for three days. Likewise, the watercourse traversing either the clan's original homeland or the region it presently inhabits furnishes the cognitive map legitimating the filial and blood bonds shaping it into a single exogamic group. Autochthonous and leading lineages thus claim for themselves a territory delineated by a particular river, forest, or stretch of savanna. Spatial framing and residence are the primary idiom for delineating outer bounds and inner segmentation. The distance between the territories of related patrilineages and their cradle serves to differentiate the lineage segments and their respective rights and attributes one from another.

A lineage quarter or hamlet is the largest residential kin group, literally, "of the inhabitants of an elder's territory" *(besi nongonu).* A hamlet comprises two to five neighboring and closely related homesteads, and it unites from thirty to eighty individuals. In general this includes the compound of the patriarch himself, of one or several of his brothers, and those of their married sons. The houses are placed at distances of eight to fifteen meters from each other and are usually aligned in a concentric pattern and in such a manner that their doorways are facing the patriarch's house.

The *village* or *locality (hata)* constitutes the largest but least marked of the residential units and in general is comprised of two to four hamlets. Except for those villages along a track, there is no straight road traversing the whole of the village. It is within this space that the individual seeks solidarity and support, and here justice is meted out. Public or communal activities take place, in the shade of a tree, somewhere in the center of the village's oldest lineage quarter. This is the site where the council of elders meets, in the morning, to tackle common issues regarding, for example, succession or territory. There they may discuss familial affairs relating to marriage, illness, and death, or more general juridical matters and disputes between individuals of related or nearby hamlets regarding land, hunting rights, domestic animals. Here, as well, take place some wedding and mourning ceremonies, diurnal dancing with masks, the yearly encounters with the civil authorities, and Christian religious services, which are held possibly once or twice a year, when a pastor or priest is available. Goods are distributed or exchanged out in front of or inside the dwelling of the lineage elder and might involve handing over matrimonial goods or mortuary compensations and sharing alcoholic beverages (palm, pineapple, or honey wines). These various councils and meetings unite all the adult men, who are seated in a semicircle, ideally according to some order of seniority or prestige; their assembly is depicted by the expression *baluungana ndze n-kaandzu myameenu,* "to be complete like teeth in the mouth." They form "webs of solidarity" *(kuumi dya baatu).* The women observe the discussion and negotiation only from a distance.

In some cases, it is the eldest hamlet or quarter, but in other cases it is the most marginal one that establishes contacts with the foreign world, namely with the administrative, medical, educational, and pastoral services. It is from former, similar contacts with the colonial administration that these villages obtained their proper names and some kind of renown. Mutual aid actually takes place as much between households or hamlets of nearby villages as it does between those of the same locale.

Each lineage duplicates itself in as many homesteads *(ndzo)* as there are elders, or patriarchs belonging to that lineage who are recognized as capable of unifying and representing the domestic group with authority. It often happens that in the entourage of a prestigious patriarch, as in any other residential group counting more than four or five elementary families, a certain number of individuals seek the support of a close elder before consulting the lineage chief. By building their homes near that of one of the elders and by sharing their produce, they and their households gain a certain autonomy. This virtual form of segmentation increases in intensity when misunderstandings between elders are exacerbated through accusations of murderous ensorcellment. A section may leave the lineage quarter and build their relatively autonomous homestead along another track of paths. Nevertheless, only an elder who has given daughters in marriage—thereby becoming the recipient of matrimonial goods—and who has marriageable sons can take it upon himself to represent their interests in the assembly of lineage elders. In this way, he can assure his family a certain independence.

The homestead forms the individual's commensal group and niche. It usually comprises two to five conjugal homes, one or more houses for adolescent boys, and kitchens. It is in this context that the individual, day after day, participates in the weaving of a most vital web through the sharing of physical contact, commensality, and mutual aid. These relations are such essential components to his or her existence that, according to the oral lore, the individual who is rejected by or alienated from the household body either perishes or is reduced to the status of a slave, literally "of the other" *(m-phika* or *n-hika):* a slave is by definition an individual whose parental ties, rights, and privileges are unknown and who therefore has nobody to speak up for him in family councils. In reality, it is possible for any adult man, single or married, to go live with his own or his wife's maternal uncles, and his children will then belong to respectively his own or his wife's matrikin. Similarly, a married man may seek integration in the patrikin of his wife. Within the commensal group one does not easily suspect another of hostility or serious threat, while potential or former commensals are quite likely to do so. In the case of some misfortune—a lasting illness, failure in the hunt or any other productive enterprise, loss of one's job, a traffic accident, loss of valuables or domestic animals—one first suspects members of the lineage quarter to have attracted the misfortune as a retaliation for an injury, for, that is, an act of sorcery, offense, or intrusion once committed by a lineage member. Deviant behavior such as assault on one's conjugal shell, the refusal to perform required services, a wife's refusal to do the cooking or share the marital bed, obscene conduct, a man's failure to provide clothes for wife and children, or a lack of respect for the spouse's family—and the list is hardly exhaustive—arouses fear and complaint if it emanates from members of the household.

The status of the elder or senior male *(mbuta)* is principally acquired by virtue of his place in the generational continuum. Relations between elders and juniors, literally forebear *(mbuta)* and descendant, are expressed in terms of engendering *(-buta)* and paternity. The fact that one has marriageable or married children—indicating that a following generation has been ensured—procures the parent seniority. Related elders nevertheless are ranked according to their genealogical proximity with the ancestors whose status and prestige are carried down through the agnatic descendants. Genealogical hierarchy, at least as much as personal merit or competence, determines one's access to the status of patriarch or the role of priest in a communal cult of agnatic tradition (see 4.4.2). The antagonism which risks raising the new generation up against the older one is diffused inasmuch as those individuals considered as belonging to the generation of elders in fact vary immensely in age. Because the elders relate to the young members of the kin group very often as grandparents, there is between them a kind of mirroring, a symmetric reciprocity and joking relationship that may help to balance out strained relations between the generations of classificatory fathers and sons. At any rate, a son is expected to assist his father in preparing the fields or in the hunt, but most notably in providing him with valuables through cash labor. People are convinced that a lineage head or patriarch who finds himself in rags is likely to ensorcell his sons who refuse to share their income. If a dispute divides father and son, the latter is usually blamed for his lack of respect. Even when his children are grown-ups, a man will still avoid outdoing his older father in titles or valuables for fear of raising anger and ensorcellment.

Elders are highly respected and enjoy an incontestable authority. They see to it that norms remain in vigor within the household and seek to balance the sharing of goods and services. They also interpret the failure of a hunt, bouts of illness, or any other negative turn of events in the household by relating these to other inauspicious signs they are aware of in their life-world or in dreams; they may therefore consult diviners. Yaka elders enjoy a monopoly on the communal rites inherited from the agnatic ancestors and whose legitimate practice is authenticated through success in the hunt (see 4.4). They make the decisions as to the distribution of the ordinary game caught in the hunt, and the vital organs are reserved for them. No alcoholic beverages may publicly be consumed in the village or neighborhood except in their company. Activities which a lineage member undertakes outside the household are generally decided upon in deliberation with one or more lineage elders. It is finally the elders who weigh any decisions concerning marriage (the choice of a spouse or a request in marriage, its annulment, and the inheritance of a widow), taking into consideration the interests of the group as well as any hindrances or objections.

The social fabric embraces a structural concept of time rather than the assumption that time can be mastered through events that may shape a new future. The tradition-oriented time perspective in palavers, divinatory etiology, and ritual practices—all highly valued activities in the public world of Yaka men—is centered on the patterns of lineage segmentation and the succession of generations, that is, on spatial order and social seniority, rather than on one's real age. Palavers, oracles, and rituals, by definition, seek to discover or reenact a continuity with the past; this continuity is not essentially material or rigid, for changes may occur, but structural. Rituals and councils pursue a spatial, hence vitalizing linkage of the sociocultural institutions and organizations with their ancestral source. Cosmic phenomena, such as the diurnal movement of the sun or the watercourse, offer patterns regarding migration and settlement. In their turn, these patterns depict agnatic descent and the establishment of society and political power by bloodshed and hunting. The foundation of social order, rulership, and lineage divisions is distinctly associated with transformative movement, masculine sexuality, and hunting. And yet the agnatic order that shapes one's social personhood *(muutu)* ties in with uterine life-giving: as a being of "flesh and blood" *(luutu)*, in his most individualizing outer appearance (skin) and innate capacities, the individual is a sprout of the uterine source of all life. Birth-giving is seen as an eversion of the mother's womb—a basic issue in transition and healing rites, which I would like to term 'exvagination' or 'exfoliation.'

3.4.2 *Uterine filiation, even more than patrilineal descent, underscores the individual's health and uniqueness.* As such, it does not give rise to residential units. The northern Yaka hold that physical and innate characteristics such as health, blood, and inborn capacities *(yibutukulu)* are passed on to the individual primarily through maternity and the uterine line *(yikheetu, yimaama, yingudi)*. Uterine filiation is thought of in terms of birth-giving *(-buta, -vwaala)*, and of the mother-child and brother and sister relationships. Siblings who "come from the one womb" share privileged bonds of bodily contact, of commensality, and of warmth, trust, and mutual aid within the household, along with their parents. The blood ties between siblings are permanent. Analogously, maternal relations typify the bonds between the coinitiates themselves and with their healer in the context of a cult; coinitiates may share their lifeblood or vital flow *(mooyi)*, weakening or strengthening each other's physical condition through the exercise of these same bodily activities.

The aptitude for the roles of divination and healing are also thought to be transmitted through the uterine line.

Motherhood weaves bride-takers and bride-givers, agnatic and uterine relations together. Since residence is patri-virilocal, uterine links allow the exogamous agnatic group to break open at each generation: women join the group through marriage and pass on life to their children, who will marry in their turn. Uterine links may thus envelop people from many different villages in webs of vital bonds, but bonds that have no particular political value. To honor his wife's capacity to bear offspring, a man bestows her with the honorific title of *mwaadi,* which is derived from the same root *-aad* as *-vwaala,* literally, "the one who regenerates (through) the blood."

The tree, particularly its stem and branches—strictly speaking only the left-hand side (literally, "female hand side")—depicts the uterine links with the source of life, whereas the right-hand side ("male hand side") refers to agnatic descent. Each ramification of a branch represents a matrimonial alliance by which a household cedes a woman to another lineage for whom she will also bear life. This metaphor is transposed to the human body: the youngest descendants are the buds or leaves of the uterine tree, as the fingers of the left hand are the buds of one's arm and body. When referring to their mother, grandmother, great-grandmother, as well as to the respective brothers of these mothers, people successively point to their left wrist, elbow, shoulder. Pointing over their shoulder to their back, they refer to the uterine ascent of their great-grandmother, that is, to the stem of the life-tree. Conversely, while speaking of paternal descent, their gestures indicate that they have come, as if it were, from between the legs. Thus, left is to right as uterine relations are to agnatic ones, and as the river source and the sap rising up in the tree are to the downwards flow of the sap and of the river. At night and outside the protective family shell, children and young or weak people are addressed by the term *lukaya,* literally "leaf"—it is said that this anonymous name seeks to mislead the sorcerer who is laying in wait.

Uterine physical bonds with the life source are represented, on the social scene, by the three generations of maternal uncles. They are the classificatory brothers of the mother, maternal grandmother, and great-grandmother. For want of more colloquial terms, I might call them the maternal uncle, granduncle, and great-granduncle. They weave the vital webs with the mothers and uterine life source into the social fabric. These avuncular relations are also pictured in terms of the tree metaphor. The primary uncle is referred to as uncle from the top *(leemba dyamathaandu),* the granduncle as the uncle from the middle *(leemba dyamakati),* and the great-granduncle is called uncle from the base or at the roots *(leemba dyamasina).* Normally it is the primary uncle who actively assumes the avuncular role *(buleemba)* delegated to him by the uncles at the ascendant generations.[9] The primary uncle is responsible for keeping the other uncles informed of any events in the lives of the uterine descendants: marriages, births, cult initiations, grave illness or death, and so on. The latter also share in any gifts from their uterine kin.

The maternal uncle plays a particularly important role in the individual's health and destiny. Motherhood and avunculate (that is, the relationship between brother and sister and the role of maternal uncle) intertwine both agnatic and uterine relations in analogous ways. First, the Yaka address the uncles of successive generations in the uterine ascent by a term of respect: *ngwakhasi* or *ngudyakhasi,* "male mother, male wife, male source." These generic terms refer to the sovereign potency of the uterine life source. Being the mother's brother, the uncle is "of the same womb" as the mother, and "of the same blood" *(meenga mamosi)* as she and the maternal grandmother. As such, the maternal uncle has a most vital function of interweaving the physical or maternal ties that connect the individual with his uterine source of life. Second, the uncle is referred to as *leemba,* literally, "the one in rest, the one who unleashes, unbends." The maternal uncle acts as a keen mediator, a meeting place or intermediary between the genders as well as between bride-givers and bride-takers. All reciprocal gift-giving passes through him. Though he is of the same blood as his sister and her offspring, he moreover represents the bride-givers in the context of his sister's alliance and toward her husband's group. In relation to his sister's husband and the latter's patrikin group and progeny, the maternal uncle represents the group of wife-givers *(buko)* and the line of transmission of physical health, blood, and innate abilities. In this same capacity he is the one who at his sister's marriage dictates prohibitions to the husband that should secure the transmission of life: he sees to it that these prohibitions protect the uterine offspring. The uncle combines the register of uterine filiation (extended via the marriage and progeny of his sisters) with that of the agnatic rights that he as bride-giver, in the name of his own patrikin, maintains towards this uterine offspring. In this latter position, he is called *buko,* "in-law," that is, he is assimilated with his father's household, which has given a daughter in marriage. The maternal uncle therefore plays an important role in the structuring (and possible de-structuring) of an individual's identity. He is able to either diminish or exacerbate the gap or tensions between the individual's physical and hereditary makeup and his or her social position.

The weave of uterine ties is ego-centered and most vital for the individual. It is a paradigm for other forms of exchange as well. Through the agency of their maternal uncles, that is, via their uterine links, maturing males discover themselves as individuals on which the group of their compound of birth have no total claim. Once married and enjoying some seniority, a man may join his mother's brother to assist him in an avuncular task, particularly at mourning or to collect his part of a bridewealth. It might be said that uterine filiation comprises as many webs of life transmission as there are living persons owing their existence to the maternal line of mother, grandmother, and great-grandmother. Each uterine web ties together, on the one hand, a married man and the ascendant generations of mothers and maternal uncles and, on the other, the man and his household. A married man is expected, at different stages of his life, to compensate the uterine forebears of his children inasmuch as they represent the life source of his wife and children. This occurs at the time of puberty, marriage, pregnancy, major changes in social position, ritual initiation, and death. Inasmuch as matrimonial alliance founds a basic web of exchange, it serves as a paradigm for other forms of exchange as well. Mortuary compensations *(n-kuundu)* have the function of bringing the life of the individual, including both personal as well as hereditary characteristics and even his faults, back to their uterine point of origin (see Devisch 1979:138–40, 156–57). Mortuary rituals transform the particular individual into a structural position within the agnatic ancestral order, and they recycle his idiosyncratic and innate characteristics back to their origin in the uterine life source. It is via the uterine line as well that the consequences of any of an individual's misdeeds may befall a particular descendant.

The uncle is the purveyor of the *pheemba,* the kaolin drawn from marshy ground near the source of rivers. In applying this kaolin on the left arm from wrist to elbow of his sisters' children, he renews their ties with their uterine life source. He thereby bridges the successive generations of mothers and bride-givers and acts as "the male giver of the uterine source" *(ngwa khasi).* Those acts which negate or pervert exchange—ensorcellment, selfish benefit, theft, all acts that "unbind" or "hamper" life transmission—are considered causes of illness, death, and disunity. The uncle offers tonics *(makolasa)* to victims of infringements in order that they regain health *(-kolasa).* In many people's view, the uncle may also exercise an existential control over his sisters' children that is far more powerful than that of their father. An individual also avoids at all costs serious disagreements with an uncle, for fear that his own health or life, or that of a child or any other close relative, will be threatened. Before committing his son to any choice affecting his future—such as a profession, marriage, or the conferral of the gift of sorcery, or even, as may happen, before allowing the son to be ensorcelled—the father will "hear the uncle's advice" *(-bidisa);* the uncle's seeking the father out for his advice would rarely happen and in any case is not compulsory. Adults tend to consider the uncle as a respectable person yet nonetheless one to be dreaded. Once acquiring seniority titles, an individual may fear his uncle even more than any one of the patrilineal consanguines who is capable of conspiring with him.

3.5 Hunting versus Sorcery, and the Fabric of Kin

In the view of men, the fabric of domestic kin relations is sustained or rewoven in the forest realm through the hunt and sorcery. Hunting and life transmission offer images for one another. The hunter captures life forces in the forest for the benefit of his family. He reenacts the deeds of the culture hero inasmuch as he domesticates violence into life-bearing. Conversely, the sorcerer is considered a selfish hunter who abuses the relations of descent and the blood ties. Seen from the perspective of established society, sorcery negates or inverts (*-loka, -balula*) sociality and reproduction: the sorcerer draws down the principles of kinship, alliance, and life transmission; he breaks down the balance between day and night, red and white, giving and receiving, and so on.

3.5.1 *Hunting displays an exploration of the void between violence and order, bloodshed and life-bearing, genitor and genitrix, forest and village realm.* The hunter is compared to the genitor inasmuch as through bloodshed he produces highly prized food that strengthens the life force in his family.

Hunting and conjugality are one another's omen. An essential part of social life is played out within the confines of the nuclear family and the household, soldered together through conjugal union and the sharing of hearth, meals, and bed. Each of these elements, touching on the integrity of the community, is reflected in the hunting domain and vice versa. The man who has a house built and the one who constructs it for his commissioner are required to share equally the fruits of their hunt so long as the work continues. Every rite to enhance the unity of the household, the hamlet, or the territory, and the health of its members, naturally leads the men into the forest in a collective hunt. The success of this hunt "gives shape to or confirms" (*-saka* and its causative *-sakwasa*) the very reality expressed by the hunt, that is, it shows off that the contrarieties of fortune in the village realm do no exhaust the order of the world, and that on the contrary the world is an ever-renewing source of forces and chance. In the event the hunt fails, an oracle (of the sort outlined in ch. 5) is invoked in order to bring to light any hindrances and disunity among the members of the household or among the elders of the lineage which must be "cleared away" (*-sakwala*). It is also forbidden to hunt so long as prohibitions are in force regarding conjugal relations or the exchange of fire between conjugal homes, for these are interdictions which themselves signify disunity. Within the framework of the family group, the relation between hunter and game is considered structurally analogous to that between the genitor and the fertility of his first spouse: she can only release fertility to the extent that his hunt is successful, and success in the one is an omen for the other. The conjugal rights conferred on her at the moment she arrives in the conjugal home equally imply her "rights of the hunt." The day that the young wife leaves her paternal home, her father instructs her in the rights that her status as spouse bestows on her to the spoils of her husband's hunting, as well as of her influence on its success. In offering his daughter a "hen for the hunt" (*khokwa busuungu*), which she in turn must present to her husband, the father of the young wife

124   Chapter Three

forswears any attempt of his to negatively influence the new household. On the morning following the nuptial night, before the husband departs for the hunt, the wife is assured her rights over the product of the hunt. In presenting the "hen for the hunt" given her by her father, she invokes, by repeating the traditional formulas, the future success of her husband as witness to her conjugal commitment and the exclusivity of the marital rights:

1   Tala leelu meni kundzo ngeyi yika yikota.
2   Yina kwaama ye bayakala bahikaku;
    nge yakala yatheti.
(*Variant:* Yina kwaama ye bayakala bahika,
    leelu yukaamba bwoku.)
3   Leelu khoku yaayi,
    yam-funu ya tsoombi, yan-kuundya ngulu.

1   Today I am entering your house
    [and becoming your wife.]
2   I have not known other men;
    you are my first.
(*Variant:* I have known other men
    whom I will not name here.)
3   Today, I present you with this hen,
    in order that you may be successful in the hunt.

The fertility of the wife augurs a productive hunt. Conjugal commitment in fact revolves essentially around the transmission of life through the uterine line. Whereas the success of the hunt witnesses to this contract, the fertility of the wife signifies the fertility and abundance of game. Inversely, any impediment to human fertility symbolically denotes a corresponding obstacle to animal fertility, with all the repercussions for the hunt that might entail. To establish the young woman in her role as wife equally implies that she be invested with the function of life-bearer in the maternal line and in her role as "guardian or holder of the rights of the hunt" (*yiluunda kyabusuungu*). The mother of the husband incarnates the last link in the chain of the transmission of life for which the young wife will hereafter be responsible. In order to fully transfer the maternal role, the mother of the husband, at the moment the newlywed comes to live with her son, will bequeath her daughter-in-law with the rights over the spoils of the hunt that she has held up until this time. From this moment on, the husband will no longer give certain parts of the animal (the *n-loongu myambisi,* literally, the "reserved parts" of the animal; see Devisch 1979:171 n. 62) to the mother but to his first wife: from now on she may also be called *yiluunda kyatsiingu,* "bearer of the rights over the neck," since the neck of the animal is always reserved for her alone. In giving over her rights to the game, the mother also relinquishes in favor of the daughter-in-law any powers to influence her son's hunting. The rite of renunciation of the rights of the hunt takes place in front of the home of the young couple, where husband, his mother and father, and the young wife gather. While pouring water over the hands of the wife, the mother declares to her son:

1   Meni yin-khetwa mwaadi, kyeleka,
     ngwaaku wabuta ngeyi.
2   Bwaleelu meni yikedi kudya n-loongu.
3   Bwaleelu ngeyi wuka ye n-kheetu.
4   Meni leelu ndobukele:
     moosu meka kwan-kheetu,
     kadya n-loongu.
5   Mwaana kayedi,
     kalala mumayenu mangudiku.

1   I, in fact, am your first wife, (a)
     I, your mother who brought you into this world.
2   To this day I have eaten the portions of the game reserved for the wife.
3   Today you have married yourself a wife.
4   Today I relinquish [these rights]:
     may they be passed to your wife;
     may she eat the portions of the animal reserved for her.
5   When the child has grown,
     he no longer remains bound to the breasts of his mother.

Comment:

(a)   The mother of the youth is compared to the son's first wife in the sense that, before her son's marriage, the right to eat the parts of the game reserved to the wife fell to her.

Her own son's welfare in mind, the mother of the young man presents the young wife with the symbols of the successful hunt: red ointment, *yikula*, which serves as a stimulant, and a hen for the hunt that the spouse will later prepare for her husband, who will eat it alone. The young wife hands over the *yikula* to the husband to wish him a fruitful hunt. Once in the bush, the husband proceeds with the hunt after spitting some *yikula* on the trigger spring of his rifle. The divinatory oracles would have one believe that the omission of just one of these rites would not only provoke a long-lasting failure in the hunt, but would also prevent his wife from conceiving. As long as the mother has not given up her rights over her son's hunting, conjugal relations remain illicit and are treated as equivalent to "assault, rape" *(yidyaata)*, as the oracle states. As I have noted in a previous work (1979:116–17), the wife must be stripped of her rights of the hunt, under pain of the appropriate calamities, when the marriage ends in divorce or in the event of the death of the spouse.

Blood is not to be spilled in the hunt if it cannot add to the fecundity of the hunter's wife. In general it is considered foolish, and even dangerous, for the man to go off on a hunt or to handle a knife without having taken ritual precautions during periods in which his wife is evidently infertile: while she is menstruating or when she suffers from a gynecological disorder. In such periods, the wife should avoid contact, even visual, with hunting instruments (rifle, knife, bow and arrow), which connote violence and the shedding of blood, as well as with ritual objects belonging to the hunt. Inversely, any gynecological anomaly or sexual abuse on behalf of the wife is capable of causing the husband's hunt to fail. Extramarital relations on the part of the wife or her refusal to have sexual relations with her husband are seen as equivalent, in the terms of an appropriate expression, to "twisting the neck of the animal" *(-zeka tsiingu)*, that is, compromising the fortune of the hunt. In order to remedy the situation, the husband will demand that the wife produce more propitious signs with regard to the hunt. If it is a new marriage, those responsible for the match are expected to intervene in the conflict. On the other hand, the husband redoubles his hunting efforts when his wife is pregnant or nursing a child.

3.5.2 *Maleficent sorcery is the means to represent and control the agents of social disruption.* At the end of the previous chapter, I argued that the imaginary order of sorcery unsettles and reaches beyond the many polar concepts and arrangements on which the world order rests. But from the perspective of the legitimating discourse of elders at the village center regarding order and authority in the kin group, the disruptive sorcerer embodies conflicting definitions. In lines with customary demands, family elders in their councils as well as diviners in their etiological statements compare sorcerers to dwellers of the forest intruding upon the village, subverting the social order, and feeding on the blood of the relatives. Conflict and misfortune in the homestead are ascribed to the sorcerer who figures as the 'demonized' extraterritorial identified with the blackness of charcoal and the obscure night, or with an acrid or pungent smell that arouses revulsion. Seen from within the center of diurnal and established village life, sorcery is considered maleficent, the emblem of anger, greed, wickedness, indecency, filth, folly, incontinence, concupiscence, and aggression. Whereas in the utopian and imaginary view sorcery opens up to a realm of wonder and unexpected forces, called *yipha,* the 'norm-alized' view inverts the boundlessness of the extraterritorial wanderer in search of vital resources, called *mboongu,* into an epitome of *mboongi:* obscenity, lechery, incontinence, adultery, intrusive greed *(yiphala).*

There are three basic modes or sources of fatal ensorcellment, namely, as a form of abusive feeding on the uterine blood ties, as an effect of visual intrusion implicating agnates, or by occult means that outreach blood relations.

First, fatal sorcery operates along uterine lines and is considered a form of "eating the other." It thereby sustains the basic rule of sharing and commensality. The capacity to ensorcell is considered congenital, for it may be transmitted to the individual from birth either by the mother or by the father in league with the maternal uncle. It means that beliefs and accusations concerning sorcery basically aim at domesticating in-married women and in-laws, and thereby sustain exogamy. A sorcerous attack or fatal curse *(-kasa pfuundu; yifwaandu)* is never deadly unless "an uncle has entered," that is, has become an accomplice to the affair. Sorcerers tap the vital flow *(mooyi)* from other kinsmen. The transmission and exercise of congenital sorcery is largely a question of the matrikin, the three generations of uncles and their sisters' children; this is evidently a strictly exogamous sphere. Ensorcellment in the uterine line is spoken of as a form of eating or feeding oneself selfishly from the blood of a consanguine.

Second, in the agnatic line, sorcery is transmitted and exploited as a form of sharp vision, a correlate of the elders' super-vision. The agnatic life force *(ngolu)* that flows from ancestor to descendant is most powerful in the agnatic elder and grants him clairvoyance, that is, the piercing gaze of super-vision. It may turn into an intrusive and ensorcelling eye by way of which a senior member of the patrikin may steer his junior victim by intruding upon his thoughts, heart or inner vision, motives and dreams. A junior fears the lineage elders, except his father, and through gifts and deference he prevents their anger and revenge. According to shared conceptions, the patriarch sees to it that the elder in his lineage will avenge any of his descendants who suffered from ensorcellment, and that the sorcerer will pay back the damage caused *(-laandila tsita)*. The lineage elder is assumed to know through a kind of clairvoyance of any fatal sorcerous acts occurring between members of the lineage in order to compensate a prior "debt of the night." The elder's intrusive gaze can dispossess the victim from his selfhood and inner life force *(ngolu)*, but cannot kill unless there is complicity on behalf of the mother or mother's brother: together they may "eat away" his physical life-essence or vital flow *(mooyi)*. The sorcery that is transmitted in the agnatic line from father to one or another of his (classificatory) sons is termed *-teemwasa*, "to open the eyes to." It occurs at the first cock's crow when the realm of the night cedes to the diurnal one. One of the most important marks worn in this occult transmission of sorcery is the white clay that the father applies to the temples of the apprentice-sorcerer in order to "enlarge the sphere of the eyes" *(-vuumbula meesu)*. When agnates conspire with the matrikin to fatally ensorcell a descendant, it is said that the ancestral kaolin is "soiled with the blood of victims." When the ensorcelled person is made aware of the impending harm through an oracle, he or she may legitimately respond by placing a curse on the suspected culprit.

Third, there is sorcery that can be acquired through clandestine ritual initiation, often far away from home or from a foreign magician, and one which deploys the forces of poisons, "medicines or ritual articles of fight" *(binwaa-nunu),* and occultism.

Representations regarding sorcery underscore in a subtle way social order and social cohesion through an indirect coercion in the realm of the imaginary. On the one hand, sorcery situates individuals in a kind of 'placebo' interaction with the imaginary world of dreams and fantasies: sorcery arouses potent and empowering images that enhance the social order through carnivalesque inversion and the revivification of desire, delight, and fascination with the monstrous. On the other hand, and conversely, the dream-like desire and lust *(ndzala)* that motivate the sorcerer is characterized as capable of sheer selfish greed or envy *(yiphala).* The sorcerer may engage in a solitary and transgressive quest for force. He may join nocturnal and promiscuous meetings in the dark and remote forest. In order to remain young and vigorous, he then feeds on the blood of his relatives. The sorcerer thus personifies the antimodel, the very inverse of the reproductive family unit with its highly valued ideals of commensality, bodily contact, and sharing of smell, sleep, and hearth. As antimodel, sorcery depicts a realm of greed, vice, horror, and aggression that turns social life into a nightmarish scene, into nocturnal banquets of cannibals in the forest. And yet, when powerfully displayed, these imaginary phantasms of sorcery come to work their power of fragmentation, assault, curse. They issue into 'nocebo' relations between kin that may victimize some vulnerable members: the latter seem to open up themselves to the group's anxieties, nightmares, and vicious speech and forces of repression.

The fantasies regarding cannibalism, literally, the "cooking pot of sorcerers" *(ndzuungu zabaloki),* in the remote realms of the dark night and deep forest depict, in an inverted way, the ideals of commensality in the family. The sharing of meals and the conjugal communion between partners and children at home in the evening normally transform the bodily boundaries and orifices into means of exchange. Sorcery is about agencies of empowerment through the violation of limits (see Devisch 1986). Openness towards the other in commensality and conjugality, however, can be perverted into any extreme violation in the sorcerous banquets that are held in the black of night in the deep forest. Fantasies regarding the promiscuity of sorcerers demonstrate the extent to which the realm of the night, the imaginary, dream, sleep, and desire are replete with forces and agencies on which sorcery feeds beyond the grip of the social and conjugal order. The sorcerer's reign is one of the senses over the mind, of desire over reciprocity: sorcery undermines the reproduction of the community. The sorcerer is a solitary actor who feeds himself selfishly, without sharing, and perverts intersubjectivity. Whereas conjugal union inaugurates a most vital intersubjectivity, sorcery encloses the self-absorbed sorcerer into selfishness, conflates fields, and perverts sociality into wickedness.

The imaginary discourse on sorcery, in which people project on 'the others' their own unconscious images, expresses in its own right society's deep fears regarding a dissolution of the self and the household, and thus formulates negatively basic social rules and arrangements. Terms such as ensorcellment and evil sorcerer allow an individual or the group to give vent both to fears and to basic expectations; beliefs concerning sorcery are all expressed in a self-evident way in the third person, which contributes to generalizing their applicability and at the same time preventing any criticism or contestation. The speaking subject is unknown: it is inconceivable to depict oneself as a sorcerer or to make an accusation in one's own name as if one were a witness to a given individual act of sorcery and cannibalism. Popular imagination, through the use of the imagery of cannibalism and extreme sexual deviance, constructs boundaries that allow one to vividly imagine and, at the same time, to temper any such wild desire that could pose a threat to society and, in particular, to the household from within. The discourse of ensorcellment figuratively expresses the family's deeper fears facing the succession of generations and matrimonial exchange: it may dispel the group's fears in opening itself up to women marrying into it, to children who are born and members who die. At the same time, the discourse exorcises or dissipates evil and misfortune, and further gives an indirect expression to social rules. The figure of the evil sorcerer—in popular stories and etiologies as well as in many antisorcery practices—is the living example of what the average Yaka should not become. Conversely, it depicts what will necessarily happen to individuals who depart from the way of the elders and ancestors, who neglect to transmit traditional knowledge and customs, or disdain social boundaries, and so on. In the popular mindset, dogs and goats that in the diurnal village realm mate with the females that dropped them also belong to this gloomy world of sorcery. In order to attest to the boundedness and inviolability of his homestead, the married man will claim compensation from the head of a neighboring but unrelated household whose goat or dog has repeatedly entered the house or, worse, crossed and thus defiled the hearth.

The theme of evil sorcery sustains the rule of exogamy. In the context of sorcerous banquets, themes of nudity, incest, and quasi animal feeding habits characterize a nonsocialized sexuality, or a sexuality that is too endogamic. These themes serve to circumscribe the set of socially acceptable alliances through images depicting the equivalence between the nonmarriageable and the noncomestible, inasmuch as each kin group has its particular food taboos. Popular imagination relegates the world of sorcery, cannibalism, incest, and other abominable behavior to the gloom of the forest where primary kin walk about naked in each other's presence, practice incest, and eat raw human flesh. This reference possesses an integrating function, a means by which the group may represent itself to itself with the proposition: "That is the other, of course, in that it is the inverse of what we are," all the while remaining open to the incomprehensible, to the 'new' and unexpected event that it will have to face.

The panoply of protection paraphernalia against sorcery vents deep anxieties in the kin group regarding dismemberment. The protective measures may be compared to a hunt or a war against the intrusion of figures of the night into the heart of family life: the homestead, its unity, fertility, and vital commensality. Ritual articles of war *(mateenda, loombi, binwaanunu)* turn means of mixture and intrusion—for example, the amphibious animals that are the disguise of the sorcerer after metamorphosis—through incineration self-destructively against themselves (as we noted in relation to blackness, at 2.2.3). The patriarch or family head closes off the homestead from the intrusion of a monstrous forest realm: he places ritual arms of attack in the center of the homestead, at threshold points such as the doorway and entry to the sleeping place, or attaches them to the beam that sustains the roof. The house is transformed into a protective cell for life-bearing.

Who engages in these sorcerous journeys, who is the witness to their deeds? This sort of question may be the concern of the guardians of customary order and the diurnal village realm inasmuch as these guardians sustain seniority relations and settle people within bounds, values, and categories. Both sorcerer and hunter are depicted as unsettled wanderers and predators whose aim it is to re-empower their world through the kill. Whereas a hunter may openly tell the public of his endeavors, a narrator of sorcerous journeys and plots, however, has never himself been a participant or a witness to the journey. A successful hunter may enjoy immense prestige by reason of the almost superhuman power that he holds over the animal world and of his capacity to empower his kinsfolk through the kill. At times settled villagers may attempt to reappropriate this extraterritorial vagabondage. It happens that the too successful hunter attracts suspicion because the imagery, in bestowing an almost sacred power over the forest realm onto his person, also ascribes to him an equally extensive hence subversive power over the village realm. Besides, established diurnal society draws a fundamental distinction between these two extraterritorial figures: hunter and sorcerer are depicted as moral opposites. The hunter is praised as a founder of diurnal society, for he leaves the village domain only during the day and provides the community with its most rewarded sustenance, reinvigorating blood and meat. On the contrary, in the moralizing discourse, the sorcerer is considered the antithesis of civility, settlement, community, and commensality. Like the hunter, the sorcerer sets traps, lies in wait for and attacks his prey, and carefully chooses the choicest cuts from his prey. But the sorcerer's prey is a close relative, as it is commonly said, the one whom the hunter purveys with food. In other words, the sorcerer feeds himself on the life force of the very person for whom the hunter provides sustenance. Disgust that established society expresses with regard to the evil sorcerer is the same as that for the pig's and hyena's eating habits: the sorcerer feeds on his children just as the pig and hyena respectively eat feces or corpses. The dog and goat in turn are like sorcerers: they commit incest (see 4.1). In these various associations, the despised figure of the evil sorcerer is thus variously a powerful censor of semantic conflation and extraterritorial vagabondage, as well as of oral greed, sexual desire, and threats to life transmission.

4

Body, Group, and Life-world
Between Maze and Weave

Yaka cultural symbolism and healing practices suggest that the ways in which a person inhabits and represents her or his body deeply affect the connections that person has with others and with the world. Day after day, coresidents or coinitiates weave a multilayered fabric of relations between the fields of body, group (in essence the kin group), and life-world. A consonance or resonance is brought about and modulated between these fields. It is in this connection with others and the world that personhood is achieved. For pubescent boys, the focus is on exploration and on permeability to others. The value of the female self both of the young girl and of married woman is on exchange of services and some qualified openness in the domestic and conjugal realm, and on closure and restraint in the diurnal, public realm. Paradoxically, the more the senior adult man extends his authority over several wives and a growing number of descendants and in-laws, the more he grows towards a bounded, yet autonomous self: the elder will eat alone, speak with great moderation, or even refrain altogether from speech during formal meetings.

Illness and misfortune disrupt the fabric: they close up the body in a maze of contrarieties, or they disconnect or unthread the weave. It is largely in their iconic language that the various symptoms are conceived of. The cults of affliction and communal sodalities are the many weaving looms through which Yaka culture renews itself. They produce each their own types of interlacing, braids, plaits in and between the initiate's body, group, and life-world.

The Yaka regard the body both as a limit or bounded expanse in space and time, and as a possibility of opening up to the other and the world. The body *(luutu)* limits the individual *(muutu)*. In spatial terms, the individual is more or less confined within his or her envelope of skin, shell of dress and adornment, and conduct of modesty and restraint *(tsoni)*, that is, within the social skin; temporally, the individual is caught between birth and death. At the same time, the body also constitutes the site, medium, and filter of physical and sensory exchange with the others and the world. Contact with other persons and the world is a function of the way in which the individual inhabits his or her body. The orifices serve as the media for both exchange and separation between the individual and others, between inner and outer, and so on.

Inheritance and transmission of life are equally constitutive of personhood. It is this exchange which forms the basis of social individuation, of social identity and personhood; in the exchange, the subject inserts himself in the outer world and thereby "becomes a person" *(wuka muutu):* "he becomes a whole" *(-luunga).* The person is a stitch of the fabric of kin, and as yet separated from other webs of nonkin. According to Yaka culture, spouses and children living together in one dwelling establish intense physical and sensorial contact with each other through bodily transactions such as the sharing of table and bed, intimate fondling, olfactory contact, physical intimacy at night, conversation, and eye contact. These olfactory, acoustic, tactile, motor, and visual fields of transaction serve to model hearth, home, and kindred, and through them the Yaka offer to one another signs of identity. The bodily shell, orifices, and sense organs ensure the reciprocal identification of the family members (see above 3.1), and, transposed symbolically upon the domestic space, they form a rampart around the household within which the basic life-giving functions occur. The house marks the shell into which the family withdraws and devotes itself to life together, to a shared search for health. Bodily, family, and domestic space are in day-to-day basic activities symbolically extended to the life-world.

The twofold function of the body, namely of bounding off and interrelating, forms the underlying dynamic in the construction of the individual's universe (Devisch 1990b, 1991c). The physical body provides the most immediate and tangible frame of reference within which the individual forms and comprehends herself or himself in relation to the kin group and the life-world. This bipolarity of being connected and yet apart underlies the integration of the social, cosmological, and bodily domains. In this "domain cross-referencing" (Dougherty and Fernandez 1981:413), the body metaphorically intertwines itself with the social body and the life-world while it is itself patterned and consolidated by this integration. According to the Yaka, the core of this dynamic and vital interaction between, for example, inner and outer, boundary maintaining and crossing, is formed by mediational tactile, olfactory, oral, sexual, and interactional experiences. As the Yaka see it, these experiences are related to life-giving or life-promoting acts and exchange such as the intimate contact within the family, the exchange of corporal smell or bodily shade, eating and digesting, transmission or reception of semen, gestation and delivery.

Through taste and touch, feelings of hunger, attraction and repulsion and the like, the skin and bodily orifices filter a wide range of sensations, perceptions, and reactions that may or may not enter or affect the body. Interaction via the bodily openings thus serves to construct a basic polarity: the orifices differentiate between inside and outside of the body, upper part and lower part, front and behind, before and after, all the while permitting or preventing passage and contact. At the same time, taste, touch, and feelings tie in with perceptions such as of savoriness, niceness, delectability *(nyeki, mbote)* versus disgust, harshness, hurtfulness *(phasi, mbi)*. It would appear that the experiences of conjugal intercourse, breast-feeding, weaning, and, more than any other, the strict rules of commensality, serve to fashion the imagery relative to fellow-feeling and concord as opposed to separation and dissension.

There is a close relation between the spatial position and posture of the body, the type of sensory contact, and the type of identification that together serve to constitute the identities of persons living together. Our attention is drawn here to the position and posture of the body with regard to other persons inasmuch as these relations are qualified along vertical or horizontal, lineal or concentric, progressive or cyclical axes of space and time. The Yaka do in fact share the meal seated in a circle on the ground. The husband lies in bed with his back to the door as if to cover, protect, and enclose the wife, who lies on the side of the rear wall. Insemination is perceived as a movement from high to low—a man should be above his wife during conjugal union; erotic songs associate insemination with the image of burial, inasmuch as the genitor prefigures his death by engendering a son who will succeed him. Birth, by contrast is perceived to occur in an opposite vertical movement: the parturient leans slightly backwards in the arms of a senior woman kneeling just behind her, so that the infant comes into the world in an almost upright movement. The emergence of the newborn is thus a prelude to the movement which must gradually separate him from the mother and from mother earth. A child or youth is expected to interiorize the words of the adults, as if by means of a horizontal and centripetal movement. The adult man stands erect and speaks with authority, while the aged person, likened to an eagle, is thought of as being above all others by virtue of the clairvoyant gaze that places him in a position of super-vision.

Spatial logic constitutes a norm and serves to 'norm-alize' the activities of the orifices and the sense organs. Spatial partitions and prescribed movements function as the criterion of the normal or the normalized over against any deviant or pathological state. The spatial code acts very much as a preverbal means of socialization. It is the informal and often tacit eye and tactile contact and the transmission of language, etiquette, and the code of interpersonal behavior that insert the child and the individual in the symbolic and ethical order shared by the group. Space ties in with time: the more important transitional phases in the course of one's life initiate the individual into the ancestral past through its ritual reenactment and link him or her up with the group's development.

4.1 Physical and Sensory Modes of Contact

Many of the criteria of partition, transition, and mediation deployed in spatial and temporal categorizations are equally applicable to the human body. Age, gender, patrilineal descent, matrilineal filiation, genealogical proximity, initiations, and various forms of socio-professional activity and status are by means of ritual and social code (re)inscribed in the body, the group, and the life-world that they themselves help to fashion. Certain social and spatial differences involve corresponding bodily distinctions.

When referring to the nose, the Yaka are aware of more than the simple sense of smell, for to them smell represents something unconfined that easily crosses corporal barriers and spatial limits. Olfaction and sexual appetite, which is compared to hunger, are considered to be manifestations of the vital flow *(mooyi)*. In informal talk, people confide that seduction and sexual desire are stimulated less by games of touch, speech, or sight than by sharing in a meal of the fruits of the hunt, and even more by another form of sharing vital flow, the exchange of body smell or heat. In the amorous encounter, the sense of smell alternatively plays the roles of source and witness to the sexual desire of the partner. The term for erotic transport, *-nyuukisana,* translates literally, "to cause to mutually scent the odor that one excites because of the other." In olfactory as in coital exchange, each of the partners gives and receives at the same time. The desire and pleasure that the partners incite in the other reflect and reinforce the excitation and the reciprocal giving in sexual union. Scent, breathing in and out, and sensation—in other words, bodily odor, heat, rhythm, and energy—are all intimately related in Yaka thought. The excitation of scent increases the rhythm of breathing and heartbeat and gives the sensation of a higher temperature. (The lungs have no particular social signification.) The olfactory domain is, according to the Yaka, a generator of vital flow, vital impulse, and regeneration.

The link between olfaction, sexual attraction, and vital flow in life transmission and health is transferred to the fields of social relations and life-world. Cigarettes and tobacco are the gifts par excellence for tacitly soliciting, maintaining, and symbolically representing ludic sexuality outside marriage. As its odor is highly appreciated, tobacco tends to function in a way analogous to the use of perfume in many other societies. An apparently insurmountable disagreement between partners, for example, may be explained as an incompatibility of odors. This accounts for the Yaka belief that aromatic forest plants, for men, and savanna plants, for women, may be used to remedy infertility. Fragrant essences are employed in smoke or steam baths, ablutions, anal or vaginal douches, or for covering the bed with plants in the *khita* 'gyn-ecological' healing. The sexual connotations of the sense of smell are also symbolically expressed in the phallic nose adorning the *kholuka* mask used in the circumcision rites (Devisch 1972; Bourgeois 1984:135–77).

Bad odor, by contrast, may also evoke the obliteration of boundaries, witnessing to a perversion of reciprocity. Stain and repugnant odors can thus be found at the base of moral sentiments such as rejection or condemnation of the behavior of a foreign individual or group. The behavior of the dog which is attracted to the bitch in heat, sniffing at the genital parts and even mating with its own mother, provides the imagination with an example of the nocturnal promiscuity of sorcerers. In any case, the Yaka do not pet their dogs, nor do they exalt canine habits. Hence, a suitor may be rejected on grounds of the accusation that he or she consumes dog meat. If a strange dog enters several times into a particular home, the household chief may demand compensation of the owner. An incestuous person—literally, "the genitor who chokes down the foam of his own fermentation"—is believed to expose himself to leprosy. In my interpretation, the association with leprosy shows how much incest is regarded as negating the very role of skin, that is, the minimal limit between consanguines. The revulsion pertaining to incest and leprosy refers to the tainted genital smell, as do the aversions to the uncircumcised adult man and to hemorrhoids, which appear to mix anal excretion with menstrual blood. Such forms of pollution may "bring misfortune" (*-beembula*).

The link between odor, sexuality, and health is also expressed in the cultural conception of the relation between decadence and prosperity, between death and life. Fecundation is considered as the partial death of the genitor, followed by a "fermentation" and "cooking" within the womb of the male semen and the lifeblood of the genitrix. Genital odor is considered a particular form of organic energy that, through sexual excitation, transforms decay into regeneration. The exchange of genital odor in sexual intercourse exercises a function of welding together vital forces and is compared to the odor given off by the carcass of game; through its incipient decay, compared to fermentation, while remaining one night in a hide outside the village, and through its subsequent cooking, the product of the hunt is transformed into force-giving and vital nourishment. In other terms, attraction, odor, food, sexuality, and health are all metaphorically connected as conversions of death into rebirth.

The sense of touch as it is exercised by the fingers or skin is also a keen faculty of sensation and perception. To identify plant life, people will touch the plant with the fingers and lips, or smell it, as much as visually examine it. The various sensations are expressed in terms of compactness, roughness, liquidity, flexibility, or in terms of taste. However, a meal is appreciated not so much for its taste but for the spices that heat up the body and for the nutritional quality of the meat and fatty sauces—indicating their propensity to renew the blood—as well as for the feeling of having the stomach well filled, a sensation best attributed to the thick manioc porridge. While men seem to particularly enjoy spiced and salted dishes of meat, condiments, and sauces whose consistency or savor—as is said—connote virile hardness and alertness, they disdain soft, juicy, or sweet comestibles or sugary snacks and drinks reserved for women and children. Taste or distaste do not connote any moral evaluation, although in the game of love or playful seduction a girl may be described as "savory" or the boy as a "tonic."

Great care is given to properly bounding off one's bodily space: it is a function of selfhood. One's clothing, shadow, and bodily emissions—such as hair, nails, urine, feces, saliva and sweat—are all closely associated with the body and yet may be separated from it. They thus serve as substitutes for the body in a large number of rituals and in the confection of means of protection and ensorcellment. One should never step on the shadow of an elder person, or take some leaf or sand from where he was just sitting. These bodily extensions are to be bound off, cleansed, or removed at the beginning or end of a ritual seclusion in which the initiate, or the widow or widower, undergoes a profound change through ritual death and rebirth. The individual is conducted at dawn to a nearby stream in order to bathe. His or her old clothing is allowed to be swept away by the current and the body is washed with an ointment; the head may also be shaved. Any bodily pollution is thereby removed *(-katula mbvi-indu)* and the individual is "purified, made bright" *(- seemasa)*. The housewife bathes the baby, washes her own and children's clothing, and sweeps the house; it is the task of the married man to sweep the courtyard, and he does his own laundry. Cleansing not only marks a rupture with a previous condition, it also resets the limits of the body and invites the individual to re-own his rejuvenated body as his. The pagne or belt *(tsibu,* or a substitute cord) offered to the circumcised, initiate, or widow by the uncle at the end of the seclusion are the signs of this renewal and reappropriation. After birth-giving the mother ties a woolen cord around the waist of the newborn for the name-giving ceremony. In passing through the threshold of palm leaves that close off the ritual dwelling or screen off a compound, the initiand enters or leaves a foetal condition. Congruently, leaving the state of seclusion signifies birth or delivery. Towards the end of the rite, in order to sever initiatory ties, the initiated pays a fee consisting of a cloth or its equivalent "to his master to clothe him and come out from between his legs." In other instances, such as in a lawsuit, the offering of fabric connotes rehabilitation as well as bounding off.

Even more than clothing, which is to some extent an artifact of recent date, diffidence or shame *(tsoni)* has a concealing or individualizing function in that it keeps the more uncontrollable of the bodily or emotional reactions—such as sexual desire and bodily emissions, as well as handicaps—from the gaze of others. Shame also attests to a certain inviolability of the body, thereby making the person impermeable to intrusion. At daytime and in the village space, for example, it is strictly forbidden to denude oneself, excrete, or make sexual allusions in the presence of close kin towards whom one owes respect, the same set of persons, in fact, who are mutually held to respect the rules of incest. Men will refer to this kin group as *phaangya kaanga n-kapa,* "relatives of the closed belt." In the diurnal village space, an intentional act of disrobing in the presence of this close kin is considered a most serious obscenity, an attack, as it were, on the very eyesight. Such an act brings misfortune *(mbeembi)* upon the witness who, according to popular wisdom, is liable to suffer injury from a knife or other accident. Insulting a person by making reference to his genitals or those of his mother amounts to an assault on or a deflation of his identity or to an accusation of ill-fated promiscuity. It may in fact result in the near ostracism of the person who has been insulted. On the other hand, rules of decency governing interaction, speech, and dress are less strictly enforced on the periphery of the village or at nightfall, as well as among agemates of the same gender when meeting outside the compounds during the day. Firm breasts *(mayenu mandzaanga)* along with the hips are, within the circle of joking relations, the object of teasing and erotic desire. Fallen breasts *(mayenu mabwa),* because of their nourishing function, are synonymous for childbearing.

The head, as the seat of the main sensory organs, is a major focus of perfection in sociality. The elder should display a stable mood and gravitas *(zitu,* literally, "weight, rest") in movement, gestures, and facial expression, especially of the eyes; he is expected not to reciprocate eye contact or to show signs of sympathy, surprise, seduction, anger, or disdain. In everyday expression, hunger, cold, pain, joy, sadness, jealousy, anger, and fear are all described in terms of visual awareness *(-mona ndzala, kyoosi, phasi, kyeesi,* literally, "to see hunger, cold, pain, joy," etc.). One refers to epileptic fits, trance, fainting, drunkenness, madness, and several other forms of loss of control by stating that the "head is softened, impressible" *(n-twa wukooka).*

Blood and belly, and more generally the soft tissues of one's body, make up one's vital ties with the mother and the uterine source of all life. Giving birth to children, being and having a mother provide a profound experience of human connection, "of being of the one womb" *(mu yivumu kimosi).* Healthy blood and the function of the belly, it is believed, depend on a good balance between proper intake and regular excretion. The Yaka believe that the belly absorbs food and excretes that which it is not able to transform into blood. Blood is thought to be either produced or corrupted specifically in the abdomen and especially in the heart and liver. Anemia, rectal piles, and stools with blood are indications of a deterioration of the blood. Because of this dual function, the belly may serve to signify many other types of ambiguities, polarizations, and reversals. The production of healthy blood requires not only a good diet but also the regular evacuation of the intestinal tract. Facilitating bowel movement, it is said, directly contributes to improving one's health, and efforts in this direction are especially recommended in periods of transition, whether seasonal, life-cyclical, or during pregnancy. Enemas—and very rarely vaginal douches—are taken with the goal of purging the body of any interior ill. The abdomen is the seat of digestion and human reproduction. Like hunger, sexual desire is a function of the "master of the abdomen." Coitus, childbirth, and menstruation defy the bodily limits and vividly point to the outside/inside polarity. This is the reason why the belly may also designate the maternal dimension of the homestead enclosing parents and children, as a place of departure or arrival for newly wed women. The belly, more than any other bodily part or function, symbolizes how much, because of their common uterine origin, consanguines have a direct, physical influence upon one another. Thus an elder who has reached an exceptionally great age is thought to have done so by feeding on that very uterine life source at the expense of others.

4.2 The Relational Body

The Yaka perceive of the body as the pivotal point from which the subject gradually develops a sense of identity. One gradually becomes a person through the progressive formation of a center of interiority, spoken of as the heart. The major achievement of childhood and youth is the capacity to listen attentively, that is, to learn and educate oneself through hearing. Except for the communal rites and initiations, traditional education is rather suggestive and informal. A child is expected to understand by her- or himself, that is, with the aid of the heart: the latter allows for the formation of images or insight, depicting by way of some inner vision what the ear has heard and decoded. A child is rarely corrected in public, though she or he may be chased away. It is the privilege of the fully adult man, notably the father of marriageable or married children, to speak on the occasion of a palaver, ceremony, or tribunal. The aged man, having attained the summit of socialization, rises above all others thanks to his piercing gaze and superior vision: he thus distinguishes himself in a relation of verticality vis-à-vis his group.

Listening *(-wuula)* is an active and demanding process. It permits the child and youth to progressively establish in the heart a center of inner understanding, evaluation, and remembering. In the process the child is not taught to hear, value, and strengthen his or her own voice. In Yaka thought, socialization derives essentially from listening and particularly from the capacity to enclose and ponder in the heart the ideas and ideals that one hears in the words of others. Most talking in the family is not during the meal, but in the evening while sitting in front of the home. The grandparents are more likely than the parents to draw out the voices of the young children. In turn, grandparents and grandchildren love bringing up or commenting on what they believe, on their journeys to fields and river. Meanwhile, there grows a sense that there are but a few versions of the same story. The grandparents in particular take time to explain to children, through story and play, how they are expected to behave towards their relatives in terms of respect and sharing. The questions adults often ask of children are of the type: "Who told you that?" or "What did your uncle say to you?" The ear, and therefore hearing or listening, are a prerequisite to membership in society. To listen and to learn to speak is to accept the social rules and the order of culture expressed by the word. The ear deciphers the signification of the voiced. "The ear is its own master" *(pfumwa tu)*, say the Yaka, as it is itself able both to decode the message and to convey it to the heart to ponder for a correct response.

Listening and speaking in diurnal and public village space are even more coded. Here the complementarity between junior and senior is one between listening and speaking, between reception and emission, between "those who snuggle together" (pl. *baleeki*) and "genitor" *(mbuta)*. For a chat, people hug together in a circle, sitting on a mat, a tabouret or a low rattan chair. In these daily conversations, the relationship between speaker and listener is not thought of in terms of verticality, as would be a relation of submission and domination, but rather in terms of centripetal and centrifugal movements. In public diurnal space and till seniority, identity is very much received through the voices of others. Children and youth are not encouraged to express their thoughts spontaneously in public. They are to adults—both men and women—what the ear is to the word: they are an ear to the adults. In other words, they are encouraged to subordinate their own words to the representations and values that they hear in the voices of others. From the age of five or six years girls remain in the company of women or peers, while boys often remain in the company of male elders: they know that they should keep quiet when joining their fathers in a council. Elders will seldom tell a junior what they want him to do; they apparently expect of juniors to know in advance. It is in the community of elders that the child learns the rules of respect and how to behave himself or herself when in public. Juniors learn that knowledge is received and only to be displayed at invitation and as a means to come to terms with a *dyaambu*, "an affair, critical situation, adversity, or predicament." An adult will rarely praise the unique traits or skills of a child in public. Adults do not usually ask a child what he thinks or desires yet nevertheless are careful not to offend a child emotionally. And a child, or even an adult, will never ask, "What do you think of me?" or "What would you want me to become?"

The heart *(mbuundu)* is the core of the individual, namely of inner understanding or inner sight. The individual hereby gradually identifies herself or himself with a core of received knowledge of kin, of things good and evil, trustworthy and dangerous, and of proper ways of speaking. The heart is not a capacity for loving or helping others. The child is supposed to progressively acquire a certain interiority, and to become capable of maintaining some distance with respect to others, and to sift out the meaning of their speech. In the Yaka view of the person, the heart has the ability to envision the message captured by the ear and to empower it from inside. Specifically, it allows the imagination to picture what the ear has captured and thereby offers a visual translation of what has been heard. It appears that the child or youth is in fact encouraged to observe and scrutinize with the aid of the heart rather than the eyes. The usual question directed to children is "Have you heard it?" and not so much "Have you seen it?" Meanwhile, the child learns to spontaneously share its food and bed with brothers and sisters, without an adult having to intervene.

The heart is the center of moral vision and the source of "concord and cordiality" *(-buunda, yibuundwa)*. It enables the person to review his or her past and to envision how essential plans should be carried out in the future. A moral decision springs from the heart's inner vision while attending to the expectations of others and to conceptions of right and wrong. The heart is the seat of stability and patience, of feelings and reflection upon these, of virtue and conscience; with age the heart becomes the source of wisdom, memory, and commemoration. It is in the heart that is borne one's sense of difference from others—a difference understood in terms of knowledge and status, rather than of life project. The heart sustains fellow-feelings such as sympathy, joy, concord, sadness, and regret. In sum, it is in the heart that the individual grows towards a responsive and centered subject, thus acquiring a core of being or interior space. The more the person echoes or ponders within himself his perceptions and becomes capable of well-balanced comprehension, the more he enjoys the goodwill and acceptance of others. Persons incapable of listening or demonstrating any receptiveness are, in contrast, considered obtuse and consequently less than human. Should it ever happen that the ears, eyes, or hands become repeatedly unable to correctly filter or decode messages given by others, it is assumed that the heart and body of the individual are inhabited by a malicious spirit or are ensorcelled. The afflicted person closes in upon himself or begins to lose his senses (see 4.3 below). It is considered a sign of death when the person in mortal agony no longer responds when addressed.

The liver is the polar opposite of the heart, literally "at the bottom of the heart" *(kutsyambuundu)*. In contrast to the heart's ability for listening and for envisioning the message so as to enhance cordiality and conscience, the liver—also called *katika*, "what is closed or turned inward"—is seen as the seat of unbalanced feelings that may be too hot or too cold, as are aloofness, anger, and fierce hostility.

In praising the man as hunter, Yaka culture domesticates violence in favor of reproduction and sharing. The virile life-generating force is complemented by a metaphorical equivalent from the forest in the image of the hunter who, in drawing blood, transforms game into highly valued nourishment. For a man, "life transmission is a manifestation of force" *(ngolu mubuta baana)*. Both the acts of life transmission and catching game in the hunt give a vertical dimension to virility. A vast tradition of folktales and hunting cults as well as the complex of joking in the context of the hunt exalt the virile power which flows through the stiffened muscles and the tonic vigor (*khoondzu*, "erectness") of the hunter's whole body as it tenses for action, compared to the manner of a bow ready to launch an arrow towards the prey. From time to time, seemingly more often in rural than in urban milieux, a husband beats his wife under the influence of alcohol, after a difficult hunt, or on the occasion of a palaver with in-laws during which he has been countered. He will do so in plain view of his neighbors, preferably around mealtime in the evening. And conversely, one may hear a woman complain that her husband no longer beats her, implying his lack of endearments. On the contrary, divorce would issue if a man repeatedly beat his wife, out of sight, at night in the conjugal home. By relegating this violent behavior to the public and diurnal domain, the cultural code seems to disconnect aggressive virility from the intimate and hearty sharing in the conjugal encounter as it is usually lived in the privacy of the darkened home. In their public discourse, Yaka men do not conceptualize sex in relation to love or intimate partnership. Sex is formally spoken of with regard to the reproduction of society. But the patriarchal ideology and masculinist life-style celebrated on the public stage appear to praise virile generative sexuality mainly as an act of domination. Public exaltation of virile sexuality in songs, jokes, and rituals seems to have a tonic effect, largely because it reassures the men of their masculine power to control or dominate.

Seniority grows with multiplication of the self in descendants and initiates. Life transmission, productive work, and various initiations in communal sodalities and affliction cults increase one's seniority and weave the individual in a multilayered fabric of relations. Gender differences dwindle with seniority: *kha* or *khaaka,* literally, "gran" or "grandparent," are terms of both address and reference for fully senior people. Seniority channels an assertive sense of self, and seniority in women is socio-centered. Young women turn to senior ones, namely grandmothers or mothers-in-law, for information and advice. The senior female is the beloved grandmother to a numerous offspring, the one who fondles the grandchildren and who is "the guardian of the hereditary kaolin clay" *(yiluunda kyapheemba)* to her husband's office as patriarch or priest in a communal sodality. Cult initiation moreover bestows seniority and empowerment on the woman, shared with the coinitiates. Faithful conjugality and generous commitment by women to domestic tasks are rarely a topic of praise in formal public discourse. They may form topics of conversation or of edifying narration in the homestead. Conversely the more men grow in seniority, the more they affirm autonomy, not as an embodiment of 'logos' but of totalizing sociality and worldliness. The senior male is able to augment his social status by responsibly exercising the roles of husband to several wives and father of married children, family head, judge, healer in a cult, or ritual specialist. These roles allow the man to extend his matrimonial goods, word, and ritual commissions over an ever-larger territorial space. The more he deploys contractual and spatial forms of status, the more he must prove his mastery—of a more or less ritual character—over the sensory body, including the demonstration of etiquette, restraint, and a certain corporal continence. In other words, the more his identity is amplified in terms of territorial space, the more a dense and self-centered individuality is constituted. By contrast, any uncontrolled or extrusive behavior by a senior male who is incapable "of keeping a level head, of containing his passion or vengeance" inverts or perverts the norms of seniority and is a threat to community life. The impatient heart that is easily enraged and just as quickly empties itself in insinuations and hypocritical accusations is equally disdained; such behavior leads to quarreling, jealousy, insults, intractable moods, and finally to what is labeled as madness.

Authoritarian and authorial speech, *-zweela,* is men's form of "birth-giving" *(-vweela).* In recycling received knowledge and tradition, men join in a wider process of regeneration. They do not so much aim at reasserting the ancestral master narrative about a basic project or telos in society. Men's public discourse is not a narrative of mastery, but aims at renewing the fundamental interwovenness or vital solidarity between group and life-world. Palm wine fosters the elders' speech, and important councils are preceded and prolonged by sounds of drum and gun which link up the birth of words with a more encompassing cosmic and social space: it is a *n-samwa mata,* "a bearing of a message with a salvo," often followed by "a bearing of a message with the great drum or the talking one" *(n-samwa ngoma, n-samwa moondu)*—drums whose respective male and female genital significance is glaring. They echo the resonance between body, group, and life-world.

Authoritative speech is an art of senior men, and it implies the junior as listener. The senior orator stands to listener as partly recycled tradition and constructed wisdom stand to received knowledge. Formal speech is not so much concerned with truth as with empowerment and regeneration of group and life-world. It happens that facts of genealogy or relative seniority are redefined into facts of meaning rather than of objective factual remembering. More readily for men than for women, seniority involves a transition from receptive, that is, interiorizing, listening to assertive speech. To speak with authority and organize rituals, that is, to generate society through the word, is the privilege mainly of the male elder. A man whose children in turn beget children may himself play a prominent role in the verbal and ritual reproduction of culture and the interweaving of group and life-world.

In councils, younger women are spoken for by the patriarch of the homestead, and elder women lack any central position. In her function as *mwaadi,* co-dignitary of a senior man, the eldest wife gains some access to public and authoritative speech. While sitting in a row of women, with lowered eyes and often rhythmically tapping on the ground with the back of the left hand, she may bring a complaint, reveal an imperfection, tell experiences in great detail, draw attention to events in the homestead, or invite the audience to hear the voices of this or another housemate. Her speech witnesses to her tendency to shape her thoughts to match those of others. She is less self-indulgent than men, but very settled and connected with kin and life-world, displaying a strong sense of shared self. Similarly, in a communal ritual, any individual woman may stand up and assertively bring out a wish or grudge; when necessary, a woman may also defend her rights before a tribunal. Women do proffer curses just as men.

In certain relations, silence may have as much social significance as speech. The individual may not speak to persons toward whom he is expected to feel respect and modesty, at least not in public or on his own behalf. In the private sphere, the refusal to speak with those who share the table augurs ill.

Assertive speech *(ngaandzi)* and authoritative knowledge of the traditions *(bumbaku)* display force and vivify the listener and life-world. They are the privilege of the patriarch, family head, ritual specialist, and respected elders. This speech enacts and imposes distinction, that is, the normative and hierarchical order. Elders take for granted that palavers honor their concerns, that is, authority and tradition as the source of order and well-being. When speaking, the orator maintains an erect posture, with shoulders raised and chest protruding. The speaker is admired for his vigorous voice *(ngolu)*, erect stance *(khoondzu)*, combative attitude, and sense of surprise *(ngaandzi)*. The upright stance of the orator expresses a judiciary power and sovereignty, contrasted with the receptivity of the seated participants who adopt a subordinate role. The rhetorical stance differs very much from the commoner in the audience who replies, or from colloquial, nonceremonial speech: a junior who replies is expected to maintain a moderate tone of voice while slightly lowering the eyes. Palavers are held in the presence of kin regarding disputes over the hunt or land, or over juridical and political affairs. In a formal council authority and authorial speech are multivocal or shared among the leading elders: a few orators join in and are the only authors. By definition, they refuse to enter in a dialogue on equal grounds with the audience or be involved in any discussion, and their voice may never falter. The orator, in a surprising profusion of metaphors, rejuvenates ancestral wisdom *(ngiindu zambambuta)* through his magistral rhetorical art *(bumbaku)*. This reweaving of the ancestral traditions at the same time guarantees the legitimacy of discourse. A speaker tries to outdo a former orator in rhetorical techniques rather than in argument. Orators enunciate statements of belief and order, not of criticism or self-doubt. They assess the matter at hand in terms of its aspects of disorder, lack of boundedness, and transgression.

Authoritative speech is understood to be the ferment *(fula)* of the group and world order. The stiff posture of the orator is associated with the tense poise of the spear hunter about to strike or of the bow about to let fly an arrow. The word vivifies the ancestral wisdom in a creative fashion and contributes to the production of cultural and social order. This generative capacity of the word is associated with palm sap that is collected from the male inflorescence and transformed into palm wine through fermentation *(fula)*. Moreover, in order to solicit the services of a judge, uncle, or family chief for the resolution of a conflict, one is first required to offer some wine, serving as an invitation. By offering the orator some wine, the word is given to ferment, that is, to develop its inner capacity of transformation, inasmuch it is connected with the ancestral life force. More wine is shared at the beginning of the palaver in order to create fellow-feeling. The wine produces relations of reciprocity analogous to those of commensality in the private domain. The wine offering links up the present council with the ancestral life force. Similarly, ancestors are offered wine on their grave when they are solicited to release the game in the forest and sustain the fertility in the kin group (see plate 3). Moreover, the meeting is thereby situated in the 'euchronic' time frame of fermentation and maturation.

Glass and bottles as well as the barrel of a gun may signify the mouth or voice, in that they all predispose to or prolong the spoken word. In order to represent the deceased in a funeral council, one may deposit his drinking cup or gun in the circle of the elders. Narratives and proverbs explain that the mouth is not indifferent to gifts or flattery and that it may accuse, curse, or speak ill of a person. If an elder were to do so, a dispute would be sure to follow. When an oracle has established a connection between misfortune, illness, or an unsuccessful hunt and maligning words, the victims have the right to invite the elder in question to recant, *-fyaawula,* that is, to renounce his unfortunate words and to offer instead a wish for the prosperity of the individuals concerned. The instigator accompanies his abjuration by rinsing the mouth with water and spitting on the ground.

The piercing gaze, that is, the capacity of keen super-vision *(-tala)*, gives to the elder a status elevating him above all others. In the public realm, control through the gaze is on the side of the male. Paradoxically, the more the elder has incorporated cultural tradition and social order, the more he becomes self-sustaining. The prestigious elder preferably sits on a spotted hide or a raffia tissue. The patriarch personifies fullness and accomplishment, the very restful state of inviolable stillness *(zitu)* of all order within his dominion: he is worthy of full respect *(luzitu)*. The keen eye of the elder scrutinizes and watches over the fabric, that is, over symbolic integration of the various domains. To signify that he is "the knot" that holds all beings in his domain together, the patriarch has his large loincloth—originally a weave of raffia—in an abundant fold, called *n-koondzi,* hanging over his belt as an effusion "from between his legs," as it is said. Superior sight enables an elder to perceive persons and situations that are distant in space and time, such as the ancestors, those absent, and his people in the course of their activities belonging either to diurnal society or to the nocturnal world of the forest. The piercing gaze of the elder is generated by a very powerful life force and has the capacity to awaken, smother, deviate, or absorb the vital flow of the victim. The gaze spoken of here is a nonreciprocal one and constitutes a veritable intrusion. (It hardly need be recalled that traditional Yaka culture knows no mirrors, writing or printing, or photography, which could help people to detect the effect of their gaze on others and vice versa, that is, to manipulate a certain reciprocity in gaze.) Whereas the diviner's clairvoyance or second sight is associated with the keen sense of smell linked with that of the dog, 'super-vision' proper to elders metaphorically refers to the sharp vision of (nocturnal) animals and birds of prey, particularly the eagle. This keen sense of super-vision is also an essential attribute of sorcerers. For the Yaka, a person's gaze does not necessarily express his thoughts, nor is observation a sufficient basis for the evaluation of another's behavior. On the contrary, an inquisitive, hence piercing gaze is considered a synonym of penetration or expropriation of a person. Super-vision is ambiguous: because of its supra-social powers, it may be turned against the order it is supposed to supervise. Defects of vision are considered the worst form of anomalies and a decay of the life force.

4.3 The Body and Its Afflictions

As I have shown elsewhere in greater detail (Devisch 1990b, 1991c), in the popular mindset and in divinatory discourse illness is basically considered a problem of boundaries and relations: it alters the uterine vital flow *(mooyi)* and agnatic life force *(ngolu)* by way of contraction or enclosure as opposed to effusion. The focus is on symptoms in the physical and social body, rather than on discourse.

A first syndrome concerns *closure*—that is, contraction, withdrawal *(yibi-inda, -biindama)*, deflation, a state of coldness or frigidity *(kyoosi)*, a cooling down of the blood *(-holasa meenga)*. In this state the individual closes up, turns inward in a state of helplessness, or no longer responds when spoken to. There are many interrelated expressions of closure: extreme timidity, sorrow, grief, prolonged anger, pent-up rage, refusal to speak or to share one's income, senseless speech, being stiffened by sadness or despair, apathy, melancholy, and withdrawal from social contact. A backache that ties the person to the house or to the ground—to sitting or lying the whole day—is a threatening symptom of closure. These symptoms are further believed to be manifested in disorders such as severe cramps, chronic constipation, dumbness, otitis, deafness, sore eyes, blindness, madness, paralysis, and sterility. In these ailments the body boundaries act as fences or lines of cleavage. Through ensorcellment, the victim's body and vital flow are turned inward "like a fermenting cassava paste that is indissolubly bound in a bushel."

A second, and related or inverse, syndrome involves *dispersal, effusion (n-luta, phalu)* as an effect of intrusive outside forces. Included here are states of excessive heat or fire, connoting fever *(mbaawu)*. An assault or rape *(yidyaata)*, particularly one committed by agnatic kinsmen, may feed on a person's life force and reverse or counteract the individual's functions of sociability: the afflicted suffers from effusion and weakens, or displays an 'extrusive' behavior or severe temper. These symptoms are all the more threatening for an adult man. He is said to have an impatient heart that bursts out in rages; he is no longer able to keep cool and control his temper. Such excessive heat is also exhibited in hypocritical speech, inconsistent thought and discourse, general irascibility, wild cursing, obscene speech, sexual harassment, and an inability to get along with others—the latter especially indicating failure to agree with the elders and disrespect of family ties. These forms of asocial behavior may eventually lead to a loss of the senses, for they undermine the life force by subverting commensality and the normative social impetus to personhood. Such insane persons may wander around and finally get lost in the forest and die.

A third syndrome concerns a fragmentation, an incontinence or emptying of the body *(seendu, -selumuna)*, a withdrawing or gnawing away of the victim's vital flow and life force: the bodily boundaries may be weakened or deflated *(-lwaala)* to the point that they are no longer able to withstand many of the impulses to which the individual is exposed. It dissolves selfhood. In this state, the presence of another person may be experienced as an intrusion. The life source of the victim subsequently is obstructed *(-keyisa)*, dwindles, and fails, or conversely, may spill over uncontrollably. The envious and deprecatory gaze of another may penetrate the other's bodily space and obstruct the vital flow. This deflation may thus produce any number of disorders in the victim, such as dysentery, lasting diarrhea, depression, respiratory difficulties, disorientation of the senses, fear and nervousness, suffocation, fainting and anesthesia, physical injury, wounds, ulceration, and discharge of pus. An 'assault' on the part of another may further bring about insomnia and nightmares or incite the afflicted individual to words and acts of aggression, epileptic fits, apparent intoxication, and obscene speech or sexual misdemeanors. Intrusive afflictions are usually transmitted through agnatic bonds, and particularly those ailments brought on by the hostile look or gaze. Other persons living in close proximity to the afflicted agnatic relatives may also be attacked by means of envious looks, backbiting, ghosts sent at night, or even by an aggressor who enters the victim's body in order to prey on and obstruct the vital flow and life force.

4.4 Cults of Affliction and Communal Sodalities

The Yaka practice some twenty initiatory cults *(phoongu)*. Cults provide both spiritual and practical devices and methods for handling crises in the life of the individual and of the collective. They are associated with ambivalent agencies, capable of being both destructive and regenerative, persecuting and healing, deflating and empowering. The initiation leads to a life-long membership. They involve "middle-range spirits" (Janzen's term, 1989:237) that surpass in space and time the ancestral shades, which are bound to relations of descent. The cults reach beyond lineage barriers and cross partitionings of kin and gender. Some of them include alien spirits from neighboring cultures, as they seek to come to terms with migrant labor or long-distance trade. Two particular categories may be distinguished according to the means of their transmission and their association with community and family life respectively. Communal sodalities are linked with values and afflictions regarding agnatic descent, masculinity, public community life, and government in the center of the homestead. Some offer spirit legitimation to the major masculinist values. The major cults of affliction, in turn, are transmitted along the uterine line and concerned with complexes of afflictions and social pathology in relation to maternal values. Their seclusion rituals take place at the edge of the patient's hamlet, at the gateway between the village realm and the alien world—that is, the realm of the liminal. While the rites in each category reflect a formal similarity in terms of procedure, each of the cults differs as to its deployment of specific metaphors that tie in with the wider life-world and cosmology. Each cult has a number of core metaphors, dances, chants, ritual texts, and medicinal preparations. The therapeutic initiation may last from a few days to even a year or more depending on the gravity of the affliction, the efficacy of the healing, and the familial means for payment. On the one hand, communal sodalities convey, in lines with rules of agnatic inheritance, a privileged social identity or role onto men, or seek to reconnect a group of men with the agnatic ancestral life force: in recycling the deeds and words of the founding ancestors, they regenerate and re-empower the agnatic group and the world order. On the other hand, affliction is the only access to initiation in the cults of affliction. These healing cults focus on the physical body, its innate traits and ailments, in relation to the basic values of social exchange that sustain the uterine transmission of the vital flow through marriage, maternity, and the avunculate. Both divination and healing, like physical health itself, belong to the maternal, uterine, and avuncular domain: they are resistant to control by masculine power or by the political game of the elders in the center of diurnal village life.

In order to address the question regarding the importance of cult healing, it is necessary to understand the political control of health and the degree to which healers enjoy autonomy within the structure of power. This topic (in lines with Feierman 1985) raises a number of questions: Are healers only delegates of the ruling class? Does cult healing seek to enforce the political control the elders have over issues of descent, marriage, and the transmission of life? Are healers allies of the patients or representatives of gerontocratic and patriarchal power? Do healers keep some categories of people or of suffering outside their sphere of concern?

4.4.1 *Cults of affliction and healing (phoongwamooyi) are inherited in the uterine line only through misfortune called on by a curse.* In case of a lasting illness or other recurrent misfortune of some ill-fated kind, the family of the afflicted may consult a clairvoyant diviner, whose oracle is somehow the voice of his own *ngoombu* spirit within a cult that stands independent of and above all the other cults. In many cases, the oracle discloses that the misfortune has been brought about by a curse uttered by a matrilineal forebear in retaliation for a "theft"—a notion that stands for ensorcellment and any other offense or ill-threat—by relatives that the latter had been suffering from. In his curse the forebear has invoked the support of one or another cult, or more precisely he has summoned a nonancestral cult spirit to avenge the offense and persecute the wrongdoer or one or another of his uterine descendants. Only the victim of that retaliation may join a cult and devote herself or himself to her or his cult spirit to domesticate the persecutive relation and foster it into a supportive one for the rest of her or his life. It is thus the divinatory etiology regarding the particular affliction that orients the afflicted to one or another cult for initiation and treatment: as such, a similar affliction may be caused by and thus treated in rather unrelated cults. It is the therapist's aim to reverse the ill-fated process by lifting the curse of the matrilineal forebear and thus the origin of the illness or misfortune, after which he then will treat the afflicted by means of initiation *(n-saku)* in the same cult. The cults thus cure afflictions that are thought to be, in a sense, congenital: as they are passed down from mothers to (classificatory) sons and daughters, a son is exposed to the persecutive action from the cult his (classificatory) mother has been initiated in, but his children may be under the threat of a cult in his wife's uterine kin. Four of them—*khita, mbwoolu, ngoombu,* and *maawa*—are "cults with a demonstrative trance" *(phoongu ya kaluka),* caused by the spirit of the same name: the trance is both a major congenital affliction in the uterine line and a resource for the healing of the initiate and the revivification of her or his life-world. In these same four cults, carved statuettes of human figures constitute a vital intermediary space between initiate and spirit. (These are to some extent documented in Dumon and Devisch 1992.)

Cults and sorcery are intimately but conversely connected. Uterine cults of affliction appear as an unauthored extrahuman management of retaliation and redress that reverses evil—basically ensorcellment—into a process of healing in the matrilineal line. Ensorcellment feeds greedily on vital forces in people, whereas a cult reverses the evil—both the agent and the misfortune—against itself self-destructively so as to restore the larger weave of forces. Thus, in using the term *phoongu* ("cult") Yaka people refer to a chain of forces or causal agencies, namely curse, spirit, retaliation, misfortune or illness, and healing. The drama of retaliation for an evil, and thus of the misfortune that issues from it, is an unauthored contrivance of the self-governing rule of exchange in the uterine line (see 5.2). The term cult can stand for the entire drama of self-governance of the rule of exchange or any of these agencies at work, according to a feedback mechanism, congruently in the fields of body, family, and lifeworld. The drama of retaliation and misfortune enacted by the cult spirits—so to say, operative in the cosmological body—both shapes and echoes co-occuring ones in the social and physical body. In other words, for the Yaka, *phoongu* denotes both nonancestral and unlocalizable spirits that may cause misfortune or bring healing, as well as the institution itself for cursing and curing seen as a field of forces to be domesticated by a proper cult. The curse and the divinatory etiology tend somehow to consider *phoongu* as named spirits. However, they are not regarded as self-steering entrepreneurs of vindicative actions or authors of their own script or plot. Inasmuch as the therapy brings about an autoproductive drama (see ch. 7), the notion of *phoongu* concerns also the entire cult and process at work within consonant fields of multiple forces that may bring about both illness and cure. Cults thus bear and manipulate forces in transgenerational time. And, as the divinatory oracle often brings out, sorcerers may conceal their plot so that the misfortune they cause to happen in their close kin of the same or following generation appears as if it were only the work of a cult, that is, of a cult spirit. Renowned diviners however can unmask the sorcerous plot. The divination cult is thus the pivot of the entire system of healing cults in the uterine line. Because of its importance, divination—including the becoming of a mediumistic diviner—receives a close look in the following presentation of cults.

Healers, called *ngaanga*, are former patients whose initiation in the appropriate cult led to their recovery from the incapacitating illness they now address in their client. A boy born shortly after or as a result of his mother's initiation is predestined to becoming a healer. All this enables a great identification between healer and patient, and, since healing draws heavily on interdependence, Yaka healers are intent on making allies among those people who suffer an affliction similar to the one they have experienced. To put it frankly, healers may also need patients like them in order to heal themselves. Consequently, in cases of severe illness such as severe psychosis, wild epileptic fits, blindness, deafness, or serious infection, healers feel unable to intervene.

The cults of affliction are similar to the *mahaamba* in the Luunda cultural zone of Angola, Zaire and Zambia (De Boeck 1991a; Lima 1971; Turner 1967, 1968; Yoder 1981). Most of the cult names prove to be untranslatable. In the following discussion, the most popular or prevailing cults are listed first, followed by the more marginal or fragmentary ones.

(a) *Ngoombu* or *ngoombwaweefwa* is a major cult with trance behavior (see Devisch 1991a). It deals with patients who intrude on another's private space through hysteric or epileptic-like crises, or, on the contrary, who withdraw from social contact and suffer from respiratory and pulmonary disturbances such as expectoration, persistent cough, forms of bronchitis, and asthma. Some patients seem very shy, and confess how much they see the shade of a deceased diviner relative. These are in fact all symptoms which may moreover manifest an individual's vocation as mediumistic diviner.

When the hysteric or epileptic-like crisis tips over into a trance state that shows the pattern of the *ngoombu* cult, the patient may be considered a candidate for the divinership. The trance in fact inaugurates the initiation and transforms the patient into a spirit medium. The medium—who may be a man or a woman—is led to metaphorically integrate the regenerative capacity of the chicken. Entranced, the diviner-initiand, like the fully certified diviner, may without any help whatsoever climb to the crest of a palm tree, or jump up on the roof of his house, and then leap to the ridge and tear away at the straw (Devisch 1991c). In the entire mime, in the movement of his eyes, head and body, prancing about, walking on the balls of his feet and crowing "coo, coo, coo," the entranced imitates the hen. The possessed medium then reveals the name of a matrilineal forebear who was also a diviner and who now calls a successor. These various aspects of entranced behavior are termed *-puumbuka*, "to leap," *-kaluka*, "to release, deliver oneself," or *-vuula*, "to slip away." Such a trance authenticates or reminds one of one's calling to the divinership. After going into the trance, diviner-to-be is secluded for nine months in a ritual hut to the edge of village space. The seclusion aims at healing, and the prescribed behavior, songs, paraphernalia, and the group's consent attune the diviner to the gift of clairvoyance that is awakening in him or her. During this initiatory seclusion, the diviner may enter in trance any time he or she hears about or witnesses sorcery. When finally led out of seclusion, at dawn, the medium withdraws to the stretch of wood at the edge of the homestead, and there behaves like a predator. In a trance, the diviner bites off the head of a hen and holds this head in his mouth. Then a close parent carries the diviner on his shoulders into the village. Reaching the seclusion hut, the diviner prances about in a trance-like state and identifies again with the brooding hen as during the seclusion. The initiation is completed when a senior-diviner, literally "who has acted as his mother" *(ngula ngaanga),* completes his paraphernalia so as to release his full mediumistic capacity and protect him against sorcerers. Since the clairvoyance is meant to be most bright in the newly initiated medium, his divinatory oracles are usually given great credence: he acts as a highly respected, public, and independent consultant who authoritatively identifies the problem and then directs the patient to the relevant family intervention and healing cult (see ch. 5).

My reading of the symbolism in the context of the initiation procedure that is specific to the cult of divination indicates how much the cock crowing at the sunrise and more strikingly the brooding hen act as symbols of intermediacy and mobility, not only between night and day, forest and village, low and high, but also between the one who engenders and the one who is engendered. By singing at dawn like the cock, the diviner-medium announces the end of the realm of the night and sorcery. By momentarily likening herself to a predator, she overcomes the persecutive dimension of the spirit of divination which made her ill. The diviner-to-be is thus a patient, and initiation into the divinership is also a healing procedure. The spirit's aggression from which she had until now been the victim is displaced onto the animal, and the spirit may then release its capacity to sustain her mediumistic art of divining. From now on, the medium identifies more fully with the symbolism of mutation and re-origination by metaphorically enacting the role of the hen brooding an egg. The house where the diviner-to-be undergoes the initiatory seclusion acts like a shell enveloping the initiate, who is her- or himself in a process of incubation that leads towards a new identity. The house moreover stands for *ngoongu*, the primal, egg-like womb of the world. The trance is a corporeal dramatization of this mutation and in it the diviner transcends all those demarcations upon which the Yaka worldview depend (see Bourdieu 1980:348). In this manner the trance of the diviner-medium becomes an ontological transformation: it establishes the order of the demarcations by transcending them in a decisive way. Trance thus permits the diviner to become the measure of both norm and deviance. Trance, mortal agony, orgasm, and birth are all symbolically associated in that they constitute either limit-experiences or the trespassing of human limits and therefore offer a model of self-healing in the manner of integration of the corporeal and the sociocultural.

Consulting a diviner occurs near his house, in the open, and in the presence of the representatives of the husband's patrikin and the wife's father and uncle. The client, namely the afflicted person, is rarely present. Upon arrival, after a formal exchange of greetings, the most senior among the consultants, without words, hands over to the diviner a *yiteendi*, "a piece of cloth"—often substituted by a coin—which has absorbed the client's shadow or double by being rubbed over her or his chest. It constitutes a kind of intermediary object between the client, the consultants, and the diviner. From now on the oracle proper may take place. During the entire meeting, the consultants avoid offering any information to the diviner; by their discretion and evasiveness, they seek to test the clairvoyant or paranormal nature of the oracle. The consulting parties have faith in the diviner's message to the extent that its truly clairvoyant or divinatory quality manifests itself. The diviner should bring out by himself the subject placed before the oracle: he should answer himself the fixed set of questions that he is chanting in the idiom of his cult with high-pitched voice and accelerated breathing. More and more overtaken by his inner vision, as if in a dream, he moves into some kind of trance-like state of expanded consciousness when he is about to trace or bring out the reason of his clients' consultation and indicate the cause of the misfortune they are facing. At that moment, shocked by the sorcerous complot that they are unmasking, young diviners may leap into the ostentatory trance behavior that marked their initiation. Calming down and in a more colloquial speech, the diviner then further elaborates upon these revelations by analysing by himself the illness on the basis of an etiological grid provided by his cult tradition (see 5.2).

Several minor divination procedures that are part of the *ngoombu* cult may be consulted in the case of bad dreams and certain material misfortunes, as in hunting, agriculture, or business, or death and loss of animals and damage to or loss of tools. In the past, ordeal by fire *(ngoombwa luufu)* was used. Some people are specialized in a kind of inductive oracle using an adhering horn of a duiker *(ngoombwa n-seengu),* or a rubbing stick board *(ngoombwa n-ti).* Because it is thought that these oracle forms can be manipulated by those concerned, people do not accept their results without skepticism.

(b) *Khita:* This cult first causes and then treats afflictions relative to female reproduction, namely incapacity to conceive, temporary cessation of menstrual flow, excessive flow of the menses, irregular menstrual periods, miscarriage, stillbirth, and recurrent death of infants. Such afflictions are, according to some therapists, the province of *khita mandzandza.* Congenital anomalies of human reproduction, including the birth of twins, albinos, and dwarf or malformed children, are the specific concern of *khita lukobi.*

(c) *Mbwoolu:* The term derives from *-woola,* meaning both "to impair or deform" and "to reerect, revalidate." The cult is first and foremost directed to disabled and rehabilitating patients. It is secondarily invoked in the treatment of grave and chronic fevers by which the fluid substances of the body are wasted away, particularly those occurring in children or due to sleeping sickness or malaria, exceptional emaciation, chronic diarrhea, black urine, chronic and productive cough with fever, and river blindness. Thirdly, it addresses patients suffering from severe 'implosion,' those having lost all sense of self and living 'beside themselves.' They perceive themselves in terms of frightening nightmares where they see themselves sucked into whirlpools and rivers, lost in deep ravines, encountering snakes, or being struck by lightning. The *tsyo* or *tsyoowa* cult, associated with the elephant hunt, is an auxiliary to *mbwoolu.* From about 1910 onwards, *mbwoolu* practice, moreover, has sought to domesticate the unprecedented intrusion of colonial trade and influence in Yaka land (Devisch 1991b; Bourgeois 1978–79; Huber 1956).

(d) *Maawa* is associated with water spirits, and it is invoked in some cases of closure and coldness, such as in feminine sterility, amenorrhea, anemia, and "swollen or extended belly" *(yivimu kiviimbidi).*

(e) *Ndzaambi,* also referred to as *ndzaambyaphuungu yiluunda,* causes as well as treats a number of afflictions of implosion: the belly is seen as a peel or cocoon hiding a greedy or parasitic core that sucks in and hides the body's entire vitality. Conversely, *Ndzaambi* figures also as some kind of bird hatching out of a primordial egg-like state. This name has been recycled in Christian discourse to indicate the Supreme Being.

(f) The *n-kanda* cult is directed mainly to skin diseases of various kinds such as boils and abscesses.

(g) The last cultic category, *yimbala,* is also held to treat various skin diseases.

Cult healing in Yaka society is a domain withdrawn from the political realm and public authority, and consequently cult healers enjoy a great professional autonomy. This is not to say that the social aspects of sickness are dismissed, but that they are dealt with in the homestead during public councils of family elders. The latter deal with the social origin and effects of the misfortune. Yaka therapists, however, do not seek to influence the public issues affecting or related with health and sickness. Concerned with reweaving the vital flow *(mooyi),* the healer operates within the realm of uterine filiation at the margins of the diurnal order of village life. Healers countervail and challenge indirectly the bases of the political power of chiefs, elders, and family heads, that is, of the virile order. They witness to the incapacity of agnatic descent to do without the input of uterine filiation. Healers, so to speak, look back at the social order 'from the edge,' that is, from the resources of the forest and the transitional zone between village space and savanna or forest.

Yaka mediumistic diviners do not function as political advisors; they will never intentionally serve a chief's political ambition. A diviner is only willing to examine a case of affliction if it is submitted by those directly concerned. Diviners will not unmask cases of sorcery, theft, adultery, or other kinds of abuse at the mere demand of a chief in his search for coercive control over his subordinates. Nor will a chief seek a diviner's advice in order to organize rites for communal well-being, to settle disputes, to resolve public crises, or to prospect a collective hunt or the proper site to choose for the village.

Cult management may variously weaken patriarchal assumptions rather than merely submitting the patient to society's control. Yet it clearly offers the patient and the support group an important chance to frame and reassert their experience within the cosmological order of meaning and the intimate social network proper to the translineage cult. Membership in a cult gives the initiate a vital support group and a relative autonomy vis-à-vis patriarchal authority.

4.4.2 *Communal cults or sodalities are agnatic, and are concerned with power, public skills, and masculinist values.* First, they are concerned with paramount rulership, corporate kin interests, family traditions, male fecundity, and the arts of smithery and of hunting—which are privileged masculine professions. They do not require an illness to indicate a vocation on the part of the initiate, and initiations are public and communal. Second, inasmuch as these cults may provoke affliction, the ailments are not considered to be congenital, though, in some cults, a misfortune may indicate a vocation to becoming a cult priest. The symptoms involve loss of vitality, impotence, surrender or weakness and dependence, great anxiety, repeated failure in the hunt, being struck by lightning or succumbing to other brutal accidents, lasting withdrawal from social encounter, or, more rarely, physical ailments such as wasting diarrhoea or 'swelling' of the belly or limbs. Healing aims at social integration in the lineage order very much through a communal ritual that reenacts some of the mythical deeds with regard to the foundation of social hierarchy and agnatic descent, while conferring on the patient and coinitiates the marks of social identity or status. The term *phoongu zan-niku* indicates the great extent to which these cults involve apprenticeship in the use or fashioning of medicines or power objects *(n-niku)*. Public male cults—like virility itself—focus on *ngolu:* force, strength, and control. That is to say that the agnatic cults are only for men, and in a few cases their spouses. These agnatic cults are presided over by the lineage chief, whose responsibility it is to guard the major sacred objects of the cult. They are comparable to the *lemba* cult that, among the neighboring Koongo, addressed the role of merchants in trade (Janzen 1982). Family heads are titleholders of the agnatic cults: patients treated in these cults may share the use of the hereditary artifacts with the titleholder. The *haamba, khosi, mbaambi,* and *n-luwa* cults display carved statuettes and a number of hereditary cult relics and regalia that pass from one titleholder to the next.

(a) *Lukhaanga:* This cult bestows the ruler in the Luunda tradition with sovereign power and the capacity to personify unity and perpetuity. *Lukhaanga* priests and initiates may counterbalance, particularly in the realm of night, the chief's pretense to paramount power. The sodality comprises three cultic traditions or associations for the elite. First, *lukhaanga* involves the political title-holder at the regional or subregional level, and his fellow-titleholders: namely, the chief's highest-ranking wife (she here represents the uterine source of life and prosperity to which the chief has access for the benefit of his people); the chief's son; the subchief; one of the chief's classificatory brothers in the collateral line (and therefore his heir); and finally, one of the chief's senior classificatory sisters. At the onset of the enthronement the chief and his fellow-titleholders form one collective body (see Devisch 1988). Enthronement in the sodality identifies this collective body with the 'parthenogenesis' proper to the founding ancestors: it is as if each successive titleholder embodies anew the ideals and forces at the foundation of the sodality. Impersonating the founding ancestor, the chief and coinitiates make present "the primal and permanent space-time order" *(yitsi khulu);* they reembody or 're-present' and impose the perennial hierarchical social organization, territorial unity, and order. In the enthronement and subsequent reign, the chief and fellow titleholders must reenact the founding dramas of conquest and life transmission. Sacrificial death, mortuary ritual, rebirth, purification, and other rites reenact the founding dramas of the coercive political order and provide transformative metaphors, by virtue of which the chief is enabled to transcend partitions or differences—such as those between the genders and between ascendants and descendants—and to conceal his own bodily transitoriness. Moreover, *lukhaanga* includes powers to provoke or treat cases of insanity, respiratory or pulmonary infection, hemorrhage, leprosy, and certain forms of swelling of belly or limbs due to anemia.

Second, *lukhaanga* patronizes the maternal *mwani kabwanga* cult for the fertility of land and people. The chief acts as the supreme mediator of the regenerative processes and resources in and between the cosmos, the land, the society, and humanity. *Mwani kabwanga* bestows upon the collective body of ruler and fellow titleholders the life-giving capacity that links the generations together, even overcoming death, and that secures the fertility and well-being of the chief's daughters and by extension of all women and the land in the chief's territory. He and his co-dignitaries link the people, the territory, the land, and the cosmic order with *ngoongu*, the primal womb—the cosmic and egg- or tree-like source of life which ceaselessly emerges and regenerates.

Third, *n-ngoongi* is another sodality linked to *lukhaanga*. This sodality is called *mwiingoony* among the Aluund to the south of Yaka land (De Boeck 1991b). It associates the initiates with the responsibilities, virtues, and secrets of the title-holders, and enhances the bond between the ancestral line of Luunda rulers and the living male and female members of the chief's lineage. Moreover, *n-ngoongi* bestows upon the ruler and his regalia the capacity to overcome the dominion of the night, death, and drought, thereby sustaining the cycles of sun, moon, rain, and the seasons—as is also enacted in the chief's ritual enclosure, *ndzo malala* (see 2.4.1 above).

(b) *Yikubu*, also called *mbiimbya n-khanda* or *n-khanda*, is the cult that marks the passing on of male fecundity from the older generation to the pubescent boys just before or during sexual awakening and "coming in force" *(-kaanda)* (see 3.3 above). Circumcision aims at "getting the body better" *(-tomasa luutu)*. The cult accompanies circumcision and puberty, and it offers healing in cases of masculine sterility, bone fracture, or leprosy—the latter is considered an effect of incest. It is also the cult in which impotence is treated. Under the supervision of the family elders and patriarchs, boys undergo initiation into manhood and virile society. The blacksmith is sometimes responsible for the circumcision proper or for making the masks which enable the newly circumcised to pass from one state to another at the conclusion of the puberty rites (see Devisch 1972). The *kyandzangoombi* priest, also called *yisidika*, prevents *(-sidika)* the boys from experiencing a fatal loss of blood or ensorcellment. By spitting aphrodisiac chewings on the genitals, he urges the boys to become potent, brave, and energetic. In contrast to the *khita* 'gyn-eco-logical' initiation, circumcision initiation does not focus on experiences of death, gestation, and rebirth. *N-khanda* initiation is much more concerned with the foundational deeds and ideals at the base of society: the original migration of the founding ancestors, violence, sorcery, the origins of generations, the invention of fire, hunting, smithery. The collective initiation into manhood thereby bestows the initiates with the ideals of the culture heroes and the hunter. The house of seclusion *(ndzofu)* for the circumcised is associated with the elephant *(ndzyoku)*. It is situated in the savanna bordering the village to the east. The circumcision cult, centered around symbolism of the gregarious elephant, celebrates male force and potency as collectively shared among the commoners. The cult suggests that men of the same age group, through unity, may collectively attain the force of the elephant and thereby become capable of facing the monocracy and violence of those among the chiefs and patriarchs who, like their totemic animals the leopard, crocodile, and eagle, behave as aloof predators (Devisch 1988). This suggests that while fostering unity among age-mates, the puberty initiation interjects a note of tension or contrariety in the physical and social transformation from boys to men. Access to malehood faces the circumcised with the rule of subordination and potential terror imposed by elders.

(c) *Haamba, mbaambi,* and *n-luwa,* the latter also called *mwani phutu,* are sodalities that link up the Luunda dynastic families with the chiefly values of bravery and splendor and with the chief's totemic figures such as the leopard, crocodile, a type of large chameleon, and the rainbow. The cults "recall" *(-aamba)* the invention of smithery, hunting, and the coercive use of power. They are paired with the exercise of political power of Luunda patrimony and serve to perpetuate the myth of the civilizing heroes of the Luunda empire in the Nkalaany homeland in Shaba. Initiates in these cults may act as commissioners between rival chiefly families. On the other hand, when transmitted equally along agnatic and uterine lines, these cults may include possession-trance and provide treatment for some kinds of "splitting head," mental disturbance, epilepsy, high fevers, difficulty in breathing, sprains, and for several injuries caused by firearms in the hunt.

(d) *Khosi* and *n-hwaadi* are related cults, sometimes involving trance, that are capable of causing fatal afflictions by way of retaliation for a murderous ensorcellment that was once committed by a uterine forebear or cursed in the same cult. They may cause a brutal death, and may either bring or cure dementia, bone fracture, hemorrhage, and high fever. Other conditions indicating treatment in these cults include injuries due to lightning, firearms, near drowning, or snakebite.

(e) *Leembi, yindongu,* and *yipfudila* represent another group of cults that make up a particular art of healing transmitted along the patriline—though cases of uterine transmission are not unknown—offering treatment for epileptic seizures *(-pfudika),* mental disturbance, and tetanus.

(f) *Ndzuundu* is the cult associated with smithery, offering also treatment of those forms of anemia involving "swellings of the legs or the belly and the blood turning into water."

(g) *N-laangu* (literally, "male sex") and *n-kuba mbadi* (literally, "purse to contain a hernia") address impotence, hernia, swellings of the testicles, and elephantiasis.

(h) *Khiimbi, malemu, mataamba, mandongu,* and *ngola* are mere fragmentary elements of cults known for their formidable panoply of ritual defense and attack *(-taamba).*

Public cults or sodalities hint both at making alliances with and at counterbalancing the political order and chiefs. *Haamba, n-luwa,* and associated cults are principally concerned with deadly cursing with the intent to attack *(-lwa)* or to exact revenge *(-aamba),* and a family elder could level a curse even against the entourage of a political titleholder of middle rank, the vassals included. Recent sorcery cleansing movements, as I observed in 1974 and 1991, may be rooted in Christian faith healing and may be a reaction to colonialism or the ill-fated intrusion into Yaka land of unequally shared cash goods or of urban (sexual) license. These movements do not confront chiefs or even seek their support, but attack cult healing and, most violently, the heart of it, namely divination. Communal sodalities seem to lose much more of their vitality than healing cults do once they are in lasting contact with a cash economy, school education, and the urban mixing of people. The circumcision ritual is very much shortened, if not reduced to a mere physical intervention, when practiced in the urban context. In Kinshasa, initiates in communal cults—with the exception of the other great political titleholders—do not enjoy major privileges or prestige.

All cults have shrines that contain numerous medicines or power objects—such as small statuettes, cowries, bracelets, hangers, shells, horns, and bundles—contained in decorated ritual artifacts. Most shrines act as standing medicines since they are set up to prevent ill or to avenge an attack or evil. Major herbalist or phytotherapeutic practices are the monopoly of some cults and their specialists. Each cult has its proper initiatory art of herbal remedies and prophylactic, purgative, or tonic medicines, called *n-kaanda,* "bouquet of leaves." The same term may also designate any external element—skin, bark, surface, etc.—that would allow identification of the substance in question. Although every "bouquet of leaves" is of a unique combination, certain plants or plant products may be found in all ritual specializations and/or cults. Name, color code, smell, habitat, and association with some animal are as important as its vegetal properties. They are each time, however, combined in a manner which endows each with a particular signification: here one speaks of *n-tyabungaanga,* "a plant of common ritual usage," whose specific value is designated by a surname or a form of motto. In order to express his request to be initiated into the legitimate and expert use of a particular bouquet of plants, the novice or client will offer the specialist a *lubongu lwataangu kataangila bungaanga,* literally, "a skirt of the sun, a cloth with as many shades of colors as those of the sun, in order that he reveal his specialist knowledge." According to the exegesis offered by ritual experts, the "sun-skirt," namely dyed cloth or the hide of a spotted animal, notably refers to the set of medicinal leaves of a great variety of plants. Should the novice undergo a period of seclusion, the bouquet of plants is suspended from the ridge pole of the seclusion house. The novice lying underneath is forbidden to look at it until the last night of seclusion. It is during this night that the ritual expert will report to the novice whatever the "bouquet of leaves has to say" *(-taangila n-kaanda)* and authorize him to employ it. Medicinal preparations may involve incantations to invoke the powers of the ingredients, and they may be combined with gestures of reconciliation and purification, aimed at rendering harmless various forces that are attributed to sorcery, curse, or infringement.

Enemas are often practiced and consist of introducing a small amount of an herbal concoction into the rectum with the aid of a small gourd that is shaped like a pear with a long thin neck. Having withdrawn to the house or to the periphery of the domestic space, the individual may administer the enema or douche to himself while lying on his back. *-Soobuka* is the term used for the lukewarm douche—mainly resorted to by adult men—made from a cooled concoction of boiled ligneous forest plants. For an anal or vaginal rinse, women employ either lukewarm mixtures of ligneous savanna vegetation or cold infusions drawn from herbs of the savanna *(yifutu). -Nwa ndzaba* is a douche consisting of a cold infusion taken principally for the purpose of sedation, as is expressed in the ritual vocabulary: "to give shade *(pheelaka)* or to cool" the belly, womb, or bowels. This is the prescribed treatment for the novice—likened to the fetus—and for anyone who seems to have lost his senses, who vomits blood, or who has a high fever. Other decoctions aim at "sweeping the belly clean" *(-koombula yivumu).* Still others "give whiteness or purity to the belly" *(-seemasa yivumu)* so as to prepare the patient to be fully interwoven again in the social fabric.

There are countless medicinal preparations and treatments practiced as a domestic tradition or under the advice of a healer. Emetics *(bilukisa)* help to discharge 'poisonous' food. *Yifutu* is the bunch of nonligneous savanna plants employed in the preparation of washes used exclusively by women. Only ritual specialists and uncles may prescribe, concoct, and offer the *yifutu;* the phrase *-tolwala bifutu,* "to compose bouquets," is in fact a synonym for *-ta buleemba,* "to exercise the avuncular role." These concoctions and infusions are widely used by the *khita* therapy and, as we will see, indicate the necessity of modifying certain relations between the living and the dead, or between living relatives. Vegetal and symbolic qualities underlie the many homeopathic medicinal preparations for use with enemas, cupping horns, small incisions, bonesetting, immunization against smallpox, or used for calming, for their lactogenic properties, against intestinal parasites, or in obstetrics. Most treatments and, in particular, child care, prescribe rest and indicate categories of food and other matter to be avoided. As soon as something is prescribed by a healer, an elder, an uncle, or in the context of a cult, or even by a medical doctor, it becomes a *n-kisi,* literally, "a treatment, a practice."

Plate 1. *Khita* healer in Kinshasa-Masina.

Plate 2. The jar depicts the world (see 2.2.1).

Plate 3. Family elder addresses the ancestral shades at their graves (see 4.2).

Plate 4. Addressing, in the *kataku* virile stance, the agnatic cult spirits at the shrine (see 2.2.2, 6.2.2).

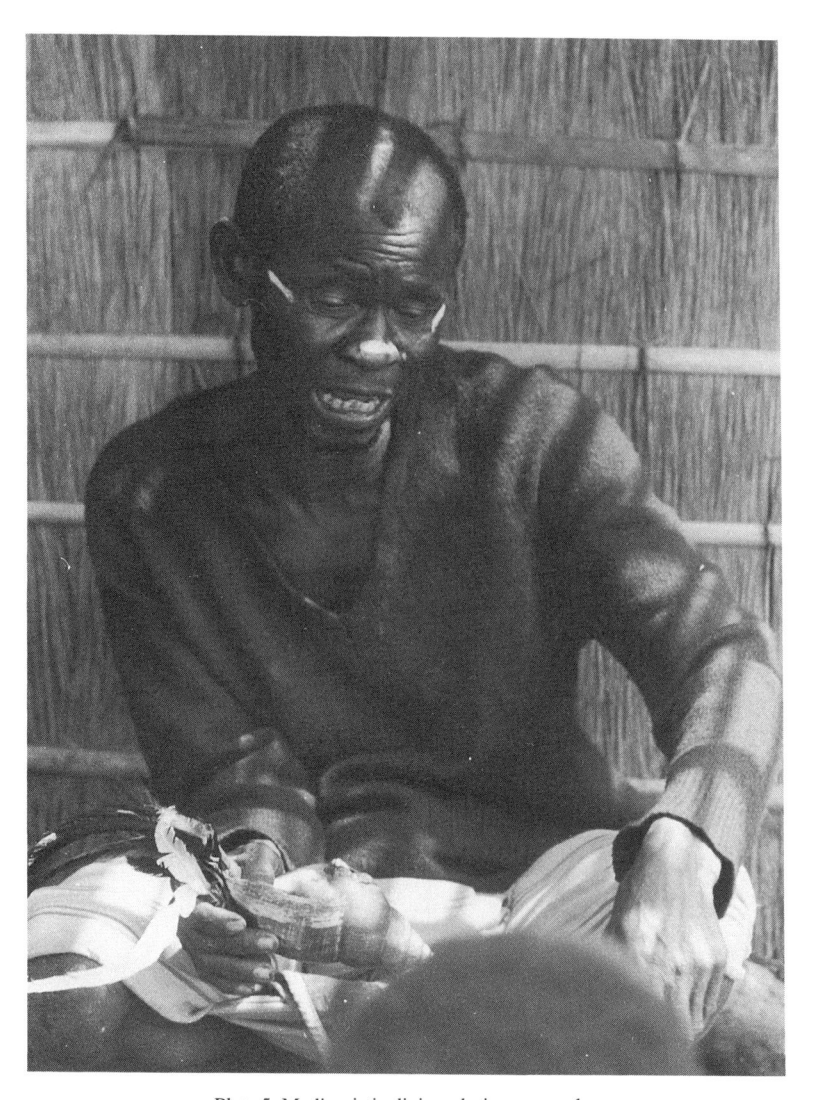

Plate 5. Mediumistic diviner during an oracle.

Plate 6. *Khita* seclusion hut for gynecological healing.

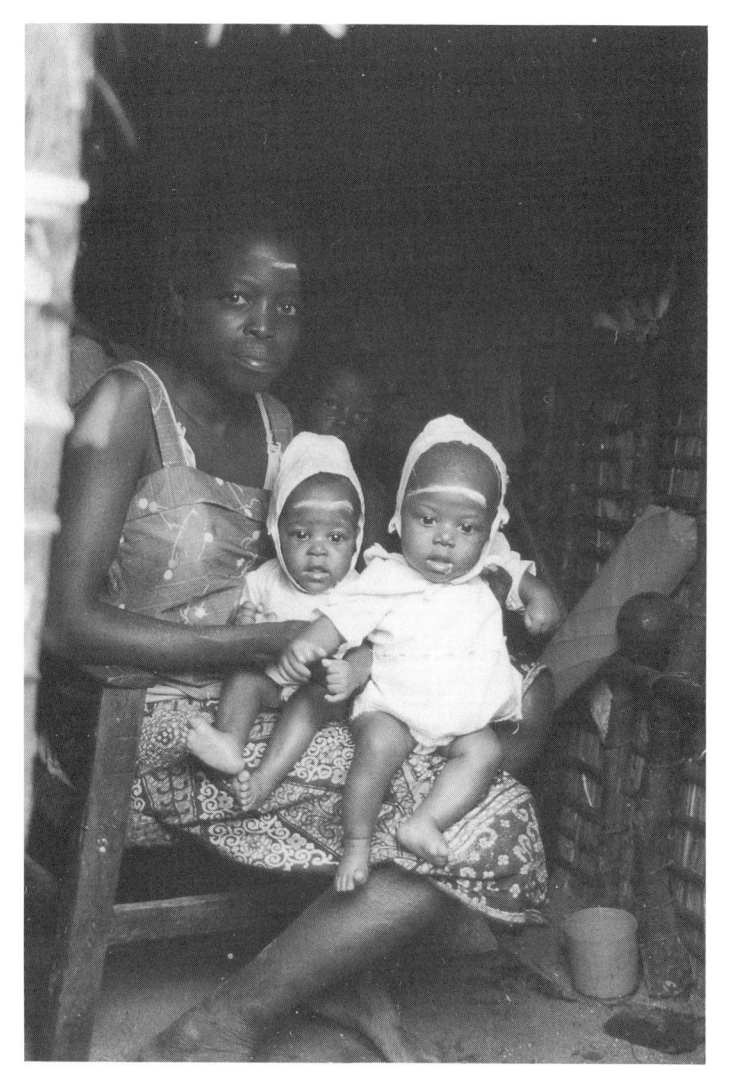

Plate 7. Mother with twins in seclusion.

Plate 8. *Khoofi* shrine in front of seclusion hut. The long stick in the entrance is the parasol tree (see 6.2.2).

Plate 9. Seclusion hut as cosmic womb.

Plate 10. *Luleembi* raffia curtain closing off the entry to the seclusion hut. The elbow-shaped *lukata* branch evokes deformities; the black termitary, *yisiimbi,* makes the cult spirits present (see 6.2.2).

Plate 11. Twisted liana and hiltless knife serving as barrier to the entrance of the seclusion hut (see 7.1).

Plate 12. *Kamwaadi* fork and *lwuila* termitary representing the founders of the cult (see 7.1).

Plate 13. Parasol tree, at the entrance, topped by the head of a hen.

Plate 14. *Khita* initiates and Maleeka servant in the company of the healer at the end of the seclusion.

Plate 15. *(Left to right)* Receptacles of both evil and healing forces; *N-noongu:* weaving-hook of the *khita* cult (see 7.2.1); *N-seenga:* a powerful ritual object of the *mbwoolu* cult; *M-bindusi:* a twisted liana serving to reverse evil.

Plate 16. *Phaandzi* pharmacopoeia (see 7.2.1).

Plate 17. *Tsaanga* calabashes with medicines (see 7.2.1).

Plate 18. The *khita* initiate identifies with the squirrel by wearing its pelt (see 7.2.4).

Plates 19–20. Weaving is rhythm, and rhythm underscores the weave of life. The participants' experiences are rhythmically interwoven with the ideals and norms of the community. Health is interwovenness.

5 Impediments to Life Transmission

Life transmission issues from an alliance between the husband's patrikin and the wife's kin group. The former transmits 'standing' onto its descendants, both the bony structure and capacity to stand upright *(ngolu, khoondzu)*, as well as social identity. Alliance connects this capacity for social standing with the wife's uterine descent which transmits life *(mooyi)* from the uterine source through the line of mothers. Inasmuch as transmission of life is the prime concern of the bride-takers, impediments to it put into question the very nature of alliance, matrimony, and descent and urge a thorough scrutiny of the principles, history, and nature of the social fabric, including the matrimonial alliance and the uterine flow of life. I would venture to say that the etiological narratives about impediments to life transmission in Yaka society do not dispossess women of their bodies.[1]

On their side, the elders of the young husband, in command of the masculinist strategies to control and manipulate group issues, tend to attribute hindrances of life-bearing primarily to social wrongs. They conceive of group members as knots within the weave of kin. It is therefore commonplace for any affliction, in particular a gynecological one, to be seen as having its origin in the kin and thus involving the social fabric. An altered state of health *(-beela)* becomes social in character from the moment that coresidents and in particular those in charge of the ailing person have formally acknowledged the disorder, literally the "impediment" *(yibiinda)*. This acknowledgment requires that the elders interpret the specific way in which a person's state of health or style of behavior deviates from the norm and that they mark out or stigmatize the deviation with regard to the interests of the group. A social definition is thereby given to the affliction, and it is identified as a disorder or "affair" *(dyaambu)*. The divinatory oracle that follows broadens the scope by considering moreover and in particular the body and the uterine life flow. However, this broader focus is narrowed down again at the subsequent family council that meets to hear the report from the consultants at the oracle. Indeed, the agnatic elders are first and foremost concerned with the social origin and impact of the sickness, that is, with the social weave in which the afflicted is entangled or from which she or he is cut off, and why this occurred. The appropriate term here is *-beelala*, "to be stricken with such and such an ailment for this or that social reason": it concerns the group's reception and intersubjective experiencing of the affliction in line with its aims. The palaver of elders to a large extent develops as a kind of sociodrama that brings to the fore conflicts and debts in the kin and alliance while trying to overcome them.

As such, agnatic elders are principally concerned with social rule. The elders in council examine the wrongs in the group that are reflected in or have produced the sickness, and they consider the many intricacies in the family history and the complex motives at play in establishing marriages. They face the reports on divinatory oracles that may unmask their own paradoxical games of ensorcelling their proper offspring: the oracle reveals the nightly plots in which uterines, agnates, and in-laws succeed one another in purveying or receiving a new catch from the "nightly hunt." The discourse of elders reinforces the virile ethos of hunters, that is, the very masculinist views on life transmission and woman's role in it, and reinforces beliefs about cursing, ancestral wrath, sorcery, and evil spirits. The ills in the family history are occasions to revise or confirm the social weave. In other words, in men's view health is linked not so much to individual virtue but to moves and countermoves in the social fabric. It is the family elders' due to examine whether the problem at hand is to be turned over to the oracle of the clairvoyant diviner.

Mediumistic divining is more of a birthing process than an arbitrament, an anamnesis rather than a diagnosis, and a hermeneutics more than a causal or moral inquiry of disorders. Divinatory revelation stands to the council of elders as 'aletheia' or visionary exploration of potentialities stands to truth as correctness (Levin 1988:438), as dreamwork to representational and discursive argument, as "speaking from the womb" stands to men's rhetorical reassertion of power relations in the agnatic order of seniority. Clairvoyant divining is concerned with the source rather than the cause of events, with the consensual moral order, with the interplay between good or ill health, the strategies in the group and the life-world. It examines how much the patient who is subjected to the power game in the agnatic descent owes her or his physical life, in both good and ill health, to the uterine flow of life. Though the divinatory approach is not causalist in a deterministic sense, but brings out moments of correspondence in the worlds of the client and the client's family, I will nevertheless speak of etiology. Divinatory etiology sees the patient as a weave and also as a hunting ground: the diviner traces back the sets of knots that are untied or loosened, or traces the plots of sorcery and evil spirits. The ill is compared to knots that have become inextricably entangled or untied. The agencies of ill— such as the ancestral shades, spirits, uterine life flow, human agencies, forces of plants and ingredients of power objects, prohibitions and words—are compared to competitive hunters and the victim to a hunting ground. The fate of good and ill health is as cyclical or reversible as the fate of time: the day never fails to emerge from the night. The flow of life inevitably leads through both bright and dark, warm and cold phases. One's fatal ill or state of entanglement is the work of a nightly plot. While tracing down the intricacies of the social fabric, the diviner never adopts the vertical stance of the paramount ruler who in the name of law arbitrates conflicts with authority. Facing the diviner—who can be a woman or a man—the consultants sit in a semicircle (see plate 5). Drawing on the basic metaphors of divination, the oracular discourse is to be seen as a weaving from the womb, speaking the message of the uterine life flow and ancestors and spirits. But the diviner disavows authorship of vision and pretends that whatever he or she is voicing is initiated by the rhythm of the slit gong—an icon of the 'vaginal mouth'—and stems from the dreamlike vision received in sleep. The cowrie shells on the diviner's front, her gong, and her trancelike behavior—like a hen that lays an egg—all suggest that the oracle is borne as clairvoyance in the diviner's heart, and further elaborated as a message coming from the diviner's belly. The shape of the slit gong is both womblike and phalluslike, and it is considered "the diviner's very image" *(yidiimbu kyaandi);* the set of three cowrie shells—a vaginal symbol—is called *diisu dyangoombu,* "the divining eye." It is in her or his body that the diviner appears as the androgynous agent and locus of the uterine flow of life, the metaphorising author and scene of rebirthing of meaning. The metaphors of weaving, of life-bearing, and of childbirth underlie the divinatory seance and pattern the whole plot. The consultants are ultimately made into an audience of the uterine rule of (matrimonial) exchange that underpins the never-ending flow of life in the body in resonance with the life-world. The oracle is the voice of the self-reliant uterine life flow from which the individual taps in both good and ill health.

Clairvoyant divining that serves as a voice of the self-maintenance of the uterine flow of life differs from the authoritative speech in the council of elders, as uterine filiation differs from agnatic descent. The divinatory oracle is not a discourse of truth and a verdict concerning social rules of right; unlike the judicial council, it is not an exercise of redressive power or domination. In naming deviancy in the rules of exchange and reciprocity, it does ask not so much for redress but for growth, healing, or 'whole-making.' Divining and council, uterine and agnatic are seen as pairs in some kind of solidarity, and they are compared to the way palm wine and tonics are the necessary adjuvants of the speaker and drummer for speech or rhythm to become forceful and compelling. During the nine months of initiatory seclusion, the diviner-to-be should feed him- or herself mainly with cola nut and palm wine, drinking it from the slit gong. The diviner's word is one of life-bearing fermentation that, when conveyed to the consultants, impels them to tap in their turn from the uterine life source and to arouse growth in their group. The divinatory oracle may unmask the elders' pretense to authoritative power and their self-serving manoeuvres for taking the goods and lives of their descendants. Divining recalls for the public how much the uterine flow of life is a maturational process that escapes full agnatic and patriarchal dominion: life's inner and passionate impetus vitalizes the social weave. The diviner acts as a master-hunter who tracks down the nightly plots and thereby sets the conditions to convert the sorcerous hunt into a life-bearing one. He is the antipode of the nocturnal hunt on which the sorcerer embarks. Unmasked and reversed, the aggression is turned and focused on the sorcerer himself. Following his verdict, the diviner summons the person accused of sorcery to add charcoal—the mark of sorcery—to his gunpowder. If the firearm loaded for this purpose actually kills the prey at the first shot, "the head of the downed animal is irrefutable proof" *(n-twa mbiimbi)* that the accused has himself commissioned or committed a fatal ensorcellment. In other words, the diurnal hunt may unmask the nocturnal one, and the game, conversely, sets the initial conditions for the renewal of commensality between the families of accused and victim.

5.1 Masculinist Views on Human Agencies in Infertility

Popular opinion and ridicule confirm patriarchal views on life transmission. The bridegroom's patrikin enters into a matrimonial alliance with the aim of acquiring rights to the woman's fertility and over the couple's offspring. Delayed fertility is severely censured by members of the couple's hamlet who charge, above all, that their quest for "florescence and fruit" *(mboongu*—a term which denotes also offspring) is a poor harvest of mere agricultural produce rather than of fruit of the womb. In this respect the names given to a child born after a long wait are revealing. Sometimes they include a nickname given to that member of the couple believed to be infertile:

Kabutaaku, "she doesn't produce."
Khobu, "the impotent one."
Mboongu, "harvest": for long the mother's sole contribution to the marriage was merely in the field and in the house.
Sela makhondu, "father of the banana plants": the father had to content himself with growing banana plants while hopelessly waiting for offspring.
N-ledi myakhatwa, "pointless finery": after several years only did the bridewealth issue in offspring.
Kamonaaku, "for long, she still hasn't seen one": the mothers saw her first child born after several years of marriage.
Yibandulula, "I've tried a number of times": the newlywed suffered several miscarriages.
Wusamwasana, "the one people talk about": the name of a child whose parents' infertility was subject of gossip.

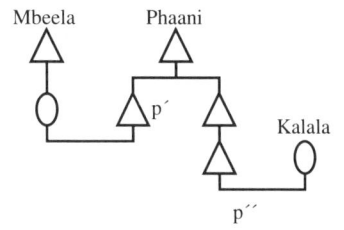

Figure 1. Circulation of Bridewealth

Those who concluded the matrimonial alliance are the first to act should reproduction be impeded. After the husband's mother has alerted the head of the homestead that conception is overdue, the family head may convene the husband, the patriarch, and a male representative of the woman. First of all they examine the antecedents and the specific circumstances of the alliance. Had some essential step or formality been forgotten? Perhaps some payment still had to be made, or additional portions of the bridewealth *(biloombi)* and other matrimonial gifts had not been handed over to the woman's family. Or perhaps the young couple, by intrusively coming to live together in the homestead, encroached *(yidyaata)* on the very means of intimate insertion—meals, hearth, bed, odors—and as a result have corrupted their own conjugal union. It is also possible that the alliance between the kin of bride-givers and bride-takers had once been banned, or that the goods exchanged in the interests of the alliance were 'stained' or corrupted.

Elders in the agnatic group see infertility very much as a casus belli, as both an effect and point of dissension and retaliation. To give some idea of the kind and the intricacy of the discord which these family elders bring to the fore I shall first of all summarize the etiological argument of a case of infertility as established in the course of a family council. I shall then retrace in schematic form the various stages of the treatment arising from this palaver (see fig. 1).

The case of infertility, as put before the council of agnatic family elders, concerns a young girl of Kalala patrilineage married to a boy (P″) of Phaani lineage: the Kalala girl was slow to become pregnant. Patriarch Phaani reports that in order to remove the impediment to the fertility of the in-married Kalala girl, he turned to the Mbeela lineage, to whom the boy's father was allied, and requested a "goat for the prohibition." Indeed, the Mbeela woman had died a few years ago and shortly after she had joined the boy's father as his third cowife.

In his report on the divinatory oracle, patriarch Phaani only mentions that the Mbeela woman's fathers were alleged to have ensorcelled her and brought about her death. Moreover, before her death, the woman had uttered a curse on her paternal forebears. Thereafter the Phaani widower (P′) had not only rejected a replacement marriage with a sister of the deceased but also had called for repayment of the bridewealth he had offered in order to marry the Mbeela woman who now had been ensorcelled to death due to her fathers' initiative. Once this bridewealth was returned to the Phaani lineage, the patriarch had transferred it to the Kalala group in view of marrying his grandson (P″). According to the divinatory oracle, "this bridewealth the Kalala group had received was bloodstained" *(n-teti bakusidimya meenga)* because the Mbeela lineage, after having already received the bridewealth in return for their daughter's marriage, had reappropriated her life through sorcery. By shedding the blood of their victim, the sorcerers had stained the bridewealth they had received at their daughter's marriage. As a result, the curse the Mbeela daughter had uttered against the sorcerers also fell upon the bridewealth, just as it formed, literally, "a threat from the deceased" *(yindaanda kyambvuumbi)* to the various persons involved in the subsequent remittal of that bloodstained bridewealth to the Kalala group. The bridewealth under the threat of the curse acted as a trap: the Kalala girl was exposed to the same sort of fatal illness which struck the Mbeela woman. The bridewealth that patriarch Phaani handed over for the marriage of his grandson with a daughter of Kalala bore misfortune: the girl's infertility was proof of the corruption of the alliance.

The agnatic elders sought to restore fertility through social redress. It was their view that the removal of any debt, curse, or 'trap' ought to clear the field of life transmission. The case just mentioned depicts the essence of the social procedures intended to restore fertility or to remove the hindrance to it. Certain conditions need to be met for the fatal curse to be lifted. According to the Yaka idiom, the sorcerer—in this case, the Mbeela lineage—must "pay the proprietor of the deceased [her uncle] for the victim they ate." Thereafter, the Mbeela lineage must in some way increase and thereby revalorize the bridewealth they had abused. By giving several goats and other goods to the Phaani, the Mbeela first of all compensate for the "blood which had stained the bridewealth": this compensation is known as the "goat for the prohibition," so as to restate the rule against murderous ensorcellment. Moreover, the Mbeela have to compensate the damage suffered by the Phaani husband because of the loss of his young wife and to repair all the ill caused by the bloodstained bridewealth. Once such compensation has been paid and now that the curse has fallen upon its victim, the curse itself no longer has any point; it can then be lifted. The uncle and the ritual expert of the cult invoked for the curse are invited to go to the grave of the Mbeela woman who had uttered the curse; there they proclaim that justice has been done and call upon the deceased to renounce her vengeance. On his return in the homestead, in the victim's name, the uncle addresses the various parties involved. He offers the Phaani elder a number of hens so that he, in turn, can address himself to the Kalala girl. The Phaani patriarch offers her a hen to compensate for the wrong already done her by the curse; then he hands over a second, which will take her out of the power of the curse, while saying:

> Taa khoku. Kola.
> Taa khoku dyaaka, lubuka,
> nge meni yuzeeyi n-taanduku.
> Muutu basya n-sasu, buko bwamwana yakala.
> Nge, kan-saswa ngeyiku.
>
> Here is a hen. May your health be strengthened.
> Here is yet another hen; escape from this curse,
> because we are not of a common uterine ascendancy.
> This curse has been cast by the in-laws of your husband's father.
> The curse has nothing to do with you.

All these acts may involve a great many other dealings depending on the success or failure of the hunt which is set up to augur any further step.

Nondivinatory or popular etiology of infertility, as it is elaborated in council by the husband's elders, restricts its scrutiny to the latter's patrikin. My comparison of the case reported with other ones confirms that nondivinatory etiology with regard to fertility problems pays privileged attention to the patrilineage of the husband, which is of course most interested in ensuring that the alliance be fertile. Given the fact that a gynecological disorder in itself does not constitute sufficient reason for divorce, action is the responsibility of the husband's patrikin among whom the woman whose fertility is hampered is living. It would also seem that this popular examination always brings up the same argument. Somewhere among patrilinear forebears, some alliances remained sterile as a result of a divorce, a gynecological disorder, or death due to sorcery. Very specific circumstances had left their mark on this divorce, illness, death, or restitution of the bridewealth. In the case of a subsequent marriage of a patrilinear descendant anything which serves as a reminder of one of these circumstances can indicate that the present situation is analogous to the past one. In order to remove this obstacle to fertility and prevent its fatal repetition, the reason for the previous evil must be paid out or levied, as well as the cause of the present and similar evil. Moreover, treatment calls for requital of the harm wrought by the sterility both in the past and in the present. Last but not least, it is important to heal the disunion within the present kin to prevent its being a reminder and thereby a presage of misfortune.

Popular etiology to a large extent pertains to the agnatic domain where relationships are coercively subject to the rules of respect, seniority, and power.

Councils reproduce the fabric of seniority and the imperative rule to share income with the elders; they report how negligence of ancestor worship or tensions within the hamlet—for example, because of jealousy, insubordination or lack of respect, sexual abuse, the failure to share income or the booty of the hunt—inevitably anger the elders and the agnatic ancestors. The anger will fall upon a descendant in his social disposition or attribution: either he will lose his self-control, or he will have mental problems, and yet again his marriage might be childless, or he will constantly return from the hunt empty handed. Even if popular interpretations of misfortune reach beyond the sociologic, they rapidly develop into linear, causal, and deterministic explanations. Elders may claim either that the affliction is a direct retaliation by cult spirits for the wrong that had been committed by some forebears or that a family quarrel led the elders to reassert their authority and rights through ensorcellment. Jealously, envy, offended honor, and anger are seen as the motives for malevolent vengeance or ensorcellment.

In the intimacy of the home, in contrast, a couple confronting an illness will apply remedies that directly concern their bodies rather than issues of oratory, ideology, and power. In the case of delayed fertility, reproduction or 'propagation' is ritually anticipated by forms of vaginal rinse that may arouse sexual desire. The husband seeks to bestow fertility on his wife by symbolically conveying an 'offshoot' to her: he gives her leaves from a parasitic plant, and she takes the prepared infusion as a vaginal rinse, literally "drinking it." This is a well-defined usage, and it may be repeated during the second or third month of pregnancy. At dawn the husband goes into the forest or savanna and gathers a parasitic plant, *yikhundakhunda,* which grows on the branches of certain trees. He climbs up into one of these trees, undresses, gathers the plant, and descends before he dresses again. In the evening, the woman boils the parasitic plant and in the conjugal home administers the lukewarm liquid as a vaginal rinse. As with any rinse or enema, she lies on her back and administers the concoction by means of a gourd with a long thin neck. This practice may evoke the marital act, for which the couple prefer to undress and the wife to lie on her back. Commentaries develop a homonymy between the name of the parasitical plant and the verb *-kuunda,* "to catch, to hold back," which also is a reminder of this plant's capacity to breed and root itself in the tree; the expression "a plant which is implanted in and breeding upon another" is a more faithful translation of the term *yikhundakhunda* than "parasite." The plant acquires an even more specific meaning in the context of the usage I have just described. Indeed, if we consider the sexual significance evoked by the sun at daybreak and the gourd—in other contexts, as well, the latter symbolizes the vagina and the uterus—we can see that the vaginal douche and this parasitical plant gathered by the husband refer to the role of the woman in the marital act. The meaning thus brought forth is that of the successful propagation and gestation of life freed from the threat of accidental abortion and in tune with generative processes in the life-world and cosmos.[2]

5.2 Divinatory Etiology and the Work of Cults

Serious and lasting gynecological disorders are brought before the oracle of the clairvoyant diviner in the *ngoombu* cult (see 4.4.1; also plate 5). I base the following discussion upon a detailed analysis of twenty-six oracles related to gynecological disorders, compared with some two hundred other oracles in related domains. Most of these oracles took place in rural Kwaango, although some twenty were conducted in Kinshasa.

Using an etiological grid, the oracle addresses the complex intricacies between the physical ailment, the family politics of fertility, and concomitant disorder in the life-world. In short, the oracle lays bare the way in which the webs of kin and marriage tie in or unbind the afflicted. The diviner seeks to discern the points of likeness between the present disorder and an abuse of rule, or an illness, or an anomaly which in former generations might have struck the descent groups—and especially the uterine one—of the sick woman. The oracle reads the present in the light of the past and vice versa in terms of prohibitions that may have been broken and curses that, within the framework of a cult, call for retaliation. Because the diviner is able to voice his own dreams, and hence to reveal some of the patient's dreams, as well as to unravel the nightly plots of sorcerers, his etiological reading of the case proves very singular and compelling.

A *first* etiological assumption at play in divination regards the uterine life source from which the great-grandmother taps and from whence physical life flows down in the uterine line *(yikheetu)*. It invokes the principle that life and its innate qualities *(yibutukulu)* are passed down to the individual by the mother, from her maternal grandmother and great-grandmother.

The *second* etiological assumption concerns the basic consensual rules or prohibitions *(tsiku)* that regard the propagation of the uterine flow of life in the matrimonial alliance and for the social benefit of the patridescent. These rules are at play in the uterine line as a means of consolidating the flow of life and its passing down through matrimonial alliance across blood communities. The rules are like an impersonal voice that states the minimal conditions for the uterine flow of life to be life-bearing. Any infringement of rights, or any offense which seriously and unjustifiably hinders the transmission of life or its flowering, is said "to kill or pervert the rule or prohibition" *(-hoonda tsiku)*. Just as flower is linked to fruit, it is supposed that any infringement that hampers physical life calls for and links up with redress; in the same way life ceaselessly atones and revives from within itself, as the rules of exchange at the base of the social fabric speak for and mend themselves. Sorcery or illicit sexual relations, that is, conduct in the homestead which infringes on the rights of the married couple and spoils or hampers fertility, are stereotypically labeled theft in ritual as well as in popular idiom. According to the oracle, a serious illness stems from a theft committed by a uterine forebear. To the extent that the oracle concerns facts of the past, their bearing is not so much measured by their objective or exhaustive enquiry but rather by the hermeneutic value of the oracle's showing how present facts of life respond to deeds from the past.

A *third* register of divinatory etiology relates to the question of why an affliction has struck this particular individual instead of someone else, in other words, why the personal history of the afflicted has converged with that of some former "track of offenses in the family and their trap—that is, the retaliation called for by a curse—along the path to the village." According to divinatory etiology, the victim of a distant misdeed will have uttered a curse *(n-sasu)* condemning the evildoer and his uterine descendants to bear the appropriate affliction. Such a curse persists in the uterine descent of both the author and the evildoer: it fosters the intervention of a cult and its spiritual agencies, that is, of an agency of revenge capable of driving its prey as does the hunting dog. This etiological register holds that affliction will befall the original wrongdoer or anyone of his uterine offspring who may attempt a similar misdeed: that deed will be deflected upon them—they will 'aim' a wrong at another but end up hitting themselves. It also establishes that the maternal kin of the victim also experience a similar affliction, if they ignore the separation and wrong, by allying again with the wrongdoer as if nothing had happened.

The divinatory etiology closes off with a verdict and a sentence: one of the parties—the agnates, or the uterine kin of the first generation, for example—is accused of sorcery or of an offense that has reactivated a past curse. Blame may be laid as well on the other party—perhaps the uterines of the second ascendant generation—for their having angered the first generation. The sentence regards a sacrifice, restitution, contact with an uncle, in particular the great-granduncle, or a cult that must be organized.

Among the uncles of the afflicted it is the great-granduncle who stands for the origin of the rules and prohibitions regarding matrimony; he therefore also represents the cradle of forces and ethical axioms from whence the curse's persecutive action stems since a curse calls upon the self-governance of these rules. He possesses this authority because he represents for society the point of origin of the transmission of life and the web of life-bearing of which the afflicted is part. The curse that is passed down through the uterine line acts as a trap, that is, as a kind of self-supporting threat within the uterine tradition. The resurgence of the curse, that is, the hereditary effect that acts as a trap, is ritually neutralized within this same tradition. The synergy entailing infringement or offense, curse, persecution, affliction, misfortune, and consequently the ritual management of the misfortune thus constitutes a cult.

Divining, by referring to cults and curses, confirms how much good and ill health, like flowering and decay, are reverse sides and phases of the same flow of life. In every uterine line of descent, the curses uttered—like the wrong that they avenge or the distressing consequences they might eventually bring— depend on one or another cult. Cults safeguard and stimulate the blossoming of life, but do so in a negational or homeopathic manner by self-destructively reversing some hereditary ailments that seriously hamper the flow of life. Curses too aim at turning evil into good health and are compared to a trap in which the game that is caught frees its life-giving force through rotting— which is associated with fermentation considered as a masculine form of cooking. They represent the persecutive side of a prohibition, whose infringement is avenged by affliction; such infringement leads to persecution and finally to redress. Prohibitions are the self-reliant 'voice' of the uterine flow of life that by its very vitality seeks to overcome hindrance or impairment. Ill health is decay, good health is florescence rather than individual achievement: both ill or good health occurs, befalls to someone. Cults constitute the moral framework to conceive of how prohibitions exert life's self-reliance, that is, how curses reassert uterine life transmission by calling on retaliation for major offenses that have choked off the uterine flow of life. Through their persecutive attribution, cults provide an etiological framework of the illness, and consequently a therapeutic framework: curing the victim of such a curse and its effects amounts to initiating the ailing person into the corresponding cult. Each of these cults brings together, across lineage boundaries, all the initiates who have undergone a cure; as a result, throughout Kwaango land there are a great many translinear networks of initiates (cf. 4.3). Fertility problems and congenital deformities are almost always—although not exclusively—related to the cult of *khita:* both the gynecological disorder and its cure are manifestations of *khita.*

Divinatory etiology traces the evil in the life of the sufferer and the webs of kin, as well as in relation to the fundamental order of exchange that underscores life transmission; it locates the disorder in the resonance within and between the fields of body, group, and life-world. The oracle will blame the self-seeking or treacherous behavior of family elders, on the one hand, and point to the self-governance of the uterine flow of life through curse, affliction, and cult, on the other. A gynecological impairment can arise from the fact that the patient has been involved in a confusion of conjugal hearths, in other words, from some strain or infringement with regard to the frontiers of the domestic and corporal spaces of the couple, as I mentioned above. Moreover, the patient may have been cut off from the source of life because an uncle has given up his avuncular care. The woman may be afflicted by an ailment in precisely the same way as a uterine ascendant who was also the victim of a similar confusion of hearths, or of some form of familial intrusion or rupture.

This *khita* curse links the present ailment to the past one. Like the distortion of conjugal frontiers, the disorder is perceived as having denatured the corporal frontiers in some way. Since the body is no longer capable of being simultaneously a confined space and a place of exchange, it either becomes excessively "closed" or completely "incontinent." The victim is seen as suffering from some kind of impediment imposed from the outside, hindering or preventing her from conceiving or bearing life. As I shall demonstrate later, the link established between the past and the present misfortune arises less from reasoning in terms of empirical causality but rather from a metaphorically meaningful interconnecting of past and present, of body, group, and life-world. I call this form of interconnecting the hermeneutics of structural causality.

The divinatory oracle ascribes the gynecological affliction or problem to several forms of offense or infringement.

First, the problem is ascribed to some form of infringement of or offense against a prohibition. The wrongdoings most commonly brought out in the oracle are adultery, sorcery, and infractions of avuncular duties or rights. Five of the twenty-six oracles revealed that the infertility was preceded by adultery. Three of these oracles stated that these extramarital affairs led to an ensorcellment: either the man with whom the woman was having an adulterous affair hinders fertility out of vengeance on the woman for her having regained the conjugal shell, or the betrayed husband ensorcells those of his brothers who have trespassed on his conjugal bed. The two other oracles reported that the woman failed to ritually cleanse the adultery and prevent a rupture from occurring; consequently, she herself suffered from closure or effusion. Indeed, the woman should have offered ritual compensation for the offense to her uncles (cf. 3.3). By omitting this, she has failed to acknowledge their avuncular role. In one of the cases, the uncles did not protect the 'unclosed' woman from exposure to the retaliatory logic of curse and cult; in the other case, the uncles condemned the adulterous woman; literally, they victimized her as "a gift" *(kabu)*. In other words, they ensorcelled her to compensate for a "debt of the night." Other oracles—a third of the total—attribute the patient's wasting illness to the "uncles who entered the affair and took their portion of prey, and are gnawing her away."

According to divinatory etiology, uncles may abuse their position in several ways. It can happen that the primary uncle, or the granduncle, passed on ritual gifts and tonics to his sister's daughter or granddaughter within the framework of a cult for which he has received no mandate from the great-granduncle, or to which he was not entitled. By failing to address himself to the great-granduncle and to share the benefits arising from the exercise of the avuncular role, the uncle who abuses his avuncular position is considered a thief. The oracle sees this abuse of rights as prejudicial to the uterine offspring and likens it to sorcery. It can also happen that the uncle and the granduncle were guilty of the death of a uterine descendant through ensorcellment. By omitting to pay the necessary compensation for this murder to the victim's great-granduncle, the primary uncle and granduncle lose their avuncular rights and corrupt the uterine ties they stand for. If, however, they further abuse their position by dispensing ritual tonics and prevent the competent uncle from administering these, they share responsibility for the illness or even the victim's death. For this reason, any abuse in the exercise of the avunculate equals sorcery.

Second, gynecological affliction, in particular in its symptoms of effusion or incontinence, is attributed, in a third of the relevant oracles, to the encroachment of conjugal bounds: *yidyaata*. Indeed, it can happen that a novice or patient resumes marital union without loosening the vital bond with her initiator or healer, or that the newlywed reaches the conjugal home without having been dismissed from under the paternal roof. The one who did not sever her conjugal ties at her partner's death or at divorce, and similarly the one who has omitted to announce the marriage to his or her uncle, is considered liable to a similar encroachment.

Third, a number of oracles accuse the elders of the afflicted woman of having drawn misfortune upon her as the result of their contradicting the curse they had uttered to protect the woman. They turned the curse against the woman by "sharing the fire and meals anew" with those they had cursed, thus denying the fact that the curse was founded on family rupture. Many other kinds of machinations, ill will, envy, and pollution are moreover considered to channel forces among people and lead to breakdown of health.

5.3 Etiology as an Indication of Therapy

When a newly wed woman is slow to become pregnant, remains troubled by heavy or painful menstruation, or fails to menstruate, it is said that this "woman has been hampered" *(n-kheetu wabiindemene)*. Divinatory etiology stresses the dimension of impediment, entanglement, or effusion of the body in gynecological ailments and birth difficulties, including interruptions of pregnancy due to accidental abortions or premature birth, stillbirth, or the death of an infant before the mother has become pregnant again. Since the latter are generally considered more serious and alarming, they are at once placed before the divinatory oracle. The transmission of life constitutes the principle reason for a matrimonial alliance and it is through childbearing and -rearing that a married woman succeeds her mother, thus binding herself to the former generations from mothers to great-grandmothers in the uterine line, that is, to those who have transmitted life from a common source. Socially, gynecological ailments are therefore considered as problems bearing on the matrimonial alliance and uterine life transmission. As for the impaired, she is seen as suffering from an impediment afflicting her from outside, some illness that gnaws away at her *(yibeefu kin-diidi)*, that binds her in *(yibiinda)*, and that hinders or prevents *(-biindama)* her from childbearing. In other words, the council of elders or the divinatory oracle pays little heed to the physical symptoms as such. The etiological enquiry is in fact a means of probing the matrimonial alliance and the basics of family life and world order, in particular the web of uterine ties that link the sick to other uterine kin who tap from the same source of life.

Divinatory etiology regarding fertility or birth disorders principally scrutinizes the extent to which the matrimonial alliance and the web of uterine ties are ill fated because of self-serving elders, offense, or curse. On the couple's side, the transfers of matrimonial goods, their circumstances, and their antecedents, as well as the proper boundedness of the conjugal cell are all examined. With regard to the woman's uterine filiation, the succession of alliances in the generations of great-grandmother to mother, each of which conditions the one succeeding it, are studied, as is the degree to which the gifts the uncles may or may not have received: they remind them of their task to pass down the uterine flow of life. The oracle may point to a recent offense against the rights and the obligations of the bride-givers and -takers, of wife and husband, of the uncle and sisters's daughter, of the patriarch and the in-married wife.

The oracle may disclose acts of sorcery or of any other ill-fated infringement on the conjugal space that seriously hamper fertility. The couple thereby gets caught in the 'trap' that a uterine forebear has set by his curse following an intrusion, abuse, or spiteful act of a similar kind. Proffered in the uterine descent, this curse resolutely threatens the uterine offspring as a whole. In other words, divinatory interpretation apparently operates by means of a kind of structural redundancy which entwines rule, offense, and affliction in a common logic of persecution. Bride-givers and bride-takers share a common project of life transmission for matrimonial goods; it is the very ground and reason of their mutual relations. Offense—ensorcellment of offspring, lack of matrimonial compensations, adultery, infringement of the taboos the wife's father conferred to the offspring—calls for persecution and redress, since life requires to be transmitted and flourish.

The assumptions on which divinatory etiology draws similarly inform a curse: they imply a kind of structural causality. A curse draws on a fundamental—implicit, hence optimistic—axiom that good and ill health, life and death, regeneration and destruction interrelate like right and left hands, and that to the extent that life equals gift, life outreaches death, society creates and overcomes its forces of destruction. A curse consists of invoking the inevitable application of persecution and revenge, if there truly has been theft, that is, offense against the rules of exchange or reciprocity (see Devisch 1981). The following injunctions render in shortened version the steps in cursing:

If it were not true that he who has stolen falls ill, then, if I myself have stolen, may I fall ill or die.

Even if I have taken nothing from the one who has stolen my property, and if it were true that I am not indebted to him, then may he who has stolen my property fall ill.

In the uterine line, it is the rule of exchange which governs the transmission and the blossoming of life. In return for the bridewealth and regular gifts throughout her reproductive life, a wife is ceded to the husband's group to bear and elevate offspring. Acts that are injurious to this exchange—theft, ensorcellment, and sexual abuse, also labeled theft by ritual idiom—create both social disunion and physical symptoms that threaten the body's capacity to give and take. The curse clarifies the axiom by first assuming an unescapable link between theft and persecution: the one who utters the curse provides a guarantee by calling down upon himself an automatic persecution should he himself have stolen. In an analogous manner, he affirms that the culprit cannot escape persecution if he really has stolen, that is, if he perpetrated a wrong without having a legitimate provocation for doing so.[3] It is equally implied that the curse will turn against the protected party if the curse is false, when the author himself has taken part in the accursed deed, or when those who are protected duly reestablish fellowship with the accursed party.

Concretely, both the divinatory oracle and the curse order facts of life according to the structural hermeneutics interlinking rules of exchange, prohibition, offense or infringement, curse, persecution, affliction, and death. The oracle thereby enunciates a fundamental narrative or story of inevitable recurrence in social life: it is the story of the existential interdependence of kinsmen—through marriage, offspring, or descent—that always will reassert itself, of life overcoming restraints, of evil calling for retaliation, of reciprocity in life transmission constantly restating itself. The narrative unfolds an axiomatic paradigm or a set of principles taken for granted regarding the social fabric. It does as yet not have the outspoken and socially coercive character of law which, I would contend, comes into being only with the institution of the sovereign ruler and associated court. By applying this structural paradigm (regarding exchange—prohibition—offense—curse—persecution) to the problem placed before it, the divination makes no judgment with regard to moral responsibility, but it does permit a hermeneutical reading of various constituent elements of the situation of misfortune. By relating the past and the present, which reveals the reason for the misfortune to be recurrent, the oracle, moreover, sets the social scene for the therapeutic intervention to happen. In other words, according to divinatory etiology, there is talk of a binding rule or, more properly, of an offense as long as there is misfortune that harms the group interests and that was caused by the retaliatory action issuing from a curse.

Second, and moreover, a palaver or oracle should have judged the evil act to be illicit or unfounded, that is, infringing. The threat of further retaliation ceases when justice is done through the oracle and indemnification offered by the wrongdoer to the wronged party. Divinatory etiology, like the curse, consists of recording anew the narrative of misdeeds in the family, from the first affliction it has caused and the curse it has provoked, to the chain of subsequent misdeeds and retaliations.

The etiology of divination and cursing subjects evil deeds to the self-sustaining rule of exchange, which by its very nature urges continuance and is itself a condition for the transmission of life. The divinatory oracle registers a sequence of contingent facts in an order of first appearance. Parallel to this, the oracle—like the curse—deals with facts that have eluded the uterine and matrimonial circuits of social reciprocity and reintroduces them into an order of discourse which the oracle implements by its public declarations and symbolic function. Through its assumptions regarding the primacy of exchange and their contextual application for the etiological scrutiny, in other words through the symbolic function and foundational discourse which the diviner and the clients exercise publicly in the fashion laid down by tradition, the oracle achieves its aim: the reintegration of a disorder into the order of discourse and exchange that forms the basis of life in society.

The value system that underpins divination is also at stake in the therapeutic approach, such that the aim of the cure is to reenact these values. The singular case history of evil and its retaliation in the family particularizes only the initial stage of the cure in the course of which agnates, uterine kin, and in-laws redefine and renegotiate their mutual relations and their ties with the afflicted person. The other stages surpass the single case history and concern more the body of the afflicted and the cosmology of life transmission.

The divinatory oracle relativises its own etiology and leaves room for individual freedom and genuine initiative in the moral space. Given that it establishes multiple links between the illness and various social and axiological (cosmological) registers of meaning, the oracle domesticates the doom of destiny, or the fatal nature of the disorder: its antecedents are both many and reducible. Let us recall the various kinds of situation which are linked together: illness or misfortune, social disorganization, and the rule of exchange that underpins the uterine transmission of life. All this is related to prohibitions, offenses, curses, and persecutions, for which, moreover, cults provide an adequate institutional framework. The multiple nature of the etiological levels and argument underscores the value of the diagnosis should the treatment fail. For example, if an initial intervention applied by the uncle proves ineffective, a whole network of other factors—such as curse, offense, or inheritance "of debts of the night" from father to son or uncle to nephew—could come to the rescue. In other words, a treatment which fails does not invalidate the etiological model or the divinatory art. It demonstrates that the etiological enquiry is inadequate because it is incomplete or vitiated by the duplicity of the consultants to the oracle who, knowingly, have neglected or violated the procedure at consultation. Another divination should follow.

When it comes to unmasking the evil and its antecedents, the etiological interpretation of the disorder contributes in a number of ways to redress the situation and to recovery.

First, the etiology has linked the fertility disorder to a disorganization within the alliance and the uterine relationships. The therapy is therefore set up as a ritualized drama in which the representatives of the alliance and the uterine descent are actively involved. They reintegrate the afflicted woman in the uterine descent and reinstitute her in her conjugal role of life-bearer. At the same time, when linking the affliction to an evil which took place in the past, the etiology prescribes compensation for this evil. It allows for the *khita* curse to be lifted and the persecution affecting the sterile woman to be neutralized.

Second, the oracle authoritatively sets up the scene for the healing intervention by reading the bodily affliction of closure, entanglement, and effusion in line with wickedness and self-serving conduct, or with breaks and revenge in the social body. It moreover connects all this with the life-world of fundamental values and spiritual agencies that link up, as in a spiral movement, misdeed, curse, persecution, and affliction. By giving little heed to the somatic dimension of the affliction, but widening the scope, the oracle may contribute to temper the anxiety of the couple and close kin. In fact, the oracle anticipatively sets the scene for the subsequent healing that leads the woman to metaphorically identify with processes in the group and the world that sustain life-bearing.

Third, the divinatory etiology somehow recycles what first appeared as social deviancy into a cosmological disorder. The woman's disorderly conduct and loss of tools, or her husband's hunting accidents, announce a disorder in the physical and cosmological body. The disorder, loss, or accidents may be caused by cult spirits eager to become honored. They foreshadow an illness that will urge the patient to seek help in a cult and to develop an alliance with the spirit. The patient is considered a hunting ground involving elders, ancestral shades, cult spirits, and those of the kin whose neglect or hostility contributed to the couple's marginalization. The divinatory oracle reintegrates the sufferer and her life-world into the moral community. But, since there is no accusation of fault, the oracle—unlike the prophet in healing churches (see Devisch and Vervaeck 1985)—does not set the scene for a therapy as part of a salvation history.

The divinatory seance is itself a first and major step in the healing intervention. In the *khita* cure that may follow, the patient is made further the center of attention by the family elders, household, and local community. At the end of her period of seclusion she is brought back within the sphere of domestic and conjugal life empowered to more fully inhabit her body and life-world. The whole therapeutic drama further displaces the obsessions with gynecological failure and with the persecutive elders and cult spirits, and enhances the experience of body and life transmission through incorporating the potent mysteries of "florescence and fruit" in the life-world.

6

The *Khita* Fertility Cult
Reversing the Evil

The principal cure for gynecological disorders—both for infertility and for what is considered anomalous birth—takes place within the context of the *khita* cult. *Yiphasi,* literally "the place of both enhancement and diminution, excitement and suffering," designates the whole of the cure in the *khita* cult. There are two main movements, one redressive and one emancipatory. The redressive intervention comprises the several weeks needed to raise the support of the kin group and invite the healer, and it culminates on the evening the patient goes into seclusion. On that evening, the *khita* patient is led to reverse the persecutive forces at work in the kin group—namely the ensorcellment and curse she has been suffering from—into bonds that channel again the uterine life flow. The *khita* cure brings to the fore and aims at domesticating a betwixt and between world, namely *hita,* "the suffering, the monstrous, what is genderless and untamed," also associated with the blurring of night and dark forest. The intervention strikes fear into the world of the monstrous and expels it from among the kin group. Moreover, by acting on the connections between people and world at the interstices of space and time, the therapeutic initiation leads the patient out of the maze of dualisms and contrarieties in which her fertility is entangled. For the local community, the onset of the cure is an occasion for uncensored, transgressive, and joyful dance and song at dusk at the edge of village space.

Following the redressive intervention and initial capturing of forces, the emancipatory action may start: it concerns the seclusion proper—a dimension studied in chapter 7—which may last from a few weeks to several months. The seclusion develops into a cosmogenetic drama that leads to the patient's ritual rebirth and capturing of new forces in resonance with similar processes in the group and life-world.

There is a difference between cultic enhancement of male and female fertility, which reflects the doubly unilineal descent in Yaka society. Masculinist discourse primarily associates infertility and physical handicap with the uterine line. *Khita* is in some respect a parallel to the *n-khanda,* which is a communal cult for the social transformation of the newly circumcised that is called upon to assure the continuity of the patriline and virile values. Indeed all the men of the group share the role of reproducing patrilineal descent. Agnatic descent is a collective and hierarchically ordered good surpassing individual ill, wickedness, or impairment. Uttering a curse to harm male fertility is considered devoid of sense, since it endangers the further social reproduction of the group and thereby deflates one's social self. Conversely, it is through his mother and uterine forebears that a person taps the lifeblood or vital flow in a most individual way from the uterine life source. It is through the matriline that innate traits and agencies, like persecutive curses and deadly ensorcellment, befall the individual. It is also the woman and the bride-givers who are primarily brought into question whenever a couple remains sterile.[1] Both the flowering and the deterioration of physical life, which is both self-sustaining and vulnerable or needful, mark the fundamentally cyclical flow of life between uterus and fetus, between grandmother, mother, and child, as well as between the phases of day, moon, season, and vegetation.

6.1 *Khita* and Similar Cults

In the Koongo area, *khita* has been documented as an ancestral or spirit cult for the fertility of women and the land under the guardianship of particular landowning lineages. The notion of *khita* (and related forms *kita, nkita, nkira, nkit*, etc.) can be found over a vast geographic expanse covering the ancient Kingdom of Koongo and the surrounding area. According to Georges Balandier (1965:216–69), the *kimpasi* (a term equivalent to *yiphasi*) was well known throughout the Koongo kingdom in the seventeenth century. As initiation in the *nkita* cult, the *kimpasi* rites aimed at connecting the living and their world with the original fertility of the primordial couple further impersonated by the *nkita* or founding lineage ancestors (1965:50).[2] Regarding the Ntaandu, Mbata, and Mpaangu, all eastern Koongo peoples, Joseph Van Wing (1920, 1938:ch. 6–8) was a witness to the *kimpasi* devoted to *nkita,* those first ancestors of the Koongo who had died violent deaths. The ancestor cult aimed to enhance fertility and resistance to disease and death. *Nkita* appears in the central and western parts of Koongo land as a cult of affliction particularly addressed to fertility-related troubles, mental and epileptic disturbances, and swellings anywhere on the body. These ailments are attributed to certain spirits associated either with the guardianship of the inhabited areas or with certain "pools and falls" (Bittremieux 1936:153; Buakasa 1973:158–63, 212–20; Dupré 1975; Janzen 1978:213; MacGaffey 1986:101). *Nkita* is a cult belonging to the chiefly lineages. Initiating new members in each generation acts as a regeneration of the principal institutions of the group—political power, seniority, life transmission through marriage—through a re-enaction of major deeds of the founding ancestors.

Jan Vansina (1973:221–25 et passim) has dealt with the meaning of the notion of *nkira* among the Tio, a subgroup of the Teke people of the east, situated in what is now the Republic of the Congo, in the nineteenth century. For the Tio, the *nkira* are those beings or first causes residing in the sun, among whom figures the Supreme Being *Nzaa*. Andersson (1958:218) defines *nkira* as an ecstatic sect among the Teke. More specifically, the *nkira* convey fertility to the women and land of the cult leaders. A similar cult is found among the Kuyu to the northwest, and it crosscuts lineage and hierarchical divisions (Bonnafé 1969). According to a study by Jozef Thiel (1977:92–94), the notion of *nkira* occurs in very similar traditions found among those populations inhabiting the area of Zaire between the rivers Zaire and Kasai. In Angola, among the Shinji, Holo, and Kadi populations, *nkit* is a term used to denote a particular form of divination.

To gather data on the *khita* cult among the northern Yaka, I attended on several occasions its various phases as they occurred in the Taanda settlement and the neighboring area to the west. While this included observing the rites leading to seclusion on four separate occasions, and three times the rite of coming out, I was never able to witness the purification and rebirth rite at the riverside that marks the end of the seclusion period. I met three mothers of twins who had undergone *khita* therapy, and I attended the burial of a one-month-old twin. During the whole of my stay in Yaka land in the 1970s, I recorded nineteen cases of *khita* seclusion in the villages of the Taanda group alone. In the same period, I was able to meet twelve officiants of the *khita* cult. In Kinshasa, I noted some four detailed life-histories of *khita* patients and followed parts of their treatment. In addition, I made a detailed comparison with the notes drawn from observations carried out in 1939–40 by Father Léon De Beir (1975a:37–76, 1975b:84–106). The brief and very general remarks made by Father François Lamal (1965:174–75) concerning the Yaka and the eastern Suku do not appear to have been based on detailed information or first-hand observation. For his part, Igor Kopytoff (1980) reports on the *kita* as practiced among the matrilineal Suku of the Upper Kwaango, neighbors to the southern Yaka. There the cult is organized at the initiative of a lineage chief, perhaps one who has just been installed, and is intended to revitalize the lineage group and its life-world. The cult is however not meant to enhance the power of the chief or of the lineage, but aims, it would appear, at the cyclical renewal of the life-promoting capacity of the chief, as well as the resolution of crises arising between lineage factions and generations. For the neighboring groups to the west belonging to the so-called matrilineal belt, Trudeke Vuyck (1991) offers a comparative study of fertility rituals seen in relation to family organization and gender related division of labor.

In Yaka land, *khita* very probably has distant links with the *nkita* cult of the Koongo area. The refrains of some *khita* songs specifically evoke bonds with the former Kingdom of the Koongo, as well as with the related cultures of the

Mbata, Zoombo, and Tsootso who were the intermediaries in the trade centralized in Luanda. The Yaka of the northern Kwaango attribute the origins of most of their affliction cults to commercial contacts, encroachment on the land, and conflicts that arose subsequent to the arrival of the Mbata and the Zoombo. In the Kwaango *khita* is not properly speaking a fertility cult handed down by the ancestors as it is held to be in the Koongo region. In the case of the former, neither the reference to the spirits nor the sacralization of certain aspects of the life-world—thereby considered imbued with extrahuman powers—form the heart of the cult. Moreover, I have not been able to record a myth among the Yaka relative to the origins of *khita*. In summary then, among the Yaka *khita* is above all a healing cult directed to issues of uterine infertility and abnormal birth, meanwhile seeking to enhance fertility in the community of fellow-women and in their life-world.

The term *khita* also refers to the bride's departure from her parental home to the conjugal one and to the fact that she brings new life and knowhow to her new home. *Khita*, moreover, refers both to menarche and giving birth, as well as to departure on and return from long journeys for purposes of trade; it therefore connotes the rare goods (particularly those that constitute bride-wealth) and the knowledge and skills that come with such trade. In the popular mindset, long-distance trade is further associated with polygynous marriage as well as with sexual liaisons that might threaten the in-group through the spells and illnesses that such offenses may provoke. All the healing cults are said to have spread to Yaka land via long-distance trade *(phoongu ziisa muyikhita)*. There is a direct association between the notion of matrimonial alliance, that is, the arrival of a bride in the husband's homestead, the coming of cults, illness, and death. (This intriguing association may reflect tensions between the principles of patridescent, patri- and virilocal residence, and uterine filiation.)

The term *khita* may by extension carry an even broader meaning among the Yaka. It derives from *-kita*, "to transform, evert, reshape, metamorphose, transfigure." As an auxiliary verb, it refers to the effect of initiation, as in *-kita ngoombu*, "being initiated as diviner." The term designates the seclusion of both initiands and major cult objects in the various affliction and communal cults, as well as the seclusion of the chief to be installed and of the widowed and primary kin for mourning: "they are undergoing the initiatic mutation or metamorphosis" *(-buusa khita)*. The term *khita* thus serves to indicate their symbolic death to a former condition in view of rebirth into a new identity.

As a fertility cure, *khita* involves the various phases of a transition rite. Within one month after an oracle has established the necessity of organizing the cult, the husband of the afflicted woman and the family head or patriarch bring together a set of valuable goods which will serve to establish a matrimonial-like alliance with the healer and to solicit the aid of the uncle of the afflicted. In a first stage, all those concerned gather around the patient.

They meet at sundown near the ritual dwelling erected at the edge of bush and the homestead of the couple in question. The initiate is the target of a series of inversions and transformations: the ritual leads her through the experiences of death-agony, of being turned upside down comparable to a bat or like an animal killed in the hunt and brought home suspended from a pole, or also like the weave hanging from the loom. Then follows the seclusion phase.

I will describe the successive sequences of a stereotypical case in order to disclose the overall dynamic and pattern of this therapy, leaving aside a number of idiosyncratic variations—called *tsakulu tsakulu*—which do not affect the general form of the rite. In Kinshasa, the cult as a whole is not organized, and women in need return to their village of origin for proper therapeutic initiation.

6.2 The First Stage: Reversing the Persecution into Uterine Bonds of Life Transmission

Once the therapeutic group is constituted, it delegates, first, the uncle, and, then, the healer—who adopts an avuncular relation with the patient-initiate—to address the problem in its family origin of offense, curse, and persecution. The onset of the seclusion is usually planned for a new moon. The following make up the therapeutic group. Included are of course the healer, the patient's uncle, and the patient; from now on she is addressed as *Yihoonda*, literally, "the thing that kills, strikes, breaks, the breach or dissonance," as *Makhedi*, "shambles," or as *n-twaphoongu*, "the cult's head or face." The patient's husband or the patriarch, called *n-kwambeefu*, "the one in possession or in charge of the afflicted," must be present. One other important relative is in attendance: *pfumwaphoongu*, literally, "the chief of the cult," namely the representative of the uterine line of descent through which the cult is active; this person is one of the patient's maternal uncles—hereafter referred to as uncle. Two or more pubescent girls who are the initiate's classificatory sisters—hereafter called coinitiates or novices—are usually invited to share the first days or weeks of seclusion. A prepubescent daughter or son, often a classificatory one, is a stable caretaker and relay with the village during the entire seclusion: the girl is called *Maleeka*, literally, "the one who shares the condition of rest" and the boy *Saamba*, "the one who induces the singing and dancing."

6.2.1 Phase 1: The Uncle and the Uterine Source of Life. The uncle of the patient is the first to intervene inasmuch as he represents the uterine line both of the transmission of life and of the cult. This means that he also stands for any of the consequences of a *khita* curse placed on the patient and for the restoration of proper life transmission. The uncle is therefore considered responsible for the cult: his goodwill is sought in order that he release the uterine stream of life and vital flow with which, it is hoped, the patient can be reconnected through the healing. If the great-granduncle—who represents the closest ties possible with the uterine source of the patient—is not actually present, a primary uncle will at least act in his name. On the evening when the therapy is to begin, a large group gathers near the seclusion hut, including the coresidents of the patient, the patriarch of the husband's family, the chiefs of the adjacent homesteads, most women, men, and children from the locale, and some people of the villages around who share with the afflicted the same river place or have their fields in adjacent valleys. Through its songs and dances, this larger support group provides a containing or holding function for the therapeutic group.

Once night has fallen, the patriarch of the husband is seated near a fire lit for the occasion in between his compound and the seclusion hut. He faces the uncle—behind whom the patient crouches—and says: *Mwaana waawu, nge leemba, phoongu yaayi yatukuundidi, weetusaka,* which means, "this woman to whom you are uncle (whom we have acquired through alliance) is paralysed in her bonds with us following a *khita* curse operative in your lineage; do whatever is necessary to take her into your charge." He then offers the uncle three to five pieces of cloth. Given the context, the gift indicates a compensation for a wrong suffered by a uterine ascendant of the patient, an offense which consequently has been cursed. Such a compensation serves to reverse the chain of retaliation (as analyzed in 5.2 above). The uncle, in turn, addresses the group at length (an example of this speech is given in Appendix A). He identifies the patient by tracing her genealogy (*-sasa,* see ch. 3, n. 3), that is, he indicates the exact place of the woman in the uterine line and recalls the major events that mark its history. In doing this the curse responsible for the ailment is also traced. Insofar as he is considered the representative of the patient's great-granduncle, the uncle embodies the point from which the life of the woman originated, as well as the source of the prohibitions which protect her and the curses which threaten her. The uncle therefore has the ability—as it is said— "to acknowledge the distress and thereby bring the curse to rest" *(taambwala dyaphoongu* or *taambwala dyapheemba).* Next, he pronounces the wish that the avuncular line look kindly on the patient as it has done in the past for the uterine descendants. In order to lift the curse and reestablish the uterine bond with the life source, the uncle approaches the woman and, clutching a hen in the fingers of his left hand, takes her left little finger in his. With the right hand he brushes kaolin clay on the inner side of the woman's left arm, beginning at the wrist and moving to the shoulder. He hands the chicken to her while formulating a vow, the very inverse of a curse: *taa khoku, kola,* "here is a hen; may your health return." The coinitiates and the elder *khita* initiates present each rub their heels or throats with a feather from the hen, signalling their wish to benefit as well from the uncle's intervention: the heel stands for the action of walking in the footprints of others *(-dyaatasana)* and the throat for commensality *(-diisasana)*, both evoking that which intimately links them to the patient and her uncle.

Healers' comments indicate that the gestures made by the uncle reverse the persecutive logic of the curse; one speaks of *-katula pheemba,* "to break the kaolin's hold," where the kaolin stands for the cult, the curse, and its persecutive action in the uterine line of the offender. As is true of other ritual contexts, the uncle's application of kaolin *(-kusa pheemba)* to the left arm of a uterine descendant indicates his renewal of the uterine bond. This gesture reverses that of the kaolin involved in the curse, while the uterine bond is signified by the "hooking," called *yikho,* of the left little fingers. As we have seen (in 3.4), the reestablishment of these bonds unite the descendant (the fingers of the left hand) through the intermediary uncles (the wrist and the elbow) with the great-granduncle (the shoulder). The same gesture transforms the curse's hold—or that of the kaolin which signifies it—into a renewed uterine bond which from this point on will serve as a conduit of life rather than of debilitating persecution. The entire act of vowing good health casts off the ensorcelling effect *(-loka)* of the curse so that the woman may again tie in with life *(-kola)* and life-giving. Somewhat later, as we will see in the second phase, the patient herself denounces the source of her affliction and rids herself of anything which may remind her of it. In comparison with other ritual contexts, one could interpret the offering of a hen as mediating the transformation and bringing about the renewal. As is said in ritual terminology, the hen serves as *makuumi,* its function being that of bringing back the patient to "sociality and community" *(kuumi),* in particular with her uterine kin, for these are the persons who deprived her of avuncular care and severed her ties with the uterine life source. The hen may at the same time serve as *makolasa,* "sanative" (the nominal form of *-kolasa,* "conducing to health, making healthy"). In other words, the hen compensates for the wrong the woman has suffered in her body, and the uncle hereby conveys a most exemplary source of life-renewal to the patient. I may recall here my analysis, for Yaka culture (in 2.2.2), of the hen's potency to straddle worlds, and to depict as well as convey the egg-like source of all life.

6.2.2 *Phase 2: Entrusting the Patient to the Therapist.* Having lifted the curse, the uncle publicly entrusts the patient to the *khita* therapist, who proclaims his holding function to the patient as it concurs with that of a mother's brother or uncle. He then begins to chant while the community in dance and song joins in.

Who is the therapist? Cult healers in rural Yaka land are always men, but in town Yaka women beyond childbearing age may act as healer in the cult into which they have been initiated. A healer is deliberately chosen from outside the circle of close relatives. A therapist is only designated to care for an ailment which he or she has experienced, or which has been suffered by his or her own mother while she was pregnant with him or her and whose cure has meant an initiation into the therapeutic art specifically dealing with the affliction in question.

The act of handing over of the patient to the therapist is a pass-over in a plot: exegesis renders it as -*diimbula mwanambeefu kwangaanga,* "to detach or to help to circumvent a hindrance." It is the healer's task to stimulate the patient's inner force to retort the illness threatening her existence. Here begins the second phase of the *khita* therapy. The healer welcomes the woman and grasps her little left finger with his in the *yikho* gesture, thus expressing the maternal bond which is about to develop between both; the healer tends to refer to himself as "uncle." Speaking in the first person, the healer now pronounces an incantation for the protection of the initiates:

1 Tala mwanambeefu ban-diimbweledi kwameni.
2 N-kiindzi kum-fula, bangaanga kuhata. (a)
3 Kaseedi mwaana bawuku, wuka kwameni phati ye ngaanga.
4 Mwanambeefu bapheele, meni yileemba.

1 Look at the patient they have handed over to me.
2 The edge of the village is bounded by protections and the center of the village is the domain of healers. (a)
3 The patient is no longer their child but belongs to me, Healer.
4 They have left me, in my capacity as her Uncle, in charge of her.

Comment:
(a) By using this idiomatic expression, the therapist defies the patient's enemies: any plot to ensorcell her will be uncovered and turned against the aggressor.

The healer fulfills the transitional and emancipatory functions of the maternal uncle for the duration of the cure and thus symbolically integrates the dual, somehow androgynous identity of the uncle. He thus assumes the maternal role and represents the genitrix of the patient as well as the group which ceded the mother in marriage. The healer may therefore offer the patient a model of idiosyncratic identity while ratifying the desire experienced by the patient for a symbiotic relation with her uterine origin. The therapist becomes very involved in the therapy and partly takes on himself the particular emotional problems of the patient. In a series of addresses, he speaks, in the first person, to the patient, to his deceased master (as in the following incantation, verse 2), and to the *khita* spirit.

At the same time, the therapist brings into play his virile and paternal function, that is, his capacity to give away the woman in marriage as childbearer. For this, he displays his professional competence and his identity as a representative of social order and of the norms that underscore life transmission in the uterine line and that redress any infractions committed against the uterine life source. To illustrate this capacity, the healer holds his primary insignia, the *yihalu*, in his right hand as witness to his initiatic knowledge and its attributes. In this, the therapist acts as wife-giver and gives the woman in marriage to a spirit, the male component. The spirit then alights on the patient in the course of an orgasmic trance. Further, the therapist invites the patient to relive and reconsider her past and origin, and to weave it once more back into social life.

The healer displays a holding function and a perspective both on reversion of the ill and on recovery. It is as representative of the ancient therapeutic tradition and the sacred cult that the healer carries out the healing. In virtue of this function, and thanks to his clairvoyance, he is able to offer no small means of protection from misfortune and certain guarantees for the patient's future welfare. In his incantation, the therapist refers to the bonds of attachment shared with his master that assure the effectiveness of the treatment. The incantation largely consists of affirming that the harm already caused is reversible. This is for the Yaka an indubitable or axiomatic principle of ritual action, expressed in the cult idiom as: "*khita* ties in, hampers, but undoes or removes it as well." The success of this principle depends on bringing the curse to rest and on the legitimacy of the particular art of healing. The following incantation *(-sasa)* was recorded in the course of three treatments, each of which was presided over by a different healer. The idiomatic and rather enigmatic wording was almost identical in each case.

1 Khita kaziinga, m-baangu kaziingulula.
2 Teembedi mbuumba,
  mwaana fwa bukata kabukataku,
  kyeendolu Ndzaambyaphuungu.
3 N-kubwangoondzi wahoodibwa.

1 The illness entangles the body and the competent therapist disentangles it.
2 The deformed, one whose legs are misshapen,
  not that his legs are 'of nature' deformed,
  but this gait is god-given [is a work of curse].
3 It was my tutor so-and-so [he quotes his master's initiatory name] who handed
  the secret down to me.

An interpretive version might be offered, based on common exegetical considerations:

1 *Khita* prevents conception or causes the ailment, but the competent healer can remove the hindrance.

2   Deformities, infertility or any other anomaly originate at the same secret source as their cures.
3   Legitimate filiation endows me with the potency for healing.

The opening pronouncement of the incantation is the same as that closing it off (line 14 below): "*khita* transmits the ailment and through the therapist heals it." A *khita* affliction is understood to be a maze that hinders or impairs, closing in or entangling *(-ziinga)* fertility, while the cure is said to unbind *(-ziingulula)* and reweave the patient's fertility into the uterine fabric of life transmission. The fundamental homeopathic assumption of reversible damage is expressed with the transitive suffix of opposition or counteraction, *-ul-ul-*. The therapist responsible for handing down the tradition possesses the secret of a successful cure and has access to its source. This is the meaning of the expression *kyeendolu Ndzaambyaphuungu,* for which the recent christianized ascription of the term to God would by no means be exhaustive. As I have shown (in 4.4), in Yaka tradition, *Ndzaambi* is a cult spirit. Authoritative commentators trace this saying back to folktales. Here both *Ndzaambi* and the palavers of the elders[3] are equally taken as the highest instances capable of disclosing why there are things and beings of a paradoxical, irresolvable, incomprehensible, or bizarre nature, in short, anything beyond common knowledge or reason. Line 1 echoes idiomatic references in folktales to the diviner's capacity for revealing the origin of the ailment.[4] Once the affliction has been successfully diagnosed by the oracle, it is thought that healing will be certain as long as the cure is carried out according to tradition. The therapist also demonstrates faithfulness to the tradition by ascribing the relevant homeopathic postulate to his master, whom he designates with the honorific title *N-kubwangoondzi*. Some healers may cite names of several different masters. In the *khita* cult, these masters form a dynastic line of titleholders, since initiation and installment as healer are spelled out in the idiom of descent.

What follows in the incantation amounts to a challenge thrown at the sorcerers:

4   Babetu bangaanga kakasa moodi ye matatu,
    khitu zikituka, mbvuumbi zivuumbukidi.
5   Yibwe, yisala kupheemba.
    Yabalula, luphoonda.
6   Taata katsonga biloongu n-leeki,
    ndzeeyi bwoku.
7   Dyakala bwoku,
    yizendzedi n-twa ndzawu,
    phuungi bakuna hatadi.
8   Bababuti babadidiku.

189   The *Khita* Fertility Cult: Reversing the Evil

4   If those who desire my care turn against me, Healer,
    may the ancestors and the dead awake [intervene].
5   I serve under the mark of the kaolin clay [my intervention is legitimate and my intentions as a healer are pure like kaolin clay].
    If I turn myself into a sorcerer, kill me.
6   I was still a youth when my father showed me the medicines.
    I am ignorant of all these things. (a)
7   If this is not the case,
    it is as if the elephant lowers his head
    and attempts to drive its tusks into the rock. (b)
8   May she (the patient) give birth to what one need not cry over. (c)

Comments:
(a) The therapist indicates that his healing force is not feeding on the death of the one who initiated him. A succession under such circumstances might imply revenge or a debt of sorcery imposed by the dying person. The present healer thereby claims that he is free and thus not suspect of sorcery.
(b) If the therapist is both competent and innocent, the lack of success will be due to the clients themselves. The healer is also stating the axiom that any failure caused by third persons should turn against them.[5]
(c) Tradition has it that one does not mourn the birth of any monstrous or deformed being.

The incantation involves a dialectic of conditional substitutions according to the following argument. It is taken as evidence that the cure will succeed if the healer possesses the required competence and does not ensorcell the patient. In other words, such pronouncements push aside the probability of an unsuccessful treatment and ascribe the failure to external and intrusive forces, namely sorcerers who are deemed to bring upon themselves the evil they have intended for others. Any failure may thus be presented as devoid of sense. The therapist vows that death will strike him should he ensorcell the client. Further, he contrives that death or sterility come upon any who ensorcell the woman. This is once again a negative affirmation that the success of the cure essentially depends on his own ability and authority (line 6). By employing terms borrowed from male fertility rites (lines 7 and 8), the healer vows that the success of the therapy confirms his ritual competence.

The incantation concludes with another evidence of the homeopathic principle:

9   Kyeedi kwabaphati, dikabwedi kwangaanga.
10 Khita wun-ziinga, m-baangu kan-ziingulula.
11 Tuululu dyakedi kundzo kutseki.

12 Maambu kuna hata mazekedi.
13 Kambetekedi twan-butaku, n-kawa twan-butaku, kawoonga yizila.
14 Khita kaziinga, m-baangu kaziingulula.

9 The wrong brought before the healers and the cult invoked by a curse should return to the therapist in the guise of the ailment to be cured.
10 *Khita*, you bind up the woman whom the [competent] therapist unbinds [from injury] and reconnects [with the uterine fabric of health and life transmission].
11 May the seclusion dwelling on the edge of the savanna and the village be a place of beneficial rest.
12 May plotting cease in the village.
13 May we therefore bear no dwarfs, serpents, or lizards [that is, deformed children].
14 The illness binds her and the competent therapist unbinds her [and reweaves her in the fabric of health and life transmission].

At the end of the incantation the therapist once more spreads kaolin on the left arm of his client. He then applies his pharmacopoeia to those parts of the patient's body believed to be the seats of intense life: the forehead, temples, heart, shoulders, and lower back. These gestures signify that the healer intends to deliver the woman from the hold of the *khita* and to proffer her his care. Their effectiveness is founded in the avuncular relation that the healer develops with the patient, which allows him to work on the latter's uterine web that now bears persecution. Having defied his client's enemies, the therapist takes on the responsibility of protecting her. Following the incantation, he cuts the ends of the client's fingernails or some hair and hides them in a ritual weapon hung from the ridgepole and intended to protect the client. These residues are simultaneously the marks of the unboundedness of the patient's body and carriers of the body's inner forces and growth: mixed with an amalgam of untamed forces from the wild, these residues come to constitute the *mbuundwaphoongu*, "the heart of the cult," that is, the core of the cult's and patient's regenerative capacity (see 7.2.1).

In his role of reversing evil forces into life-bearing ones, the healer acts as a hunter-trapper. The events leading to the hiring of the therapist *(-laangula ngaanga)* invest him in this role. They always occur in the same fashion, independently of the healer's field of specialization or of the type of cult involved. The goods, called *n-koolu*,[6] are offered to the healer by the patient's family head or husband, some time before the seclusion. They invest the healer with the hunter's role by offering him replicates of the hunter's accessories (or substitutes, such as coins) and objects that are considered to be a reminder of the theft or ensorcellment committed by some of the patient's uterine ascendants. As such, these objects exemplify the evil consequences which have befallen the descendants as a result of a curse invoked to revenge the theft or sorcery.

This offer, which once more compensates for the wrong which has brought on the curse, deprives the persecution or illness of its raison d'etre and indicates an inversion in the state of affairs.

The *n-koolu* may be composed of a large variety of materials:

(a) The first category is that of objects often subject to petty theft; it includes small quantities of agricultural products or other objects of value more typical of ancient trade and of accessories of the hunt. The latter group consists of an iron arrowhead *(luhuundza)*, an axe *(yiphangu)*, knife *(mbeedi)*, needle *(ndoongu)*, gunpowder *(n-zoongu)* sufficient for at least three volleys, and a small bag of salt *(fuunda dyamuungwa)*.

(b) A gift of nine cola nuts *(vwa makaasu)*, it is said, expresses a wish for the health of the healer. According to some commentators, the number three *(yitatu)* or its multiples do not in fact indicate a determined quantity—for eight or ten nuts may be given—but indicate that the practice is "strictly prescribed" *(sumunu dyayizila)*. It seems that the integer nine, insofar as it is associated with the red of the cola nut and therefore with the morning sun, signifies fecundation and with it the nine months of pregnancy.

(c) Gifts of skins from the weasel, genet, or Gambian rat specifically summon the competence of the therapist by evoking his initiation to the therapeutic art. The choice of the animal is relative to the cult in question, and the gift is said to serve as "a colored cloth in order that the healer enumerate his knowledge" *(luboongu lwataangu kataangila bungaanga)* (see 7.2.1).

(d) The "three raffia cloths" *(mboongu tatu)* (today they may number from three to ten colored pagnes) constitute the price of hire, properly speaking, which may vary according to the prestige of either the client or the healer.

(e) Concerning the "small bag of earth" *(fuunda maafu)*, the commentaries explain that the expression has been borrowed from the *mbwoolu* cult in which appears the phrase: *ngeendza maafu mwaana hwa lutalu*, "the dust of the earth is like a child who cannot come to the end of the numbers." Just as the earth is infinite and inexhaustible, the causes of afflictions and their compensations have no end. In offering this present, the givers metaphorically express their request that the healer neutralize all the possible causes of the illness, including the secret ones.

(f) Lastly, the offer of a "hen for the hire of services" *(khokwan-laangu)* represents advance compensation to the therapist and his family group inasmuch as he is straddling conjugal hearths: he must hand this particular gift over to his first wife before sharing meals and bed again.

The healer reaches the site of healing as a hunter and converts the patient into a hunting site. One week, at the earliest, after he has been called upon, the therapist presents himself in the village where the seclusion is to occur. If this happens to be the first initiation that he is presiding over since the death of his master, he must announce the news at the cemetery. In order to protect the ritual site and to transform it into an appropriate place for the rite, the healer stealthily approaches the site like a hunter-trapper, as if he intends to take an unfamiliar area by surprise assault (see Devisch 1990a:220–22). Popular exegesis explains this element of surprise as a tactic intended to outwit the evildoers. Usually the healer spends the first night in an adjacent village. He will return to the patient's village just before dawn the following morning, but not by way of the usual paths: he crosses the bush, and in his conduct may imitate a cock. The first cock's crow and dawn put an end to the reign of night; at this moment, it is said, the sorcerers abondon their night-time machinations and put off their disguises. The healer is in fact believed to be able to witness unharmed this matinal conversion of the sorcerers and to unmask those who conspire against his client thanks to the clairvoyance he has acquired through his initiation. He secretly hides ritual arms at the crossing of paths leading to the village and proclaims his arrival to the inhabitants by singing *khita* chants. The healer begins by chanting a verse to which his client, soon joined by other women who have been initiated to the *khita* therapy, should respond with another verse, and so on. The therapist will not enter the homestead until the household chief and the patient's husband signal their welcome by offering a cola nut or a bit of kaolin clay. In the evening, he will install the *khoofi* shrine.

The *khoofi* shrine enacts a kind of cosmological hunt and reverses evil and wasteful forces in the life-world into life-bearing ones: its installment is like a beat across spaces and agencies to collect benevolent agencies while reversing their opposites. It is literally "an announcement" (sing. *lukoofi*) to society and the life-world that an initiation is about to begin. By installing the *khoofi* near the site where the ritual dwelling is to be erected (see plate 8), the therapist invites the kin group for a kind of collective beat against the agencies of evil. He fosters a climate of solidarity among the different members of the therapeutic group and attests to their bonds with the ancestors and tutelary spirits of the cult. The success of the cure is assured by the fact that any potential malevolent interference has been foiled in advance. Sometime during the day, the healer and members of the therapeutic group will collect a series of plant substances (branches, leaves, bark, roots, vines, fruits, and so on) in the forest or the savanna to be used in installing the *khoofi* that evening. When collecting the plants, they adopt the manners of hunters organizing a beat and rousing the game.

That evening, the therapist prepares the *v-vwa myatatu myamakoti*, "nine times three small sachets of ritual ingredients." (These in fact amount to no more than a half-dozen.) He now sets out on a hunt against the evil forces of the night that move under the ground or through the air. He digs out a hole about fifty centimeters wide and deep. The therapeutic group gathers here at dusk. The healer scatters manioc flour around the hole, climbs into it, and digs some more. Meanwhile, he takes toxic ashes (*loombi* found in ritual arms) and with the point of his knife spreads them on the ground. In a low voice, he utters curse formulas, similar to those described above, that serve to defy any would-be malefactors—spirits, ancestral shades, and sorcerers. The healer then invites the participants to help themselves to the sachets that he has prepared and to rub them on the vital parts of the body *(-dikumyanga)*. The bag is then thrown into the hole. A trunk of the *n-saanda* tree is brought and placed in the hole; it has been cut to the measure of a person's height and in such a fashion that it is able to take root. The healer, patient, and family elders all take hold of the trunk with the left hand, while other participants place theirs on the shoulders or hips of the one in front of them. They each repeat three times the invocation that is customarily pronounced at the installation of an ancestral or cultic shrine:

1 Nyeenge nyengeneke.
2 Sina mundzila, kitika.
3 Khi twadiinga?

1 [A cry marking the rhythm of the gestures of planting and pulling out the tree.]
2 Take your place among us and stay.
3 What are we seeking?

While they let the tree down into the hole, the participants straighten their right arms and respond:

Mooyi.
Life.

Once the hole has been filled in, the healer lays the *lundzilandzila* and *kitu* plants as well as a black termitary *(yisiimbi)* at the foot of the *n-saanda* tree (see plate 10). The termitary is meant to contain and restrain *(-siimba)* the cult spirit, also called *yisiimbi,* which has "taken hold or possession" *(-siimba)* of the patient. He also plants a number of branches of other trees and bushes around the trunk, including an elbow-shaped branch a half-meter in length which is unique to the *khita* cult.

The erection of the *khoofi* establishes a protected zone for the benefit of the therapeutic group. It thwarts the plots of potential evil and evildoers and particularly turns the consequences of past offenses back against the malefactor. Seen from this angle, the construction of the *khoofi* begins to "demarcate and delimit" *(-siinda)* as well as to "protect" *(-sidika)* the ritual space against sorcerers and their evil powers. As it is incumbent on the healer to transform this space into a habitable area, one apt for the enclosure of the therapeutic group, the healer avoids straddling diverse containing spaces and shuns all communicative means—like commensal or sexual relations—within his own homestead. He thus presents himself for the rite dressed in a *yibati,* the pagne knotted between the legs as a sign of continence.

In summary, the following six elements contribute to the complete possession and protection of the ritual space: (a) The ring of flour demarcates the area and places it under the sign of expectation (signified by the color white). (b) The therapist's descent into the hole and the erection of the *n-saanda* tree link high and low, earth/sky and underground, that is, any setting in which sorcerers move about. (c) The various plants composing the *khoofi* protect from harm and turn any evil deed against the doer, as indicated by their significative properties. Most *khoofi* are composed of the plants *m-mvuma, luteti, mbaamba, yiseleti,* and *n-kungwa yiteki.* These are found in various ecological habitats, and they intertwine the ritual space and intervention with the cosmology of life transmission. Their specific usage determines the dual signification they may carry (benevolent and diurnal as opposed to maleficent and nocturnal) as elements in the preparation of medicinal substances and ritual statuettes.[7] (d) The elbow-shaped branch erected at the *khoofi,* according to specialists, protects against deformities of the feet or legs that are the result *khita* curses. This branch is indeed known by the name *lukata,* that is, a "misshapen leg or foot." Its protective capacity is also signified by its other name, *kuundzi,* "pillar or support." (e) The sachets of plant and animal materials thrown into the hole, called *lukuunga,* "assortment," signify the panoply of ill forces that the therapy as a whole intends to "trap" or to turn against the evildoer.[8] The small bags invariably contain a supposedly complete series of plant samples, hair from ferocious animals, kitchen refuse connoting sterility—"that which no longer reproduces," and the fatal ingredient of ritual arms.[9] (f) Finally, by rubbing the sachets on the vital parts of their bodies, the participants mark their consent that they themselves be afflicted should they cause injury to another of the group.

The *khoofi* proclaims and 're-presents' the uterine origins of the initiates, and also the intent of the cult; that is, it interweaves the cultic space and entire endeavor with the archetypal history of affliction and its reversal, as well as with the resources of life transmission. It calls for the benevolent intervention of the cultic *khita* spirits and healers-ancestors who have been responsible for handing down the cultic institution. As with other rites, the circle drawn with white manioc flour—white being the color of the ancestors—points to the unambiguous character of the activity and more specifically delimits the site of a cult; the flour's ordinary name, *pfuupfu,* is not used here but rather the term *wuunga,* "resource, mine." Indeed, the *n-saanda* tree planted at the *khoofi* to take root there, as in other ritual contexts, points to the origin and the uterine transmission of the cult itself. By taking part in the planting of the tree, the participants renew their bonds with life or uterine life transmission *(mooyi),* and they express the hope that life may be transmitted through the uterine line in the same fashion as the sap rises up to the very leaves of the life tree.[10] The act of planting the *n-saanda* tree renews the bonds with the uterine origins of all life and its never-ending transmission. Having pronounced the appropriate incantation and climbed down into the *khoofi* pit, the therapist there adopts a *kataku* posture, connoting potent virility (see 2.2.2). The healer continues by spreading some of the drug *ndzaku*[11] in the hole, thus expressing his wish that his relation with his master (who has engendered him, so to say) may be preserved. The healer grasps the *n-saanda* trunk and climbs out of the *khoofi* hole with the aid of bystanders. After having raised and lowered the trunk several times he sets the tree straight, declaring that he is searching for *mooyi,* life at the uterine source.

Additional components of the *khoofi* and other acts as well "call down and confirm auspiciousness" *(-saka, -sakwasa).* They underscore the cult's basic assumption that life is more powerful than death.[12] As soon as the fruit of the hunt organized for the occasion has "confirmed the auspiciousness" of the *khoofi,* the healer waits until dusk before planting a thick *kitu* plant or a small black termite's nest from the forest, *yisiimbi,* at the base of the *khoofi* to embody the shades of the cult founders.[13] The success of the hunt notably points to a positive turn of events. A family elder will then stand at the site, turn successively towards each of the cardinal points, and loudly proclaim to the surrounding villages, chiefdoms, rivers, forests, and savanna the news of the rite and its expected beneficial effect (De Beir 1975b:98–99). The same message is communicated by a forest plant, *masamuna,* erected at the *khoofi:* the evil is from now on reversed. Since it is composed of plants signifying "good fortune" *(swaaswa),* the *khoofi* itself also bears the name *luswaaswa.*

A successful hunt confirms the rite's auspiciousness because the remote forest realm is a most vital resource for, and witness to, renewal. The day following the installation of the *khoofi* those men who have participated in it will go to the forest and inspect their snares, for this hunt has a divining function as well. Before leaving the village the men rub their firearms with a bouquet of leaves collected by the healer and composed of the same plants as those used in the construction of the *khoofi.* The capture of at least one large animal is a good omen and "sustains the good fortune called upon by the *khoofi*" *(khoofi yisakwedi).* As we have seen, any assault on the integrity of the household body or on any of its vital forces and functions—sharing of blood, table, bed, smell, touch—has repercussions on the hunt and vice versa. The sharing of the booty of the hunt, literally *-bukwasana,* "to share, to cut the animal in parts in order to allow for exchange," renews the commensality *(-diisasana)* and vitality of the household. The consumption of the game both augurs, and extends to the commensals, a renewed strength, for the Yaka consider that eating meat directly enriches the blood. Failure in the divining hunt held at that phase may reveal the group's disunion, thereby forcing the kin to speak out the grudges and conflicts and start rethreading the social web. The success in the hunt correspondingly testifies to and strengthens the integrity of the therapeutic body, thus sustaining the efficacy of the rite. Conjugal union in the homestead, having been prohibited with the planting of the *khoofi*, may also be restored as correlate of the commensality following the fruitful hunt. Popular interpretation affirms that "the ancestors enhance consent through the successful hunt" *(mbisi zisakwedi, bambuta bataambwesi)*. The audience of elders therefore "rhythmically applauds to witness to its regained strength" *(basika makoondzu)* when the hunter announces the fruitful hunt. In the case of a failure, an oracle will be consulted before continuing with the *khita* rite; the oracle of the horn (see 4.4.1.), held to be more accessible than that of a mediumistic diviner, is preferred. The steps are now inverted: the patient must first be strengthened again before forces can be aroused in and tapped from the life-world. The patriarch offers a hen to the patient in order to reaffirm the household's newfound vigor and restored integrity. Then, the hunters may leave for another divining hunt. The healer prepares the hen in a manner intended to restore fertility, *yikosa,* adding manioc flour, red *khula* paste, and aphrodisiacs. On the eve of her seclusion, husband and wife will share the meal in their conjugal home before proceeding to the ritual site. The following day the healer attaches the slaughtered hen's head to the peak of the parasol tree erected at the entry to the ritual shelter.

6.3 The Second Stage: The Decay and Cooking of Generative Forces

Transforming the origin of infertility into a life-bearing force forms the essence of the second or seclusion/mutation phase of the healing rite. This phase commences the evening of the seclusion period, following the incantations of the healer in the presence of the therapy group. Prior to it, the interventions of the uncle and the healer in the first phase have put an end to the cause of the ailment and have let the woman begin her quest for fertility. Now, in the course of the seclusion, the woman is brought in successive stages to identify herself with decay or death in the expectation of a return to life, or, at another level, to assimilate in her experience the meanings of defloration, self-fecundation, cooking, and the fetal condition. The local community and life-world are intimately associated with this pregnant effervescence of generative forces.

The local community joins in for dance and chant. It may be recalled that a large number of relatives and neighbors, including former initiates, join the present initiate at dusk at the outskirts of the village. The chants which they take up renew the bonds between the larger group and the therapy managing group. The rather improvised songs bring in local news and stories. Chants belonging to other initiatic cults may also be sung at the same occasion (De

Beir 1975a:56ff. offers a large number of these). "Chants" *(makana)* are intoned by the healer and consist of "expressing the anxieties and hopes, the intentions and resolutions" *(-kana)* of the patient and the community. These chants aim at expelling evil and are meant to call down the spirits' benevolence. *Yitoolu* designates the more cheerful songs delivered for the amusement of the public. These allow for some improvisation by the lead singer, but the principal theme is ludic or reproductive sexuality as it is also depicted in the mimicry of the dancers. On such evenings village inhabitants gather indiscriminately—without distinction as to age or gender—at the edge of the village, where women's dancing occurs. There is much sexual banter, for the carnivalesque and transgressive atmosphere reduces the inhibition against joking licentiously in front of close kinsfolk and the other gender. The group is in fact setting the patient on her way in the quest for her own health and fertility, and that of the whole community, through its exaltation of sexuality and fertility in gestures and games of seduction.

The drums and chants provide an atmosphere of sounds and melodies which envelop and carry away the person thanks to their rhythm, harmony, and modulation. The patient vibrates with the rhythm of the music and approaches a state of trance. This signals the beginning of the corporeal process of unbinding the patient from her affliction and of liberating her from her pathological isolation. At this moment the differentiation between the self and the world of the others has become blurred.

In what follows, examples of several chants specific to the *khita* cult will be given. These chants accompany the activities in preparation for the seclusion period (phases 2 and 4) and are sung by the group of initiates and some kin and former initiates each evening throughout that time.

Chant 1
1 Lusingee zeengenekeni.
2 Mundzila maamba lukweekwee.
3 Lusingee lusingee lukweekwee.

1 The liana, the liana swings,
2 on the path to the water, if you go there.
3 The liana, the liana [you will meet it] if you go there.

The interpretation given by the initiates blurs the sexual metaphor in the commentary: *khita* was in wait for you and has caught you in your offense.

Chant 2
1 Bakwa n-teti,
   saambidila n-ndzeendza mundzila,
   yindeengwa ndwa.

Chapter Six

2   Makhedi, ndwa;
    saambidila n-ndzeendza mundzila,
    yindeengwa ndwa.
3   Maleeka, ndwa;
    saambidila n-ndzeendza mundzila,
    yindeengwa ndwa.
4   Saamba, ndwa;
    saambidila n-ndzeendza mundzila,
    yindeengwa ndwa.

1   Those who transport goods [suspended from a pole], or the traveler on the road:
    invite them to share their news, (a)
    and show them your approval. (b)
2   You Makhedi, approve them;
    invite the traveler en route to give his news,
    and approve them.
3   You Maleeka, approve them;
    invite . . .
    and approve them.
4   You Saamba, approve them;
    invite . . .

Comments:
(a) Among other things, this verse refers to transporting the matrimonial goods in view of a marriage, as well as to the scene in phase 4 of hanging from the trunk of the parasol tree.
(b) Commentators are not sure of the precise meaning of the expression *yideengwa ndwa,* and believe it to be an archaic formula formerly used by elders to mark their respectful approval at the end of a speech addressed to an assembly.

The exegesis provided by the healers themselves tells us that the chant signifies that it is the *khita* spirit who detects the thief and retaliates theft, and that it is also *khita* who receives the victim of the distress and her companions in the initiation.

Chant 3
1   Pwa yoku.
    [Response:] Yoku (a)
2   Besi Yeengwala N-yaambi yoku. Yoku.
3   Kiima kibuula bihiinga mbuundu, yoku. Yoku.

1   Answer the sound.
    I am answering.
2   Members of the Yeengwala N-yaambi clan
    [that is, the *khita* initiates], answer. We are answering.

3   Pay attention to that which frightens those who have not yet been initiated into *khita*. We are paying attention.

Comments:

(a) According to several competent informers, *pwa* is an onomatopoeia designating a thing which breaks. Here it carries genital connotations relating to intercourse and birth. With the pumping movements of their hips, the performers allude to the meaning of *yoku*, from *-yokula*, "to launch, to cast," which evokes the particular responsory manner in both singing and sexual communion.

According to common interpretation, this chant incites girls and married women to distrust the boys and married men who seek mere sexual pleasure without further concern for the welfare of their partners.

Chant 4
1   Yitatu, yitatu dihika, yoku. Yoku.
2   Yokwedi kyoku,
    makutu kyadya ye meesu.
3   Pya tata taata pwa se.
    [Response:] Ya ki.

1   Pay attention to what comes in threes. We are paying attention. (a)
2   If you do not recite the *khita* chants,
    you run the risk that *khita* leave you deaf and blind. (b)
3   [A cry whose connotation is unknown].
    We are listening well.

Comments:

(a) *Yitatu* (a set of three) in the first instance probably indicates the pregnant or laboring woman. The second time it refers, according to interpreters, to the mother and her twin children.

(b) It is generally believed that offense against the taboos imposed on mothers of twins or other birth anomalies render the mother and children deaf and blind. The anomaly is thus an attack on sight and sense, but proper avoidance and specialized treatment prevent contamination.

Chant 5
1   Khita nyaangi,
    ngoombwa nyaangi, yoku. Yoku.
2   Khita biteelu,
    ngoombu bilaku byamaangu, yoku. Yoku.

1   May you learn that *khita* makes ill and heals,
    and that divination discloses how to treat. We are learning it.

2   May you learn that the *khita* healers are praiseworthy
    and that the diviners, revealing truths, are praiseworthy too. Yes, we do.

Chant 6
1   Besi Mweela N-yaambi, yoku. Yoku.
2   Besi Tsuumbwa Biluka
    balukidi Khosi ye Thaambu, yoku. Yoku.

1   Members of the Mweela N-yaambi clan [the *khita* initiates], listen. Yes, we are listening.
2   Members of the Tsuumbwa Biluka clan
    who have received the initiatic name Lion, listen. Yes, we are listening.

Chant 7
1   Yityeetya banuni, maama,
    khi nuni wabutila hatadi?
2   Yitsidikiti banuni baluwaanda,
    khi nuni wabutila hatadi?

1   Of all the reed warblers and other birds [whose favored habitat is thick riverine brush],
    which one makes its nest in stony places?
2   Of all the warblers [who live in the woods] and the birds who perch on a branch,
    which one makes its nest in stony places?

Chants 6 and 7 warn all those who seek to harm the initiate, declaring that the evil they seek will fall on themselves.

Chant 8
1   Weenda n-situ wakoonda ye kotya keti fuunda.
2   Weedi ku tho Kheni maama wako keti fuunda.
3   Kaamba wusala weesala wakoonda ye kotya keti fuunda.
4   Kaamba wubuta wubutaanga wakoonda ye mwaanaakwa mwaana.

1   He who departs [to the forest] at the crow of the cock, returns with neither sachet nor packet [of therapeutic plants].
2   If he has gone to the source of the river Kheni, he returns without a single leaf.
3   It seems that he has gone to work yet he returns with neither sachet nor packet.
4   It seems that he has tried very hard to father a child yet he is still without any children.

This very popular song among initiates develops the following theme: If a common mortal goes into the forest or to the stream he will find nothing useful; he resembles a sterile man. If the cult specialist does so, however, he will bring back therapeutic plants.

Chant 9
1   Baana bambviinda,
    n-zaandweetu mosi.
2   Pwa yoku. Yoku.

1   We are the offspring of the long-tailed monkey,
    stepping in one another's footsteps.
2   Yes, we are.

The parent long-tailed monkey accompanied by a cluster of young furnishes an appropriate image of the therapists who, faithful to the traditions, follow in the steps of their masters and predecessors. The long ring-patterned tail of the monkey and its manner of carrying its offspring suspended beneath it associate the animal with the patient's swinging on the trunk of the parasol tree (see phase 4).

6.3.1 Phase 3 of the khita cure aims at putting the ailment to death; it simultaneously evokes menarche. One speaks of *-fwa ndeembi,* literally, "to destroy the curtain of palm leaves."

The healer now takes into his charge the patient and her coinitiates. He moves to the head of the group and leads them around the ritual dwelling to the rhythm of the chants. The direction of this circular movement is not fixed. The number of times they do so is significant, however, for in parading three times *(yitatu)* around the house they demonstrate that they have taken possession of the circumscribed space. The therapist invites the initiates-to-be to lie flat on their stomachs on the ground, parallel to the back wall of the seclusion house and with their left-hand sides towards the bush. The healer and several other men stage a mock battle around the initiands while exchanging a mix of sexual banter and death threats. Brandishing large clubs, they strike the ground close to the patient's and girls' bodies, rhythmically crying out, one after the other: *hoonda, hoonda,* "kill, kill."

This last practice may represent an attack on those who have caused the trouble or a ritual putting to death, an exorcism, of the evil. This meaning would be corroborated by the following custom. Before inviting the girls to stand up again, the healer unlooses them from the affliction: he makes a spiral movement with his small *tsaanga khita* calabash—the ritual remedy for birth pains—around the legs and bodies of the prostrate girls. He declares (reduced in an interpretive translation):

1   Khita waziinga, m-baangu kaziingulula.
2   Khita nyaangi, ngoombwa nyaangi,
3   khita biteelu, ngoombwa bilaku byamaangu.

1   Whatever has been bound by *khita,* the competent therapist is able to unloose.
2   This ailment is diagnosed by the oracle of the diviner
3   and is successfully treated by the *khita* therapist. [Cf. chant 5.]

According to the established exegesis, this gesture, called *-ziingulula,* "to undo or reweave that which has been enmeshed," here evokes the action of untangling vines that have been entangled *(m-bindusi).* The healer frees the patient, a prisoner of the ailment, as if she were a vine or a maze hopelessly entangled with others. The healer must at the same time disarm the evil action and turn it against itself. Another meaning of this practice refers to defloration seen as setting the condition for weaving the threads of life transmission. Only those men who, by virtue of their position in the kin, may develop joking relations with the initiate-to-be and exchange sexual banter with her are allowed to approach her. The whole context and atmosphere of this stage of the rite—its occurrence at twilight and at the edge of the village, the drumming, chants, dances, and banter—celebrate sexual union. The sexual, highly licentious wording, mock battle, and very vivid gestures convey sexual arousal to the community and the life-world. This phase immediately precedes another depicting fecundation. It might also be argued that the defloration indicated in the rite is an autodefloration. Indeed, from this moment on the woman is called *n-fwandeembi,* "she who has torn the curtain of palms," this expression being used of both the present and former *khita* initiates. *Ndeembi* designates the curtain of palm leaves suspended at the entrance to the ritual dwelling and evoking the female pubic hair.

6.3.2 *Phase 4 comprises, literally, the "hanging from the trunk of the parasol tree," -zeembala mun-seenga,* as an act reversing infertility into the capacity for self-fecundation with the support of the therapy group.

When they have been given permission to stand,[14] the coinitiates are conducted around the assembly that has gathered in front of the ritual house. They are immediately brought in between village space and the seclusion house, where the healer orders them to once more lie on the ground. The husband of the patient grasps the felled trunk of the parasol tree that has been placed at the entrance to the hut: while bearing one end on his shoulder, the other end is placed above the entryway. The patient suspends her body parallel to the now horizontal pole by her arms and legs, with her legs at the end closest to her husband and her head toward the ritual house. Her uncle, and sometimes the husband's patriarch, stand on one side of the patient and the healer on the other: by pushing the woman in turn they cause her to swing from left to right. As we will see, the chants accompanying this part of the rite clearly evoke both illness and generation. When there are two patients, the ritual house will have two entrances and each patient will have her own trunk to be swung from.

At first sight, the position of the woman evokes the image of a slain animal suspended by the feet from a pole borne on the shoulders of two men; an alternative image is that of a man carrying a packet (which might be cut meat wrapped in an animal skin or in *lunguungu* leaves) attached to a stick. Yet no commentaries have to my knowledge explicitly compared the patient to captured game in this way; perhaps this is because such an interpretation would be too intimidating and, hence, reductionist. It seems, however, very plausible if one takes into account the intimate correspondence between the hunt and fertility; moreover, the preceding phase of the rite aimed at putting something to death. To further strengthen this argument, it may be noted that the name of the ritual house, *yisaasulu,* also designates the shady clearing at the edge of the forest where the carcass is brought "to be cut up" *(-saasa).*

Both popular explanation and the exegesis given by experts specifically state that the "woman is suspended from the trunk like a bat, in order that she recover her health." This association is most evident in the following chant, which is one of those accompanying the rite in which the patient is swung from the pole.

Chant 10
1   Ngeembwee ngeembu n-waangye ngeembu.
2   Ngeembu mbuta n-ledi vweeti taya.
3   Ngeembwee ngeembu n-waangyee.
4   Wadya kudya ngeembu kuzaanya.
5   Ngeembwee ngeembu n-waangyee.
6   Ngeembu hakadiila hakalokala.
7   Ngeembwee ngeembu n-waangyee ngeembu.

1   The bat, the bat, listen to what they say about the bat.
2   The bat is like an older brother who is dressed in rags. (a)
3   The bat, the bat, listen to what they say about the bat.
4   The bat eats upside-down. (b)
5   The bat, the bat, listen to what they say about the bat.
6   Where the bat eats, it brings bad luck. (b)
7   The bat, the bat, listen to what they say about the bat, the bat.

Comments:
(a) This expression probably alludes to the hairless parts of the bat's body.
(b) Since the bat is suspended upside down, its mouth takes on an anal connotation. This ambivalence indicates how much commensality may become perverted, either by a violation of its bounds, by ill fate, or by direct aggression due to evil sorcery plotted by kin.

In this association between the initiate's state and the bat, attention is particularly drawn to the ambivalent nature of the species, which is described as a "small mammal in the form of a bird" *(phuku mubununi);* since the bat hangs upside down, it is said that it eats where humans defecate and defecates where humans eat. Because of its ability to hang from its claws *(siimba),* the bat signifies the link between the individual and that which is entrusted to her, for example, between the patient and healing, or between the genitrix and her child. The bat is uniparous, and this is human-like, yet on the other hand it is a nocturnal bird-like mammal. Moreover at birth the baby bat is able to deliver itself by hauling itself by means of its rear limbs. It is then held in the wing membrane of its mother and may itself cling to the mother with its teeth. Bats may feed themselves by sucking blood from people in their sleep. They shelter in abandoned houses, hollow trees, or caves in a state of torpor—so-called hibernation—for several months. In the context of ritual intervention, the ambivalent nature of the bat signifies the transition conducting the patient from one form of life to another.

The fact that the patient is found in an elevated position, when swung from the parasol trunk, also carries a social signification. One might indeed favorably compare this particular scene with practices found in other rites of seclusion and at similar moments in the successive phases of the rite. The patient lifts herself, in a manner of speaking, above the audience, thus capturing everyone's attention and demonstrating her illness, in order to be finally integrated into the group along with the ailment that has marginalized her.

The whole scene leads the patient to engaging in androgynous self-fecundation. Indeed the representatives of the matrimonial alliance join in; the woman's uncle, the father of the groom, and especially the husband have active parts in the event. Moreover, the position of the woman and her swinging and the accompanying rhythm all lead the patient to relive sexual intercourse as part of the marital alliance in view of life transmission. Let me spell out in more detail this structural and contextual interpretation of the transformative effective of the ritual drama, especially since none of the given exegesis explicitly furnishes us with such an interpretation.

The parasol tree is the first plant to grow back onto fallow land, where it attains its mature height within the very short span of three years. Foliage only develops at the top of the otherwise very smooth trunk. Like the palm tree, which also has a straight and branchless trunk and a leafy crown, the parasol tree signifies the vertical link between the sun and its zenith, which has male connotations, and the earth's surface, which has female connotations. (Both the palm and the parasol trees carry equivalent cosmological and virile significations.) The trunk of the parasol tree is erected at the entrance to the house of seclusion, which connotes the womb. It is topped with the head of the hen which the initiate and her husband have shared in a sacrificial meal the previous evening. In this context the parasol tree and the "cock standing on one leg who announces sunrise" *(khokwa khookula)* metaphorically evoke the genitor and his role in fertilization. The chants accompanying the swing rite speak of a palm tree, while the patient is in fact suspended from a trunk of the parasol tree.

Chant 11
Yeezeemba kumbatya
tsoombu ye mbuundi. Elele.

I am going to swing from the palm treewhich has one nut with little pulp and one nut with much pulp.

While I hold that this ritual scene evokes fertilization, I do not claim that the parasol tree is taken as a straightforward icon of either fertility or of the virile member, nor that the rite reproduces the conjugal act. Nor do I seek to justify this interpretation on some similitude of the elements signified, pretending that the woman is attached to the trunk of the parasol tree like wife to husband. An understanding of the internal dynamic of the ritual production suggests that it does not as such draw on associations or substitutions anterior to the rite taken as genre. No exegesis or classification given mentions or refers to an association between the fertility of the parasol tree and female fertility. The ritual practice of swinging from the parasol trunk presents itself as a genuine production, predominantly metaphorical, capable of generating meaning and arousing an intense field of forces. The rite fashions meanings and forces which did not previously exist outside of the rite. Turning to the interactional drama, it is because the rite produces and enacts a setting relative to fertilization that the participation of the husband, the patriarch, and the woman's uncle may signify the restoration of the matrimonial alliance while reasserting the conjugal role of the patient. Because the rite aims at human fertility through its cosmological replicates, the parasol tree becomes a contextual transferral of potent fertility from life-world to the initiand and coinitiands. It is not because the parasol tree shows off an exceptional fertile capacity that the rite signifies and conveys fertility, but it is the rite which brings about and enacts the experience of potent fertility both in body and in world in rhythmic unison, of course drawing on certain palpable characteristics of the intervening elements. In other words, a set of cosmological and interactional dimensions constitutive of the ritual drama give form to sexual reproduction in the body, and to a resonance with life-bearing processes in the life-world. The sexual dimension is not reducible to some preexisting connotations of intervening gestures or ritual items. It does not come about except at the level of the whole of the generative process— that is, of the entire ritual drama.

6.3.3 *Phase 5 concerns the cathartic denunciation of the evil agent: -fuundila fula,*[15] signifying, literally, both (a) "exposing the sap that is oozing from the palm tree," and (b) "disclosing sexual excitement." It is simultaneously a trance-like attack against the persecutive agencies in the uterine line that hamper the patient's fertility, and an intense enactment of sexual arousal and union both in the patient's body and in the "uterus of the world." Taking into consideration the cosmological signification of the parasol tree and the ritual dwelling, it may then be understood that the event is moreover a metaphor of the patient's androgynous capacity for rebirth, that is, of her capacity for self-generation.

Following the swinging, the healer, patient, her husband, uncle, and coinitiates gather round the *khoofi* for a mock battle. They get down on their knees and simulate a struggle for the possession over a weaving-hook (a small rod measuring from about twenty to forty centimeters long) called *n-noongu* (see plate 15). Two small sachets are attached to this object. They are filled with an assortment of bits of agricultural produce, animal hairs, and other residues, representing any of those things that witness to unbounded forces but whose theft or abuse may have been responsible for provoking the illness in question. The participants repeatedly stab this *n-noongu* into the ground and pull it out to the rhythm of the chants. While the rhythm of the chant and the movements progressively quicken, the woman suddenly takes possession of the *n-noongu,* pulling it from the others' grasp. In a cathartic trance, she frantically sways her torso and head and cries out in a raucous voice, a state in which she is said to "allow the foam in fermentation to gush" *(-taaka mafula).* Her barely articulate words denounce the wrong or the offense (a theft, ensorcellment, or intrusion) at the origin of the illness and indicate a lineage name identifying the line and the generation in which the offense had been committed. Her state of fermentation releases the life-flow from *ngoongu:* the uterus of the world.

The patient is led to expel and reverse evil so as to release fertility. As we have seen, the patient exposes the origin of her affliction and takes possession of the marks of the evil incarnated in the ingredients of the *n-noongu* sachets in the course of the mock combat. The simulated battle thus seems to reenact in a most vivid way the lifting of the curse. Indeed, shortly after the uncle has removed the curse alleged to be at the origin of the ailment, the victim herself now denounces the illness brought on by the curse. It will be recalled that the uncle is considered responsible for uterine transmission both of what sustains or, conversely, of what may hamper the individual's physical life. By naming the evil, the woman expels the affliction from her; by offering compensation for the wrong at the very origin of the affliction, she redeems herself. During the combat the patient gains some mastery over the marks of infertility by tearing them away from the grasp of the *khita* therapist and her uncle. She recompenses the wrong committed by a uterine forebear by offering her uncle an object equivalent to that which had been stolen or abused and which thereby incurred the curse in a former generation. By means of these acts of inculpation and redemption, the misfortune is turned against itself, allowing the sufferer to withdraw from the persecution and to reverse the deadening forces into life-bearing ones.

Trance turns the impediment into an extremely transgressive experience of arousing the ancestral life-stream in the patient's body, the group, and the life-world. The presence of the *khoofi,* the gestures of stabbing the *n-noongu* into the ground, and the content of the songs all suggest that this ritual practice aims to rejoin the patient with the ancestors so as to cancel the effect of their past evil acts which could still hinder the transmission of life. As for the expression *m-fuundwa mbuumba,* "exposing the theft of a wild cat," which also used to designate this ritual event, interpreters explain that it is an allusion to the theft of a cat or other animal committed by some ancestral malefactor as the occasion for a curse responsible for bringing on the *khita* illness and consequently the cult itself. More specifically, it is said that in the course of the struggle the patient envisions in a dreamlike perception the past offense and perceives an ancestor who informs her as to what lineage and generation were involved in the evil and subsequent curse. The victim only communicates this vision in esoteric language and in a heightened state of awareness or trance, called *-kaluka,* "release, as if one was lifted up into the air"—an expression of dense sexual connotation.

The experience of trance is molded through various metaphoric layers, five of which I spell out.

First, the trance is an experience of mortal agony, of social death; as such it is considered akin to an epileptic fit. It is spoken of as *fula* (overflow, foam, saliva), a term evoking the froth emerging from the mouth of an individual suffering an epileptic-like crisis. In the framework of the *khita* cult, such crises are not expected to occur except in a controlled and moderate form. If a *khita* patient fails to fall into trance and name her persecutor, one speaks of *pfuumbvu,* "groping": it is said that she is totally bound in by sorcerers. The uncle is then required to step in and name the persecutor who victimized a matrilineal relative who previously became a *khita* initiate. This would mean that the same curse would have hit them both, because its cause would not have been reversed properly.

Second, the act of "denouncing the sap that is oozing from the palm tree" is also a kind of judicial procedure in which "a charge is brought against the impediment or source of the illness" *(-fuundila fula).* The charges made reflect the whole of the patient's past and the history of her ailment. The songs sung by the group serve to give rhythm to the battle over the weaving-hook, and they refer to the various elements of the original wrongdoing. The uterine ascendant held responsible for the act and the person who pronounced the curse may both be called by the generic names *Khaaka N-loki,* "Great-granduncle sorcerer," or *Khaaka Mayeengedi,* literally, "Maternal origin of that which torments us." I refer to these characters as the "Maternal ancestral malefactor." The following chant lists, in the form of a communal enquiry, a complex of social relations and possible wrongs whose curse may well explain the present affliction. It urges the patient—addressed in the second person singular—to uncover and denounce the evil. The patient's past and her difficulties are reflected in the series of denunciations of possible injuries. When the chant mentions something resembling the origin of her misfortune, the patient falls into a trance.

Chant 12
1 Fuunda mbuumba,
 [chorus:] fuunda mbuumba wakhaaka mayeengedi. [twice]
2 Fuunda wanuunga,
 [chorus:] fuunda wanuunga, khaaka mayeengedi. [twice]
3 Yiba bayibidi,
 [chorus:] yiba bayibidi, khaaka mayeengedi. [twice]
4 Fuunda wabelasa,
 [chorus:] fuunda wabelasa, khaaka mayeengedi. [twice]
5 Musaka byakala,
 [chorus:] musaka byakala byakhaaka mayeengedi. [twice]
6 Nguba, zangani,
 [chorus:] nguba zangani, khaaka mayeengedi. [twice]
7 Basiidi khita,
 [chorus:] basiidi khita, khaaka mayeengedi. [twice]
8 Makuba mangani,
 [chorus:] makuba mangani makhaaka mayeengedi. [twice]
9 Bangulu, bangani,
 [chorus:] bangulu bangani bakhaaka mayeengedi. [twice]
10 Muyiinda bakala,
 [chorus:] muyiinda bakala, khaaka mayeengedi. [twice]
11 Makhondu mangani,
 [chorus:] makhondu mangani makhaaka mayeengedi. [twice]
12 Handaba makalabi,
 [chorus:] handaba makalabi makhaaka mayeengedi. [twice]
13 Luku lwangani,
 [chorus:] luku lwangani lwakhaaka mayeengedi. [twice]
14 Hayitsaku, lwakalabi,
 [chorus:] hayitsaku lwakalabi lwakhaaka mayeengedi. [twice]
15 Bambisi bangani,
 [chorus:] bambisi bangani bakhaaka mayeengedi. [twice]
16 Muhuumbwa bakala,
 [chorus:] muhuumbwa bakala bakhaaka mayeengedi. [twice]
17 Mun-taambu bakala,
 [chorus:] mun-taambu bakala bakhaaka mayeengedi. [twice]

18 Muyikita lwakala,
    [chorus:] muyikita lwakala, khaaka mayeengedi. [twice]
19 Bambuta badiidi,
    [chorus:] bambuta badiidi, khaaka mayeengedi. [twice]
20 Pwa yoku. [Response:] yoku.
    Yitatu dihika, yoku. [Response:] yoku.
    Pya tata taata pwa se. [Response:] ya ki.

1   Denounce the flight of the wild cat [and all other wrongs]
    [chorus:] committed by the maternal ancestral malefactor.
2   Denounce the wrong to save yourself.
3   If there has been a theft,
4   denounce the thief in order that he be condemned,
5   if the stolen goods were in a room given to a guest,
6   if someone has stolen peanuts
7   which were under the protection of the *khita;*
8   if pieces of raffia have been stolen,
9   or pigs,
10 or goats,
11 or bananas,
12 in the banana patch,
13 or manioc belonging to another
14 laid out on the dryers,
15 or the bounty of another's hunt
16 stolen from the pitfall,
17 or from the snare,
18 if there has been theft while the owner was away trading;
19 if the ancestors have killed through a spell:
20 listen well and denounce. [Response:] yes, we do.

Chant 13
N-kooyi samuna mana wamona.
Shrike, tell what you have seen.

Commentators explain:

"You, patient, denounce the source of your trouble." It is the 'homeopathic' effect from reverting a misfortune by another mark of ill-fate that turns the invocation of the shrike, itself an ominous bird *(nunya mbeembi),* into an augury of good fortune. The shrike feeds on the fruit of the *n-lolu,* that is surnamed "an ill-fated bush" *(n-tya mbeembi)* because menstruating women use dried leaves of this bush or of the *yiyeembi* suffrutex as loincloth [or: sanitary towel], and if a miscarriage would afflict them, they should bury the aborted embryo at the base of this bush.

Chant 14

1   Fuunda yisa fuunda. [twice] (a)
2   Eh yaaya ngulwan-situ katima.
3   Eh yaaya. [twice]

1   I have come to denounce the small packet [that is, the source of my trouble].
2   Ah, my brother, the anteater tunnels into the ground.
3   Ah, my brother.

Comment:
(a)   The homonymic association between *-fuunda,* "to denounce," and *fuunda* "small packet," refers to the following custom: after the initiate has brought to light the object causing the ailment, then a piece of the stolen object—to take the example of a theft incurring a curse—is taken and placed in the small packet.

The song alludes to the *ngoombu* cult in which the entranced initiate may dig into the soil with his hands, like the ant-eater and water shrew which tunnel under the ground.

Third, in the trance, the patient overtly accuses the evil agent and exposes the offense at the origin of her ailment, and thereby frees herself from the persecutive agent. By making compensation for the wrong denounced, the victim seeks to rid herself of the sanction and the ailment it brought about. Further contact with the object of the offense is strictly prohibited because of its contaminating effect, and it becomes a lifelong alimentary and linguistic taboo for the patient. The wrong *(fula)* most often exposed is theft, such as of a goat, the bounty of the hunt, a firearm, bridewealth, agricultural produce, and so on. In order to compensate for the theft, the husband or patriarch hands over to the therapist the same good as that which was stolen or an appropriate substitute.

Fourth, the patient identifies with the bract and inflorescence of the palm tree from which palm sap oozes before it develops into a flower cluster and later an array of palm nuts. The Yaka consider that through its fermentation *(fula)* in the inflorescence of the palm tree, the (male) inflorescence grows into (a female) one that produces the growth of a stem of red palm nuts at the center of the palm tree. Through the swinging from the trunk of the parasol tree, a symbolic equivalent of the palm tree, the ritual drama transfers this transformative value of the palm or parasol tree onto the patient's body and the cosmic body. The scene is named *-fuundila fula,* an expression designating, first, the patient's cathartic indictment denouncing the evil, and the subsequent act of tying up the *fula* object (the reminder or substitute for the evil denounced) to the patient's *n-noongu* weaving-hook and to the raffia leaves hung at the entrance to the ritual house. Second, *fula* connotes the goat's rut, something boiling over, froth from the rising sap of the palm tree that is tapped, foam of the rapids, and the foam on a gourd of palm wine, which in turn refer to the crescent moon. In sum, I interpret all this to mean that the patient, in the combat involving the weaving-hook and leading her into a trance, enacts a sexual arousal and orgasmic union of the sexes that elaborates on that of the swinging on the trunk: the sap rising in the trunk stands for the flow of life stirred up to ebullience in the patient.

Fifth, the rhythm in the trance both of body and of the up-and-down movement with the weaving-hook, as well as the act of tying the reminder of evil, are a *weaving* of the life force. The *n-noongu,* sometimes called *n-seenga*—a term for the wood of the parasol tree—is generally a pointed batten from the parasol tree with a lateral notch in the pointed end, thus giving it the appearance of a hook. Several commentaries have associated the *n-noongu* to a weaving-hook or knitting needle, smaller but with the same shape and bearing the same name, used as a shuttle when weaving cloth from raffia. After the mock struggle for gaining hold over the *n-noongu* weaving-hook belonging to the therapist, the latter removes a part from the substitute good which reminds of the evil and attaches it as a reminder to the palm branches hanging over the entrance to the ritual house. At the end of the period of seclusion, he takes the reminder and wraps it in a pouch fastened to the *n-noongu* weaving-hook which is thereafter returned to the initiate. The therapist employs all the known types of knots in order to fasten the *fula* to the palms and later to the *n-noongu.* The act of tying evokes and reverses the ailment seen as a maze, which is henceforth denounced and undone in the course of the combat. The gesture untangles the maze and, in the context of the *khita,* reweaves life-bearing. The patient then will receive her own weaving-hook, carved from the wood used to construct her bed in the ritual hut. She must henceforth keep it under her conjugal bed. The child born following the therapy will in fact be named N-noongu or N-seenga.[16] The term *n-noongu* thus indicates first the object of the mock battle, therefore signifying the process by which the cause or origin of the infertility is mastered, and secondly the child who is born, once fertility has been reestablished. This double meaning demonstrates that the principle of homeopathic reversion underlies the ritual cure.

In sum, the actualized trance and concomitant acts have a metamorphic effect. The cathartic trance arouses a deeply lived and bodily enacted experience of freeing and channeling life-bearing in the body, therapy group, and life-world in unison. While the weaving-hook initially refers to the cause *(fula)* of the affliction (where the life-channel has been choked or cut off, according to my reading of the symbolism), this process is reversed at the end of the rite to become one of unhindered fertilization. By gaining control over the weaving-hook and clinging to it tightly during this state of trance, the patient dies to her former impediment and regenerates herself, thus bringing about her own recovery. The patient then pronounces the name of the evil and denounces the origin of her affliction. She thus annuls the debt she has inherited from her uterine ascendants and redeems herself by offering the wronged party a symbolic equivalent of the object whose theft or abuse lay at the origin of the curse.

The trance is truly cosmogenetic. The polysemy of the term *fula* sustains the homeopathic process of turning disease and evil against itself so as to restore the vital flow and its regenerative potential in the patient. The victim may thus return to a social existence in harmony with the community and its environment. In this way *khita* therapy may be described as 'ex-static' and cosmogenetic. It allows the patient to establish a new set of relationships with her body, her fellow-initiates, and the world; this process occurs through the ritual drama. The *khita* ritual therapy also allows the afflicted person to achieve a certain amount of autonomy to the extent that she attains a degree of bisexuality, along with a capacity to regenerate herself.

7 The *Khita* Fertility Cult
Reorigination of the Fabric of Body, Kin, and Life-world

The *khita* seclusion celebrates and arouses *ngoongu*, the primal womb, the uterus of the world, and it calls on and disencumbers the resources of regeneration. By being reconnected with the uterine source of forces and signs, the patient in seclusion is enabled to reweave the fabric of body, kin, and life-world. Besides the healing of the patient's infertility, *khita* aims at 'gyn-ecology' in a broad sense, namely a rebirth of the vital resources in the life-world and the group, in particular of the women tapping and transmitting them. The cult seeks at reenergizing the group and life-world from within intensely lived resonance between bodily rhythm and arousal and rhythm and enhancement in the group and life-world.

The seclusion-mutation phase—the third stage of the *khita* cure—may last from one week to several months; through the basic metaphors of flowering, fermentation, and incubation, it focuses on the initiate's life-bearing capacity in concert with the same capacity in the cosmos. By virtue of the cosmological and sexual meaning pertaining to the seclusion and the ritual hut, the patient is led to regenerate herself through assimilation with both the fetus and the pregnant woman. Seclusion is a transition from decay into cooking: it alleviates the suffering within the body and frees and fosters the inner forces into a self-generative process of reweaving. It is an act that reintegrates the body into the cosmic realm while re-empowering both, in a process leading the patient to relink with the multilayered social and cosmic fabric of life, itself in a process of revitalization. The fourth stage is that of the coming out ritual and the patient's reintegration into the homestead. Her passage through the river and an animal sacrifice are potent transformative methods. The initiate emerges from seclusion late one morning and is reintroduced into her homestead, where she once again may take up her conjugal role. She reaches the inside core of society while she is herself becoming regenerative of social self and the social world.

The *khita* initiates achieve both powerful nonconformity and fullness through their androgyneity, and following initiation they are accorded a mixed and privileged status on the public scene. In contrast with other women, they enjoy a relative autonomy from their husbands and their husbands' families.

They move in the dim zone between the customary order, the initiatory universe, and the 'imaginary' world of dream and forces. When addressed in public by coinitiates or teased by men, in particular by their in-laws, *khita* initiates behave in a similar joking manner, and hence they are able to participate in the seductive games usually restricted to the youth at nightfall and the outskirts of village space. Senior *khita* initiates, more than other women, may join men's meetings such as the palaver and palm wine drinking sessions. In these circles the men tend both to praise and to tease the *khita* initiate, in playful and allusive language, as if she were both a young and ideal candidate for marriage and a queen figure or "arch-mother" *(khaaka mwaadi)*—"the mother of all people" *(ngula baatu)*. According to the audience, she impersonates and arouses *kyeesi,* "bliss, grace, generosity, concert"—in my terms, a basic socializing energy, as opposed to *kyoosi,* "coldness, frigidness, withdrawal," and to *-keya, -keyisa,* "to reduce, torment, obstruct, disconcert."

7.1 The Third Stage: Seclusion in the Uterus of the World

Following the cathartic trance, the patient is entered in the ritual house for seclusion. This is phase 6 in the *khita* cure. The seclusion period prolongs the search—which has been gradually unfolding throughout in the previous stages—for protection against the evil in an attempt to reverse it. The house of seclusion converts persecution into life-bearing through the symbolism of trapping. The seclusion further leads the patient to experience what autogeneration and gestation mean in her body in connection with the forces of life-bearing that are channeled by her uterine kin and her life-world. The ritual house connotes the pregnant womb, the hen that is laying and brooding an egg, the palm tree, the cooking of palm oil or game from the hunt, and the intermediary world encompassed between the heavenly and subterranean paths of the sun and the moon. In the house of seclusion, the patient is reborn from the uterus of ceaselessly emerging life in the world, and her initiation leads to its renewal.

After nightfall (sunset is around 6 P.M. throughout the year) and close to bedtime at approximately 8 P.M., the therapist, singing all the while, conducts the initiate to the initiatic dwelling. He there invites her and her coinitiates to "put themselves at rest and sleep" *(-niimba)* on the specially constructed bed, in order to "undergo the initiatic mutation" *(-buusa khita).*

The ritual house, like a forest hide, links the habitable space with the ever renewing life of the dense forest. On average, the seclusion hut is 1.60 to 1.80 meters in breath, 2.50 meters long, and 1.80 meters or less high at the ridgepole (see plate 6). If the seclusion hut is to receive two patients, it will be longer and comprise two chambers whose entrances are built either alongside or opposite each other. At least one of the entries is always oriented towards the village. In the course of the seclusion period a small enclosure is constructed of palm leaves to hide the entries (see plate 9). The *khoofi*, situated not more than two paces from the dwelling, is to be found inside this enclosure. Lianas called *luteti* and having a breadth of about two fingers are generally used to construct the wall of the seclusion hut; in other instances the walls have been constructed of various sorts of lumber. The two ends of the vines are planted in the soil about one foot apart so as to form a large archway. These vines are further bound horizontally by others of the same species. A beam made of a parasol tree and resting on two forked uprights forms the ridgepole and supports the cylindrical vault. All the walls, including the roof, are generally covered with large *lunguungu* leaves which are impermeable but, when dry, easily torn. These leaves are regularly used to wrap and store seed, various provisions, cooked foods, or cut meat. These particular species of vines and leaves are not normally employed in construction, except to erect a very temporary forest shelter where one might remain to dry meat after a hunt or to escape from the civil authorities. The ritual hut in fact looks very much from the outside like a large packet wrapped up with string, an impression reinforced by the way in which a vine-like grass called *n-phemba* (see n. 3) is tied around the exterior.[1]

The seclusion house reverses evil in order to release potency from the world onto the bodies of patient and coinitiates. The ritual practice called *-siinda* converts the ritual house into a protected space. As in the conjugal home, a number of ritual objects including weapons are installed at different significative places in the ritual dwelling—the walls, entry, ground, roof, and bed—in order to protect the patient and to trap any maleficent force.

First, tangled bundles of twisted lianas *(m-bindusi)* are fixed to various locations around the dwelling: two at the bed, at the distance of a sleeping person curled up; one each at the interior and exterior of each wall and of each section of the roof; one above the entrance and another on the ground barring the entryway. Specialists explain that the twists of liana may represent either the illness which binds *(-ziinga)* the patient or the body hampered and afflicted by it. The treatment thus consists of untying *(-ziingulula)* the impediment, as one would unravel entangled vines. According to the commentaries, the impediment or any other agent of evil is trapped by attaching an assortment of plant substances *(mbakunumbakunu)* to the extremities of the twisted pads.[2] Such collections of plants represent the multiple forms and means of evil as well as of *khawa*, the aggressive and explosive characteristic attributed to the ritual weapons.

Second, a long bouquet of plant cuttings, including the *yinwaani* vine and other leafy branches signifying the arrest or entrapment *(-nwaana)* of the affliction or another evil, is placed against the wall.[3] This bouquet links low to high since it is tall enough to reach the roof; it is set just over the spot where a small packet containing *mbakunumbakunu* and *khawa* has been buried. All of the routes in vertical or horizontal space, in the underground and air, by which an evil force or evildoer could possibly enter are thus fenced off and controlled. The formidable ritual arms are buried at the feet of the forked poles supporting the ridgepole, as well as at the central point of the beam. Each aspect of the work of constructing and equipping the building connotes the struggle against potential evildoers and harmful influences. Protection is seen as a means to recovery. With the installation of the ritual arms at the center of the ridgepole on the eve of the seclusion period, the therapist completes the defensive work begun the moment he arrived on the scene and began the construction of the *khoofi*. According to commentators, the loud incantation the therapist makes before the therapeutic group after having installed the last of the ritual arms under the roof further aims to ensure the efficacy of the redoubtable defenses of the ritual house.[4] By establishing a homology between the dwelling, the family, and the body of the patient, the system of protection conferred upon the house metaphorically contributes to the patient's recovery of her bodily integrity and protective boundaries.

Entering the house of seclusion is an 'invagination': the patient identifies with both the fetus and the pregnant woman. Seclusion teaches the patient to make the fetal condition her own and to identify herself with the phase at which life seeks to burst forth. The furnishings of the ritual dwelling and the prescriptions governing seclusion transform it into a womb of this world. In fact, the patient's entry into the ritual house and her introduction into the interior chamber have a genital signification. A raffia curtain hangs down to the ground at the doorway to the hut, "closing it off" (see plate 10). This curtain of palms is called *luleembi* or *masasa,* whereas in the Koongo language (according to Laman 1936) *sasa* (plural *bisasa*) designates pubic hair. The use of raffia palm recalls the wrap-around, raffia skirts worn by initiands. A *n-seengedyambeedi,* literally, "a knife or machete without a swelling, a purse," namely one without a hilt, is buried under the pad of twisted vine "in order to kill any sorcerer who tries to enter" (see plate 11). This knife is employed by women only; they carry it in a basket on their backs which in many contexts is understood to signify the uterus.[5]

Seclusion and nuptial experience overlap. Entering the hut is called *-suumbuka n-kiindzi,* "to climb onto or pass above, or, to straddle a barrier." It reenacts the nuptial event when the young bride enters the conjugal home on the eve of the nuptial night. The bridegroom must on that occasion purchase his marital rights in order that the bride be willing to enter the home and "cross over [that which impedes] and climb into bed" *(-suumbuka kuthaangi)* (see 3.3). Similarly for the seclusion, the husband must purchase the right of entry for the patient by giving the therapist several white cloths as *kuba dyan-kiindzi,* "a half pagne for passage over the barrier." The manner of entry is characteristic of all seclusion and differs from the way in which one otherwise crosses the threshold of a dwelling. For seclusion, the patient enters the house backwards and leaves it—any time there is need to do so, and at the end of the therapy—facing forwards. Exiting in this manner most likely evokes a head-first birth, the sole position considered normal by the Yaka. It may be recalled here that from the moment of their entrance to the ritual dwelling, the patient and the coinitiates are called "the ones who have torn the palm curtain" (see 6.3.1); they are further distinguished from noninitiates, who are referred to as *yihiinga*, "she who awaits her turn," in the same manner as the circumcised initiate is distinguished from the uncircumcised. If one is to trust the commentaries, any indiscreet glance by a noninitiate on the patients in seclusion has the effect of nearly blinding them and of "injecting their eyes with blood" *(-hweeka meesu)*.

By identifying with the fetal state, the secluded patient enters a subsocial condition. She is excluded from all "commensality" *(-dya)* and, at the beginning of her seclusion, is content to nibble *(-tafwala)* plant foods that have been prepared by members of her family.[6] When the seclusion period is drawn out into a matter of months, it is the young coinitiate Maleeka who plays the role of a house servant. The use of fire is prohibited in the seclusion hut and one may not speak in a loud voice. The patient is dressed in nothing but a small wraparound during the whole of the seclusion period. She in fact spends the larger part of her time resting in bed. Relaxation is the rule and any activity undertaken on behalf of another person is suspended. She may pass entire mornings, crouched down and singing if she wishes, at preparing rouge. To do this, she rubs a piece of *khula* wood against a rough stone, mixing palm oil with the powder. She will later anoint her whole body with the mixture which, as we have seen, evokes the belief that the fetus is surrounded by the maternal blood that shapes its soft tissues and skin.

The fetal—initiatory—condition means undergoing 'cooking' in the uterus of the world. Rhythmically preparing *khula* paste and anointing oneself with it also associate the initiate with the process of cooking palm nuts. Once the palm nuts ripened, the reddish oil may be extracted from the nuts through a laborious process of cooking. The same symbolic complexes also provide alternative images of the genitrix's contribution in gestation. The appearance of palm nuts, the descending movement of the sap in the palm tree, and the cooking of the sap in the red earth all function as metaphors of life-bearing in the uterus of the world. The macrocosmic significance and field of forces proper to the palm tree are transferred to the space of the seclusion house and to the patient's body. The patient is brought back to "the egg-like womb of the world" *(ngoongu)* by being confined in this special dwelling. Here in seclusion, the patient returns to the fetal process of gestation and self-creation, *ngoongu,* by sponsoring in her body the cross-fertilization of the white sap and the red life-giving fluid.

While in this condition, the patient must seek to prevent any contamination of her fetal state that might issue from contact with any analogous regenerative processes in her surroundings. The patient must therefore avoid any contact with water and is prohibited to see the light of day. When she exits the house to relieve herself, she wears leaves on her feet and covers her head with a towel. She must, moreover, walk haltingly, with her back bowed like a chameleon *(lungweenya)* and with her head bowed: the ability of this animal to adapt the color of its skin according to its environs undoubtedly sustains the initiate's submission to change. The initiate is otherwise prevented from leaving the premises or resuming married life.

The healing is a gestation from within the inflorescence or bract of the palm or parasol tree. Plants specifically belonging to the *khita* cult are placed in the patient's bed and signify the force of life about to burst forth. The plant substances making up the infusion which the patient administers herself through the vaginal douche, on the other hand, symbolize those forms of life which in all their fragility nonetheless blossom out under difficult conditions. The bed is in fact placed as far as possible from the entry to the hut. What distinguishes this bed from an ordinary one is less its form than the type of wood used to construct it and the plants that are laid on it. As it is made of wood of the parasol tree *(n-seenga),* it is called the "bed of the parasol tree" *(thaangyan-seenga).* Two large logs support the two long perpendicular poles linking the head of the bed to the foot and across which the transverse slats are laid closely together. These are in turn covered with a thick layer of plants: large *lunguungu* leaves used to roof the ritual hut, *mangangatsaanga* foliage, and a bract of the parasol tree *(phwan-seenga).* A simple sleeping mat is placed on top. *Mangangatsaanga* is a climbing plant which grows well in humid areas and on steep slopes; its fine foliage closely resembles a covering of hair. Even though its meaning is never made explicit, in different ritual uses this evergreen plant often carries a genital connotation.[7] As for the bract of the parasol tree, its process of blossoming and leafing is transferred onto the initiate in seclusion.

Each evening the patient renews her invaginating of the life-resources of the life-world. The therapist offers her a "bouquet of plants" *(yifutu)* from the savanna (a female space) or from the forest (a male space). Every evening, the patient will "drink an infusion or concoction of these plants" *(-nwa yifutu)* by way of a cold enema. As such, this practice metaphorically associates oral and genital 'intake' and explores the capabilities of the genetic processes both in the environment and in the human body as if they implicitly resemble one another. The therapist acts as a mother-healer *(yingula ngaanga)* to his patient in the gestation process of her new identity. The therapist has the ability to combine maternal care with virile qualities. When gathering the required plants, the therapist adopts the behavior of the hunter in order to reverse the significative value of the evil or misfortune that is attached to savanna plant species, notably because of the annual brush fires which destroy them.[8] Upon his return from the morning expedition to collect these plants, the therapist prepares the infusions by leaving the gatherings to soak and then by boiling them in water contained in an earthen pot covered with *lunguungu* leaves.

The composition of these infusions varies slightly from one *khita* therapist to another, yet the significative value of the whole set of ingredients used in the infusions is not affected. Anal douches use savanna plants that survived the ill-fated annual fire.[9] The vaginal douches are made with an infusion of *yifutu* prepared by cooking a certain forest liana.[10] A luke-warm infusion is occasionally used as a vaginal rinse. Yet another type of infusion is reserved for a cold vaginal or anal douche giving "shade to the abdomen" *(ndzaba zapheelaka);* in other words, it has an antispasmodic effect and arrests hemorrhaging.[11] At the end of repeated douches with these cold infusions, the therapist may prescribe another vaginal rinse involving plant substances—the same ones as those used to construct the bed—that signify fertility.[12] Where the divinatory oracle has attributed a disorder to one or another offense and to its entangling effect on the patient, the therapist prepares a cold infusion which the women will administer as a vaginal douche in order to loosen the maze. Several climbing plants or tendrils, herbs, and the base of a palm tree's leafy crown make up the components. The tendrils give the infusion the capacity to arrest the affliction's power to entwine the victim, while the other plant substances signify the denouement of the disorder. Other ingredients signifying fertility may also be included in this infusion.[13]

Enemas and the ointment with red paste are powerful devices through which the patient may reappropriate the phatic function of skin and orifices. By anointing her own body and the body of the young coinitiate Maleeka with red *khula* paste, as well as by administering lukewarm enemas to herself and to Maleeka, the patient is led to remold the pathic and liminal functions of the bodily envelope and orifices. She thus reappropriates the sense of touch and the body-self ("moi-peau," cf. Anzieu 1985) linked to a sensation of comfort and tonus, and of being intact and cohesive. The red paste symbolizes the sacrificial blood as well as the uterine blood and unison with the mother; the anointment develops a kind of mirroring interaction between initiate and spirit, as well as between the coinitiates. All this mobilizes in the initiate a sensation of surface, volume, and brings her in a vivid contact with her body and its sexual characteristics. In the process of this anointment, and the murmuring of initiation chants that accompanies it, the *khita* spirit obtains a tactile body. At this moment the initiate begins to embody the spirit—at least in its benevolent dimension—that is her mirror image. To anoint her own body is like entering into the skin of the spirit or like remaking her own skin, a process that is also mirrored by her young coinitiate Maleeka. The anointing thereby displays a very powerful transitional capacity or intermediary function (Winnicot 1971), capable of evoking all kinds of sensations and affects from early childhood, from both her personal and family histories. The skin thus acts as a surface of sonoro-tactile exchange, of sensation, excitation, and engrafting of very primary experiences, of pictograms enclosed in the skin (Castoriadis-Aulagnier 1975). "Le massage devient message" (Anzieu 1985:38), and it remolds the patient's social skin. In other words, enemas and ointments are devices that may be variously employed to open up the body's closure, to expel intrusive agents, or to reinfoliate a body in a state of effusion or dissolution. The enema may also include strong-smelling herbs and plants from the savanna that arouse sexual desire, intense enjoyment, or repugnance, or attract some animals and evoke flowering or decay. Smell binds the patients and coinitiates together in an almost organic fusion, a kind of intimate sensing and tasting of the copresent others and the surrounding life-world. These devices aim to bring the patient to a new experience or sense of the bodily shell and its various orifices and their culturally encoded functions.

Food taboos prevent contamination with any form of ill-fated intake, both oral and genital. The patient's diet is more frugal and monotonous than is the average daily fare. Alimentary prohibitions *(yizila)* imposed on the initiate are intended to protect her fertility by ensuring avoidance with any element signifying her specific ailment or any other gynecological disorder. The prohibition against taking meals, that is, against commensality, refers to her fetal condition as well. Any pregnant woman, if she wishes, might in fact observe the same alimentary prohibitions in order to prevent malformation of the embryo or other anomalies related to conception and birth. The prohibitions against eating a series of foods—including small mammals who live in holes in trees or the ground, fish caught with the aid of a hook, and eggs[14]—seek to prevent any reference to or contact with forces of miscarriage, sterility, and birth complications. The forces of gynecological misfortune should in fact be turned back upon themselves in a self-destructive manner. Nor are these alimentary restrictions automatically lifted at the end of the seclusion. An initiate may continue to respect them as long as she sees fit, for it is then permissible for her to lift a prohibition simply by infringing it.

Seclusion leads to embodying the self-generative potential of a core cosmic metaphor: the hen laying and brooding an egg. At the peak of the parasol tree, erected at the entry to the house and dominating it, is fixed "the head of a hen" *(yizuumbi)* (see plate 13). The patriarch will have offered this hen to the infertile couple following the successful hunt that was conducted in order to cast good fortune on the planting of the *khoofi,* and they will have eaten of its meat the evening marking the beginning of the period of seclusion. Specialized exegesis limits itself to the indication that the head of the hen, on the one hand, is meant "to announce the news of the seclusion to all those in the vicinity and to the life-world," while on the other hand, "it is surveying the area especially for sorcerers" who might emerge from the forest and enter the village by night. The manner in which the hen is consumed and the fact that its head is fixed on top of the palm—whose symbolism also contributes to the meaning of autogeneration—indicate that it may, in the context of the seclusion rite, signify the hen about to lay or "engender life." The "hen ready to lay" *(khoku yabutama)* thus serves to symbolize the patient in seclusion who auto-engenders herself, as would an androgynous being, in assimilating both the condition of the fetus and the state of pregnancy. In the same context, the egg about to be laid also signifies the patient, and this would adequately explain why she is prohibited from eating eggs or the meat of the weasel who steals and eats chickens and eggs. The prohibition therefore prevents her compromising the process of self-generation mobilized by the act and context of seclusion. (As I will argue in 8.3, the value of the 'hen and the egg' entails an ontological problem, which engages the question of bipolar unity: the one issues from two, two issue from one.)

Heart, womb, the state of seclusion, the game caught in the hunt, and the bat are all associated as regenerative potentialities, as sources of inner growth and self-delivery.

First, the patient is associated with the *mbuundwaphoongu,* literally, "the heart enclosing and maturing the secret powers of the cult," which is called "her double" *(yidiimbu kyaandi).* It is made out of a small termitary *(mbaambakhuku)* of a reddish-brown color and is attached to the center of the ridgepole. The termitary is wrapped in the fibrous scales taken from the base of the palm *(mbuundyambati).* It contains, aside from a ritual weapon, the patient's residues or double, namely some nail clippings referring to her shadow entities *(biniinga).* A person's shadows comprise both her invisible interior dimension and her physical quintessence. In the bush, one finds this type of termitary suspended from a branch in the top of a Rotin palm; it is seen as an icon of the setting sun, and it bears a fetal signification. As its name indicates, the termitary is attached to the tree with a *mbaamba* liana signifying the bonds of descent. The sun passing through its rising and setting phases is symbolically compared to the cluster of palm nuts at the center of the foliage and to the *mbaambakhuku* termitary suspended to the liana emerging from this foliage.

Second, in the initiatory state of both pregnancy and fetal life, the patient is associated with the transitional capacities of the bat, in particular with its capacity to deliver itself (see 6.3.2). The *mbuundwaphoongu,* when suspended from the ridgepole of parasol wood, carries the name, among others, of *siimba dyamwanambeefu,* "that which the afflicted woman clings to." This particular expression refers to the bat which hangs from its perch or its mother by its claws, and which, according to the interpretation, symbolizes the patient suspended from the trunk of the parasol tree or connected with her mother and the uterine life source. The termitary attached to the rafters is hidden by bunches of suffrutex leaves from the savanna hanging one next to the other the whole length of the ridgepole. It may be recalled that the *yiyeembi* suffrutex is the first plant to become green after the annual bush fires blacken the savanna (see 2.3.7). The initiates call these bunches *ngeembu*. The interpretation of specialists establishes an explicit relation between the patient suspended from the trunk of the parasol tree, these packets of suffrutex, and the ability of the young bat, also called *ngeembu*, to hide itself in the wing-membrane of the mother.

Third, the patient is associated with the the game caught in the hunt, wrapped in its everted pelt and hanging from a pole. Seclusion is an experience of dying that leads to rebirth, through exfoliating the inner new core while infoliating a new skin from the vital life-world. The act of skinning an animal killed in the hunt is transposed on to the patient hanging from the parasol tree, as well as on to her state of seclusion which leads her through a process of rebirth, that is, of shedding her former self for a new being. *Saasulu* may equally designate the shady site in the forest where the game is butchered as well as the ritual house. This substitution corroborates that of swinging from the trunk of the parasol tree, which not only evokes the manner in which game is transported but also the ritual hut. Both share the form of a packet carried on a stick or pole over the shoulder and perhaps containing cut meat wrapped in a skin or *lunguungu* leaves.

Fourth, there is moreover an implicit association between, on the one hand, the bat for its value of inversion and transition and, on the other hand, the seclusion of the patient and the vegetation which quickly grows back in the savanna—a feminine space—once men have set fire to the plains. The patient's suspension from the trunk as if she were a bat which hangs from its perch—itself associated with the bunches of suffrutex foliage hanging from the ridge pole—is reenacted by the initiate in seclusion. Lying on her bed of parasol wood and bract, she is like the foliage of the parasol or the palm tree which blossom out while feeding themselves on their rising sap. The variant name given to the suspended bunches of suffrutex, *n-kaanda*, "bouquet of leaves," also evokes renascent life with all its potentialities. This term is a synonym of *lubongu lwataangu*, "a cloth or surface as varied in color as the sun," for the matinal sun connotes the act of fecundation.

Fifth, the genet is moreover a metaphor both of the secluded patient sleeping on her bed and of the termitary attached to the roof. A tree-loving animal, the genet sleeps high on a branch with its snake-like tail curled around it. As is expressed in one of the initiation chants, this habit of the genet evokes the fetal condition of the patient in seclusion. The genet may further signify the capacity of self-generation, and the patient will cover her head with a genet skin at the end of her seclusion. Genet and civet cat, both tree-loving animals, are symbolic substitutes for one another. The civet cat has a speckled pelt and a tapered snout, which is compared to that of a dog that sniffs the genitals of the female it has mounted. The following chant—which is very popular and which arouses vivid banter—expresses certain of these connotations:

Chant 15
1 Tuutila mbwa, mbala weedi kwaandi; [in chorus] tuutila mbwa.
2 Tuutila mbwa, mbala mosi bisaangi; tuutila mbwa. (twice)
3 Tuutila mbwa, mbala mosi mayiinda; tuutila mbwa. (twice)
4 Tuutila mbwa, mbala n-kwa yinyoongi; tuutila mbwa. (twice)
5 Bunyoku. (twice)
6 Tuutila mbwa, mbala weedi kwaandi. (twice)

1 [one person sings:] Recall your dog [to make it return to you]; [the other answers:] the civet has already gone; [in chorus:] recall your dog. (a)
2 Recall your dog, the civet has entered the little forest; recall your dog.
3 Recall your dog, the civet has entered the great forest; recall your dog.
4 Recall your dog, the civet has bowed its head in a gesture of chagrin; recall your dog.
5 It is lying down, curled up. (b)
6 Recall your dog, the civet has already gone.

Comments:
(a) According to the statements of the initiates, these verses are intended to encourage the patient and family leaders to follow the ritual specialist's instructions scrupulously.
(b) The term *nyoku* is also used to describe the advanced state of pregnancy; this expression refers to the fetal curled position—comparable to that of the snake *(nyoka)*—characteristic of the sleeping civet and the secluded initiate at rest.

Seclusion is tapping from the uterus of the world, *ngoongu*. The esoteric meaning of *ngoongu* is difficult to disclose. In the context of the *khita* rite, this notion designates the fibrous scale-like coverings from the crown of the palm tree: pieces of these are fixed to the extremities of the tangled bundle of lianas placed at critical points around the ritual dwelling. Yet *ngoongu* may equally indicate the patient's habits in seclusion of wearing shoes of leaves or rags and of covering her head with a cloth on her brief absences from the house. In another usage, the archaic term *ngoongu* designates objects that cover, envelope, or insulate. As such, it signifies, in the image of the celestial vault, the dense vegetation of the forest cover enveloping the hunter. It also designates the bud of the parasol tree that is placed, at burial, on the head of the diviner or of the therapist specializing in virile fertility.[15] It would appear that, in the context of cults, *ngoongu* connotes the state of autogestation and fetal development. When the therapist brings the initiate into the house of seclusion, he sings *Kongoongu (Ku ngoongu) a mwaneetu,* "into this pristine seclusion (or primal womb), we carry our child." The seclusion reenacts the cosmogenetic significance of *ngoongu,* the pristine cosmic emergence of (re)generative forces in the universe which are constantly renewed at their point of origin.

Seclusion brings into play cosmological and mythical icons of the autogeneration of life. More precisely, it explores in the cosmology and myths the instances of autogeneration in order to tap from these. Some articles found in the ritual dwelling seem to refer to mythical entities, *lwuila* and *kamwaadi,* who are vaguely perceived as spirits of the earth and founders of the local population at its most archaic and prelineage stage. Between the bed of the initiate and the bouquet of plants laid against the wall will be found a small blackish termite nest called by the ritual name of *lwuila* and an object of wood sculpted in the form of a fork, called *kamwaadi.* A similar sculpted object and a *lwuila* termitary are placed against the opposing wall. Still more black termite nests are sometimes placed in the corners of the dwelling near the foot of the bed. The *lwuila* and *kamwaadi* are installed the evening preceding the seclusion. These particular termitaries and sculpted objects attest to the line of continuity between the therapeutic group and the founding spirits and ancestors, respectively male and female, of the *khita* cult, representing the most ancient period of the society (see plate 12). *Tsuumbwa,* a nickname for the *lwuila* termitaries, is also an esoteric term designating the trunk of the parasol tree from which the patient is swung. In mythical language, however, the term *tsuumbwa* refers to one of the clans of the Kwaango that is believed to have started the *khita* cult (see chant 5). The name *kamwaadi* appears to point to the archaic mother-ancestor of the group, while the term also denotes a forked branch of a savanna wood, *n-heeti* or *m-booti,* approximately 40 centimeters long and planted in the ground with the fork in the air. The extremities of the fork are tapered. Notches are made on both the front and back sides of the fork, just below the bifurcation, creating a Janus-faced silhouette. Ashes and red clay *(muundu)* are applied to the notches (see Devisch 1987).[16]

7.2 The Fourth Stage: Emancipating Forest Forces into Social Fecundity

7.2.1 *Initiation into the therapeutic art represents phase 8 of the khita cure.* (See 7.2.4 for discussion of phase 7.) Initiation is a form of nightly cooking to 'feed,' in a trance-like state, the androgynous body from below. To a certain extent the therapeutic initiation renders the aid of the healers unnecessary; it corroborates the healing as a form of self-generation and also marks the end of the period of seclusion. The patient is introduced to a number of medicines, as is her husband, for he is authorized to prepare some of them for her.

The therapeutic art is a form of nightly cooking to arouse and tap the forces of the forest and the earth. The art is handed down in the course of a vigil and on the morning immediately preceding the end of the period of seclusion. Throughout the night, a small therapeutic group gathers round a fire lit close to the house of seclusion. From sunset to sunrise, in chants and ritual, they celebrate the forces of the dark forest realm. This night of transition is described as *-niimba yizalala kyaphoongu,* "to watch all night in lustiness while dancing or trembling in tune with the cultic spirit." The dance is meant to evoke the movements of the hen, while brooding, crying, and scratching the ground. All engage in a sham fight similar to the one at the beginning of the period of seclusion that leads to the denunciation of the evil and the appropriation of the *n-noongu* weaving-hook (phase 5). They all then take part crushing the *phaandzi* pharmacopoeia (see plate 16).

Initiation into the healing art is above all a way of weaving the patient into the vital forces of the life-world. This process is doubled by the references to the hen. At sunset, close to the *khoofi,* the sham fight begins, using the *n-noongu* intended for the patient. It looks like a weaving-hook and is made out of the wood of the seclusion bed (cf. 6.3.3); attached to it is a hen and also a sheet folded to form a bag containing agricultual objects like the ones that forebears had stolen once upon a time, and whose theft had been cursed and caused the initiate's illness. The cock or the hen will be put to death as a sacrifice at the end of the period of seclusion (phase 10). The *n-seengedyambeedi,* the large knife whose wooden handle has been removed and which was placed at the entrance to the ritual house (plate 11), is plunged into the earth close to the *n-noongu.* The fight begins anew, to the rhythm of the chanting; it breaks off a number of times in the course of the night and comes to an end at first cock crow. When the patient enters the state of trance, her entire mime—the movements of her eyes, head, and body—imitate the chicken ready to leave its nest. This rhythmic plunging is simultaneously a way of interweaving the patient's capacity for life-giving in concert with the resources of life-bearing in the world. In trance the patient cuts the *fula,* namely the content of the bag— in fact, the persecutive agent—in pieces with the large knife which has been plunged into the ground. She has her fate and development more firmly under control. The therapy group thereby reverses the nightly realm of sorcery and retaliation into a means of life-bearing. At sunrise, it is then up to the patriarch of the couple to "redeem the evil condemned" *(-kuula fula dyaphoongu),* by handing over to the therapist the equivalent of the object whose theft in the past led to the curse and created the impediment. It may consist of two or three pieces of cloth. The therapist then collects the *fula*, namely the content of the bag which the patient has cut into pieces and now mastered and reverted. He wraps a few pieces of this *fula* in a small piece of cloth and fastens it to the *n-noongu* weaving-hook intended for the patient.

The sham fight evokes the arousal of and union with the vital resources of the world. It is a reminder of the initial denunciation of the cause of the problem (phase 5). While working through the persecutive experience again, the therapeutic group turns the impediment or the misfortune against itself. The sham fight thus also involves the representatives of the matrimonial alliance, the patient, her husband, her uncle, and the one who represents the uterine line of descent through which the *khita* cult has been handed on, as well as the therapist. This combat involving the *n-noongu* weaving-hook to a certain extent reflects the marital union, while the knife without a handle and the *fula* (which is understood to represent foam) have genital connotations of femininity and virility.

Patient and therapeutic group are engaged both in a quest for healing and in the transmission of medical skills. These activities occur within a context that involves engenderment, agnatic filiation, and initiation.

First, the therapeutic group once again transforms the patient's search for health into a family endeavor and thus considers the patient's health as part of a larger fabric. The act of plunging the *n-noongu* into the earth alternates with rubbing a bag attached to the patient's *n-noongu* weaving-hook against the earth in time with the rhythm of the successive chants. This bag is full of rinds and medicinal plants. The participants rub it back and forth against the ground so that the contents are crushed. The therapist intones chants, from time to time breaking off to explain the medicine, or the master-pupil relationship, or to remind the family leaders of the honors due to him.

Second, in the initiation the master conveys knowledge and power to his pupil. Here are some of the elements of this teaching, which are directed initially to the patient and her husband. The therapist begins with the following chant, which is nothing more than a list of the ingredients of a warm purging enema:

Chant 16

1. N-ndolundolu yabonga yibala;
   betu boosu mu yibala yibala, betu boosu.
2. N-nkheneti yabonga yibala;
   betu boosu mu yibala yibala, betu boosu.
3. N-kwaati, yabonga yisaka;
   betu boosu mu yisaka yisaka, betu boosu.
4. M-mvuma, yabonga yibala;
   betu boosu mu yisaka yisaka, betu boosu.

1 I will take a piece of bark from the trunk of the *n-ndolundolu* bush;
   all of us, we will put this bark in the infusion, all of us.
2 I will take a piece of bark from the trunk of the *n-nkheneti* bush;
   all of us, we will put this bark in the infusion, all of us.
3 I will take leaves from the *n-kwaati* tree;
   all of us, we will put these leaves in the infusion, all of us.
4 I will take leaves from the *m-mvuma* bush;
   all of us, we will put these leaves in the infusion, all of us.

The specialist continues his instruction by enumerating the plant substances that may not be employed in the douche: *n-kooki, m-buungi,* and *n-dzimba.* These plants are not to be used because the first causes hemorrhaging, the second is toxic, and the use of the last—whose name evokes menstruation, usually indicated by the verb *-ziimbakana,* "to miss or err"—might provoke abnormal bleeding.

The following chant provides instruction as to the means of "administering nasal instillations" *(-ta m-mweemwa)* against headaches the initiate or her colleagues might suffer from. To do this, several drops of palm oil or wine are poured into the nose through a funnel made of the leaf of an aromatic plant. Sometimes this leaf is simply rolled up and placed in the nose for a day or two:

Chant 17
1 Matsutsuutu m-mweemwa.
   Yilumbu kyeenda ngaanga kyayaabakanaku.
2 Mabulukutu m-mweemwa.
   Yilumbu kyeenda ngaanga kyayaabakanaku.
3 Mahetiheti m-mweemwa.
   Yilumbu kyeenda ngaanga kyayaabakanaku.
4 M-fwangulusu m-mweemwa.
   Yilumbu kyeenda ngaanga kyayaabakanaku.
5 Tundala m-mweemwa.
   Yilumbu kyeenda ngaanga kyayaabakanaku.
6 N-kwaati m-mweemwa.
   Yilumbu kyeenda ngaanga kyayaabakanaku.

1 The aromatic plant *matsutsuutsu* is good for nasal instillations.
   [Refrain:] The day of the master's departure is unknown. [As the master only gives explanations once, the student must be attentive.]
2 The herb *mabulukutu* is good for nasal instillations.
   [Refrain.]
3 The savanna bush *mahetiheti* (bearing aromatic leaves) is good for nasal instillations.
   [Refrain.]

4 The savanna herb *m-fwangulusu* (having a hollow stem) is good for nasal instillations.
[Refrain.]
5 The savanna herb *tundala* is good for nasal instillations.
[Refrain.]
6 The savanna tree *n-kwaati* is good for nasal instillations. (A wisp of its bark is placed in the nose.)
[Refrain.]

Third, the therapeutic initiation is an engenderment and agnatic filiation. The following chant encourages the initiate to adopt an attitude of submission towards his master, in the manner of a docile goat that kneels, with bent forelegs *(-bokula),* before its master. The master-pupil relationship is conceived in terms of agnatic filiation; as the phrase puts it, "the pupil has come from between the legs of the master-therapist" *(tuukidi mumaalu mangaanga).* Moreover, at the end of each explanation, the therapist offers to the pupil the plant or the object to which he was referring; the pupil pulls off a piece, known as *yitoondu,* "communication, association," and thereafter master and pupil entwine these pieces of the plant in their hair in order to "pass the communication on to the head."[17]

Chant 18
1 Khoombwe lele mee, khoombu mee, khoombu.
2 Koombu kameeka mee, khoombu.

1 The she-goat says "maa," the she-goat says "maa," the she-goat.
2 The she-goat bleats, she says "maa," the she-goat.

In the next chant, the specialist reminds the initiates that the ritual instruction will not be finished until he has received all his honoraria:

Chant 19
1 Yakusweeka bungaanga,
wungyimini n-kaanga;
yakusweeka bungaanga.
2 Wundobwedi n-kaanga,
yakulobwala bungaanga.

1 I will hide the art of healing from you
if you refuse to pay;
I will hide the art of healing from you.
2 If you pay me,
I will show you the art of healing.

The following chant is sung while one crushes the pharmacopoeia *phaandzi*, here referred to with a term of respect, *yaaya*, "elder brother":

Chant 20
1 Tuudinika yaaya dinika.
2 Kabwedi thandu yaaya dinika.
3 Kabwedi banda yaaya dinika.

1 All together, elder brother, we crush you.
2 Come down, elder brother, so that we may crush you.
3 Come up, elder brother, so that we may crush you.

Fourth, the transmission of healing skills is a kind of domestication of life forces from the nightly forest realm. The person in charge of the rite starts off the next chant at the first crow of the cock, when he goes to cut the *fula*, that is, the reminder of the patient's persecutive ailment, at the entrance to the ritual hut. This act signals that the instruction in the ritual specialization is complete:

Chant 21
1 M-mwalaala mundzila ngaanga;
2 m-mwalaala.
3 Yikweenda kayedi.

1 A millipede is on the path taken by the ritual specialist;
2 it is a millipede.
3 He has gone away for good.

The crushing of the medicines and the accompanying chants are intended to enable the group to share in the regenerating forces of the life-world, both vegetal and cosmic. The patient is meanwhile authorized to make the preparations herself. The vigil, during which the healing art has been partly transmitted to the patient, links the therapeutic group to this same regeneration. The instruction with regard to the therapeutic use of plants explains and defines the meaning of the cluster of herbs (*n-kaanda*, a synonym of *lubongu lwataangu*, "a cloth or a surface whose colors are as varied as those of the sun"), which is attached to the ridgepole of the seclusion house. Indeed, ritual vocabulary refers to this teaching either as -*taangila n-kaanda*, "learning what each plant has to tell us," or as -*taangila tona*, "learning what *tona* has to tell us." *Tona* is pure color, and it is the term applied to the color of the early sun. Initiation into the therapeutic art ends in the early morning with the preparation and the handing over of *bilesi*—the ritual objects *phaandzi*, *n-noongu*, and *tsaanga khita*—to sustain the health of the patient and assist her (*n-lesi*) during the treatment she must administer to herself. The preparation of these *bilesi* cannot be separated from the nocturnal initiation into the therapeutic art, despite the fact that it only begins after the water rite of transition which takes place on the first or second morning after the night of initiation. In order to prepare the *bilesi* the initiates and the therapist sit close to the *khoofi*.

Fifth, the pharmacopoeia bundles forces from the forest realm and puts these to use for protecting, restoring, and enhancing fertility, both feminine and masculine. In the *khita* cult, to prepare the *phaandzi* pharmacopoeia, the therapist takes the cloth attached to the *n-noongu* weaving-hook containing the plants crushed the previous night (just as the *yihalu* pharmacopeia is prepared in the context of other cults.[18] He calls on the little guardian Maleeka to crush them in the oblong mortar used for grinding dried cassava roots. He then wraps the crushed plants, to which he has added redwood paste, *khula,* in the cloth, being careful to add nothing which comes from his own pharmacopoeia. Finally, he wraps the cloth and its contents in an animal skin at the bottom of which lies a *lukata,* a thick ring of woven grasses that serves as a cushion when carrying various objects or loads on the head. The *lukata* suggests that the cult and its pharmacopoeia offer a kind of self-sustaining version of the life-world. The preparation of the *phaandzi* and its handing over to the new initiate completes the initiation into the therapeutic art which began the previous evening. This portion of the rite has a three-fold function. First of all, it delegates ritual power to the initiate—an act of delegation expressed as *-taandwasana phoongu,* "to disclose all aspects of the cult." Second, by virtue of its components—the animal skin in which it is wrapped (genet, weasel, Gambian rat or squirrel) and the *lukata* ring—the *phaandzi* pharmacopoeia has the property of trapping the evil.[19] As a result, the pharmacopoeia also enables its owner to formulate powerful curses within the framework of the *khita* cult. Third, the pieces of bark in the pharmacopoeia come from large, straight-boled trees, thereby representing the forest. This reference to a virile realm underlines the sexual signification of the plants contained in the sack attached to the *n-noongu* weaving-hook; this sack is crushed at the end of the mock battle, a process which itself is full of sexual connotations. Moreover, the red paste—a connotation of the setting sun—and the animal skin, that of the civet in particular, signify the fetal condition.

Just as the weaving-hook converts the maze in which the patient's fertility has been entangled into a weave, so the therapy reverts evil into life-bearing in the life-world and group, in connection with the uterus of the world. Two small bags are attached to the *n-noongu* weaving-hook at the middle of the stick or close to the farthest point from the notch. Apart from the *fula* (the condemned misdeed, foam), these bags also contain other agricultural or commercial products which might possibly be condemned as the sources of evil *(fula)* because they are the fruits of a past theft and, through a curse, are destined to lead to retaliation or persecution. In reality, these are tiny fragments taken from the presents that the coresidents offer to the patient as a sign of welcome on the eve of her reintegration into her homestead and conjugal home (see 7.2.3). To these the therapist adds some *khawa,* the explosive used in ritual weapons. The *n-noongu* weaving-hook is coated with *khula* and is wrapped in *manganga-tsaanga* grass, gathered from the river bank. The contents of these bags enable the *n-noongu* weaving-hook to convert the disorder into a reproductive, virile force. The shape of the hook and the mock-battle contribute to this meaning. It is a force of reproduction that stems from the earth, connoting the patient, spirit, and ancestral sources of life. Moreover, exegesis explicitly develops this connotation by stating *n-noongu kabutila baana,* "the *n-noongu* is for engendering children." We find more evidence of this meaning if we consider that, at the end of her period of seclusion, the *khita* initiate plants the *n-noongu* in the soil under the marital couch.

The *khita* initiate and the guardian Maleeka receive a *tsaanga khita,* a small gourd without a neck (see plate 17). Because of its contents, its shape, and the *mangangatsaanga* grass wrapped around it, this gourd is a reminder of the maternal belly whose impediment has henceforth been turned into certain fertility.[20] The initiate keeps her *tsaanga khita* like a copy of her maternal breast and places it close to the *n-noongu* in the marital home. Once she is pregnant, she can pour a little water into this gourd and drink it if she is in pain.

7.2.2 *A coming-out ordeal constitutes phase 9 of khita treatment.* It acts as the patient's delivery and birth in unison with cosmic 'origination.' There are two variations. While different in form, the meaning is the same: water, hence the river, provides for transition, purification, and healing.

The *first variation,* which I shall call the *ordeal and augury of the live fish,* takes place approximately two days before the end of the period of seclusion. Here the patient's coresidents join her to test and augur her regained fertility. They go fishing—literally, *-yaba mayaanga,* "to fish what lies in the pools." Having caught some fish, even only small ones, they return to the village carrying the live fish in a gourd or an earthenware pot filled with stream water, covered by a *lunguungu* leaf and wrapped in *mangangatsaanga* foliage. This gourd or pot is kept in the ritual house until the following day. If the majority of the fish are still alive by the next day, the patient eats them, as the expression indicates: *-diila yaanga dyahata,* "to eat in the village what comes from the pool." This takes place close to the ritual house. Using the weaver's needle *(thuumbu),* the therapist threads a live fish onto a fibre of the *futi* creeper that grows on the river bank. He extends this little fish towards the patient's mouth, saying: *Mina, mina, mina, yingola ngola,* "Swallow, swallow, swallow; it is an eel." The patient does not in fact swallow the fish; holding it in her mouth and without touching it with her hands, she places it in the hot cinders and fries it with the other fish kept in the gourd. This is an unusual way of cooking fish, because normally they are grilled on top of the fire or fried in a pan. The initiate then eats these fish with manioc paste.

This practice of catching and eating fish enacts potent transitions. The fish caught are referred to as *yaanga,* "the pool, that which comes from the pool." The pool is the place where the stream widens *(-yaangula)* and where the water stagnates, in other words, an intermediate place, on the one hand between terra firma and the running water of the stream and, on the other, between upstream and downstream. The fish, recalling the transition, remain in the ritual house for one night, thus linking sunset and sunrise. The act of swallowing the fish can also represent the passage from raw to cooked food, that is, the lifting of the ban on food. The transition from keeping the fish a night in a gourd and then offering them to the initiate so that she can swallow them intertwines the states of being contained and containing, and is probably evocative of fetal condition and pregnancy. In addition, catching the fish and their survival augur the subsequent course of the therapy. If the majority of the fish in the gourd are dead, the therapeutic group will ask one of its members to consult the oracle of the horn to determine the meaning of these deaths. Informants hold that the oracle can offer only one interpretation: *Ho yaanga dyan-kola, futu kanyeedya,* "if the trial of the pool has failed, it is because the patient has concealed a misdeed." According to these same comments, this hidden misdeed *(futu)* indicates that either the patient was involved in an extramarital affair (in which the boundaries of the conjugal home have been encroached upon), or that she is still exposed to ensorcellment (the frontiers of the body are undone, or in disorder). Efforts are made to neutralize the impact of the offense and the intrusion by offering the therapist some form of compensation for this misdeed. The significance of this ordeal by living fish can be compared to the oracular value of the hunt organized at the end of each phase of the ritual. Just like a productive hunt, the success of the fish ordeal is evidence that all the prescriptions related to the rite have been observed and that the treatment has every hope of succeeding. On the other hand, like failure in the hunt, the death of the fish means that infringements blamed upon the patient or a member of the therapeutic group must be remedied if the cure is to be successful.

The *second variation,* which I call the *water ordeal of transition,* takes place following another rite of transition performed at the crossing of the paths at dawn on the day on which seclusion ends. At first cock's crow, the patient, the guardian Maleeka, and the therapist leave the village and go towards the stream. They chant in turn as they carry out these morning rituals. In order to prevent the transition from exercising any evil influence, the patient and the Maleeka caretaker imitate the behavior of the chameleon as they leave the ritual house and the village. To preserve their fetal positions, they wear leaves or cloths on their feet and in their hair. The small group halts when they arrive at the crossing of the paths on the outskirts of the village. As we have seen, this crossing point forms the intersection of the various horizontal and vertical spatial divisions. It is here, too, that diviners and also *khita* healers are buried. The therapist unrolls his *yihalu*, the insignia of his specialization, and spreads his *ndzaku* on the ground to indicate the link which unites him to the *khita* spirits and to his deceased masters. While the guardian Maleeka stands behind the patient and holds her by the hip, the therapist takes the patient's left arm and helps her "pass across the crossways" *(-suumbuka phaambwandzila)* three times. In the meantime, he proclaims:

1	Sumu, sumu, sumu.
2	Khi twadiinga? Mooyi.
[or:]	
1'	Nyeenge nyengeneke,
	sina mundzila kitika.
2'	Khi twadiinga? Mooyi.
3'	Muufi wu, muufi wu, muufi wu.

1	Break the ban. [Three times]
2	What are we pursuing? Life.
[or:]	
1'	Come among us and stay.
2'	What is it that we seek? Life.
3'	The patient is a thief. [Three times]

In the terms of these texts, the patient infringes a taboo by passing through this crossing point, and this offense is seen equivalent to theft. Indeed, by straddling this point of transition and spatial intersection, the patient to a certain extent gives the lie to her condition as a recluse: having been forced to remain in bed in the ritual house, the patient is placed symbolically at the point of transition, on the one hand, between village and forest, and, on the other, between high and low, that is, at the point where the bract of the parasol tree gives way to foliage. By transgressing the spatial constraints inherent to her seclusion, the patient prefigures her return to customary social life.[21]

Arriving at the stream, the initiands prepare for the ordeal of crossing the waters. Since it is equivalent to the ordeal of the living fish, if the patient has undergone the latter she will not need to go through all the stages of the water ordeal of transition. When they reach a pool *(yaanga)*, the therapist threads a fibre of *futi* creeper onto a needle which he then inserts into a cola nut. Throwing it into the water, he pronounces the same words used during the trial of the living fish: "swallow, swallow, swallow; it is eel." The patient then throws herself into the water to catch the cola nut with her teeth while it is still floating on the surface. If she fails to catch the cola nut, the therapist calls on her to reveal her *futu* (hidden evil). Having confessed the sin or protested her innocence, the therapist verifies her affirmations. If she now succeeds in catching the cola nut in her teeth, a success which he attributes "to the extraordinary powers conferred upon him by his ritual art" *(mu yipha bungaanga)*, the patient's protests of innocence are upheld. The therapist demands a goat or some other form of compensation to combat any hidden evil which might hamper the effectiveness of the therapeutic treatment. The success of the trial is an augury: it proclaims the success of the treatment, that is, of the revitalization (cf. cola nut) of the vital weave (cf. needle, creeper, or raffia) regarding life transmission as epitomized—as we will see next—by the river journey to the spring.

The patient then bathes in the stream. The current must both carry off any impurity still clinging to the patient and revivify her. Before entering the water, the therapist bounds off a propitious or receptive place in the stream for the patient. Standing on one bank, he throws water towards the other, and by thus traversing the current he links the two banks, as he would be link up bride-givers and -takers. He then takes the patient by the left arm and makes her enter the stream, saying: *nyeenge nyengeneke: khi twadiinga? Mooyi. Kesa yebala mungoluku,* "What are we seeking? Life (from its source). It is not in defiance that she has entered the water." By allowing the patient to wash herself, the therapist lifts the ban on water involved in seclusion: it is a first separation from her fetal state. This invocation attests to the fact that entry into the stream also signifies her renewed reintegration into the uterine flow of life transmission. The therapist tears off a strip of the cloth in which the patient is dressed and calls on her to let the current carry off all her clothes and to wash herself. In this way, we are told, the therapist, on the one hand, prevents a sorcerer from using for evil ends the clothes or the water in which the patient has bathed. While she is washing, the woman looks upstream. Before coming out, the therapist collects fallen leaves *(tsatsala zaseenguka)* from either bank. He stores them in his *yihalu*, together with the strip of torn cloth. Or he might tie the piece of cloth to the *m-mvuma* tree which forms part of the *khoofi*. Bathing in the stream is thus an act both of joining and of bounding off one's proper place in the bloodstream or vital flow from the womb of the world.

The patient and the guardian Maleeka walk behind the therapist in the stream bed and upstream towards a small waterfall or rapids considered equivalent to a spring. From time to time, using a bunch of leaves, the therapist sprinkles *(-yuba)* on those following him, in order to purify them. Using her left hand, the patient gathers branches from the various bushes and plants growing close to the water and ties them round the small of her back. The significance of this skirt of leaves, known as *masambala*, is very similar to that of "the assortment of young shoots of plants taken at random" *mbakunumbakunu:* healing replaces the illness following the path used by the latter and the patient links herself to the 'buds' that is the youngest offspring, of the uterine tree of life transmission. When she reaches the small waterfall or the rapids, the patient bathes herself again and then steps out of the water. The guardian Maleeka likewise takes part in the various stages of the rite. In other words, walking upstream further reconnects the patient with the maternal earth source of all life. It publicizes to the environment or life-world the change which has taken place within the patient.

Reentry into the village represents a new phase in the patient's attainment of a new social identity. On the way back from the stream the therapist collects a number of plants *(mbakunumbakunu)* which he uses on that same morning to produce the *tsaanga khita*. When the group reaches the first crossing of the paths on their return route, they stop and "take a smoke bath to redeem themselves" *(-difuta kyaangu)*. The therapist gathers trampled dead leaves from the paths which converge at that point, sets them alight, and adds certain ingredients from his *yihalu* pharmacopoeia. The patient steps over the fire, exposes her body to the smoke and waves the smoke into her face with her hand, while the therapist proclaims:

2   Lubuka, lubuka.
3   Kandzoku, n-hwangala.

1   Smoke of the leaves [penetrate]. [twice]
2   Come out, come out.
3   This house is not a house for living in, it is an empty and abandoned house.

The fumigation is supposed to chase away the affliction by bringing about its destruction. The smoke from the fire of dead and crushed leaves collected at the crossing of the paths signifies that no matter what path it has taken, the malady has no further power over the patient. The initiate has "paid off" *(-difuta)* any debt to the kin or any ties with possible retaliation. Throwing the ritual ingredients of the *yihalu* on the fire should dispel the evil once and for all. The therapist's words compare the patient to an empty house which has become inhospitable to any form of illness, because nothing remains in the woman which could still justify its presence. Indeed, compensation has been paid for any possible offense and the success achieved in the hunt forecasts the success of the intervention.

Reentry in the social world is gradual and a function of separation from a former condition. Close to the village, the patient and guardian Maleeka stop singing and again imitate the chameleon. The therapist invites them to sit for a moment on a mat placed against the wall of the ritual house, in such a way that their backs are still turned to the inhabited areas of the village. The patient's head is quite often thereafter shaved as a sign of her separation from a physical state which she has now left behind her and as a sign of rebirth; at the same time, she receives new clothing from her husband.

7.2.3 *Phase 10 of the cure involves the initiate's reintegration into the family circle, hearth, and home.* It is accomplished by means of sacrifice and a meal all the members of the therapeutic group and the coresidents share; this element is common to all the cults. The sacrifice and commensality take place at the end of the period of seclusion, immediately after the preparation of the ritual objects, and lead up to the reentry of the *khita* initiate into mainstream society. The cock or the hen offered by the uncle to the patient on the evening of her seclusion is handed to the therapist. On the previous evening, the bird had been attached to the pharmacopoeia during the ritual denunciation of the vanquished evil. Like a predator, the therapist now tears the chicken's throat with his teeth and allows the blood to flow over the patient's legs and over her ritual objects. The bird is then dressed and cooked, and after distributing bits of grilled meat to all those present, the therapist then gives them permission to use their hands to partake of the meat and manioc paste.

Firstly, the chicken is the object of "a blood sacrifice" *(yimenga),* a substitute of the possessed and victimized patient. In its original sense *yimenga* denotes the animal handed over in compensation for the evil that led to the retaliatory curse; the animal is killed and prepared to be eaten by the beneficiary and the immediate family. As though to burden the bird with the impediment that binds the woman and in this way to "unbind" *(-biindulula)* her body from all that is hampering it, the therapist coils the hen in a spiral around her body. Through the intimate relation between the patient's body and the seclusion hut, itself a metaphor of the hen about to lay or brood an egg, there is an intimate transfer between the sacrifice and the freeing of the patient out of the persecutive relationship with the spirit. The guardian Maleeka runs round the house while plucking the fowl in order to further bring about this transfer between the sacrificial animal, the ritual house, and the patient's body. Having torn off the its head and having allowed the blood to flow over the patient's legs, the therapist intones the following words, which clearly demonstrate that it is a substitute sacrifice: *nwa makhoku, mamuutu tiina,* "drink the blood of the fowl, keep the human blood," or *nwa makhoku, mamuutu masaaba,* "drink the blood of the fowl so that human blood will increase." Informants stress the need to sacrifice a "singing hen" *(khokwa khookula),* a reference to the cock which crows at dawn and, hence, the end of the reign of night. The sacrifice of this hen aims at neutralizing all murderous aggression against a member of the small therapeutic group. More specifically, the animal takes the place of the patient or any other member of the therapeutic group in danger of becoming the victim either of an evil agent or of a persecution for a misdeed committed by the ascendancy. The patient's illness is thus transferred to the sacrificial bird, and this transferral reverses the patient's relationship with the previously deadly spirit.

Secondly, the members of the small therapeutic group enter into a pact *(khalu)* by sharing the sacrificed hen in the course of a common meal; any malevolence within the group is reversed against itself and is transformed into bonds of solidarity. Having prepared the "hen of the pact" *(khokwa khalu)*, the therapist extends a piece of the fowl close to the mouth of each participant. To do this, he uses either the point of his knife or the claw of a predatory animal. At the same time he lays a curse upon anyone who, having shared the common meal—which is supposed to create an intimate union among those taking part—attacks the life of any other person; that person will find his aggression turned against himself:

1 Khita nyaangi, ngoombwa nyaangi.
2 Phoongu phoongwaandi.
3 Kitu kitwaandi

1 Learn that *khita* is at the origin of illness and treats them, that divination reveals them and shows how to treat them.
2 May the tutelary spirits of the cult turn against those who misuse them [that is, use it to ensorcell].
3 May the *kitu* plant turn against those who use it. (a)

Comment:
(a) *Kitu* is a fast-growing and expansive plant that, because of its scabs and its homonymy with *-kitula*, "to disguise, to transform into a sorcerer," is a sign of ensorcellment. Here, by repeating the term *kitu*, the phrase *(kitu kitwaandi)* commands the sorcerous action to turn against itself.

Thirdly, this meal strengthens *(makolasa)* those who take part. There are several rules governing the preparation of the fowl. These prevent the hen, which serves as a substitute for all illness, from transmitting the illness to the commensals or to those who live in close bodily contact. The therapist adopts the behavior of containment *(yibati):* he knots his loincloth between his legs and avoids any exchange through manual contact; he therefore places the pot containing the hen on the fire by gripping it between his feet. He uses no knife and avoids breaking the chicken's bones, no doubt because of the cock's connotations of virility. To strengthen those taking part, he adds stimulants such as cola nut, pepper, and aphrodisiacs to the sauce. According to ritual vocabulary, the blood of the fowl which flowed over the legs of the initiate serves to "nourish her blood" *(-tsaatsila meenga)* and to strengthen her ability to connect with the life source and transmit blood or life. It should also flow over the ritual objects *phaandzi, n-noongu,* and *tsaanga* intended for the initiate. In substituting his aggressive act for the spirit's aggressive proclivity, the healer reverses its aggressive tendency into a life-giving one.

Those consanguines and coresidents of the patient or the afflicted couple unable to attend the sacrifice and the common meal will have a later opportunity to associate themselves with the rite. In return for some small gift, the initiate will lend them the bone of the sacrificed fowl which she keeps in her *phaandzi;* they rub this against their throats, as a mark of commensality, or against the sole of the foot, suggesting intimate association.

7.2.4 *Phases 7 and 11 lead the khita initiate back into society.* Reentry into her genetic role and household tasks is foreshadowed two days prior to the end of the period of seclusion (phase 7), and is finally fulfilled when she steps out of seclusion for good (phase 11). The woman hereby finishes her initiation and regains her autonomy. She can now resume her married life and distance herself from the filial or avuncular tie with her initiator.

The rehearsal of the initiate's social reintegration generally takes place two days before the night in which she is initiated into the art of therapy (phase 8). Throughout the preceding day and evening the taboos pertaining to seclusion are temporarily lifted, in particular the bans on leaving the village and of seeing daylight: it is a "day of transition" *(yilumbu kyatsaandzu).* In the evening, the therapist, the initiate, and her guardian circle the ritual house three times; they then traverse the whole village "collecting gifts" *(-seenda, n-seendu)* and dancing to the rhythm of their songs. At each family compound the initiate stops and receives small gifts of money or food (money, sections of manioc root, yams, peanuts, maize, pepper, gourds, and so on) which she places in the basket carried on her back or on her head. At the end of this round of visits, she hides her basket in the seclusion house. According to the therapist, this practice represents first of all "the collection of gifts offered in homage" *(-diingila n-laambu)* and evokes the tribute offered to a ruling chief. It also foreshadows the initiate's return to domestic duties. It is moreover meant as a death trap for the evil, and is seen as *-kaya hata,* "ensnaring any evil influence from villagers which might still threaten the initiate." Whereas the initiate's illness is very often linked to the theft of foodstuff and with the resultant curse, these gifts to a certain extent neutralize the negative valence which any engagement in social life might eventually possess for the initiate, her family, and the former *khita* initiates of the village. The conflict—the spiral of theft, curse, and illness—is turned into healing thanks to the dynamics of the ritual. This collection of foodstuffs is also referred to as *-somuna phoongu,* "rooting out anything which might recall the evil already condemned," or *-lobula yidyaata kyahata,* "purifying the village of any intrusion or any other form of evil." The following is one of the chants which accompanies this collection; it refers to the purification of any evil that might lead to the reappearance of the disorder:

Chant 22
Ah Makhedi,
kota wadya yitoodya.

Ah! Makhedi [the *khita* initiate],
come into the village and collect the hen's droppings.

The therapist breaks off fragments of the various foodstuffs collected and attaches them to the initiate's *n-noongu* weaving-hook. As we will see, a portion of the food collected will be handed over to the therapist at the end of the period of seclusion; he will destroy a part and use the rest.

The metamorphosis brought about by her initiation authorizes the initiate to reintegrate her social position at the end of the seclusion. The initiate publicizes this transformation by altering her appearance, making up her face, and decorating her head. Once the initiate returns from the water ordeal and her hair has been shaved, an elderly woman, a blood relative or relative by marriage, joins the initiates. When the therapist gives them the order, the initiate and the guardian Maleeka stand up. The old woman assists them in taking off the skirts of leaves and the rags with which they covered themselves on their way back from the stream and in putting on their new clothes. Escorted by the elderly woman, and walking like chameleons, they go into the savanna to throw the rags, the leaf skirts, and sometimes the shaven hair at the foot of "a bush of sorrow" *(n-heeti* or *m-booti).*

Facial decoration adds to the initiate's identification with the generative potential of the hen. Upon their return, they seat themselves on a mat in front of the seclusion house. Whereas during the period of seclusion they had to "cleanse [that is, anoint and warm up] their body with red" *(-yebasa khula),* they are henceforth entitled to "cleanse [that is, expose and warm up] their body with the light of the sun" *(-yebasa mwuini).* The elderly woman then paints the faces of the initiate and of the guardian Maleeka. This act is called *-ta tsona,* "to make markings," or *-sya ngidi,* an expression whose etymology I have been unable to trace. The decorative motif is the well-known pattern of facial adornment found also on many small statuettes: these continuous or broken markings trace circles round the eyes and cross at the nose (see plate 14). Using a hen's feather, the elderly woman applies white *(pheemba)* and red *(muundu)* clay, and sometimes also a blue color made from imported powder. In the meantime the therapist plaits necklaces and bracelets using raffia and *futi* fibers. He ties a lace round the neck of each initiate, and to this he attaches a leaf from the parasol tree containing a feather of the sacrificial hen. This leaf, it is said, is shaped like a heart and represents the heart of the initiate, while the role of the *futi* fibers is to call down peace upon that heart—*mbuundwa-muutu futi,* "may the heart of man find peace and security." The therapist ties other bracelets of raffia and *futi* fibers round the upper right arms of the two women.

The initiate receives a ritual headdress made of the skin of a civet, weasel, Gambian rat, or squirrel (see plate 18). This headdress runs from the forehead to the base of her skull; it is known as *n-kotu* or *yimbondu,* terms that refer to a lock of hair plaited over the forehead. The animal skin was offered to the therapist in payment for his services. Such a skin may also be used to wrap up the pharmacopoeia. Once the period of seclusion is completed, this headdress serves as a token of safe-conduct out of all the ill-threat the patient has been a victim of: because of all the various things attached to the headdress,[22] the weasel and the civet may signify a positive fetal condition, whereas the squirrel and the Gambian rat signify the reversal of the agent of misfortune against itself. The headdress also evokes the comb of a rooster, metaphorically assimilating the *khita* initiate's emergence from the seclusion-incubation with a chick breaking out of its shell. The raffia and fibers worn by the initiate on her arms as witness *(yidiimbu)* to her initiation evoke the hen's feathers on its legs. The therapist applies a spittle *(-seengula)* of cola nuts or aphrodisiac plants *(tseengwa)* on those parts of the initiate's body believed to be the major seats of life force: the forehead, the temples, the heart, the clavicles, and the kidney area.

The healer finally acts as a midwife for the initiate's delivery and rebirth. The way in which the therapist "draws the initiate out" *(-loondzula)*[23] of the seclusion house is like a liberation, a hatching out: the same term also refers to the act of drawing something out of a hole, bottleneck, or hiding place. For her coming out, the initiate wears all the marks of her initiation: her headdress, her facial markings, and her ritual objects, namely *phaandzi, n-noongu,* and *tsaanga.* She also bears a small elbow-shaped branch formed from the wood of the bushes of sorrow, *m-booti* or *n-heeti,* and wrapped in *mangangatsaanga* foliage on her shoulder. According to commentators, this branch, whose ritual name is *n-lasya,* signifies deformity and, by extension, any other form of fertility or birth disorder. The therapist leads the initiate and the guardian Maleeka into the ritual house by the entry facing the village. Imitating a violent struggle, the therapist uses a machete to cut a hole through the wall against which the initiate's bed is placed. The three then step over the bed and through the hole, thus passing from inside to outside the hut. The therapist, initiate, and guardian enter and exit the hut three times, each time chanting:

Chant 23
Kongoongo,
a mwaneetu. [Twice]

From this pristine seclusion,
we carry our child. [See 6.3.4.]

Chant 24
Eh Tsuumbwa,
kiima kyazuunga n-leembi.

Member of the Tsuumbwa clan,
reawaken to your winding sheet.

Comment:
This formula assimilates the period of seclusion to a period of gestation.

The *khita* initiate is thereafter led off through the village to her conjugal home; the insignia of her initiation and her healing are exhibited constantly. Finally, the initiate joins her husband to resume her married life. When she arrives at the threshold of the marital home—or that of her uncle if the treatment took place in his village—the therapist invites husband and wife to sit down facing each other and asks them to "entwine their legs" (*-biindasana maalu*). The husband then offers the therapist one or two pieces of cloth in order to "buy back" (*-kuula*) the right to stand up. Some healers then call on the couple to give life to the child *n-noongu* without further ado: this child will thus bear the name of the *n-noongu* weaving-hook, which the initiate will preserve under the matrimonial bed. When the initiation occurs in a place other than in the husband's village, the *khita* initiate will return to the marital home only after she has passed through the therapist's village.

Once the period of seclusion has ended, the initiate is reintegrated into her domestic group and homestead: on that day the men who go hunting are certain that the hunt will be successful, and this will be a sign of the success of the initiation.

7.3.5 *In phase 12, the initiate emancipates herself from the therapeutic relationship.* The agnatic relationship of master-pupil and the avuncular or uterine relationship of therapist-patient change in such a way that the patient finds herself once again woven into her network of alliances, maternity, and residence. This reintegration ties her in with the customary gender roles, a situation from which the initiate, because of her androgynous identity, had been withdrawn during treatment. At the moment he draws the recluse out of the seclusion house, the therapist recalls the filiation that exists between him and the initiate and threatens her with misfortune if she ever betrays this bond:

1 Khita nyaangi ngoombwa nyaangi.
2 Kanguula dyaambu keti pfuundu.
3 Kakotala kupfuundu, n-hoonda;
4 Keti mwanaama, keti n-khetwaama, n-hoonda.

1 May you learn that *khita* makes ill and heals, and that divination discloses how to treat.
2 If the initiate knows of an attack on me, if she fails to warn me that in a secret meeting sorcerers have decided to kill me;
3 if in a secret meeting she herself proposes killing me, kill her.
4 If she wishes evil on my child or my wife, kill her.

To heighten the impact of this warning, the therapist holds a cord with a wooden hook *(m-mvuma)*; this he attaches either to the initiate's left little finger or to the string holding her loincloth. Because of its name, *yikho,* this hook represents the trigger that sets off the net or bow trap: any evil act on the part of the initiate against her master will inevitably 'entrap' the author and prove fatal to her.

The therapeutic bond has to be loosened so that initiate and healer may each regain autonomy. Soon after the end of the period of seclusion, the *khita* initiate, accompanied by her Maleeka guardian, goes to see the therapist at his home. The therapist transforms the intimate avuncular ties that link him to the patient henceforth into a bond as with in-laws, as of a wife-giver, *buko.* The therapist thus limits himself to the role of the one who gives the patient in marriage to the spirit of the cult and therefore expects to receive his share of the benefits which the initiate will enjoy from her healing or, more specifically, from her initiation. The patient, now emancipated, is authorized to resume marital life and renew her links with society.

Payment of the healer's services and a successful augury from the hunt are preconditions for the severance of the therapeutic ties. Tradition holds that the initiate should come to visit her healer on the "third day" *(yitatu)* after the end of the period of seclusion. In fact, the initiate is entitled to revisit the therapist the very next day; in other cases she may wait for a week or more—the reason being that such a visit cannot be made until all the honoraria *(yita)* due to the therapist have been paid. The step may also be postponed until a hunt has been successful. This visit to the therapist is referred to as *-fila phoongu,* "escaping from the ritual relationship," an expression recalling the one used to describe the integration of the young married woman into the marital home: *-fila mwanan-khetu kuloongu,* "to take the young woman out of her father's house." Both cases involve the "sending of a basket of foodstuff" *(-loongala n-yendi)* (see 3.3).

Ill fortune has been finally induced to destroy itself. The initiate hands over to the therapist part of the food which she collected in the village two days before the end of the period of seclusion (during phase 7). At dawn, in order to dissolve the ill-fated nature of agricultural products—whose theft has brought about the spiral of curse and persecution—the therapist places the basket containing the products on a midden on the outskirts of the village. He adds the patient's *n-lasya,* the elbow-shaped stick which she carried as she came out of seclusion and the sign of her *khita* disorder. Using a weed, he sprinkles them with *n-zoondza,* a liquid preparation consisting of the excrement of domestic animals mixed with water. This gesture casts ill fortune upon the ailment and again signifies that every form of evil finally is self-corrupting. The therapist also takes some of the gifts from the basket and buries them in the savanna at the foot of a bush of sorrows. The next morning, when the *khita* initiate offers him a hen to signify the change which she intends to bring about in their relationship, she says:

1 Khaaka, leelu ngeyi watsiimba,
  leelu wundobwedi kuphoongu.
2 Yisa tolula n-toondu.
  Taa khoku. Kola.
3 Meni yulubwedi kuyidyaata.

1 Master, in these days you have taken me in,
  and now you have withdrawn me from the influence of the cult which you represent.
2 I have come to take my leave. (a)
  Here is the hen; may your health be fortified.
3 I am making you leave my marital space to prevent you from becoming an intruder.

Comment:
(a) *-Tolula n-toondu* is the name given to the act of breaking the leaf funnel that is used to collect the palm sap in a gourd for the making of palm wine. By breaking the funnel, the initiate, having been "engendered" into the therapeutic art by her master, affirms her rediscovered autonomy in relation to him (see Devisch 1988:278).

As a sign of this transformation in their ties, the therapist in turn presents a live hen to the *khita* initiate and says:

1 Taa, ngeyi watsuumbukila; menibi yakusuumbuka.
2 Taa khoku.
3 Weenda buta batsuki ye ndzala.

1 Thus we have straddled each other.
2 Here is the hen.
3 Go and bring forth children with hair and nails [healthy children].

Master and pupil, separately, will prepare the hens they have received; then, to mark off the bounds of their respective families, each will eat her or his hen in the course of meals with the members of their homesteads.[24] The initiate will first spend one night in the therapist's village and after returning home, will have the family meal. Before this, and in order to liberate herself from the avuncular relationship between patient and therapist, the woman frees herself from the prescriptions governing such relationships. By drawing water for the therapist, she transgresses and thus lifts the taboo against working and touching water, and witnesses to her social rebirth and new position in relation to the stream of life transmission.

Upon her return to the marital home, the *khita* initiate is no longer limited by any explicit prescriptions. The day of her arrival she is welcomed with dances, and her return is celebrated that evening. She emerges from the seclusion and its tests matured, honored, and pacified, ready and prepared to take up anew her reproductive role and household tasks with greater confidence. Since she is now seen by society as virtually capable of bearing healthy children, or at least as one who can hand down the uterine life source to a child that she may adopt from a younger sister in case she would remain barren. There is a firm relation even if the child does not necessarily stay most of its childhood with the adoption mother. Moreover, while during the *khita* cure she had renounced all woman's work and had taken on an androgynous identity, she is now reintegrated into the gendered division of activities and spaces. Initiation nevertheless leads to a consecration or lasting devotion to the *khita* cult which is henceforth focused on the cultic objects, in particular *n-noongu, phaandzi, tsaanga,* and *yimbondu*. She will further observe certain cult taboos, having chiefly to do with food, and a code for handling social contacts that should enable her to escape once and for all from problems concerning fertility and birth.[25]

Her return to the marital home indicates that the initiate is fully invested *(yiyaalu)* into the *khita* cult. It remains for the lineage chief of the cult to 'bound off' the initiate from the malevolent action of the *khita* spirit: he places a plated fibre bracelet around her ankle in order to prevent repercussions of the ailment or aggression. The initiation closes with dances and chants.

7.3 Relapse of Illness

Reappearance of the illness (cf. appendix A) does not mean that the *khita* treatment has been ineffective, at least from the perspective of the cult. If the result is less than expected, when all the prescriptions have been strictly observed, it is supposed that not all the antecedents of the problem within the family were taken into account. The treatment itself is considered infallible because it is prescribed and guaranteed by the divinatory etiology. The competent therapist presides over the organization of the seclusion on the basis of very strict rules which he himself has been taught through rites of initiation. Were he to break one of these rules, he would expose himself to the persecution for that offense. Moreover, as a precaution, the treatment only advances when the time seems ripe—indicated by the success of the hunt—and these signs are interpreted as marks of approval on the part of the *khita* spirits and the ancestors. Again, once their rights have been respected and their legitimate claims have been satisfied, the families involved can no longer thwart the therapy except by sorcery. The treatment, however, takes all precautions to rule out any ensorcellment.

Since the ritual therapy is seen as an institution handed down by tradition, the efficacy of the cure can never be questioned. On the contrary, it is taken for granted. If the initiate does not recover, this will in fact not lead to skepticism, criticism, or a change of opinion. Any statistical assessment or estimate of probability seeking to establish the number of successes or failures is quite foreign to the mind-set of therapists and their clients.

Since the oracle entertains a number of etiological dimensions, since the interpretation of the disorder involves several ascendant generations, and, moreover, since the treatment gives priority to the transmission of the disorder within the *khita* cult, the failure of the treatment could not weaken the divinatory oracle. Moreover, the initial divinatory diagnosis generally attributes the appearance of a disorder to several different curses and ensorcellments for which ritual treatment, should the trouble persist, has probably not provided all the necessary compensations.

If the gynecological problem recurs, or appears in other forms, only a new divinatory oracle is capable of revealing the causes. While the second divinatory oracle, on the basis of the same given facts, rarely provides an etiological interpretation different from the first, it can nevertheless take into consideration other factors or other aspects of the same facts.

If a second therapeutic treatment within the same cult still proves ineffective, specialists from other cults can be called in, on condition that the husband or the head of the husband's family are wealthy enough to meet the costs. It can happen, however, that in such a case the husband would prefer to spend his goods to acquire a new spouse. A second period in the seclusion house is only possible if the oracle has revealed that the first period of seclusion was presided over by an uncle who, without due entitlement, had caused the treatment to fail. When the afflicted woman, while still young, has been abandoned by her husband's family, she may return to her parental homestead. If her cure be attributed to care paid for by her family of origin, this abandonment represents a valid cause for divorce. On the other hand, however, if after four or five years of treatment the illness proves incurable, the sterile women becomes marginalized within the group of cowives and within her residential group; the classificatory fathers and brothers of such a woman see no reason to take her in. Since, however, the disorder with which she is afflicted has its origins outside of herself, in family or ancestral antecedents, and since several initiations have made her the focal point for collective beliefs in extrahuman realities, she will arouse both fear and respect. As the woman has in some sense been sacralized, her disorder confers upon her a social status and respect that transcend gender categories and the frontiers between the human and extrahuman.

7.4 Fertility Rituals and Analyses Compared: A Look at Victor Turner

According to Victor Turner (1968:198), female puberty rituals among the matrilineal Ndembu are a means for social reproduction that dramatize the girls' transition to motherhood while publicly endorsing the legitimacy of certain crucial principles of Ndembu society. For him, the Ndembu thereby seek to overcome some reverberating tensions in and between the successive generations, the uterine kin, and loyalties towards the father, the husband, and the residential group. These "life-crisis" rituals attempt at a socialization of women's places in the matriliny and society. Communal cults articulate the interests of the matrikin in a situation in which the genitors and the mothers' brothers each seek power, loyalties, or wealth for themselves. Affliction cults help the patients and those concerned to accept the duties of motherhood in society, as these are regulated by male interests. His very sensitive reports and analyses of the interlocking social system and rituals are extremely rich and insightful. Although much of his ethnographic data are evocative of bodily symbolism, Turner's cognitivist analysis does not disclose how Ndembu rituals are operative beyond the level of social value and cognitive or predicative meaning. To be sure, his analysis suggests that these rituals may lead the women to a particular consciousness of their role as childbearers in the uterine line of succession from the grandmothers and mothers (see Turner 1968:81–85). However, he does not show how much the maternal body is both a source and template of meaningful action in the therapeutic drama that empowers the female initiands or patients while realigning in particular ways the forces of growth and reproduction in the body, the family, and the life-world. I argue that the healing ritual is not fully reducible to a means by which the social and cognitive order restates itself: in particular, the imaginary register and the body are a source of a plus value, of a quality change in the relationships in and between the fields of body, group, and life-world. In the Yaka view, healing is the nonauthored manifestation of the life-source: it activates the weaving-loom of life.

Turner reports in great detail on two cults concerned with female reproduction, namely the *nkula* affliction cult and the *nkang'a* puberty ritual as found among the matrilineal and virilocal Ndembu of northwestern Zambia who, like the Yaka of southwestern Zaire, have been strongly exposed to Luunda influence. He presents rituals in part as a narration that moves people to social action and in part as a rewriting of a script about how women have to give away social power to the men, be they father, husband, mother's brother, ritual specialist, or hunter. Turner conveys an image of Ndembu society in which the rituals provide a narration of a social structure and power struggle outreaching the all too subjective and idiosyncratic experience of the body, meanwhile socializing the senses, passions, and emotions. The rituals of affliction express how much the system of filiation and residence gives rise to a contradictory and messy world of difficult separation from, and problematic interdependence with, the uterine world of mothers, grandmothers, matrikin, and shades. In Turner's view these rituals are quintessential customs, basically intermingled with the group processes of human bonding, loyalty, and power: they make present the group's basic ethics through the logos of meaning. The rituals cathartically vent and constrain socially destructive urges in individuals, and redress social disunion and contradiction. They also compel the initiates and the wider audience to dramatize the core values of motherhood paired with matriliny, solidarity, and seniority. These rituals bring to light and try to circumvent the structural contradiction in Ndembu society "between *matrilineal descent,* which governs residential affiliation, succession to office, and inheritance of property, and *virilocal marriage,* which determines the post-marital residential affiliation of women" (Turner 1968:265). They therefore do not only bring about adjustments between men and women, mothers and daughters, residential unit and matrikin, but "mobilize and direct the total energy released by *all* the specific conflicts" towards reaffirmation of social cohesion, imbuing the core symbols "with warmth and desirability" (268). It is as if the purpose of these rituals is to achieve a world of order, rules, and regularity. Rituals perform on the stage of consciousness and morality by capturing the power and gratification of desire, the bonds of loyalty and duty, and by linking these up with a wider system of meaning rooted in the past. For Turner, rituals feed emotionally on the body (cf. the orectic pole), in order to escape from or master the (maternal) body in an exchange of meaning and social integration.

In the *nkula* cult (Turner 1967:41–3; 1968:52–88), a woman suffering from menstrual disorders, barrenness, miscarriage, or difficult delivery, or who gives birth to a sickly infant, undergoes a paradoxical ritual of redress and identification with maternal values. It is a 'red' ritual of 'blood,' as Turner describes it: the uterine shade first afflicts and then through cultic intervention assists the afflicted. Turner stresses that *nkula* has basically to do with a highly dramatized handing down of the 'genesic' function in the maternal line from the maternal grandmother—in the figure of the possessing shade—and via the mother to her daughter and the latter's children. Behind the patient's house a small "hut of the *nkula* shade" is erected. The patient and her male helper are several times led to the spirit hut. She is washed with medicine, and drinks it. Medicines aim at "killing the witchcraft" and the misfortune it causes, and at arousing life-giving potency in the patient: cold and hot, white and red medicines aim at reversing the misfortune. In "doing the dancing with an axe in the hand," the patient is led to ritually adopt the very virile behavior of the hunter and warrior, inasmuch as hunting and giving birth are conceived to be analogous processes. Meanwhile she is facing a core symbol of idealized motherhood and of her expected role of life-bearer in the matriliny. Namely, these values and core symbols are exemplified in front of her in the form of a treated calabash that symbolizes the womb: a carved figure of an infant is contained in it bathing in a glutinous red mixture to which 'residues' (nail clippings, hair, shadow, excreta) of the initiate are added. The figurine is made from the *mukula* tree whose 'blood' (red gum) coagulates quickly. For the Ndembu, it evokes the way menstrual blood should coagulate in the womb to form a child. Men carve this figurine with the hunter's small skinning knife, thereby reasserting their importance in society's reproduction. According to Turner, the cult is above all a positive and pervasive force in social action "overcoming divisions and restoring solidarity in the local community" (1968:80).

The rich ethnographic data provided by Turner allow me to recognize a pattern of bodily symbolism that is similar to one found among the Yaka, but overlooked by Turner. The relationship between the patient's body and the shade-hut, into which she is led backwards for seclusion, is one of encompassment. The patient's body is treated with medicines from trees chosen either because of their abundant fruit—representative of many children—or because of a large central root, which stands for the *nkula* shade (62). A pot with medicines is put on the fire in the shade-hut to the side of a meal mortar containing a part of the leaves and some of the root parings. The patient sits by the mortar while women do the pounding, and the male "doctor puts his hand in the mortar and gives the patient a little medicine to drink," or "pours some on top of her head, so that she will receive her shade" (63). She is then washed with medicines from the cooking pot: the vegetal bits of the medicines should dry and adhere to her body. The uterine ancestral shades enter the patient's body while she is in a state of possession, but they also inhabit the shade-hut which encompasses her. Movements in and out of the shade-hut, putting medicines in the mortar, pot, or house, and extracting preparations from these containers and giving them to the woman to drink or splashing them over her body are metaphors both for purging the patient's body of intrusive elements and for making her into an agent capable of inclusion and life transmission. The shade moreover articulates ties with uterine descent. The patient hereby experiences 'embodiedness' and embodiment, feeling contained and herself able to contain. This logic intertwines the patient's longing to be a baby and to have one, that is, to relive a fetal condition and symbiosis with her mother, on the one hand, with her wish to becoming herself a mother, on the other.

Nkang'a is a communal cult and puberty ritual for girls: it prefigures or accompanies their transition to marriage, childbearing, and becoming a provider of (white) food. Inasmuch as it enacts the core moral values of matriliny and motherhood, Turner labels it as a 'white' ritual of 'milk' that celebrates the girls' coming to age. Around the *mudyi* life tree (with its milky latex), the girls are led to ritually and vividly portray the tensions arising in a matricentric family living virilocally, namely between themselves or the homestead where they were born or grew up, on the one hand, and the group of their husband where they soon will settle, on the other. Through moments of avoiding versus sharing contact in the same ritual scene, mother and daughter, uterine kin and in-laws, the initiates and other participants learn to transform conflict into cohesion while gaining self-understanding. While meeting in the village shelter, men make critical comments about the female sex, while women in their songs at first mock marriage and praise adultery but later emphasize fertility. A mock battle takes place between the men of the bride's and the groom's party: the latter should win. The wedding night that follows is a test of the groom's virile potency. As such, rituals offer a social metacommentary, a narrative of the perennial social drama (Turner 1980a). The form of communal rituals is consistent with the structure of the society: these rituals resolve conflicts and generate emotional catharsis so that "actors in a ritual do feel what they are supposed to feel" (Turner 1968:238).

Adopting an agonistic view on the dynamic and dramatic role of social life, its conflicts and the inherent tendency of groups to segment, and stressing the redressive function of ritual, Turner elaborates upon central themes prevailing in the "Manchester School in South-Central Africa"—the name Werbner (1984) has coined the group of scholars working under Max Gluckman—which he belonged to during the period of his research among the Ndembu. Political anthropology was a central concern in this school. Ndembu people are portrayed in micropolitical fields: hut-plans and villages are mapped, and inhabitants are located in space, genealogical charts, and networks of rivalries and allegiances; the character of major protagonists is even identifiable. Turner sees life-crisis and affliction rituals as attempts to redress conflicts, although they may sustain processes involving changes in the social arrangements. These rituals handle the asymmetry and "propensity towards conflict" that characterize the social relations between men and women, matrilineal descent and the virilocal residence group. In stressing how much the rituals together with juridiction transform social conflict into a regularizing process of normalization, that is, of reordering and restating values and norms, Turner's sociological and emancipatory view has a 'modernist' flavor. Although he stresses the cathartic and transformative function in some healing rituals, he does not elaborate upon their capacity to allow differences and to reject a totalizing (male) order: for Turner, rituals, like jurisprudence, support the power strategies and the centralized, gerontocratic order of men. In other words, if he does mention that the liminal phase in rituals may foster some liberating insight, his emphasis is however on the redressive effect and how much core symbols through the state of fusion experienced by the coinitiands convert all too subjective demands and experience into communal and conservative ones.

Through his mother, an actress, Turner loved acting and all aspects of dramatic performance. However he sticks to a performance model proper to literary culture. In his later, post-Ndembu writings he came to develop a theory of the way social drama and stage drama are linked (Turner 1974, 1980, 1982, 1985). Healing rituals and the centripetal gaze and narratives of the ritual specialists have the quality of the theatre: Ihembi, husband and wife Kamahasanyi and Maria, Kasonda, Muchona, Mukeyi, Mundoyi, Nyakinga, Sandombu, and others are narrative voices and/or key actors in the heroic cycles of the social drama—with whom readers can identify. For his portrayal of the Ihamba ritual (Turner 1968:156–97), Turner shares the analytic center stage with Ihembi, the diviner orchestrating the healing: he subsumes himself in the narrative voice. Whatever influence this association between ritual and stage drama has gained from the scholars of dramaturgy and liturgy, I would contend that it is precisely this argument that has prevented Turner from reaching a more profound understanding of the genuine nature of Ndembu ritual. His analyses allow a vivid view on how symbolic acts under conditions of intense social and ritual communitas move experience and values. Symbolic acts—the atoms of human action and social process—instigate action because of their intertwining ideological and sensory qualities. He looks at how they condense and synthesize their ideological or normative aspects with physiological, sensory, or affective ones, thereby producing "genuinely cathartic effects, causing real transformation of character and social relationships" (1968:56). It was from Freud that he derived the idea of the unification of disparate significata and evocative ambiguities within a symbol, and of its polarization into ideological and orectic poles (Turner 1980b). Nonetheless, however rich his analysis of ritual symbols is, he fails to see their logic sui generis in their broader setting of symbolic subsystems and cosmology, just as he fails to see how ritual symbols in inventive and empowering ways reach beyond representation and cognitive meaning. Life is seen as performance and staging, that is, as "social drama." Symbols and rituals, in Turner's view, are a narrative in trials of strength, control, and conflict in the social drama. A ritual of affliction and redress, like a communal ritual, provides a narrative of the core values of society in the sensuous disguise of symbolic objects, gestures, plants to be administered as emetics and ointment, or in cupping, enemas, and baths. These symbolic devices mobilize energies, affects, and motives so as to make the social virtues most desirable while realigning people in "social processes of unification," in a communal concern "with the health of the corporate body, with securing balance and harmony between its parts" (1968:270). The pivotal ritual symbols—the *mudyi* life tree, white clay, and the *muyombu* ancestor tree—summarize uterine values and solidarity, and "customs in a single representation, and mobilize strong emotions in support of the social order" (1968:235); they moreover allow for an ingress of power into the initial situation (Turner 1980). "In ritual . . . society reappraises its ideology and structural form, and finds them good" (1968:237).

Ritual drama, in Turner's view, basically conveys or narrates meaning in a dramaturgical way: ritual is based in and generates narratives; it develops textual politics, and stage after stage a consensus marks a given sense. It develops in an order of sequences or succession, negotiating a cognitive melding of past and present, anticipating the future, and conducing the participants to conform to the ideas and norms conveyed. Neither bodiliness, senses, and emotions nor cosmology are considered as genuine sources of symbolization; these serve rather as disguised expressions of and implements for the social. For Turner, the longing for social order or cohesion is fraught with structural contradictions, conflicts of norms, and indeterminacy and is the major source of symbolic production. The more complex society becomes, the more the dramaturgical and narrative framing and symbolizing become elaborate (Turner 1980a). It would appear that in its rituals society normatively reenacts its basic script while reaching some new insight and compromise formation between subjective desires and fears, on the one had, and the socialized demands of reason and group, on the other.

I contend that, in his study of nonliterate Ndembu culture, Turner adopts a view on cognition and information partly derived from lineal writing and literacy in the West. Ndembu communal and affliction rituals display aspects of liturgical or theatrical staging. The exegetical meaning almost discloses the master narrative or basic representational truth of the ritual, and ritual specialists and other skilled informants are the privileged holders of the hidden script which they have inherited—and committed to memory—from their master and which they now convey to the initiate. The ritual specialist is seen as the "master artificer" of a play that is basically normative narration: "social actions of various kinds acquire form through the metaphors and paradigms in their actors' heads" (Turner 1974:13), through the "cultural models in the heads of the main actors" (64) that propel actors along a certain path or passage. Although Turner suggests that these root paradigms go beyond the cognitive and even moral domains, he does not offer keys to disclose this subliminal potential, and yet he studies it as a language and inasmuch as it is brought to cognitive consciousness. When performed, the ritual acts as a declaration of the past in the present, a revivification of memory or a revitalization of "deep myths," thereby articulating an intrinsic affinity between the successive events of the life of a group and the life cycle of an individual. The antistructural moments in healing and transition rituals through inversion and primary encounter—after stripping away conventional hierarchy, status, and roles—lay bare the deep structure or root paradigms of the culture, for both the participants and the anthropologist. Moreover, such an experience of existential communitas and liminality fosters new images, helps to found and re-empower the institutionalized social and cultural structures, and enhances the members' adhesion and cohesion in society: by revitalizing worn-out patterns, communitas paradoxically serves to emphasize the need for structure and becomes itself a maintenance mechanism.

Turner's attention is basically fixed on people's cognitive understanding and moral inspiration rather than on genuine creativity or on bodily symbolism and processes. In his view, ritual symbols operate on and through minds by means of illocutionary acts and by instilling a sense of duty in which memory, anticipation, and commitment combine. Ritual meaning is basically about social order, social cohesion, and the socialized person. Contingent events are too singular to become ritual, and yet they are a possible source of disorder and servitude. The subject in focus is not the experiencing one but rather the performer or co-actor who enters a discursive formation or a play role that urges reflection and conformation. The self is social, gendered, a member of a residential and kin group. A person's involvement in a group is finally one of being capable of narrating it, either by attuning him- or herself to the group through involvement in ritual or by telling axiomatic stories such as proverbs, dilemma tales, or genealogical information, or by conceiving and experiencing him- or herself in terms of life stories. The ethnographer is not a translator of a culture but a transmitter of the informants' exegesis and consciousness, of their narratives and involvement, and of the participant-observation as part of the overall narrative plot. Writing is a transmission of this record of 'texts' and relationships, in terms of narrative contexts and consequences, knowledge and meaning, to an alien audience of writers and readers.

My account of healing ritual differs considerably from Turner's. I contend that he overlooks the genuine and creative significance of the human body in healing rites, or the perspective that comes through in the ritual on life, connectedness, and generative capacity centered in particular in women's bodies. In his writings, embodied experience and, hence, the body and the concrete involvement in life transmission appear but as mere vehicles for ritual drama; they are therefore not seen as a genuine source for the emergence of symbols or for self-generative production in the transformational process. In Turner's analysis, the human body establishes itself as some kind of natural, that is, transcendental, universal value: it is a given, it is receptive rather than a genuine source of symbolic creativity. The power of dominant symbols derives from their capacity to condense structural or moral norms—the eidetic pole—and fuse them with the physiological and sensory phenomena and processes—the orectic pole. For Turner, the orectic pole is a given, an undefined force of desire, not a source in its own right of images, fantasies, and signs: by their very nature, blood, sexual organs, coitus, birth, death, catabolism, and similar physiological phenomena and processes arouse desire and appetite, willing and feeling. The human body as orectic pole energizes the eidetic pole of the symbolic so that the obligatory is made desirable and the conflict between personal aspiration and social necessity is reduced (Turner 1967:54; 1974:55ff). Turner's attention to the human body and the senses is a rationalist one, and it paradoxically reduces the genuineness of the orectic such that it becomes a mere vessel for the eidetic. In his view, the body as such appears but as an aimless drive or energy for social action.

In my view, ritual—in particular healing—is more than reenacting a script, a 'fit' between present and past: it is a generative act that reaches beyond or beneath the 'story.' In Yaka society—and I venture to extend the argument to the Ndembu as well—the link that a ritual may have with tradition is not spelled out in terms of a genealogical continuity with, for example, a foundational act or a legendary, yet exemplary performance. To the outsider, the healing drama may look like a programmed portrayal of some hidden script, displayed within a clearly circumscribed space-time order. In these nonliterate cultures, however, there is no 'script' or abstract mental mapping going on in between the performers and the performance. There is no sender and no privileged recipient of a primordial meaning. The very constitutive or transformative parts of the ritual drama are not primarily representations or means of thought and identification: they are neither primarily referential nor designative, neither are they substitutes of more original ideas or a basic narrative. A Yaka healing drama is not in the first place a categorical or an empirical exposé, nor is it a demonstrative or a propositional discourse. Healing drama is by no means a liturgy, nor a theatrical performance, nor an enacted explanation of a world order. At least, in the very creative core of the healing drama, there is no temporal gap between source and product. Unlike Turner, I do not consider healing ritual among the Yaka as a dramaturgical plot or play, nor as a kind of psychodrama. Neither the initiates nor the wider audience are simply onlookers who have the option of taking a critical stance and comparing the performance with some script or other performance.

In grasping ritual—and in particular the *khita* 'gyn-eco-logical' healing— as self-constructive and generative 'in a bodily mode' from within its own terms, I try to pass beyond Turner's sociological reading of the ritual in the light of the social dynamics at play. I see healing ritual among the Yaka as a genuine practice that stands by its own and in its own right: it is not primarily a device for social purpose, but a self-foundational and morphogenetic practice. It taps from the generative and infinite resources in the life-world and the body prior to their relocation to society and history as representation, meaning or knowledge, and power relations. Healing ritual reaches beyond 'the cognitive mode,' that is, beyond the order of narration and 'textual' representation of sociocultural reality, of knowledge and meaning. This does not mean that healing rituals are but a naive refuge outside the social and cognitive arenas, escaping the reality of oppression: it is perhaps at the fringe that the initiate gains a deeper insight and greater critical vision. As I argue in the next chapter, inasmuch as ritual creativity in healing arises from the potentialities in the body, senses, and life-world, and not as such from a narrative voice or an interpretive consciousness, ritual—and the approach I am forwarding—is not a hermeneutics of self-creation. Ritual is not primarily a means of narrating reality, nor a plot about leadership of the narrative voice, but a means of disclosing or producing reality as not yet appropriated by a hero or an author. In my account of affliction cults, I try to do some justice to the unrepresentable and prepredicative, and to the polyphonic and polymorphous meaning—beyond or outside the position of a hero and his power of action. It is a portrayal of healing in its various processes of becoming, of its constitutive principles and intentionality, rather than of 'reality' as the product of representation and self-recognition. My focus is on agency as a practice of meaning, forces, and empowerment. Healing rituals offer a space for constituting and transforming rather than for identifications and the compelling manifestation of cognitive structures. Healing in Yaka culture not only expresses but it also generates clusters of innovative meaning and forces; it integrates gratification of desire, passions and frailties, nurturance and sociability; it conveys strength and empowerment to the patient and initiates, and causes to flourish many forms of genuine reciprocity and concern for others in which separateness and interdependence, autonomy and mutuality exist simultaneously between persons, groups, and the life-world.

8 The Body as the Weaving Loom of Healing and Life

My focus is on self-healing as it relates to the practical arts of inducing healing from within the body's resources. Consequently, the perspective of the experiencing and self-reflexive subject is not central to my approach. In focusing on healing techniques and methods rooted in the body, the analysis aims at disclosing a cross-culturally relevant perspective that nevertheless takes into consideration the culturally shaped forms of healing. Despite what the Latin root suggests, 'patients' are not passive sufferers. The more I have come to know of the skills, practices, and methods of reputed healers and have been able to share in the knowledge, emotions, intentions, and empowerment of both patients and healers, the more this very participation has offered me the key to a genuine interpretation of therapeutic rite from the inside. Healing ritual occurs in a more or less predefined context at the margins of diurnal public life and power relations. It is an all-embracing rhythm, giving over the body to the senses; it is a dream of health and an incarnation of values, moving through metaphor beyond language, arousing cordiality, conviviality, and empowerment rather than distancing self-awareness. It is operative at a level that largely escapes the grasp of colloquial speech and representational thinking. Healing operates through the human body as the basic deposit and embodiment of cultural traditions. In an untutored or spontaneous way, these traditions come to articulation, in and through the body, with the community and the life-world. And through feeling and sensing out the meaning of the embodied interwovenness with the kin and the life-world, the body is deeply moved, intensified, and remolded. The very elaborate devices, procedures, and methods of healing are never the object of comment during the healing. Dedicated initiation is their resource for renewal in the transaction between sufferer-novice and accomplished, self-projecting healer (Janzen 1991). Healing starts from a singular distress in the patient and kin. Healer, patients, kin, and support group interact in a leisurely ambience. It is one of a dense and appealing interplay of metaphors and paradoxes, images and senses, withdrawal and playful exhibition. The interaction and transaction of moods, images, and symbols foster an intimate and englobing process of self-healing from within the resources of the patient's body in tune with the uterine flow of life, with processes of flowering, 'cooking,' and birth in the life-world, and with the cycles of rest and motion, decay and flowering in cosmological time. The process extends from healer and patient to the therapy managing and support groups, and vice versa.

Healing ritual draws on a pool of resources consisting of what might variously be called *transformative devices* or *embodied skills* (*phila, yikalulu, -yika;* habitus, in Bourdieu's terms). Devices respond to the questions as to what is being done or displayed, who is involved, and when, with regard to the rite. Devices thus imply rhythm, music, dance, gestural and sensory codes, interactional conventions, mnemotechnical means, space-time arrangements. Alongside these means there are the many ways of manipulating the skin and bodily orifices through massage, ointments, steam- or smoke-baths, enemas, and scarification. A Yaka healing drama also draws on dream messages and dream-like fantasy, and very much transpires as a kind of makeshift exploratory event, as "bricolage" (Lévi-Strauss 1962).

Healing is moreover a productive *process (luhaangu)* that takes place both in time and over time, entailing a skillfulness *(-yika)* that in concrete practice knows the procedures, that is, knows what to do and how to operate *(-yidika)*. Here I am tackling the question of how things happen in ritual therapy. Patient, former initiates, and representatives of the kin group or neighborhood all share in the therapeutic endeavor. Further, patient and spirit may fuse as co-actors: the patient remains herself in the drama and yet embodies or acts as the *khita* spirit. The healing drama seeks to mobilize the affects, driving them to the point of an abreaction and catharsis. While expelling the malevolent spirit, in her abreaction the patient reverses the effect of the curse put on her and develops a beneficial relationship with the spirit which from then on is identified and named. The sacrifice of a hen that follows and the spilling of its blood over the patient's body help to expel the evil from the patient, almost turning her body inside out. The internal and exclusive relationship with the anonymous spirit—like an alien body in the patient's body—is transformed into an external and exclusive relationship with a named spirit, that is, into a mirroring relationship of cooperative actors. The drama helps the patient to overcome her defensive relation to the elders and the coercive order of tradition. Ritual performance brings the sensory body and the imaginary register into play. The word of the song is made flesh and embodied in rhythm; it is therefore to be understood primarily in the realm of the senses. Healing ritual basically brings to the fore a nonnarrative realm of anxieties and feelings of persecution, poignantly differentiating them from the realms of desire and life transmission. These realms are remolded in that process proper to rites of passage which leads the patient through the motions of mortal agony, fecundation, gestation, and rebirth.

A *healing method or art (bungaanga, buphati, pfunu, -disonga)* is in fact disclosed by both devices and process: the method concerns the questions why do things happen as they do, what is being aimed at, who is the subject and/or author? The healing event unfolds a method of intertwining the fields of body, family, and life-world in a morphogenetic way, so to speak. The healing relationship between therapist, patient, and therapeutic group is itself a morphogenetic field—though my analysis, too indistinctively perhaps, subsumes the healer most often in the field of group. In terms given by Yaka culture itself, this healing method is best typified by the act (or process) of 'biological' weaving. In this case, however, the weaving is for real and becomes a living skill, praxis, or art. Healing entails the 'biological' interweaving of the various layers of body, group, and world: the one *is* the other, in an alignment of *becoming*. It is a very concrete, fertile, and powerful endeavor through the libidinal and imaginary registers, the senses, the body, engaged in communal action. The crossing of boundaries, both within and between the corporeal, social, and cosmological bodies, forms the basis of the healing method. Ritual drama unfolds a space-time staging in which metaphoric correspondents of the patient's body, the spirit of the founding ancestor, and life-bearing or life-threatening dimensions of the life-world are constituted and manipulated. Healing frees the patient from her or his state of closure or possession, effusion and dispersion. It fosters the vital flow in and between the patient and the family, so that the patient may reweave her or his inner feelings and motions outwardly into the fabric of the larger life-world. Healing is a 'technē' of worldmaking while remaking oneself into an active part and partner of it. In and through the body, the healing drama reconnects the patient, in immediacy, with a meaningful and empowering world order. But the incentive and inspiration seem to evolve out of the seminal capacities of and cultural deposits in the human body and the maternal life source. Healing method may be compared to a fabric whose weave sustains itself while engendering new meaning and renewed relationships. In the moment of ritual performance, and particularly in trance, healer and/or patient are able to fashion a fundamentally vital link with the seminal life-world itself, with the primal source as if it were, in an almost unmediated way.

My *method of analysis* entails the parallel interpretation of *various fields*. It is an *internal* approach inasmuch as it discloses the healing method from within, that is, through its own devices, processes, and perspective or intention. My analysis seeks to unravel the devices and the processes that are actively at play in the observable practices—the level of denotation, so to say. From there, it passes to the space-time dimension and gives ear to the reverberation between the fields of the therapeutic relation (body, family, and life-world), that is, to the level of connotations. Seen from the inside, healing drama is very much a self-generative practice, and the field in which the generative process and its devices are most readily observable is the bodily one. From here, the analysis moves on to deal with the resonance brought about between the bodily experience and the portrayal of family or group and life-world. It is therefore very difficult, in terms of the type of internal research I am engaged in, to take a clearly positional perspective and name the partner in my dialogue or the authority behind the ritual scene, and hence the author behind the polyphonous and polyscenic drama. The performing subject in the healing practice is not the healer, the patient, the spirits, nor even the therapy managing group. The real subject is precisely the ongoing intertwinement or mutually impressible or continuous integration of the vital flow, the senses, and the body, all of which are being profoundly linked in the interactional drama with the life-world. The *performing subject* is the *method* or *art,* namely, the ongoing multilayered weave in and between the encompassing fields of body, family or group, and life-world (see plates 19 and 20).

The weave, insofar as it is the healing method itself, embraces and opens up the whole healing system, and at the same time it allows us an insight into the cult's basic ontological assumptions concerning the nature of life, solidarity, health, and healing. Seen from within ongoing practice and the therapeutic relationship, the vital flow *(mooyi),* matrilineally transmitted, and the body *(luutu)* appear to be the very source of healing and the dominant organizing field. Ritually-induced transitions from one aspect and/or field to another— say from the corporeal onto the social and/or cosmological body—are brought about through creative transferences of sensible qualities, practical abilities, and feats of skill. For example, besides other devices, the undulating movements of the hips in dancing transform the whole happening into a weaving; by anointing herself with red paste, the patient nurtures herself in her fetal condition. In this last case the ointment evokes the blood of the sacrificial animal turned inside-out that was spilled onto her body: both ointment and sacrifice relate to the possessing spirit expelled from the patient's body and pacified into a named double. In the healing drama bodily enactment is both source and product, agent and scene of an interrelating of fields or worlds that are transformed in the same process. In the enactment, the human body reverberates with processes of life-bearing in the life-world—captured through a genuine matching with the primordial energies in the hen laying or brooding an egg, in the palm tree, and the lunar cycle in particular—and makes present what it represents, namely a resonance between the body's inner possibilities and the virtualities in the cosmic body. The healing performance embraces the body's illuminations in dream and heightened sensory awareness: it is a sensing out and passionate celebration of the body as species, the ancestral body in each individual tapping the ancestral life source in rhythm and in the imaginary register. Healing frees and taps the life flow through a metaphorical reweaving of life's diverse dimensions into a resonant whole. The bodily enactment and the more encompassing healing drama are the unfounded yet emergent foundation of healing, like a womb that gives birth, or a body in processes of 'exvagination' and taking on a new 'social' and 'cosmic skin' offered by the house of seclusion. Through this ongoing, polyphonous or multilayered, and somehow explorative drama the healer, the patient, and other participants open up to and reembody an encompassing order of values and forces that come into play, interconnect, and reveal themselves beyond mere conceptual understanding or conventional representation.

The healing drama celebrates the love of life; it is a quest to transmit, enhance, and optimize life. It makes one fundamental statement: that this world is real, prolific, all-encompassing, composite, interrelated, and thus accessible. The weaving of body, group, and world makes tangible, tasteable, visible—concretely approachable—the fact that life *is* this world, and is lived as an interactive alignment of lingering, actual or lasting power and affect. It is the weaving, by means of the body-senses, of bodies with each other and of bodies with the world. The weaving entails also the biological, and its devices or skills and methods are of a type that does exist in other cultures as well.

8.1 The Role of Music and Dance in Healing

Rhythm, dance, chant, and melody give the body over to the senses and the life-world. They form a primary resource of healing devices or crafts. Healing originates in rhythm that intertwines with intimate fellow-feeling, olfactory exchange, erotic transport, sexual communion and reproduction. Underlying the rhythm, tempo, and pace in dance is a sense of presencing-oneself-in-the-world, a sense of lustful collective celebration of body and solidarity so as to enhance the flow and force of life.

The devices creatively bring about a basic process of healing or making whole, that is, a particular interweave. Though I am unskilled in the type of musical analysis suggested here, I nevertheless can sense how therapeutic seances bring into play a variety of rhythms. The drummers who beat the oblong and shorter drums gradually test various rhythms and pulses, that is, they search out a balance between the beats and an attunement between the tonalities in the chants. The lead drummer advances the pulse or leading beat *(-sika ngoma)*. The participants respond with clapping and soon "sing to the drum" *(-yimbila ngoma)* in a mutual 'call and response' sharing of experience (see Janzen 1991). In their chants and overt allusions to the drummer's skill or to one or another aspect of desire and group life, the participants themselves probably offer the basic measure or indication of that resonance: as does the heartbeat while speaking in a rhetorical stance or in anger, running in the hunt, in laughter or in sexual arousal, and so on. Music and voice may also display various tonalities. In other words, at several crucial stages of the healing, the elements of beat, pulse, tonality, dance, chant, melody, and theme allow for a particular spatio-temporal interweave of passion, libidinal affects, senses, archaic images, spasms of verbalization, body-self, social ties, and life-world. Music, voice, and dance always come into play at transitional moments in the life of the group and the cosmos. They thus mediate between life and death, sorrow and vital flow, chaos and order, affliction and healing. They form the very core of tradition and yet foster great spontaneity and improvisation on the part of the drummers, singers, and dancers. Rather than being a formalized, ossified, and therefore "inferior form of communication," as Bloch suggests (1974), dance with chant seems to me an anterior (that is, a primary), sensuous, libidinal, preverbal, and prereflexive form of exchange through "waves of fellow feeling" (Blacking 1977).

Dance is, moreover, a method of healing which articulates affliction and therapeutic tradition, individual emotion and group values, body and life-world. The forms of dance are models for and ways of interweaving the "vécu corporel," lustful body, vital flow, affects, embodied feelings and thoughts, with the social and cultural universe. It is in particular during the dancing in the vicinity of the cult house that participants are offered a unique opportunity to dance for joy, abandoning themselves to attraction, empathy, and bliss, while voicing their affective states, subjective images, and hopes. Rhythmicity and repetition in underlying tempo, pace, dance, as well as intonation and melody in chant, comprise an energetic process in which healer, patients, coinitiates, and the local community participate in a lustful and emotional way, thereby intertwining—in a kind of morphogenetic way—the vital flow in the person, group, and cosmos. The interconnection as process is not fully predetermined: it must be explored and traced in the very performance. Tempo and pulse are somewhat negotiable, and one drummer may be preferred to another because he has a keen sense of negotiating the leading beat with the other drummers and with a playful public: one or another of the drummers may lengthen or shorten the pulse, accelerate or retard the tempo, superimpose various rhythms and tones upon the same leading beat, and so forth. Both the music and the dance—with its rhythmic rotations of hips and belly, steps, turns, and twists—display a specific and 'hypocognized' method of healing.

The resounding chorus and dancing give way to a genuine bodily method of world-fashioning and empowering. In dancing and singing to the drumming, the chant and dance patterns shape the participants' emotional and corporeal experiences, while the latter also graft their own specific spatio-temporal habitus onto the chant. Dance and chant offer an idiosyncratic, affective, and embodied display of spatio-temporal patterns such as continuous, cyclical, intermittent, or discontinuous. The dance patterns interconnect, for example, the wheeling movements of the hips with the rotating patterns in life-bearing and the agricultural or domestic tasks of the women. In their daily search for food and water, the women indeed display a wheeling pattern of movement in tune with the solar and lunar cycles: the activities of fetching water and collecting food, working in the fields or fishing, processing cassava at the riverside and near the house are all caught in a concentric procession away from and back to the homestead. The libidinal rotations of hips and belly, as well as the idiosyncratic gestures and turns in dancing give a bodily and sensuous form to waves of solidarity in a kind of reverberation with the encompassing of social and cosmic domains. This energetic and rhythmic interweave of bodies and world dispense a reciprocal empowering of participants and the life-world through a kind of morphogenetic interweave between bodily, social, and cosmic fields.

Like the vital flow, dance is rhythm, or more precisely rhythmic autogenesis in perpetual emergence. Chant and beat fill and cross space and, through the act of dancing, incite all present to participate in its very rhythm; dance and chant mold space and time. Dance acts as a fabric, namely as a genuine method of articulating the vital flow with the collective and the world. The weaving of the loincloth is both an expression of this articulation and an unspoken pattern of dance. In other words, the vital flow manifests itself as rhythm and cosmogenetic formation.

Rhythm, drumming, dance, and chant are genuine bodily methods to interweave the individual and idiosyncratic not only with the group and the socialized environment but with the cosmos as well. The communal dances and the playfully shared forms of chant between chorus and chanters foster much spontaneity and improvisation by singers, drummers, and dancers. Consequently, rhythm, drumming, dance, and chanting invite the patient, the therapy managing group, and the wider community to join in and participate, that is, to become one of the whole, to achieve one body. At the same time, they enable participants to express their most personal and idiosyncratic feelings in the improvisation. Far more than dance, chant and drumming are a socially and culturally patterned code that allows the person to express her or his affects, desires, and thoughts in an idiom that can be shared by all those involved. In the Yaka view, this achievement of an 'ensemble' arouses vital flow. Moreover, the bonding that is thereby achieved allows patient, group, and life-world to move together in real or 'historic' time: this is the music's liminal function. Yaka have but a few songs intended especially for children; a child learns the music from his or her grandparents or through observation of communal chanting and dancing. Furthermore, there is a clear continuity of style. These two phenomena explain why melodies used in healing cults readily evoke memories and experiences of one's childhood and feelings towards the group. The rather freely evolving counterpoint of the music gives the patient the opportunity to express various feelings at different conscious and unconscious, vocal and gestural levels. Rhythm and chant structure the dancing gestures and movements of the dance. At the same time, the drummers may adapt their pattern of rhythm to the dance that it inspires.

In chanting, the voice is a genuinely sensuous and emotional device and art of mediating between body and language, between very deep bodily reminiscences of archaic origins and primal socialization. (This is even more powerfully so in trance, as I will argue below.) The wording in the chants and ritual texts may join together the generations and gender groups: fragments of one's former identity and aspects of various roles are voiced. Because the wording is shared, relatively 'fixed,' and estheticizing, it allows for a distancing of the subject's emotions in tune with the other participants and with motions in the cosmos. Following Rosolato (1978:31–51) and Castarède (1991:101–24), it would seem that the voice in vocal music (and in trance) mediates between body and language in that any voice may be interpreted as a transformation of the first, mother voice that gave form to the original bond in merged bodiliness. This transformation is brought about by the father voice who separates the merged bodies in the mother-child dyad, inasmuch as his voice is heard as representative of language, position in the kin group, and the traditions of the larger community and successive generations. Rhythm, drumming, and singing in particular may therefore at the same time induce the primary experience of corporeal harmony (Rosolato 1978:35) and the child's later experience of separation and differentiation. Rhythmic beat, concord, pulse, voice, musical harmony, polyphony, and counterpoint all intertwine affect, fantasy, and body with socioculturally informed rules, evoking and regulating in a very sensuous way both fellow-feeling and distancing.

The voice of the patient, in the very emotional moment of trance, is a particularly libidinal engenderment of a cathartic indictment, a meaning and force that surpass or precede the word. For each major cult, there is a type of drumming which summons the spirit "to release, to lift one up in the air" *(-kaluka)*. This is the real liminal function of trance in which the spirit incites and authorizes the medium to speak out while the body gropes for latent resources of vitality and as it were breaks out of its limits. Trance is not an out-of-body experience; neither should it be seen as a loss of consciousness. Both the suffering and vital resources in the body may hereby creatively transform and recompose themselves—that is, heal, or "make whole" *(-luunga)*. I would postulate that in the process of impersonating the spirit, the voice is freed to bring up troublesome and intractable experiences from early childhood, fusing them with themes from folktales and deeply experienced collective fantasies. In the course of the seclusion, to handle her anxieties and clarify her experience, the initiate may create her personal song in which she intertwines an archaic and sacred idiom with her own distress, inner moods, impasses, longings, and with the world of dream, cult spirits, and cosmic imagery. Inasmuch as biographical reminiscences and mythical fragments pierce through in the intensely felt abreaction of trance, they together transform fate into a destiny. In trance the voice at first is merely a sound of accelerated breath, an inchoate phonation. Entranced, the patient gropes for words and gestures. The drummer tries to palliate her anxiety by fitting his tempo to the personality of the patient without, however, discarding the traditional rhythmic modes. Through the songs that precede and follow, the healer and group offer fragments of some mythic narrative suggesting that what is presently happening is, *in illo tempore,* as it was at the beginnings. Moreover, through his rather rare yet authoritative cultic interventions at crucial points in the therapy—shortly after the trance, for example—the healer voices the patient's needs, her ailments or handicaps. In this, the healer is speaking in the name of the cult spirit or the ancient tradition. Echoing the divinatory etiology, he transforms the ailments into the fundamental story or foundational myth of the existential interdependence between kinsmen, that is, into the story of evil calling for vengeance, or the history of social order and life-world reasserting themselves.

It is in these synesthetic ways that the very devices of rhythm and dance act as a transformative process to modify "in a profound and diversified manner the consciousness one has of oneself in relation with oneself and with the world. The modifications bear essentially on the dimensions of these relations" (Rouget 1980:22, my translation). In other words, rhythm, dance, and song integrate and reempower the body in its sociocultural context by the very sensuous, expressive, spatio-temporal interweaving of them. Rhythm, dance, and song act not only as a process but also as a method of integrating and energizing due to the fact that they are rooted in a bodily 'hexis' or habitus and realize a sociocultural logic that is enacted and recognizable through its sensuous form. If the patient fails to recognize—at least partially—that very logic, then rhythm and song may fail to have any real impact. Song or music can only be a communication from body to body (Bourdieu 1979) if this communication ties in with the habitus and makes sense within the worldview. But at the same time, rhythm, melody, and dance seem to provide the patients and other participants with an unsuspected and prereflexive enactment through which some hidden layers of the (collective) unconscious may disclose themselves.

Dance and trance develop as a method of interweaving innermost affects with the group as an encompassing whole. In this multidimensional interaction, the individual corporeal expressivity transcends its isolation and moves into the social and cultural space of the performing group. The beat, pulse, tune, or dance pattern are no longer those of an abstract tradition, an inchoate individual, of a particular group; they are the common expression of their very interlinking. It is precisely in this reciprocal interaction through music that the dancer acquires a feeling of belonging and cooperation. The group is cemented together, and everyone is given the opportunity and capacity to participate within the fluid boundaries set by the ever-changing musical interaction between the bodily, affective, social, and cultural domains. The relationship of reciprocal exchange with others in chant, music, and dance acts as a trigger that stimulates the *khita* patient to give a highly dramatized bodily, hence entranced, expression to her preoccupations. The therapeutic team and community of regular participants offer a secure and receptive group space for the impulsive flow of dance and trance whose resonance all members come to share. They create an encompassing and containing structure in which bodily sensations, feelings, and preverbal and verbal elements circulate. I conjecture that reminiscences of early relationships with parents and siblings, or of gender identification, are at the same time reactivated and interwoven with the time patterns regarding life-cycle in body, group, and world at display in the ritual. This may help the patient to work through some hidden problems and anxieties in the highly dramatized transition from inner to outer, from self to the other, from feeling to thought, or vice versa. In other words, rhythmic beat, concord, music, singing, and dance all constitute the liminal function that connects the patient with her own body and sensory awareness (while beginning to clarify its inchoateness), with her cultural tradition and life-world, embodied in the musical code and melody, and with her kin and cult members.

8.2 The Source of Healing

The human body is the central device or principal key that opens up and stimulates the whole system of healing. The process of generating the system of healing itself may be characterized as one of weaving. Weaving, moreover, is an activity that fosters a method of healing: expressed in terms of the cult, the art of healing is a reweaving and interweaving of three bodies, namely the physical body, the family or group, and the life-world. In the *khita* cult, the reweaving of a loincloth, for example, inspires a basic method for empowering and even transferring the ability to bear life from the physical body onto the group and the life-world, and vice versa. The healing cult is the patient's and group's weaving loom par excellence. Therapy comprises weaving the vital flow, the generative forces and fibers of meaning that link together the many activities, and the movements and dimensions of body, group, and life-world into one harmonious resonance. Healing draws on the patient's androgynous capacity for self-fecundation and giving birth to herself. It ties in with the basic rhythm of life transmission and enhancement in the enactment of the basic rhythm of regeneration in the group and the universe. I postulate that the connection between the bodily enactment and the parallel processes in the group and its life-world witness to its morphogenetic character. I am hereby developing a more radically generative and transformative perspective on healing, and—unlike, for example, Lyon (1990)—deliberately resist its reduction to cognitive processes.

The body as both weave and weaving loom is the major elaborating and transformative process and force that permits the transposition of meaning, structuring, and energies between the bodily, social, and cosmological fields. The therapist treats the patient's body as if it enclosed or embraced the world, as if it were both a micro- and macrocosm. This relationship is one not merely of figuration but of transformation in the very process of mutual encompassment. The healer works upon the patient's inner world of passion and affects, her sensory and bodily forms of contact, and her social and existential involvement with the group and the life-world by metaphorically regarding them as bodily-cum-cosmic processes of depletion versus empowerment, obstruction versus flow, closure versus exchange, rotting versus fermentation, killing (in the hunt) versus regenerating (through cooking), and so on. Reactivating the world also means reempowering the patient. In the healing ritual, the patient is led to reconnect with her desires, senses, bodily awareness, and inner forces and at the same time to transfer these experiences and capacities onto the topography of the healing house and onto the group and its transactions. A certain connivance develops between persons and things, between the body's forms and processes and the shapes of the objects and time-space configuration belonging to the ritual. As Zempléni (1982, my translation) so aptly puts it, "in this sense, traditional healing is the art of linking the states of the bodies themselves with the states of the social bodies by means of magico-religious symbolism."

The healing art is a very practical method of intertwining the body with the group and the life-world. It does not so much draw on the spoken word; rather, it brings into play the devices of seclusion, incantation, rhythm, dancing, mime, body decoration, colors, massage, fumigations, laxative enemas, concealment, containment, and trance. By means of these devices the art of healing makes the patient 'give body to' and reembody the social and cosmological body. Perceived in this way, the boundedness and openness of the physical body appear to provide a site and process of meaning production. Corporeal boundaries and openings act as the very locus and generative means to remake or renew the units of exchange in the social and cosmological fields: the conjugal and domestic unit, wife-givers and wife-takers, house, village, and the lived environment. Skin and orifices act as a nexus, that is, as a juncture between various orders. Orificial transitions, manipulations of the skin, and bodily postures may become means of healing, for they are whole-making processes constituted by, for example, the intensely dramatized resonance between pregnant body and fetus, seclusion house and microcosmic womb in gestation, or the hen that lays an egg and incubation. Skin and orifices thus provide both for differentiation and for bridging between inner and outer, boundedness and closure, mortal agony and rebirth, decay and flowering, destruction and regeneration, man and woman, ascendant and descendant, before and after. These poetics of modulating various domains or fields with one another—otherwise kept separate by representational thought—serve to release self-healing in the patient. The healer's clairvoyance and his profile as hunter and weaver, and his androgynous and avuncular identity as well, possess just such a transgressive and transformative, yet integrative, capacity. They link with and draw on the uterine vital flow from the primal cosmic, egg-like, and tree-like life source *(ngoongu)*.

Seclusion is one major method of healing; it transpires within the euchronic time proper to gestation. Therapy extracts the patient from the contingent social interaction and family history. Within euchronic time—that is, within an ambience of receptivity, leisure, daydream, and wonder—seclusion aims at the 'rebirth of the patient' congruent with a symbolic reordering and a powerful revivification of the patient's life-world. Seclusion itself brings about a metamorphosis of the patient and her life-world precisely through a trespassing of boundaries and a metaphoric or rather metamorphic bridging between polar conditions (such as death-agony and delivery, the fetal state and gestation, or being born and giving birth), and between the worlds of passion, senses, and vision. Both healer and patient disavow authorship of the drama: they are not the subjective source or author of the creative performance. *The genuinely self-generative body praxis is,* I contend, *the very heart of the Yaka healing art.* It is first and foremost the patient's body, acting as an interface between bodily, social, and cosmological fields, that is the scene or vessel and the very source or subject of the healing. The patient herself embodies the source of healing—or the generative patterning or interweaving proper to the therapeutic drama—and transfers it onto the social and cosmological bodies. This transference is part of what I would call the morphogenetic potential of the ritual drama. In other words, it is the gestational capacity of the trance, of the seclusion, and of the coming-out sequence—and the capacity bestowed on the patient's body to bring the fields of body, group, and cosmos in unison—which is the generative potential or source of healing.

Understood in this manner, the process of healing displays a basic ability to embody at once paradox, bipolar unity, oneness, and duplication. Healing ritual is creative in that it reflects a Janusian world order or thought movement where strongly conflictual affects (such as the overlapping experiences of agony and orgasmic sexual union) and contrasting states of life (giving birth, dying, and being born) are simultaneously embodied and enacted. The capacities of the orificial body and the senses to meaningfully intertwine and reembody the various levels of life—corporeal, social, and cosmological—as well as to display paradox and transgression, are the author proper of the healing drama. The subject or author of the ritual enactment is indeed the interweave, both self-generative and self-legitimating.

Let me briefly spell out, from the perspective of the *khita* cult itself, the transformational process at play in the healing method, as it is generated and unfolded by the human body itself.

First, the ritual enactment urges the patient to participate in a project of creativity and excitement or transport. The patient is led through hypocognized experiences, namely sensory awareness and transactions through the body that link perception directly to the realm of liminal bodily experience. This form of passionate sensing or awareness is both disruptive and extensive—in the sense of an outward linking movement—and hence precedes orderly cognition. For example, the denunciation of the evil agent in trance (literally, "exposing the sap that is oozing from the palm tree," or "disclosing sexual arousal"—see phase 5) or the seclusion of the patient (further depicted as fermentation, self-fecundation, incubation, cooking, or gestation—see phase 4) are moments that engage the body's transformative devices such as sensing, illumination and inner renewal in sleep, sexual arousal, and death-agony.

Second, the patient is then reconnected with the group. Interpersonal transactions between maternal uncle, healer, patient, coinitiates and participants in the lay therapy managing group integrate bodily and noncognitive sensing in a network and process of interactional patterns and cultural values. The therapeutic scene, community, and sequence of action together offer a space-time stage upon which the body of the patient, the affects, the senses, and the organic, bodily functions exfoliate and become linked to primary forms of social relation and action. Thus the latter are themselves enacted and transformed in the process. Through her exfoliation in ritual space-time, the patient is led to become and embody her outer, metaphorically ritualized, and thereby socialized, repatterned self.

Third, the weaving of a meaningful fabric out of ritual wording, speech, and chant, out of the course of social action and sensuous display, comprises a method of self-renewal. Specific patterns of family interaction, such as consensus over the common affliction and the course of action to take, are interwoven with the emotions and senses of the self-projecting patients, healers, therapy management group, and the wider audience. All this comprises a method of self-renewal in the context of others and the life-world. It involves a method and means of gradually opening up the patient towards a reidentification with the speaking subject and social self that is able to bear a role and responsibility in society and daily reality. Healing, from within the patient's body, inner world of senses, imagination, and life-world, displays a space-time of liminality inviting her to phatically explore the virtualities of life and death. Meanwhile, it helps the patient to shape her new self "before the eyes of the others" *(mumeesu mabaatu).*

8.3 Paradox, Transgression, and Homeopathic Healing

Khita cult healing, like related cults, is surprisingly paradoxical and transgressive. Healing is a transitional state pervaded by profound ambivalence. The healer does not seek certainty and power, but confronts disorder and pollution. Healing operates very much at the level of *luutu,* the bodily envelope, and in particular the orificial and sensory body. Cult healing is basically governed by the systematic handling of paradoxes, bi-directional movement, and the reestablishment of congruent boundaries (that is to say, of their joint functions of separation and linkage) and of points of space-time transition in the fields of body, family, and life-world. For the gynecological patient, the healing process evolves through a sequence of transgressive moments and develops along the fault line separating and intertwining the libidinal and social landscapes. Affinity or sympathy *(fiimbu),* desire *(luhweetu, ndzala),* and appeal or attraction *(fula)* are seen as predominant driving or motivating forces in both healer and patient. Therapy establishes an ambience where the ludic and serious intermingle, where the licentious and normative compete. It metabolizes paradoxes and the impetus towards 'acting out' inner conflicts by transforming a state of crisis and transgression into a process deploying curative and emancipatory virtues and effects. It fosters energies, inspiration, and incentives from the vital, undomesticated, and energetic universes of the night, the forest, spirits, dream, death-agony, orgasm, gestation, parturition, the mother-child dyad, and trance. The trespassing of boundaries and exploration of liminal experiences appear to instigate a revival or reawakening in the patient, as if inducing in her a revivification of intra-uterine and early childhood experiences. These liminal zones are reawakened by particular rhythms, melodies, incantations, themes and mimicry of the dances, prayer, gestures, posture, massage, interactional stances, the significative arrangement of the seclusion house, and many other aspects of the rite. At the margins of society, that is, beyond the repressions and social rejections proper to mainstream society, therapy aims at reconnecting these very vital experiences with the norms and attributes of initiates, adulthood, established society, gender relations, and social reproduction.

A particular set of transformative devices is charged with bringing these paradoxes and transgressive moments into play. Following Devereux (1970:ch. 1), I would label them as levers or cultural inducers of therapy seen as process. They operate at the interstices between several specific domains or dimensions of life. These dimensions are the vectors that underlie the cultural image of the body, mapped out by the coordinates inside/outside, high/low, front/back, before/after, and left/right. According to divinatory diagnosis, illness inverts, blocks, or disconnects these coordinates so that they function only in an unbalanced or unidirectional manner. Therapeutic techniques very often restore these coordinates and their vectors by bringing about their reversion or by directing the disruptive imbalance against itself in a self-destructive way. Both the clairvoyant diviner's revelations and the dream are compared to reading the underside of a leaf: it is like interpreting diurnal village reality from an insight into the nightly and forest realm. This polarity is the very core of the etiological system: in unmasking the source of evil, the divinatory oracle releases a healing potential. It is a homeopathic principle that is also at work in the use of medicinal plants, *makaya,* literally, "foliage of plants," that are toxic under some form or use, curative under another. And the notion of *-kaya,* "to fight evil by turning it back against itself self-destructively" derives from the same root. This solidarity between life-giving and death-giving evokes a basic maternal experience: in rural Yaka land death is always near in delivery. So divination, dream life, plant life, parturition, and maternity—like hunting and cooking—have in common a close connection with the circle of life processes and are prominent in healing and transition rites. Therapeutic reversion and the homeopathic reversal of evil against itself are mobilized at the interstices between forest and village, ancestor and descendant, uterine and agnatic, female and male. They spur the development of defense mechanisms. Reversion and reversal may at the same time effect the denouement of a crisis situation that has been frozen in a long history of conflicts. More fundamentally, these processes indicate how much the subject's becoming is one of doubling and un-doubling. The point where the patient is folded back upon the very root of her suffering and her history most notably reveals how much she has been dispossessed at the very core of her being. In other words, the patient is paradoxically, and simultaneously, led through processes of experiencing and cognizing based on contrasting directions and moods: for example, trance intermingles the limit-experiences of mortal agony, orgasm, and fecundation, and the sacrifice evokes the aggression proper to sorcery and unites the family for a commensal meal.

Another set of devices or cultural inducers belonging to therapy as process would appear to be operative in the *khita* cult. Either they perform reversions—such as items 1–6 listed below—or imply a Janusian thought movement or world order involving the simultaneous deployment of one connotation and its reverse—such as items 7–9. They might also illustrate the homeopathic principle (item 9) in striving for a given effect by turning an opposing force against itself self-destructively. But, as I will argue, the homeopathic principle carries a hidden risk of perversion (item 10). The key to understanding the therapeutic value of the paradoxes is expressed by the healer at the very onset of his formal oration: *khita wuziinga, khita wuziingulula,* "*khita* ties the patient's body in and *khita* may also disentangle it.*" This implies that the ritual alters and frees the patient's body and unbinds the moral relationship between spirit and patient. This alteration, moreover, induces the patient to enthusiastically adopt opposing cognitive modes or affective moods. The transformation involves the simultaneous overlapping and embodying of contrasting corporeal processes or transactions, images, affects, gender positions, and thought processes.

(1) *Processes of incorporation/expulsion and infoliation/exfoliation overlap*

in healing. Through threshold metaphors, the patient is led to abandon old identifications for new ones, to shed off her old 'social skin' for a new, to simultaneously identify with the experiences of mortal agony, orgasmic union, delivery, and birth. The underlying Janusian thought is capable of releasing very great creative potential. It is manifest in the patient being simultaneously led into a fetal condition and pregnant state; in the house of seclusion as both an egg and a hen laying and breeding an egg, or as a micro- and macrocosmic womb. In other words, the processes of 'invagination' and 'exvagination'—which are similar to centripetal and centrifugal movements—overlap since the patient is both fetus and pregnant and the house simultaneously egg- and hen-like. The convex outer shape of the seclusion house implies a concave inner shape. The seclusion house acts as the outer skin for the patient who, in the motion of being led inside, invaginates her new self and further transfers her fetal condition onto the house. The aim of the therapy is to expel whatever has invaded the body and caused it to be ill, while simultaneously (re)incorporating its reverse element or whatever is missing. Therapeutic techniques for treating the symptoms of a closed body restore, through processes of reversion, its capacity for mediation and passage. Fragrant steam baths, ablutions of the genitals, hot enemas, or even emetics may be prescribed. The ritualization of entering and exiting the seclusion house underpins and helps to reappropriate the experience of passage and to regain some control over analogous movements in the body and the daily life-scene.

The body of the possessed patient cannot be turned inside out. Instead, the healer turns the body of a sacrificial animal inside out and spills blood onto the patient who in turn may anoint herself with a mixture of red *khula* paste and palm oil. The contents become the container and the patient sheds her skin through a cycle of death and rebirth. Analogously, the blood sacrifice of an animal may appear to be a device or medium reversing the negative relationship between the aggressor (sorcerer and/or spirit) and his victim so that the bond takes on a positive healing force. The spirit is incorporated into the sacrificial animal, then transferred to the altar built to honor the same spirit, or the therapy may shift the illness or misfortune from the patient's body onto an inanimate host. This object may be buried at a crossroads at midnight, hung in a tree above a busy pathway, or thrown away in a remote spot to decompose. The evil may then be replaced by a 'good object,' such as a protective spirit. Inasmuch as the trance evolves from a passionate transgression of boundaries into a more ritualized liminal experience, it converts the illness into a controlled manifestation of the spirit that is thereafter allied with—married to—the possessed or entranced person. Anointed with red *khula* paste and her head and feet wrapped in a cloth to avoid contact with the sunlight and the ground, the patient is led into the seclusion house in an experience of both gestation and the fetal condition; she thus identifies with a process of infoliating the cosmic body and exfoliating her fetal condition and transferring it onto the seclusion house.

(2) The *left/right crossover* is a therapeutic device. In the *khita* cult kaolin is sometimes used to draw diagonal stripes across the patient's body, or raffia strings may be hung around her body in cross-like patterns; they aim to circumscribe the unity of the body and thus restore it to health. The stripes are specifically drawn—or the strings hung—through the corporeal intersections: at the navel, above the heart, or between the breasts. The drawing of these lines occurs at nightfall during the time of a waxing moon, on the edge of the village, and in the family's presence. As left stands for feminine or uterine, and right for masculine or agnatic connections, the diagonal lines or strings intertwine the patient's bilineal, uterine and agnatic, descent.

(3) The *high/low reversal* is another therapeutic means. According to the cultural body scheme and patterns of sociability, adult men should maintain the upper parts of the body, particularly the heart and head which denote the senses, cool and in poise—in a manner demonstrating weight and gravity *(zitu);* any heat is to be kept in the lower part of the body. Ensorcellment, particularly through agnatic kinsmen, erodes away or empties a person of this gravity and inverts the body order. The victim suffers on the level of the senses from a state of lightness, aimlessness, disorientation, excessive heat and effusion, or he may display an extrusive or bad temper (see 4.3). The victim may suffer from epileptic-like fainting, which is spoken of as "to fall in a faint" *(-bwa nyaambu).* Several lukewarm enemas, normally taken at sunrise, aim to correct this condition. They are made from fragrant plants plucked from tree tops and left to dry in the sun. In line with the humoral logic, the enema is meant to counterbalance and calm colds and chills in the lower part of the body, thus counterbalancing the heat that goes to the head. While vomiting denotes an inversion of the oral and anal functions, anal enemas aim at counterbalancing the defiling effects caused by the ingestion of improper food or the hearing of indecent language.

(4) Healing remobilizes the *inside/outside* dialectics of the body and the cultural valuation of the *orifices.* The orifices constitute essential markers and thresholds of the body's in/out orientation. When an orifice is inverted, the entire body is disturbed and in danger of being itself wholly inverted. Such appears to be the condition in the case of vomiting, hemorrhaging, amenorrhea, miscarriage, strong body odors, and chronic constipation. During the treatment of his amenorrheic or dysmenorrheic niece, a maternal uncle offers her young flowering herbs—gathered at the edge of the village (that is, at the site of lovers' secret trysts)—to "drink" by way of anal or, at times, vaginal enemas. The healer may prescribe saunas or massages with red *khula* paste, mixed with a fern having a rash-like appearance. He may even prescribe massages with the same paste but mixed with a pregnant woman's first urine of the day. Underly-

ing this prescription is the vaguely expressed principle that only a woman who is containing—is pregnant—can also be a container, or represent a holding function. The same logic governs the practice of blessings with saliva. In this case, the family head or patient's uncle spits on the patient's forehead or chest (over the heart): he publicly attests to the lack of any resentment or malice likely to hamper the patient's recovery, and thereby offers his protection.

(5) *Inversion of rhythms* is both a symptom and a cultural inducer of therapy. The notion of biological and social rhythms is fundamental for therapy. Loss or distortion of a rhythm is a sure sign of a major intrusion of the person by sorcerers or spirits. Trembling of the hands, legs, or entire body during a trance often indicates the loss of rhythm, for trembling, which shows the internal rhythm to be cut off from any coded or social order, dangerously exposes a person's breath and vital flow. Trembling delivers the internal rhythm of the vital flow to the covetous spirits and urges the healer's intervention. Sleeplessness is another symptom of a disrupted rhythm; it robs the subject of his most intimate possession, namely, dreaming and sleep. Daily chanting and dancing as a group at dusk serve to reconnect the patient's idiosyncratic rhythms with the collective patterns.

(6) Healing aims at rearticulating the ties between *past and present* by situating the patient in cyclic time or a in ritual cycle. Paradoxically, by reliving the basic transitions in the life-cycle in league with the cycles of sun and moon, and in fellow-feeling with the wider audience, the patient in dance experiences a kind of rebirth or immortalization: the whole drama of renewal, also of group and life-world, is possible only because of her. In this, healing recycles memory by leading the patient to jointly relive mutational experiences of childhood and adulthood: by anointing herself with red paste and by infoliating the 'skin' offered by the house of seclusion, the initiate reshapes her experiences of fetal condition, gestation, and delivery. In a very ludic way, she is meanwhile led to sense out her unconscious identifications while remolding the one experience in terms of others and embodying dimensions from among the stock of symbolic and imaginary themes that are displayed by the setting and drama. Moreover, the accompanying chants offer various themes that question the social body, the relationships elders have with both the ancestors and the descendants. The chants help the patient to roam about in the imaginary realm or to explore in her own life themes of loss, change, and renewal. Moreover, chanting is a primary experience of cycling, in the wheeling pattern between lead singer and the refrain from the chorus of coinitiates, and in step with the cycles of moon and sun. The notion of cyclic time is also important whenever plants are employed in healing. Herbal remedies meant to stimulate the vital flow in the patient should be gathered and used during the first phase of the cycle, when the sap is rising in the plant. Herbal concoctions are used at the transition from one phase in the ritual cycle to the next, or at transitional phases of the lunar

or daily cycle. Preparations counteracting evil forces might likely evoke the new moon or vegetal decay.

(7) *Therapy intermingles both gravity and playfulness, self-containment and ecstasy.* Therapy's overall ambience of dilatation and exuberance helps the patient to open up and to transfer inner tensions onto the collective flow. Healers, participants from the therapy managing group, and observers from the community join in teasing one another as they playfully intermingle in the collective dancing near the seclusion house. The therapists often display a mischievous or even malicious appearance and develop a playful rapport with their patients through their speech, looks, and touch. What occurs in the intimacy of the seclusion house—the patient's ritual skin—is, however, secluded from public view and from encroachment by noninitiates. One of the most serious offenses against the *khita* cult is the breaking of the taboo of sight. An uninitiated person, and men in particular, may see neither what is inside the seclusion hut nor the patient in seclusion, just as a man may not witness a woman in labor. Conversely, a *khita* initiate is not permitted to observe the *n-khanda* or male circumcision and initiation. Such an intrusion in the initiatory secret, it is believed, may capture the initiates' life-bearing capacities or mutilate the transgressor's eyesight. Similarly, both initiatory healing and sexual reproduction are secluded from public view. Initiatory healing is thus by one means or another kept out of public sight and outside the center of diurnal village life, where the elders impose their piercing gaze of power and where the rule of shame and diffidence counterposes men and women, old and young, public and private. At the end of seclusion, the therapist concludes his life-bearing task and the patient's delivery by "giving eyes to" or "reshaping the gaze of" *(-buumba meesu)* his initiate; this means, in effect, that he "draws signs" *(-ta tsona)* on the patient's face. I contend that the double ovoid pattern he traces, by way of metaphoric transposition, associates eyes and the genital orifice, as if upper and lower body were replicas of one another, and also, perhaps, as if the marked eyes are an invitation to meeting with the unmarked, namely, with someone of the male gender. The seclusion ends with a night of festive dancing.

(8) Both *illusion and expectation, exploration and self-examination,* are fostered by the *transitional object.* While Yaka therapy makes moderate use of speech, it relies far more heavily on the interplay of musical rhythms, objects, bodily techniques, and drama. An object (a medicinal plant, ritual object, charm around the neck) contains the memory of the transferential relationship with the therapist. Some patients say: "If I do not wear my charm, something bad will happen to me." The object socializes or attenuates both the expectation and the illusion in the healing relation. For example, a little pendant—made of lianas neatly woven into a double moebius knot, fastened to a small pouch and hung around the neck of the patient—might look rather mysterious.

It signifies in fact the pain caused by the initiation ordeals that the patient underwent as part of the treatment, and it invites the patient to keep an alert mind with regard to the rite. The patient is led to ask: "Is this rite not only a game?" or "Could the healer really harm me?" The object also commits the patient to try to reach a truth or higher knowledge that is accessible only through the ordeals of initiation and guaranteed precisely by the accomplishment of the rite itself. Without the experience of the rite, such truth would remain indefinable. Initiation may give rise to a kind of secrecy which is not so much of a particular knowledge but rather a mark of, or at least the pretension to, an initiatory identity; the rite in itself, however, is unlikely to involve much particular esoteric skill or knowledge.

(9) Healing aims both at *destruction and regeneration*. Healing operates both as a process of *homeopathic or self-destructive reversal (-kaya)* of the illness, as well as a creative or gestational kind of self-healing *(-buka, -bukama)*. For the diviner-diagnostician or according to formal etiology, health *(-kola)* and illness *(-loka)*, good *(mbote)* and evil *(mbi)*, are polarities just as the left and right hands are considered to be nearly equivalent yet reversed derivations sharing the same origin. The therapist's task is -*kaya*, to fight external evil by turning it back against itself self-destructively and thereby to gain access to the vital flow that the evil or illness would otherwise have suffocated or deviated (see 6.3, phase 5: *-fuundila fula*). In my own terms, it is the weaving of the vital flow, metaphorically connected with the processes of fermentation and cooking, that molds the cure into the form of gestation. The cure is thus a transformative process. Homeopathic reversal in fact expresses a particular ontological perspective in Yaka culture. The relation an individual establishes with the realms of ancestral shades, spirits, and forces of the dark forest and the night may appear as double-sided: they are as equally capable of hindering or harming a person as they are of bringing good luck, life, and growth. Order and disorder are not simply opposing concepts. They are seen as twin, coextensive, and solidaristic terms in the sense of conceptual pairs such as good fortune and misfortune, health and illness, fate and anti-fate, abundance and famine, excess and lack, autonomy and intrusion, and so on. All these phenomena are accepted as occurring together just as risks and opportunities are thought to do in most undertakings beyond the daytime realm of one's household. This ambivalent quality of reality shows itself, through the various images given to sorcery, exorcism, and antisorcery, to be a power whose finality can be modified or redirected by means of inversions. Yaka cults posit homeopathic reversion *(-kaya)* as a basic process in therapy: it is an action which turns the malevolent agent against itself self-destructively through symbolic means and paradox itself. The power of the sorcerous aggressor discovers its counterweight in the ritual power a victim might solicit in order to turn the aggression against the aggressor. At times it is indeed the victim who triumphs

in the struggle, with the result that the sorcerer is killed by the very forces which he intended to wield against someone else.

(10) *Decadence/fulfillment* and *deceiving/redeeming oneself* are versatile polarities at play in healing. Good and ill health appear as the mere outcome of a movement back and forth between polarities rather than as a consequence of moral conduct. The question of the double-sidedness of boundaries and of the bipolarity of transition points—that is, the turnover from what causes ill health to what brings good health, or from decadence to fulfillment, death to rebirth—also indicates the extent to which contact with the source of life or with the extrahuman is permanently susceptible to *perversion*. It would appear, at least, as if the nonancestral cult spirits were present only in the margins of social and cultural order and were fundamentally ambivalent forces lacking any stable orientation in themselves. The maternal uncle and family elders are capable of abusively appropriating a large part of this extrahuman force for their own ends and may turn some aspect of the shared agnatic life force on itself. A word spoken by one of them in anger against the ancestors may bring misfortune. The familial chief is then invited to purge himself of the incriminating outburst *(-fyaawula)* in order that the word may once again serve to weave together family bonds. The relation that one establishes with a chief, a therapist, or any other ritual specialist always carries an element of fear. An individual trapped between the contradictory constraints of fidelity to tradition, on the one hand, and the concrete demands of everyday life, on the other— between a rock and a hard place, as it were—might well appeal to the ancestors or the cult spirits for justification of his vengeful behavior. Knowing full well that his act is wrong, he might redeem himself, even in advance of the crime, by administering to himself or to his accomplices fortifying tonics of a symbolic nature. In point of fact, there is always a means of redeeming oneself from a misdeed, of righting the evil act, by effectively symbolizing—even in advance of the deed—the injurious effect turning self-destructively against itself. By offering a hen or a monetary substitute to a sexual partner, the man attempts to neutralize the effects of an anticipated act of adultery, or at least to disclaim his responsibility for it. It is therefore possible to postulate a permanent store of 'credit' for self-activated neutralization through contact with the spirits.

Drawing on these paradoxes and on the Janusian model of transgression, cult healing proves to be more of a creative art-therapy than a recompense or a group remedy. Indeed, *khita* operates on the basis of paradoxes or opposing terms that manifest themselves simultaneously. *Khita* may both cause gynecological disorders and enhance female fertility.

In short, many traditional therapies put at play the deconstruction/reconstruction principle, in line with the cultural assumption that ensorcellment *(-lokala)* and healing *(-kolala)* are reverse sides of the same phenomenon. They are rooted in a subtle handling of paradoxes, like the sculptor who 'handles' the spatial dimensions of inside/outside, high/low, left/right, convex/concave, in order to give his work the relief and depth of the past and the spiritual power of the living. Illness expresses the upsetting of the body's vectors (referring to inside/outside, upper/lower, front/back, left/right), of the dialectics of setting and transgressing boundaries, or of one's spatial and temporal place in the group and the life-world. The body, especially the skin and orifices, become the privileged means and sites of inversion, reversion, and transformation. The senses and abilities to communicate are the privileged vectors in the task of interconnecting. A myriad of invisible entities, actors, and relationships are thus intertwined with persons, social rules, and axioms. All this occurs in an in an unfolding corporeal, communal, and cosmic drama.

8.4 A Ternary Logic of Mediation and Effusion in Self-healing

The many healing cults at play at the edge of established Yaka society appear to operate partially beyond the objective conditions and conventional arrangements of diurnal social order and beyond the commonsense knowledge of unskilled informants. Unlike Bourdieu (1980), I would not consider the systems of signs, symbols, and forces at play in the healing cults as devices that merely assist the reproduction of the objective conditions, that is, as means of conferring a quasi-natural status to the conditions of social life and the cultural conventions in such a way that people tend to see them as the only possible reality. Ritual healing explicitly withdraws the patient from the coercive order of *agnatic* relations of subordination and social status, that is, from the cycle of familial history in which offenses inevitably call for vengeance.

The healing cult reconnects the patient with her *uterine* ties and with the source of life. Therapy endeavors to reweave affects, organs, energies, and bodily functions, all of which are exfoliated on the ritual scene, into an irrepressible emergence of the uterine vital flow. It has an all the more ecstatic effect in that it is cosmogenetic: it leads the patient towards a transformed presence within and in relation with (e.g., *Mitwelt*) the life-world which is itself transformed in the process (e.g., *Umwelt*). Ritual healing inaugurates a new bodily experience and a new world order while it simultaneously transforms, through corporeal acts, the subject's relation to this world.

The healing ritual simultaneously unfolds on two levels. On a first level, such pairs as bride-takers and bride-givers, genitor and genitrix, agnatic and uterine, ascendant and descendant, healer and patient, illness and health, being bound and being linked to, offense and persecution, and before and after are represented as polar terms *on the same axis*. This is the level at which we find the logic of distinct *binary* oppositions to be operative. The cult aims at mobilizing a series of polarities and paradoxically at mixing contrasting elements: as for example, in the trance-induced overlapping of the experiences of mortal agony and conception, of being both child-bearer and newborn. This involves a mixing of categories that can be both dangerous and potent. At work here is a homeopathic principle of restoration through reversal, thanks to which healing results from reversing chaos into order by trapping *(-kaya)* disorder and reversing the evil or the stain against itself in a self-destructive way.

On another level underlying that of opposition is a more embracing order, one whose function it is to provide a dynamic foundation for the polarities or, more adequately put, for the phenomenon of emergence, outbreak, and effluence. Healing brings about a unifying and all-embracing system of a *tridimensional* nature, so to speak: healing is "making whole" *(-luunga)*. At play here is a *process* or a kind of *spiral* movement informed by a *ternary* logic. It is the ceaselessly emergent movement of the life-flow from the uterine life source. The paradoxical Janusian thought in *khita* therapy destabilizes and energizes the binary folk-level oppositions of illness/health, illicit/licit, closure/effusion, polluting/pure, agnatic/uterine, and the like. And yet, there is more to this pattern of thought: a tridimensional system and ternary logic is brought into play by the various participants. Differences as between male and female, agnatic and uterine, forebear and offspring, healer and patient are not exclusionary categories. The patient enters a process of androgynous self-healing. The very paradoxical thought processes and transgressive acts display the differences and oppositions in reference to an englobing order of foundation, a realm of the sacred, of basic postulates such as "life is stronger than death; evil ends by destroying itself." This order of foundation destructures the dyads of ill health/ good health and the like, and breaks them open into a ternary logic. This realm of the sacred is not a longing for fulfillment in an eschaton; it is both a ground of discourse and a deep source of forces in the body, group, and life-world rather than a truth or an ontological foundation for the production of knowledge and ideology.

In terms of the Yaka healing cults, this *basic ground* of the healing art and healing per se *(bungaanga)* is *in the world:* in this view, the sacred is this world's *innermost, ceaselessly emerging life source: ngoongu,* the uterus of the world. In some respects, healing is fundamentally a regression into a world prior to the body: *the body stems from the world,* embodying 'the primal womb of the world.' Its unfolding regenerative processes in people and life-world bear witness to this ternary logic.

In other words, the tie that binds the authoritative or paternal function with the mothering capacity of the healer—who acts as a maternal uncle to the patient—is not obtained in terms of a dialectical process of *Aufhebung;* a ternary logic underlies the healer acting as 'male mother, male source,' or the patient being both fetus and pregnant. The ternary logic does not simply overcome the opposition or lead to a totalizing system, but completes, rather, the Janusian thought, transgression, or homeopathic reversal with growth, the effluence of life and empowerment. The bond between the two poles (paternal/maternal, parent/child, mortal agony/rebirth, incubation/hatching out, and so on) does not depend on their intrinsic qualities only but on their different relations with regard to a unifying and liminal pole. This unifying pole is like the measure, the basic rhythm in the drama, the ongoing weave, the source of tonics, vitality, and empowerment. In Yaka healing culture, *ngoongu,* 'the primal womb,' appears as a place of transformative transcendence, the space-time order of the founding and ever reemerging possibility of existence. It is not the telos of the whole, but a 'womb of cultural life,' a common source and ferment, one that sets forth vital solidarity, not appropriation and power. *Ngoongu* evokes the euchronic maternal space, the primordial, self-generating source of life emerging from the soil and continually renewing itself between the subterranean realm and the sky, in the chthonic, animal, human, and cosmic matrices. Seclusion in the ritual house, ties with the maternal uncle, the healer acting as a demiurge or a weaver, anointing with red *khula* paste or with kaolin, the healing processes of trapping and hunting—all of these events draw from and tap this erupting source, this transcendent and embracing instance. In this foundational instance and ternary logic, the principles of linearity (underpinning agnatic descent, manhood, excellence, ranking, supervision and super-vision) and circularity and cyclicity (characterizing uterine descent, motherhood, commensality, agricultural production, and relations with the autochthonous people) meet each other in the morphogenetic intertwining of the patient's body and world with, for example, the realms of the palm tree, the parasol tree, the hen that lays an egg, fermentation, being caught up in a trap, and cooking. These syntheses are metamorphic, transformative, and mutually empowering links between corporeal, social, and cosmological domains. Rather than making all this explicit in speech, the healing ritual brings forth a productive "fusion of the worlds" (Stoller 1989). The patient "has grown to fullness" *(luungidi).* It is not a locus of innocence, but a hard won recognition and achievement of a new solidarity in the unclosing and sharing of a common life source and in constructing new identities. It does not focus on consciousness, rights, or salvation but on bodily, sensuous, and communal skills and arts that enhance and share vitality, that arouse energy for regrasping a determining relation with the social world. It arouses, shares, and responds to potentialities in the person grounded in mutual caring.

It seems to me that the basic metaphors vitally informing this therapy bring into play a particular spatial and temporal logic. The process of weaving *(-kuba),* which is symbolically superimposed onto the process of healing *(-buka)* and which is interconnected with the growth of the raffia palm and fermentation of palm wine, evokes the juxtaposition of a concentric movement (from periphery to center and vice versa) and a spiraling or rhythmic movement. On the one hand we have a spiral movement of weaving. The spiral combines the horizontal and concentric (centripetal/centrifugal, infoliating/exfoliating) movement and the vertical movement (of growth and aging). Therapy leads the patient from the outer fringe to the center of her or his being. Having its starting point in the social network and brought on by depressing or harmful relationships, therapy leads the patient into the seclusion of the maternal womb, into the egg of the world. This process represents the gestation of a new being within the patient that must be born to life.

On the other hand, the healing drama seems to superimpose the movements of weaving onto the centripetal-centrifugal axis. Healing leads a patient to her or his center or source of life, while fermentation links decay to regeneration. The raffia cloth connotes the effervescent, sexual, and cosmological symbolism of the raffia palm and of the fermentation of palm wine, as well as that of cooking palm oil. Healing really means drawing on the effervescent vital flow. The cure thereby aims at an arrangement that is prefigured by the fabric: it is the weaving of the vital flow. In doubling the palm metaphor, the weaving brings about and gives meaning to a reinsertion of the subject in the world. It achieves this by means of a constitutive juxtaposition of the polar principles which characterize beings and things, right and left, up and down, front and back, heaven and earth, decomposition and rebirth, sowing and flowering, agnates and uterines, genitors and offspring, masculine and feminine. To put it in the terms of Bourdieu (1980:29, my translation): "Only someone who is completely mastered by this kind of logic can master it completely him/herself." From the point of view of corporeal movement, the cure leads the patient from violent gesticulations during the trance to an unobtrusive but active receptiveness during the seclusion. At the end of the cure, in the act of "coming out from between the healer's legs," the patient is led to take possession of her or his redefined corporeal space and to stand upright in front of the healer and the others. Informed by this morphogenetic superimposition, the cure is also a movement that integrates the physical, social, and cosmological levels, and in which the vital flow is interlaced. The Yaka healer relates his intervention to the ancestral time of which he is a mediator: euchronic time. It surpasses the contingent and linear time that the symptoms display, since they stem from disorders in the family history, namely from repeated offenses and the curses and retaliation that have followed upon them.

Through affliction and healing, *khita,* like most other healing cults, punishes an offense and reasserts the need for semantic, social, moral, and cosmogenetic order. In some of its aspects, the ritual is an instrument of classificatory thought, but more strikingly one of reempowerment insofar as it demonstrates how much social systems of descent, marriage, and reproduction are but extensions of cosmological or, better, cosmogenetic processes. Inasmuch as they include polar forces and directions, these processes are displayed in the rite of seclusion, and the many paradoxes in the healing cult are embodied in the patient's trance behavior or the avuncular role of the therapist. The cult's symbolic and morphogenetic drama draws heavily on female or maternal life-bearing powers, yet the orchestration of the meeting of both sexes mediates these powers in favor of male rights or of spirits controlled by male healers.

The *khita* cult demonstrates the great extent to which cultural symbols and metaphors are operative through the body, the being itself, the meaningfulness and power located in living experience. It is in and through the body that meaning-bearing connections are made and that the human body, group, and life-world are interwoven. Ritual symbols are not images but primarily corporeal devices, processes, and methods or patterns that originate in people's corporeal rootedness and participation in a cultural wellspring and life-world. They perhaps arise from a potential which, akin to the dream, unconceals both images and inner energy woven into the texture of the body. This view is as such a reversal of most of the linguistic and semiotic perspectives on metaphor and its logical processes known today. Only after the enactment, in the living body of tradition, do the actors of a rite become aware of a meaningful texture of the world that they have come to embody. Through ritual, the body is the weaving loom of healing, and yet of the umbilical cords of life and the uterine life source.

What the present study has been aiming at is a genuine encounter with Yaka society through a disclosure of how *khita* fundamentally associates the processes of health and life transmission in the human body with those in the world, as both share something in common and with other forms of life emerging from the palm tree, from a breeding hen and egg in incubation, and so on. *Khita* converts the patient's body and the seclusion house into resonant micro- and macrocosmic processes tapping the source of ever-renewed life. The concept of healing—as it is refracted through an understanding of Yaka culture itself—conveyed here is not simply one of change, redress, catharsis, self-control, cognitive relabeling, self-assertion, meaning production, or drama. Healing, rather, basically draws the patient and her close family into a cosmogenetic weave and empowerment. It transfigures the initiate, her body, senses, emotions, and embodied meanings, her receiving and giving, into a relationship of integration, that is, into an interweaving. And yet, it leads to or reinforces a *decentering of the individual:* emphasis is on the patient's acceptance of the condition of being a medium, that is, of a mediumistic type of 'conjugal' relation with the cult spirit for the benefit of the group, and thereby on the patient's contracting a debt with regard to others. This occurs, however, while the cosmogenetic drama releases self-generative power or stimulates self-healing in the patient and her life-world, benefiting her close kin as well. The patient, her kin, and life-world are linked up with *ngoongu,* the uterine, primal, egg- and tree-like source of vital flow that ceaselessly emerges and regenerates itself. When after the initiatory healing the *khita* initiate gives birth to a child, the latter receives the name of *N-seenga* or *N-noongu,* which evokes the weaving-hook made from the wood of the parasol tree and is itself a symbol of the inflorescence of the palm and parasol trees. This birth seems to echo the theme of the patient's being bound, the process of untying her bonds, and the strategy of reweaving her into the very vital flow emergent from the world's uterine source of life.

Epilogue

Although the healing rite is marked by seclusion and a myriad of highly charged symbolic elements and stands as a portal between the this-worldly and the other-worldly, it nevertheless remains firmly grounded in this world of practical action. Most of the information that I have received from elders and healers—some during the rite or the seclusion itself—has been gathered while informants were in a very witty or playful mood: while carving a ritual object, making basketry, weaving a mat, preparing the lianas for setting their traps, or building the house, for example. The healer's offer of information and self-revelation resembles a trapper-hunter's account of finding the right bait and place to set the trap. This is the place where routine and correct opinion are overcome by the act of stumbling over the obvious. In his behavior and in the narrative he recounts, the healer is like the trickster, deploying surprise, giving his clients a means to explore. In their very core, divination and healing are founded, so to speak, in dreamwork that owes much to the processes of condensation, displacement, and figuration disclosed in the idiom of scenes, moods, and feelings—but this makes for another study.

The anthropological endeavor I am advocating radically opposes some of the deconstructionist stances taken in postmodern anthropology. I compare my position as an anthropologist to one of a reluctant joker or trickster figure. I have been deeply and morally touched by my relation with the Yaka people with whom I have come to share so much. In my view, the fundamental authority for the anthropologist is precisely the interdependence of field and text, both in an intellectual and moral respect. In late 1974, on returning home after eight years of intense work in Kinshasa and Kwaango land—while in my full youth and having severed myself from so many friends and a world in which I had taken root—one of the last messages given me by a friend, a university professor and zealous militant of the "Recourse to Authenticity" campaign belonging to the M.P.R. (the People's Movement of the Revolution), was this: "After you have appropriated the people's knowledge and cultural patrimony, you will publish in languages and texts that are out of our reach. With it, you will make yourself a social position. This is cultural theft: it all belongs to us and should return to us." It took me many years of intense work to recover from this indictment. When, for the first time, I came back to Kinshasa after twelve years, in a conference organized by the Center for the Study of African Religions (C.E.R.A.), I recounted my having been questioned by the son of a prestigious Yaka diviner in Masina-Kinhasa, a few days earlier: "You the white man, who seems to know a great deal of our divinatory and healing art, who are you? You the white people, you have tried to kill the heart of our people by condemning diviners, healers, and fetishes as being the work of satan: who are you? Tell us who you are, you who know the innermost life of our people" (Devisch 1987:146). Then I told the conference that I had given some Yaka elders a copy of my publications in a gesture recalling the act of a widower at the end of his mourning: he is expected to transmit the fruits of his work to his uncle so that the latter may then relieve him from mourning. I further informed the audience how much Yaka cultural body symbolism had inspired some innovations in our approach to family medicine in Flanders (Devisch 1990d), just as it is, moreover, influencing my psychoanalytic practice and theory.

The type of anthropological encounter I am advocating is careful to not impose its own paradigm; it does not restrict me to looking through the window of my own worldview; nor is it a translation. Anthropology requires taking a skeptical stance with regard to the outspoken side of life, to the face value of outward behavior and information, and to the claims of reason and power. Rooted as I am in my Flemish culture of origin, I entered into Yaka society and culture as receptive, self-critical, situated, and authentically myself as I could, that is, as an intermediary onto whom my hosts in their daily and ritual practice could transfer their deeper intuitions and longings about life. Maybe it was my search for personalized encounter, open-hearted intersubjectivity, and genuine solidarity that earned me the name of reference: *n-ndedyeetu,* "the white man who became ours," or the welcome of the elders in 1991 as *mamoosu tukukeembe,* "to you we had committed everything." I do recognize difference, but in solidarity. Nonetheless I deeply resist an appropriation of all of the Yaka world into Western theories of some transcendental essence, autonomy of reason, rationality, science of the orderly and recurrent reality, objective truth, linear time and beneficial progress that would rescue them, or into Western views on otherness, mind/body, mental/manual labor, culture/nature, male/female, reason/sense, truth/illusion, or on power, social change, modernization, globalization, acculturation, and victimization. Since 1989, a team of Zairean and Belgian scholars of both genders has worked at applied medical-anthropological action-research in Kinshasa that aims at promoting, in urban Yaka culture, the cultural components in healing and a genuine comprehension of it by biomedical staff in the Community Health Care.

My endeavor reaches beyond dialogue and discursive reality. In order to deepen my understanding of the meaning of crucial notions and practices in the cults, I had the occasion to offer or share palm wine and cola nut with the elders and ritual specialists, during or after the organization of the cult. These moments served to inspire words and acts that spill out and transmit vital flow and empowerment—including those directed at me. But the more affinity and affectionate fellow feeling grow, the more the 'anthropological' encounter becomes transferential—in the literal sense of *diaphorein, Übertragung:* bearing across and conveying to one another, carrying beyond, opening up. This encounter challenges and enriches the ethnographer's social and cultural assumptions. It is not one of innocence, salvation, or sadness, but grows into a genuine human venture for a never-ending polylogue, a critical giving and receiving, and an always finite exploration of the resonance between body, family, and life-world. It is a resonance of reweaving and reempowering through limitations, paradoxes, and innovative transformations, and it witnesses to an ever reemerging possibility for meaningful existence, dignity, and inexhaustible mutuality: this is and brings *kyeesi*.

Appendix A
A Case of Infertility

The following case illustrates the role of the maternal uncle in countering gynecological disorders (as I have outlined in 6.2.1). Madila and Leewo, two full sisters who had been recently married, began their *khita* seclusion on 31 July 1972 in a village neighboring Yitaanda. (Several of the names have been intentionally changed.)

Madila has a four year old daughter named Mafuta from a previous marriage. This marriage was ended when an oracle revealed that the sterility Madila suffered following the first birth had been caused by a prohibition of intermarriage between members of her clan and that of her husband. Divorced and remarried for over a year, she has still not become pregnant. Madila and her daughter underwent the *khita* therapy together. For her part, Madila's younger sister Leewo has already suffered four accidental abortions. The young women belong to the Mbaya clan, by their father, whereas in the uterine lines they are related to the lineages of Mangaya, Moombo, Waana, and Mbela Khuumba through, respectively, their primary uncle, granduncle, great-granduncle, and great-great-granduncle. Upon the death of Madila and Leewo's father, Mbaya, the deceased's junior brother inherited their widowed mother Khuumba in marriage. She herself died soon after, the same day as did her son Kasela, the full brother of the two young women. The divinatory oracle associated these deaths and an abusive curse. Khuumba had ensorcelled her son Kasela in complicity with her brother Mangaya, a primary uncle to the victim. To remove suspicion from herself, she had then invited Mangaya to curse those in the kin group who might have caused Kasela's illness. Subsequent to this, however, the young man had gone to see his great-granduncle Waana to collect a dog for which he had not yet paid. The "mixing of hearths" that receiving this domestic animal represented was enough to bring Mangaya's curse on Kasela and his mother, who died a sudden death the same day. The dog also died. By accepting the gift of the great-granduncle Waana, the sorcerous mother Khuumba and her son Kasela effected a paradoxical union with the uncles, including the complicious primary uncle who condemned the ensorcellment, through a curse, while it was the mother herself who had ensorcelled her son.

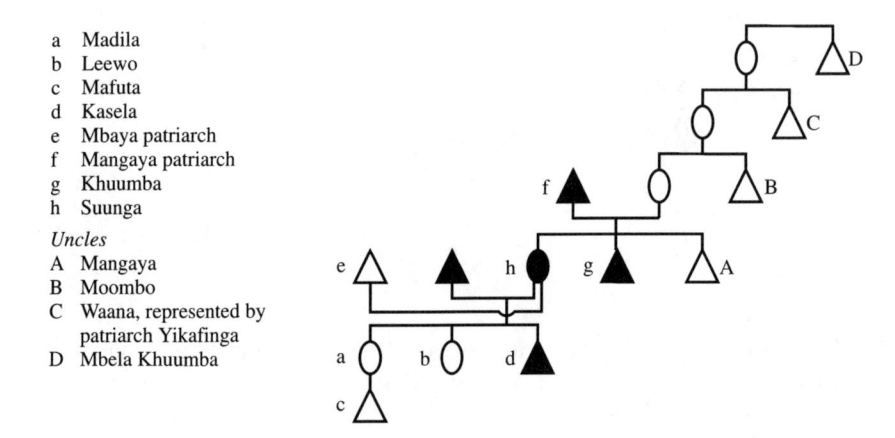

a Madila
b Leewo
c Mafuta
d Kasela
e Mbaya patriarch
f Mangaya patriarch
g Khuumba
h Suunga

Uncles
A Mangaya
B Moombo
C Waana, represented by patriarch Yikafinga
D Mbela Khuumba

Figure 2. Classificatory Position of the Afflicted Individuals

The evening of the seclusion in the *khita* cult of Madila and Mafuta, following an invitation by the head of the afflicted couple's family for him to intervene, the great-granduncle Waana spoke. His speech (recorded below), deals with the manner in which he had fulfilled his avuncular duties in the past, and has the purpose of warranting the effectiveness of his actions with regard to the two young women. Here we directly address the dimension of uterine and avuncular relations regarding the problem. Waana opens his speech by affirming his uterine ties through Mbela Khuumba, who had transmitted to him the prohibitions (named under point 2 of the speech) regarding himself and the whole of his uterine descendance. At the end of his speech he again mentions Mbela Khuumba as being in charge of the *khita* cult and the affliction that it transmits. In his oration, Waana relates how he acquitted himself of his avuncular duties on the occasion of three instances of ensorcellment.

The first was linked to the death of Suunga, who was a primary uncle to the two women. The oracle divined on that occasion attributed this death to the plotting of the victim's father (patriarch of the Mangaya family), his primary uncle Moombo, and his granduncle Waana (points 6–7). Later, when Waana fell ill, he and Moombo offered compensation to Mbela Khuumba for the death of Suunga and thereby redeemed their avuncular rights (points 8–9).

The second ensorcellment involved an affliction operative through the *maawa* cult spirits that affected Khuumba, the mother of the young women. Khuumba was healed after having been given ritual tonics, while her younger brother Suunga died soon afterwards. The sorcerers were able to keep their conspiracy hidden, and the oracle was duped into assigning the death to some presumed influence of *maawa* cult spirits. Thus, when Khuumba was initiated

287   A Case of Infertility

into the *maawa* cult, it was not expected that she enter into a trance in order to authenticate her mediumship (trances of the *maawa* type could have led to her death) (10–12). Although Moombo accused Waana of having ensorcelled Suunga (13), the latter was declared innocent because the tonics he had given to Khuumba during her initiation into *maawa* were beneficial.

The third case of ensorcellment involved Kasela, the brother of Madila and Leewo. As we have seen, Kasela died the same day as did his mother Khuumba and the dog upon reception from Waana. The oracle inculpated Mangaya, Moombo, and Waana for having killed the victims through sorcerous means (15–20). Waana continued to administer tonics to the children of Mbaya, and, as they appeared to be in good health, he was freed of suspicion (21). Finally, Mangaya and Moombo reassumed their avuncular rights—which had been taken from them following the ensorcellment of Suunga, Khuumba, and Kasela—without having paid Waana in order to regain the avuncular function. Waana therefore attributes the sterility and repeated abortions Madila and Leewo have suffered to the abuse of avuncular power by Mangaya and Moombo (27–32).

Waana's address ends with a conjuration: the fecundity of the two young women will depend on the legitimacy of his intervention as uncle, in lines with his former beneficial influence. He therefore affirms that his intervention should bring a new-found health to the women, while their healing should in turn witness to the legitimacy of his avuncular acts.

Yikafiinga, the patriarch of the Waana kin group, addresses the council in his capacity of legitimate successor to the great-granduncle Waana:

1   Khaaka wasala ndziimbu, Waana, weekotasaza mundzo Mbela Khuumba.
2   Meni buko, Mbela Khuumba: "meni wa Mbela Khuumba bun-neeti: kaanda dyaadi babata maafuku, babaluundza meenuku, bababwaaka maholuku, mbeedya n-kolu khatwa."
3   Dyakhedi bwoku, khaaka N-ziinga.
4   Baana ne babaheedi?
    Bidiimbu byameni.
5   Bikuma byoosu bikabwedi kwameni.
6   Suunga weetonguna phakasa; hakatonguna bibuudi bikuma. Phakasa badiidi, muutu bahoondedi.
7   Bubeenda ngoombu bikabwedi bikuma: Waana n-siingi, Moombo n-siingi, Mangaya n-siingi; khatwa Mbela Khuumba wako kungoombu.
8   Waana khaaka bimini; kasya nde "yibwe tsya?" Moombo lubukidi: "tweenda tweefuta lufutu."
9   "Baatu katala ngoomby kakota. Taa fuunda dyabudi, n-ledi khatwa." Beesa, bafuta mahuudi. Waana wusa kota mukaanda.
10 Khaaka fuudi. Khaaka Luvwefwa seele. Meni yakala kweenati yihalu kyamaawa kya Maa Khuumba. Tweedi kuna mbika N-dima.

11 Kuna tweenda, bahoya: "Khuumba kakalukiku, badiilama baatu, lun-sya pfuumbvu."
12 Basiidi pfuumbvu.
13 Moombo wadya baatu bahoya: "khi kuma kahaanina baana baba makuumi?"
14 Yendi n-kweedya. Bwaphaanga bwaphuna kaanda didi dikodiku.
15 Bwaleelu mwaana waawu Kasela kakweenda kumbika Waana, zeeyi Mbela Khuumba.
16 Bwaleelu mwaana weendeledi mbwa: yiyaawu yatuunga yisina. Ban-heedi mbwa keti mwaana Waana kalaanda zoku.
17 Keti besi Mbaya balobula maambu mana, ndzeeyiku.
18 Kukafuudi mwaana, phaangi wakhutidi: "nge n-loki, nge lun-diidi ye Mbaya."
19 "Maama, meni ndiidi muutuku." Budyabwa.
20 Buna maambu malutukidi mubaana baba. Beedi ngoombu. Kuna beenda, basya nde: "Waana n-loki weehya ngoombu, kakatuka mubuleemba."
21 "Meni wa Moombo, meni yinaha." Bwakahiila Waana ngoombu wadya biima byamasuka ma Mangaya. Bubuna bwababuudi phaka.
22 Hahana keti neni wafwa, khaaka mooyi kakedi. Tuhweena: maleemba bawu.
23 Bwaleelu kaanda dyaadi dibuudi bikuma; wuna kwaaku leemba bavudidi.
24 Waana watiina. Leka khaaka N-ziinga, khaaka Luvwefwa, bawu bunguumba ba-huna, betu yivumu thuna kya N-ziinga.
25 Masuka matuuka Moombo, kiima yabonga n-tuwa ye khoku ye n-ledi mitaanu.
26 Bukosa hoya meni muhata yikala, yihoya buumaku. Bubakwee ngoombu, nde: "wuna wukula Waana?"
27 Bwaleelu, meni Waana pholele bakhoombu, baana beesedi kwameni; yina muphwa Waanaku, kaanda didi dikodiku; Waana meni, watsadila ndziimbuku, maamba meni kan-kweelaku, lukodiku.
28 Benu baana baba, leelu kan-kweedi Waana, kaamba bulufwa meni ngoombu yahya.
29 Leelu meni theetemeni hayifulu kyabaana wasiisa nge Khuumba. Moodi yizaayi-didi, matatu, kaanda didi dikodiku. Ndzeeyi moodiku, meni Yikafiinga kabuta Waana. Waana wasala ndziimbu yabutukila.
30 Bwaleelu ho Mbaya maambu kabazaayila, bwaleelu meni ndzeeyi buumaku. Ya-kala kuyifwaandu kya Mbaya ku.
31 Baana baba lukhoondzu lungolu, meni yipfumwaawu yavwa kaanda, yavwa tsiku kwa Mbela Khuumba.
32 Leelu beka kwameni n-kweeba.
33 Phoongwa yihoonda ya Mbela Khuumba; kabwaanga wameni Waana; mbwoolu Mbela Khuumba, yihoonda kyamandzandza kya Mbela Khuumba.
34 Leelu bameniba bakola khoondzu. Yemeni Yibaanda tuvuudi baana.
35 Tukedi bakheeki tubaheedi; tuluukidi, tusabukidi matu, tumeeni wukabula: yi Mbela Khuumba, yikyaawu.
36 Koondzu muutu ndzilaandi kateela buleemba. Bwaleelu makumini maambu mavula.
37 Leelu phoongwa yihoonda yimonekeni ya Mbela Khuumba, khaaka wavwa ku-kaanda bwaabu yan-mona muna simwa Kwaangu keenda fuula.
38 Bwaleelu bapheedi baana baba. Makyeleka, benu bafu bakhulu, baatu mbidi, luwa mbeembu ye mbila. Baana baba bakotedi kuphoongu.

A Case of Infertility

39 Meni n-kwa masina makaanda meenda mundzo Waana. Leelu bakola, meni yavwa phoongu: yihoonda kyameni, mbwoolu wameni.

1 My grandfather Waana gathered together the matrimonial goods necessary for marrying a woman of the Mbela Khuumba lineage into his homestead.
2 Upon it, my in-laws, Mbela Khuumba, have set a rule [thus indicating the prohibitions for the descendants issuing from this marriage]: "Now that you take the bride, I, Mbela Khuumba declare: in this clan no member will throw either earth or charcoal on another, no one shall be bitten, and the knife of the night [of sorcery] will not be exhibited."
3 I speak with authority owing to my ancestor N-ziinga [to whom these prohibitions were given].
4 [A question from someone present:] These young women [Madila and Leewo], to whom have they been given? [What rights does Waana have over them?] [Waana's answer:] A portion of the matrimonial goods given for marrying the mother [Khuumba] of these young women has been returned to me.
5 Subsequently, all the avuncular rights and duties have been handed to me.
6 Suunga has hunted a buffalo. It is with this kill that the case began. The buffalo has been eaten and the man has been killed. [Waana nearly lost his avuncular rights when he was accused of conspiring against Suunga, who was fatally ensorcelled on his return from a buffalo hunt.]
7 The divining oracle revealed that the sorcerous death of Suunga had been caused by the patriarch of the Mangaya clan and by the victim's uncles Moombo and Waana.
8 My ancestor fell ill and said: "What shall I do?" Moombo replied: "Let's go pay the cadaver. The one who is responsible for men is the one intended by the oracle." [In order to receive the ritual tonics from their uncle, Waana and Moombo paid their share to Mbela Khuumba of the mortuary goods for Suunga. They hereby recovered some innocence.]
9 "Here are ten thousand cowries [as compensation offered to Mbela Khuumba for Suunga's death]; there is no fabric." They returned; they had paid and settled the question [and recovered their avuncular rights].
10 My ancestor died and grandfather Luvwela succeeded him [in the exercise of the avuncular responsibilities in the Waana matriline]. At this time Luvwela invited me to attend in the initiation of Maa Khuumba, the mother of Madila and Leewo; Maa Khuumba suffered from a *maawa* possession. We then invited the therapist Kha N-dima, to organize the initiation.
11 When we went there [to the home of Kha N-dima] we were told that Maa Khuumba could not be properly initiated in the *maawa* cult because *maawa* spirits had been abusively fostered to kill uterine kin, and such possession would therefore have brought about Khuumba's death. "Treat her without her having to enter into trance."
12 They treated Khuumba to make her to come out of the influence of *maawa*.
13 Moombo, who was an accomplice in Suunga's death, said: "Why does Waana give tonics to Madila and Leewo?" [Moombo had killed Khuumba's brother, Suunga.]
14 Waana [represented by Luvwela], who held the avuncular rights, said: "If it were

290   Appendix A

15 true that I do not have the right to exercise the avuncular duties, let these tonics be of harm" [though they proved to be beneficial].
15 This young man Kasela went to Waana who knows Mbela Khuumba [Waana and Mbela Khuumba share the avuncular rights.]
16 But this young man Kasela went to Waana to get the dog: that is what caused his death. He was given the dog but no one followed him [to collect the payment for the dog, or to offer tonics to his mother or sisters Leewo and Madila].
17 I don't know if it was the patrikin Mbaya who first wished that he die.
18 When this young man Kasela died his eldest sister Madila [unjustly] accused me, saying, "You, great-granduncle Waana, are a sorcerer; you and our patriarch Mbaya have eaten him [Kasela]."
19 "Woman, I have eaten no one." This is what I told her.
20 Since then these young women have suffered greatly. When consulted, the oracle declared: "Waana is a sorcerer [in thwarting the fertility]; let him give up his avuncular rights."
21 [Granduncle Moombo then took up his responsibilities for Madila and Leewo:] "I Moombo am here." The oracle accused Waana of sorcery, namely of having taken the lives of uterine descendants [like Kasela] to avenge for Mangaya who did not share the income from his avuncular duties.
22 When my ancestor Waana was still alive [and exercised his avuncular duties], did some die [because of him]? We were not the ones who intervened; it was they who acted as uncles. [Moombo had exercised the avuncular duties without either having the right or being delegated to do so by Waana.]
23 But today problems have appeared in the matriline [with the illness of Madila and Leewo, as witness to a lack of proper reciprocity between the different generations of uncles].
24 Waana has given up [his avuncular rights]: "Listen, ancestor N-ziinga, grandfather Luvwefwa." They are lying. I am a direct descendant of ancestor N-ziinga.
25 I have taken one full basket, a hen, and five cloths from what Moombo paid in order to recover his avuncular rights [as authorized by Waana].
26 When Moombo came to discuss the affair [with Waana of avuncular rights] I was in the village and said nothing. When they consulted the diviner, the oracle asked: "Who chased Waana away [took from him his avuncular rights]?" [Waana did not prevent Moombo from his avuncular duties yet the oracle had asked why Waana had stopped patronizing Moombo.]

Waana's oath attesting his legitimacy of avuncular rights is cited.

27 If it is not true that I today demanded that I be given goats [to compensate for Moombo's abuse of the avuncular rights under my guardianship], that the young women came to me [to solicit my care] and that I belong to the Waana clan, that the members of this lineage [these young women] are afflicted. If it is not true that I have been given the matrimonial goods for their mother Khuumba, and if it is not I myself who have given her in marriage to Mbaya, then may you yourselves be afflicted.
28 If it is not true that Waana gave his daughters [and uterine descendants] in mar-

riage and that the divinatory oracle has never accused him of ensorcellment in relation to a death among you.

29 If I have remained to watch over the place that you, Khuumba, have left, if I know two or three things [if Waana has ensorcelled these women], as did their mother Khuumba, may the members of this lineage suffer. I have not been involved in any case of ensorcellment, I, Yikafiinga, whom Waana has engendered. It is Waana who has gathered the matrimonial goods in order that I be born [the speaker really belongs to the lineage of Waana, his classificatory father who has died].

30 Even if their father Mbaya has something against them, I have nothing to do with the affair; I have not attended the meetings of the sorcerers organized by Mbaya.

31 May the health of these young women be renewed; I myself am the uncle responsible for them and I have received the prohibitions concerning them from Mbela Khuumba himself so that the uterine life flow may be transmitted and be fertile.

32 These young women belong to me.

33 Mbela Khuumba is also responsible for the *khita* and *mbwoolu* cults; I myself am responsible for the *yihoonda khita* cult.

34 These young women are my uterine descendants; may their health be renewed. I and Mbela Khuumba, these young women are ours.

Waana ends his oration by handing over a hen to the young women and anointing them with kaolin clay.

Mbela Khuumba then offers the following speech, declaring that he is the great-great-granduncle of the young women and the owner of the *khita* cult. He further acknowledges that the young women have come under the *khita* spell (sentence 38) that he is able to lift.

35 When I was still young someone else acted as their uncle. Since then I have grown up, my eyes have been opened and I, Mbela Khuumba, have become their uncle.

36 Each one exercises his avuncular responsibilities in his own way. But today the quarrels have become too numerous. [Those in exercise of avuncular duties have abused of their rights.]

37 According to the oracle, the *khita* cult operative in the Mbela Khuumba matriline has caused the women's affliction.

38 Today I have been given these children. I speak the truth; you, the many ancestral shades, listen to my appeal. These children have fallen under the power of the *khita* affliction. [Mbela Khuumba testifies before his ancestors that he is the great-great-granduncle responsible for the ailment pertaining to the *khita* cult.]

39 I myself am the root of the tree of uterine descent which has branched out into the family of Waana. Today, may the health of these young women be renewed if I am rightly in charge of the *khita* and *mbwoolu* cults.

In the case recorded here, the cure had only partial success. In April 1973 the eldest of the sisters, Madila, gave birth to a child who remained healthy. Earlier, in December 1972, the younger of the sisters, Leewo, had given birth but both mother and child were in serious condition; the newborn died ten days later. Two diviners were consulted and both attributed the death to the same cause. The oracles had revealed that the newborn had been killed by a prior curse which had not yet been lifted. As we have seen, the younger brother of the initiates, Kasela, was gravely ill. His mother Khuumba and her brother Mangaya, the primary uncle of the sick young man, had both ensorcelled the latter. Khuumba had at the same time asked Mangaya to curse anyone else who threatened the life of Kasela—in fact, a devious trick intended to prevent any accusation directed at him or his sister. A ritual compensation was offered to Mangaya, as it was not yet known that he had abused his avuncular rights. This compensation should have been given instead to the innocent uncle, that is, the great-granduncle Waana. Besides, the primary uncle of the victim Kasela would have been expected to use the avuncular right to lift the curse. Being an unjustified curse, it killed the one whom it should have protected and continued to ravage the children of the victim's sisters, Leewo and Madila. The oracle advised that Mangaya be invited to speak to Waana in order that Mangaya pay the necessary ritual compensation for the death of Kasela. Waana would have then been capable of consulting the deceased Kasela, victim of an unjust curse. Once the avuncular powers would have been properly restored to Mangaya, he would be able to lift the undeserved curse.

This advice was scrupulously followed, and once all these steps had been carried out Leewo, the sister of the deceased Kasela, became pregnant and gave birth to a baby boy in August 1974. The child, however, died almost a year later in July 1975. The husband had meantime married a second wife in order to redress his sterile marriage. In 1977, Leewo gave birth to a son who is in good health.

Appendix B
Herbarium

Mr. L. Pauwels identified the flora listed here while he was at the botanical laboratory of INERA, Kinshasa campus, of the University of Zaire. The flora are from the secondary forest and savanna in the immediate proximity of the villages of Yitaanda and Zeembi, as well as from the forest and forest galleries on the left bank of the Waamba river near the villages of N-tulumba, N-koongu, and N-saanda, in northern Kwaango. Descriptions of these milieux, such as the Taanda populations perceive and represent them, are given in 2.1 and 2.3.

diimbulu	*Landolphia lanceolata*	Apocynaceae
futi	*Entada gigas*	Mimosaceae
kaloombi	[*savanna suffrutex*]	Rubiaceae
khidi. *See* n-kidi		
Kitu dyan-situ	*Haemanthus* sp.	Amaryllidaceae
kitu dyatseki *or* kitu dyahata	*Sansevieria bracteata*	Liliaceae
lufuundu	*Lagenaria siceraria*	Cucurbitaceae
lundzilandzila	*Schenckia americana*	Solanaceae
lunguungu	*Megaphrynium macrostachyum*	Marantaceae
luteti	*Hypselopdelphis poggeana*	Marantaceae
mabulukutu	*Hyptis suaveolens*	Labiatae
mahetiheti	*Hymenocardia acida*	Euphorbiaceae
mangangatsaanga	*Selaginella scandens*	Pteridophyta
masamuna	*Pauridiantha dewevrei*	Rubiaceae
matsutsuutsu	*Ocimum americanum*	Labiatae
mazeledi	*Ctenitis lanigera*	(Fern)
mbaamba	*Eremospatha haullevilleana*	Palmae
mbati	*Elaeis guineensis*	Palmae
m-bidi	*Canarium schweinfurthii*	Burseraceae

m-boondi	*Salacia pynaertii*	Hippocratiaceae
m-booti	*Dialium englerianum*	Caesalpiniaceae
m-bosubosu	*Berlinia giorgii*	Caesalpiniaceae
m-buundzya	*Maprounea africana*	Euphorbiaceae
m-buungi	*Strychnos pungens*	Loganiaceae
m-fwangulusu	*Costus edulis*	Zingiberaceae
m-mvuma (kaseema)	*Rhabdophyllum welwitschii*	Ochnaceae
m-mwayi	[large trees with brownish nut-like fruits]	
ndiimbula	*Gnetum africanum*	Gnetaceae
n-diingi	tonic fruit	
n-haandzi	*Pentaclethra macrophylla*	Mimosaceae
n-heeti	*Hymenocardia acida*	Euphorbiaceae
n-honu	*Salacia pallescens*	Hippocrateae
n-hoondasala	*Diplorrhynchus condylocarpon* var. *angolensis*	Apocynaceae
n-kaasu	*Cola acuminata*	Sterculiaceae
n-kidi	*Mammea africana*	Guttiferae(?)
n-kooki	*Strychnos cocculoides*	Loganiaceae
n-kukubuundu	*Pachystela* sp.	Sapotaceae
n-kula	*Drypetes limosa*	Euphorbiaceae
n-kungwa yiteki	*Chaetocarpus africanus*	Euphorbiaceae
n-kwaati	*Erythrophleum africanum*	Caesalpiniaceae
n-lolu also called n-ndolundolu	*Annona senegalensis*	Annonaceae subsp. oulotricha
n-ndzimba	*Combretum laxiflorum*	Combretaceae
n-nkheneti	*Strychnos icaja*	Loganiaceae
n-phemba	*Adenia cissampeloides*	Passifloraceae
n-saanda	*Ficus thonningii*	Moraceae
n-seenga	*Musanga cecropioides*	Moraceae
n-siki	*Morinda lucida*	Rubiaceae
n-tsatsa	*Markhamia tomentosa*	Begoniaceae
phaanda	*Trichilia heudelotii*	Meliaceae
phutu	*Erythrophleum guineense*	Caesalpiniaceae
tsaamba	(synonymous to *mbati*)	
tsakutsaku	*Cyperus articulatus*	Cypereaceae
tundala	*Aframomum stipulatum*	Zingiberaceae

Herbarium

yiimba	*Raphia vinifera*	Palmae
yikayakaya	*Dalbergia bakeri*	Papilionaeceae
yikhundakhunda	*Phragmenthera capitata*	Loranthaceae
yikuumbi	*Staudtia stipitata*	Myrsinaceae
Yimbandzya kyahata	*Eleusine indica*	Gramineae
yingoombu	*Hibiscus esculentus*	Malvaceae
yinwaani	*Tricalisia dictyophylla*	Menispermaceae
yisakaamba	*Cognauxia podolaena*	Cucurbitaceae
yiseleti	*Chrysophyllum bangweolense*	Sapotaceae
yitsakudi	savanna shrub	
yiyeembi	*Helichrysum mechowianum*	Compositae

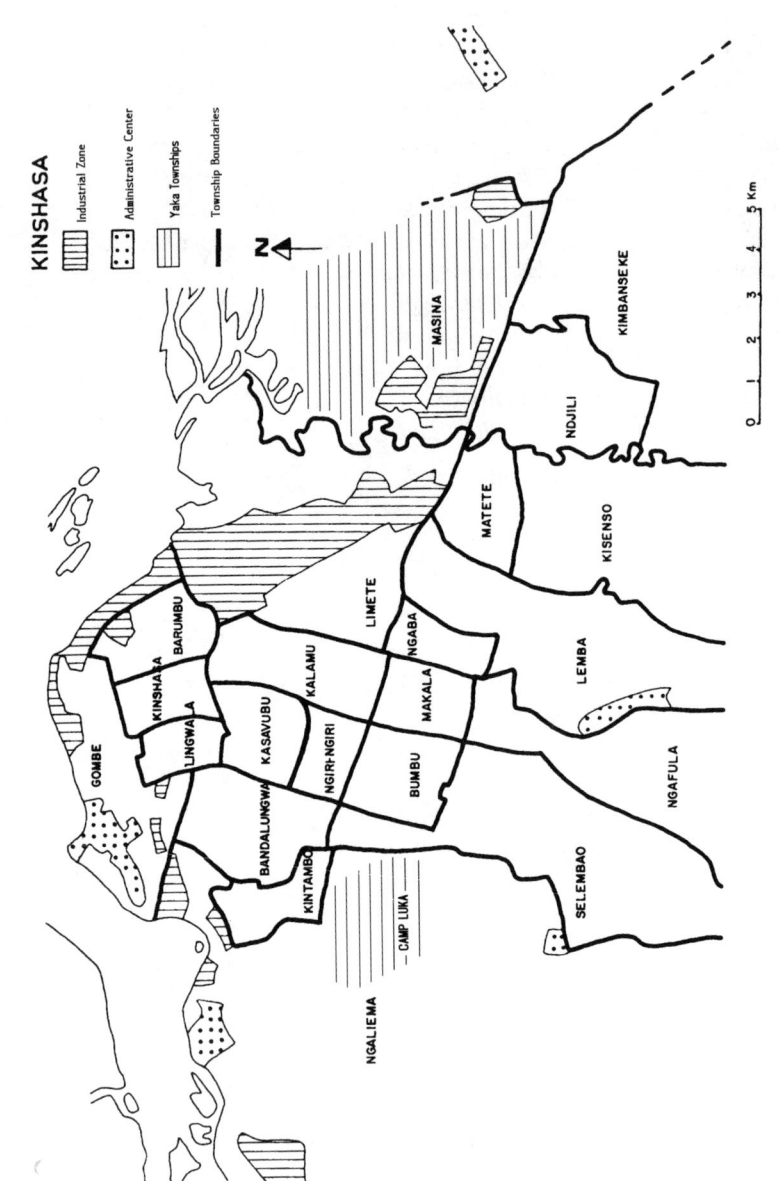

Map 1. Kinshasa: Fieldwork in the Townships of Ngaliema-Camp Luka and Masina

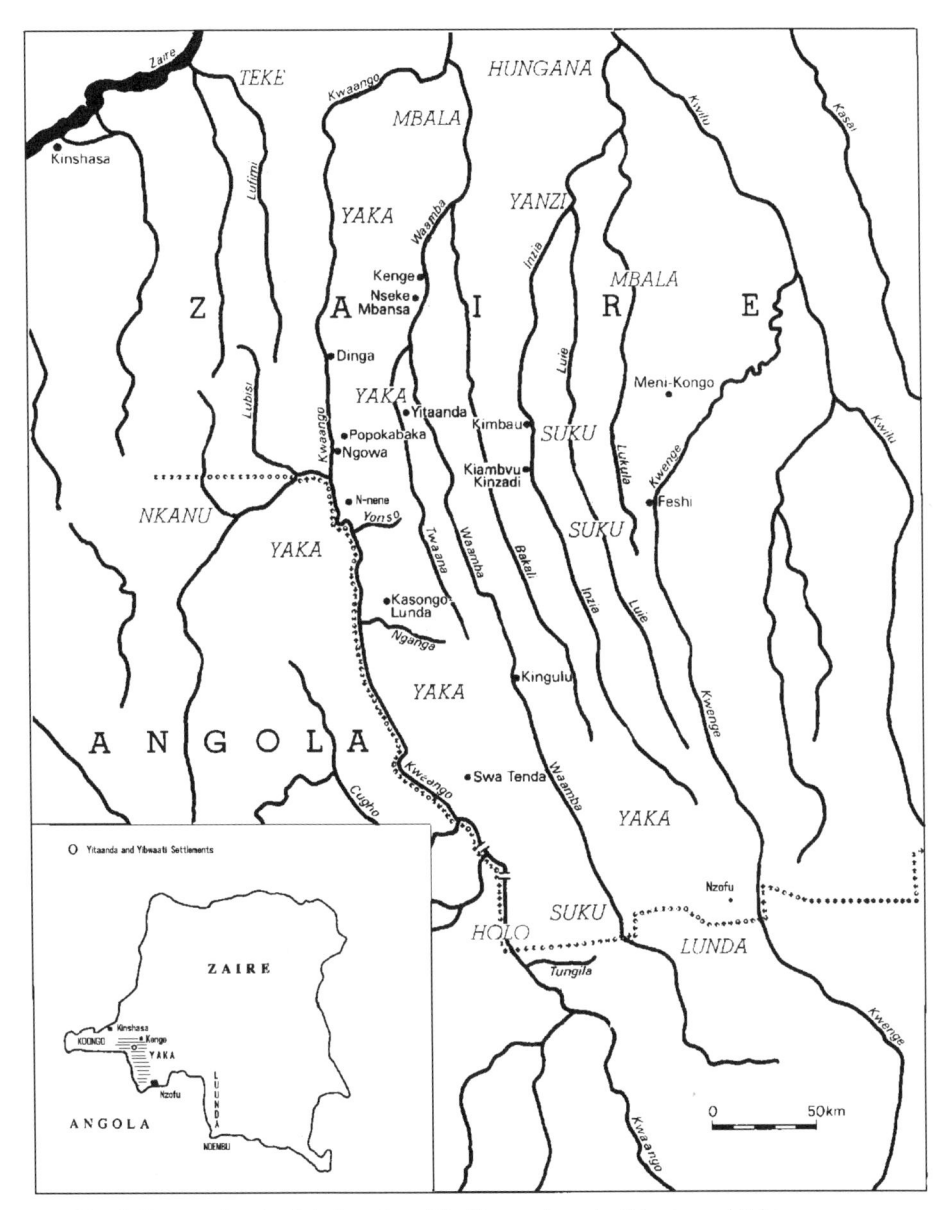

Map 2. Kwaango Land and the Location of the Koongo, Luunda, Ndembu, and Yaka

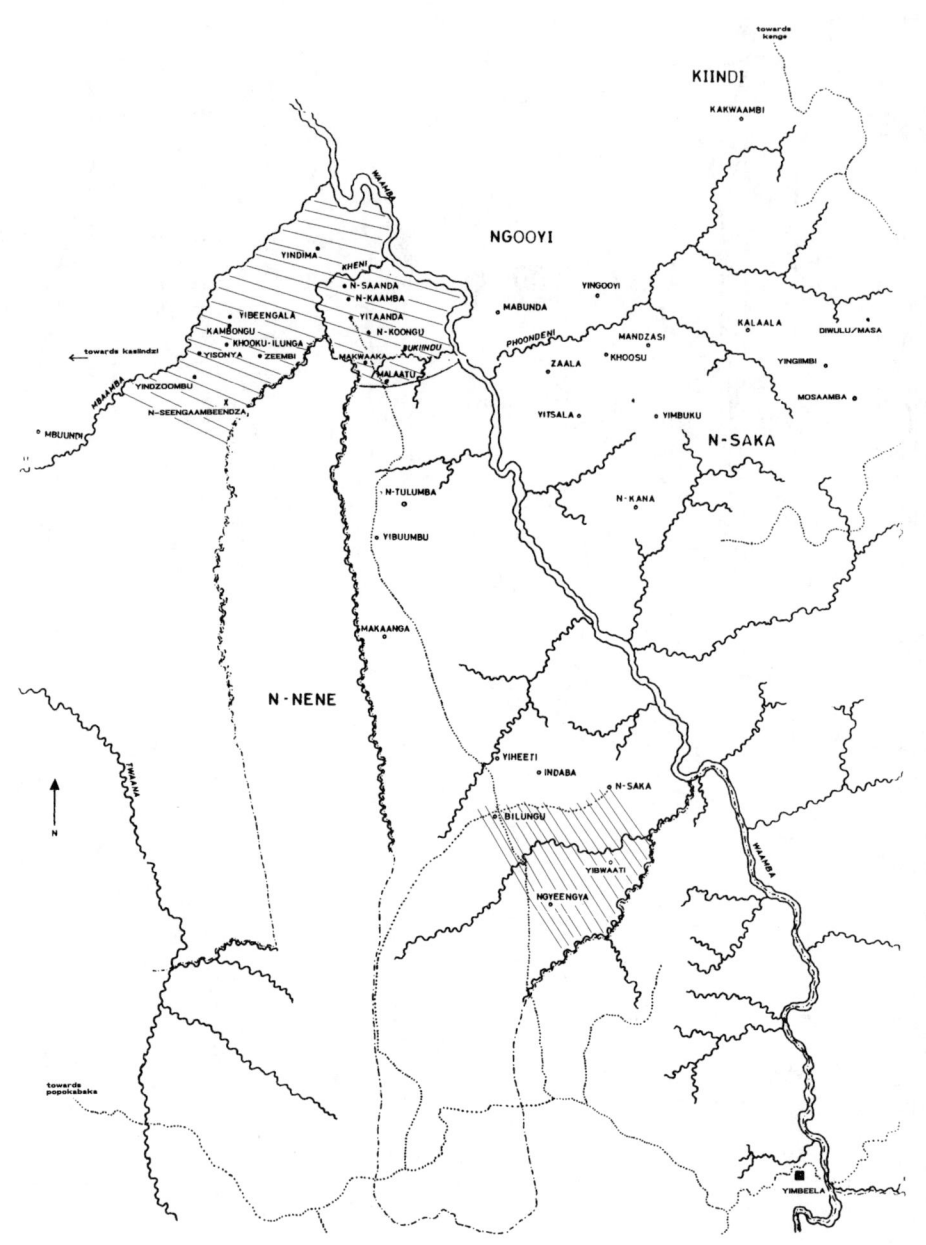

Map 3. Fieldwork in the Yitaanda and Yibwaati Localities in Northern Kwaango Land

Notes

Prologue

1. Throughout the book, I am using 'imaginary,' not with the primary meaning of fictitious, but in line with Lacan (1949). In his view, the 'imaginary' register is the subject's mode of unconscious feeling and understanding of other people as shaped by the partial projection of his own unconscious images or clichés, that is, imagoes. The more these images interpenetrate with the register of language, social exchange, and dialogical intersubjectivity, the more they transform into the symbolic order.

Chapter One

1. The most recent global estimates of population in the Kwaango area come from de Saint-Moulin (1976, 1977, 1987) and Ngondo (1980). De Decker (1968) is concerned with the largely Yaka population of the diocese of Popokabaka, covering the larger part of the Yaka region. These estimates indicate that the predictions for demographic growth made by Denis (1964), based on his research carried out in 1958–59, are quite likely overestimates, since they took neither the deteriorating health situation nor the increasing rate of rural exodus into account. Denis (1964:39) further estimated at the time of his research that the population density for at least 60 percent of Yaka land varies between 1 and 6 inhabitants per km^2.

2. It is most difficult to estimate the present Yaka population in Kinshasa since there has been no censuses related to ethnic identity. I refer to the most recent and reliable demographic investigations, namely from the 1980s by Léon de Saint-Moulin (1987). Yaka people form the majority of the very densely populated urban zones of Masina and Ngaliema-Camp Luka; large groups are also living in Kintambo and Yolo sud.

3. De Boeck (1991a, b, c; Centre of Anthropology, Catholic University of Leuven) offers in-depth analyses of the major sociopolitical institutions and cults of affliction among the Luunda in the settlement of Nzofu, under the authority of Mwaant Nzav in the Kahemba zone.

4. I wrote a critical review of De Beir's studies (1975a, b), as well as of Van der Beken's (1978), in *Cultures et développement* (Louvain-la-Neuve) 10: (1978): 324–27 and 11 (1979): 150–51, respectively.

5. Because of its preoccupation with the physical, cosmopolitan, or scientific, medicine is labeled 'biomedicine' here, for want of a better term.

6. The foundation of the ANAZA (Association Nationale des Tradipraticiens du

Zaïre), later renamed as UNAGZA (Union Nationale des Guérisseurs du Zaïre) by the "Mouvement Populaire de la Révolution," as well as the Kinshasa-based Association of Traditional Practitioners (ATKIN, with more than 1,000 members), in the late 1970s was proof of the government's endeavor to legitimate traditional healing practices and to help healers to exchange their semi-clandestine existence for a public exercise of their skills, at least as herbalists. Today, despite the recommendations of the 1992 Sovereign National Conference, there still does not exist a proper legal frame to insert the healers and their institutions into the National Health Care structures. The Kinshasa-based project Health for All has made some efforts to institutionalize and develop the links between Community Health Care and traditional healing in Kinshasa.

7. See Dumon and Devisch (1992) for audiovisual documentation of the trance of the diviner.

8. I have discussed various approaches to body symbolism and symptom formation, regarded in relation to culture and healing drama, in earlier studies (1985a, 1991c).

9. Throughout this book, I use the concept of morphogenetic field in a rather heuristic and analogical sense.

Chapter Two

1. The principal trees to be found in these rather thinly forested areas are the following: *m-booti, m-bosubosu,* and *n-hoondasala.* Edible mushrooms proliferate in these forests. In the lightly wooded savannas, the principal tree is the *n-kwaati,* "the wood of which is as hard as iron." Other vegetation growing there includes: *yiyeembi, yitsakudi, n-heeti, n-hoondasala.* The *n-kwaati* caterpillar, so-called from the name of the tree on which it develops, also flourishes in this environment.

2. As we know from the study carried out by Devred, Sys, and Berce (1958), the botanical landscape of the Taanda group offers a highly representative survey of the vegetation of the Kwaango.

3. The hyphen replaces the prefix *ku-, wu-* of the infinitives which are indicated in the text without their prefix.

4. The raffia fibers *(luhusu)* are taken from the pinnate leaves *(luleembi)* of the raffia palm. Arrows are made from the young rachises, well-grown rachises *(n-ndidi)* are used as lats to build houses, doors, or stools, while the fibers *(tsiinga)* of old rachises serve in the making of traps and baskets.

5. This position *(-lama* or *kataku)* is also the one prescribed for the administration or reception of aphrodisiacs or, in hunting, when the hunter prepares to shoot a large animal *(mbisi).* In the shrine for the ancestors of the lineage or of an agnatic cult, the esoteric name *kataku* is used both for the banana plants *(dikhondu dyakataku)* and for the small structure which is erected behind the house of those who are newly circumcised. This structure consists of two forked branches implanted in the soil with a small stick resting upon them: it seems to suggest that men in regenerating life bridge the successive generations of mothers, as the latter are symbolized by the forked branches.

6. Thus we understand why, at dawn, the body of the chief during installment is anointed with the red *luundu* clay dug out of a ravine close to the river or taken from a termite mound. This anointing symbolizes his birth as the mediator of human and animal fertility (cf. Devisch 1988). Red clay, *muundu,* to be found in a cave, and white

clay are also applied to the cheeks—red clay on one cheek, white on the other—of the initiand in the *n-ngoongi* cult, who is likened to a fetus, or to figurines which recall the founding ancestors of that cult.

7. The etymology of *kyandzangoombi,* meaning "rainbow," suggests the idea of a skirt of raffia *(ngombi)* which surrounds the female flower of the palm *(kyandza).*

8. Apart from the rodents, the other *phuku* which are held in high esteem in oral literature or ritual prescriptions are: *mbviinda* (lemur: *prosimii*); the Viveridae *lumbongi* (civet cat) and *mbala* (civet); *thotu* (striped mongoose: *herpestes*); the Mustelidae *m-fuki* (mottle-necked otter) and *mbulu* (polecat); *n-koondu* (small jackal: *canidae*); the Chiroptera *pheengi* (fruit bats: the "flying dog"), *kaphakala* (insect-eating bats: "horseshoe"), and *ngeembu* (insect-eating bat); the Insectivores *lutsokutsoku* (water shrew) and *n-pfusyambuumbulu* (mole); and *khaka* (tree-dwelling scaly anteater: *pholidota*).

9. Other ways of calling down bad luck *(-beembula,* with its indefinite form *mbeembi,* "ill fate, ominous transgression") include a man taking a woman by surprise in the process of defecating, and menstruation, which is said to represent a special threat to the husband. The leaves of the *n-lolu* bush, found in the savannas, which are used as toilet paper, also represent bad luck. We should add that in nocturnal chants and in jokes, the mention of the small tree known as *n-kakala,* which is found in the savanna, calls to mind similar bad luck—in bush fires the edges of the leaves are burned, leaving bare wispy fibers.

10. From the terminological point of view, the ligneous plants are treated with more distinction than the nonligneous. Ligneous species are given original and unique names. The oral lore provides ample information about them, and they may be classified according to both ecological or functional criteria. Not only do the plants themselves have their own names, but the different phases of growth and reproduction of each—buds, inflorescence, core, or sucker, for example—are designated by specific terms. But once these plants are employed in a practical or ritual way, the original term gives way to another technical or functional name. Some of the semantic categories are based on morphological properties which the plant might exhibit; those with branches pointing upwards are grouped together, as are plants with spotted leaves, or those which produce their leaves at the same time. Others are classified according to chemical properties, such as aphrodisiacs or toxic plants, *khadi,* that is, "with a bitter taste."

Chapter Three

1. According to popular belief, the act of giving birth, particularly when it is difficult, renders the parturient especially vulnerable to murderous ensorcellment destined to pay the "debts of the night" *(kabu).* Of course, such a conception only serves to reinforce the social exclusion of the parturient.

2. *Loonga* and *kawa* are objects offered in contexts in which one person urges another to consider a formal request for the establishment of stable and benevolent relationships. The principal candidate to the succession as political titleholder presents these objects to the chief of higher rank who will enthrone him. In cases of reconciliation, the guilty party presents these objects to the victim of ensorcellment.

3. The term *-sasa,* used to designate this declination of the identity, denotes the idea of an interpretation of destiny. The head of the household or an individual's uncle inter-

prets a descendant's destiny *(-sasa)* whenever there is or could be a change of status: it is done particularly for the novice, the fiance at the handing over of the bridewealth, the deceased prior to burial, or prior to consultation of a diviner with regard to a death. Faced with imminent danger (a storm, the crossing of a large river, some major test, and so on), the individual under threat himself plots his own fate in order to ensure a future as propitious as the past. The divining oracle also consists of interpreting the destiny of someone who is sick or has died. Depending on the etiological examination established by the divining oracle, the therapy or the funeral rites for the survivors play a role in this destiny, as we shall see in the case of the *khita* treatment. The curse *(n-sasu,* the nominal form of *-sasa)* consists basically of plotting one's fate as an inescapable revenge in lines with general destiny for similar wrongdoing.

4. The average value of the total bridewealth, including the *diwu,* the gifts offered to the uterine ascendants of the girl, was some US $130 in 1974, some $100 in early 1991, and less today; in general, it is equivalent to one year's legal minimum wage for an unskilled laborer in the Yaka region and throughout rural Bandundu. Though the monetary value—in particular of husbandry—changes, the amount of goods varies little and is not dependent upon the social status of the parties or on the economic situation of the country. Should the lineage group demand an exceptionally high bridewealth, it in fact devalues the goods received because it lays itself open to similar demands when a young man from their own group plans to marry. The cloths *(marecani, pheesu)* offered are pieces of white linen, four meters in length and an arm-span wide. Today, elders very much complain that the young couple cohabit in Kinshasa years before receiving family consent and paying bridewealth.

The matrimonial transaction serves as the model for other forms of transaction and engagement as well. The seller and buyer of a goat, pig, or dog enter in a kind of alliance, comparable to the matrimonial one, as do healer and patient at the end of the treatment. The diviner, the circumciser, the sculptor, the ritual specialist, and the master of the enthronement ritual all relate to their client as in-law *(buko).* This means that the client or the patient is entitled to special hospitality in the home of the seller or the ritual specialist. On the other hand, the profit which the client accumulates from the animal bought or from its fertility, or the cure or the initiation into a special art is, in part, returned to the seller or the master.

5. If, in order to marry a new wife, the polygynous elder uses the matrimonial property acquired by the marriage of one of his daughters, he is censured by the group, who suspect him of evil intent towards his sons. It happens, however, that the matrimonial property will be offered to the civil authority in payment of fines imposed by the civil tribunal.

The compensatory role of the bridewealth is again seen in another situation in which the transfer of this property acquires an even greater symbolic value. In the case of death through ensorcellment, the culprit's family group must offer gifts to the uterine ascendants of the deceased, as I explain in an earlier work (1979:170–76). These valuable gifts, known as *bibiindi,* to some extent restore the deceased to his uterine ascendants who gave him life. They compensate for the services which the deceased person rendered to close kin during his lifetime.

6. When someone has to commission another person, he offers a dyed cloth, known in ritual language as *lubongu lwataangu,* "raffia cloth of the color of the sun"; the

commissioned person wears the cloth to witness to his status. Putting a homonymy between the terms *taangu,* "sun, color, colored" and *-taanga,* "to narrate"; popular exegesis explains: *lubongu lawataangu kataangila n-samu,* "this cloth serves to communicate the message." The husband must pay compensation, known as *makosi mayakala,* for the first conjugal union in the consummation of the marriage, for this union "broke the back" *(-tolula n-loombu)* of the woman's genitors. Before offering two or three pieces of cloth to his wife's father and mother, he strikes both around the lower back "to cure them." Any person guilty of intrusion into the intimacy of matrimony must make similar compensation to the betrayed husband.

7. Among the Yaka the physiological process of gestation usually arouses little interest from male society. The husband is expected to have regular intercourse with his pregnant wife in order to consolidate the bony hard parts of the body in formation through his sperm. The anal douches that the pregnant woman administers herself seek to maintain the humoral balance.

8. Tradition prescribes sexual abstinence in order to prevent conception. Information would suggest that abstinence is respected by means of coitus interruptus or by some kind of cleansing: after sexual union, the woman crouches, beats her hips, and cleans her vagina with a cloth. Although young people who have lived in Kinshasa are familiar with the idea of abortion, in the rural environment it seems rare and is severely criticized for its danger and for its potential for provoking the vengeance of the elders, who want their offspring to increase.

9. That the primary uncle should act on behalf of his own uncle derives also from the asymmetrical relation with one's mother's sister's and brother's children, seen as part of a lower generation: at their mother's death, a person refers to them in the same terms as he does to his children. A symmetrical, joking relationship develops between Ego and his maternal uncle's wife, whom he might well inherit in marriage upon the uncle's death. Again, upon the death of Ego's father, the children of his father's sister enter into the category of brothers to Ego's father. The principle of polarity entitling a person to act in his uncle's name also enables him to replace his granduncle and his great-granduncle.

Chapter Five

1. Martin (1987) argues that such dispossession is largely the case, for example, in the metaphors of failure, waste, decay, and breakdown in gynecological or medical science that express American society's embarrassment with the female body's processes of fertility.

2. Ancient traditions sometimes associate a young married woman's failure to conceive because of amenorrhea or false pregnancy (pseudocyesis) with *nyoka n-kawua,* literally, "a snake [here a metaphor for the vagina] that bends and unbends like the string of a bow." In order to exorcise this "snake," according to the reports of Buakasa and Didillon (1981), *khita* initiates make small incisions on the woman's genitals causing them to bleed. Pascaline Creten (Centre for Anthropology, Catholic University of Leuven, devotes herself to an in-depth analysis of the *nyoka khawa* syndrome as it is conceived of in Nkanu-Koongo culture, at the northern fringe of Yaka land.

3. This hypothesis is further confirmed by the explanatory value given it in the oracle: to interpret a disorder, the oracle refers to the breaking of a ban which, through the

curse, must be sanctioned by an evil. The oracle thus acts as the guarantor of its own declarations and interpretations, whose legitimacy is finally demonstrated by the effectiveness of the cure indicated by the oracle's commands and the success of the hunt organized to this end.

Chapter Six

1. Responsibility for the delay of expected pregnancy is first attributed to the woman and her kin of origin. It is only in the case of impotence, characterized by the absence of an erection, that the oracle is consulted indicating that the husband is to undergo an appropriate therapy.

2. The concept of *khita* was already to be found in writings with regard to the kingdom of the Koongo dating from the mid-seventeenth century (Balandier 1965). I have, however, been unable to retrace the history of this concept in the Yaka culture.

3. In narratives, the expression *yeehyuula luhaangu kwa Ndzaambi,* "I shall ask Ndzaambi for the solution," is equivalent to another, which is just as common: *yeehyuula luhaangu kwa bambuta,* "I shall ask the elders for the solution."

4. The soothsayer therapist, known as *m-baangu,* drinks diluted poison and then interprets the divinatory message according to the spasms of his digestive tract. This quite peculiar type of therapist is familiar with certain curative procedures such as preparing ointments, potions, douches, cupping, and steam or smoke baths.

5. Lines 7 and 8 refer to a fertility which is threatened or obstructed. The ritual formula *yizeendzedi n- twa ndzawu, phuungi bakuna hatadi,* "it is as though the elephant lowered his head and tried to bury his tusks in the rock" is frequently found in the incantations against evildoers. Here the elephant tusks and trunk are representative of virile sexuality (cf. Devisch 1972). The majority of the elders invited to comment upon this expression limited themselves to a comparison, saying: "If a chief bows his head, it is in mourning; if a ritual specialist bows his head, it is to provide care." This formula amounts to saying that a patient under the care of the healer is in good hands, but if he is left in the care of the elders, he or she is in danger of ensorcellment. Moreover, two competent commentaries substitute the following terms for the first and second part of the expression respectively: *yizeendzi* (the inflorescence of the *m-fwangulusu,* a plant found in the savanna and in the forests), and *yimiikwaandi ndzuungu* (a spatula for preparing corn paste placed in a pot filled with an aphrodisiac potion given to candidates for circumcision). Such an exegesis would appear to suggest that the declaration in question warns those who wish the *khita* patient ill and advises them that in acting this way they are endangering their own fertility. The *m-fwangulusu* plant, prior to blooming, is crowned by a flower that is covered with large bracts. When this plant is pulled from the ground, the tuberous root remains fixed in the earth and the sap oozes from the stalk. The homonymic association between *yizeendzi,* "inflorescence," and *-zeendzama,* "to bow the head as a sign of affliction or mourning," expresses how much aggression through ensorcellment or from the shades might finally turn against the aggressor. Moreover, on the eve of circumcision, the master *(yisidika)* of puberty rites proclaims the same formula to call the parents and the elders to renounce any form of ensorcellment. He invites them to take turns walking around this *m-fwangulusu* plant and then spitting into an earthenware pot *(ndzuungu,* which in this context evokes the

maternal domain) held by the *yifiika,* the woman acting as mother to the initiates. The latter then employs this pot to prepare the *yikosa,* a mixture of manioc flour, aphrodisiacs, *khula* (evocative of fetal blood), and the hen offered to the oldest candidate. The *m-fwangulusu* used in this preparation is called *yimiikwaandi ndzuungu.* The practice turns the threat of impotence through ensorcellment against the evildoer.

6. At the end of a major healing seclusion, the initiate or one of his family will pay the therapist a *yita,* namely a dozen or more pieces of cloth, the equivalent of a half year's unskilled work in the rural areas of the Yaka. This compensates for the benefit the treatment offers to the new initiate. A male initiate may be authorized, in turn, to preside over therapeutic rites, and he should share "some benefit of the initiation" *(lusaku)* with his master. The total remuneration—*n-koolu, yita,* and *lusaku*—is called *n-kaanga,* which means "connecting."

7. Every *khoofi* consists of a specific set of items believed to counteract the evil agencies:

(a) A branch of the forest tree *m-mvuma,* which is erected next to the trunk of the *n-saanda* tree. Popular exegesis through homonymy attributes a defensive function to the *m-mvuma* tree, based on its similarity to the verb *-vuma,* "to arrest": *m-mvuma kavuma yibeefu,* "may the illness of this tree be arrested."

(b) The *luteti,* a climbing, thorny forest plant bearing much the same signification. Because of its thorns, this plant obstructs passage. Sometimes it is used as binding in the construction of the fences between traps during a game drive; it is also used to build the seclusion house of the *khita* rite. The *luteti* plant moreover augurs a propitious treatment; this is hinted at by the homonymy between *luswaaswa,* a term describing the shoot of this plant, and *swaaswa,* which means "good luck." Shoots added of the *lundzilandzila* weed found along the footpaths *(ndzila)* corroborate the same augury: *muna ndzilandzila kakola,* "that he may find healing without delay."

(c) The rachis of the leaves of the *mbaamba* rattan palm which is planted in the *khoofi.* The rachis of these leaves grows and extends until it eventually resembles a creeper. It is used in the making of traps and baskets and as bindings in the building of houses. This element too signifies bringing something to a halt. Through its insistence on the homonymy between *-baambama,* "to coincide with, to stick to," and *mbaamba,* exegesis recognizes the significance of an arrest, stating, for example, *mbaamba kanbaambama,* "let the agent of evil become stuck to the *mbaamba* creeper." Specialist exegesis compares the role of the plants in arresting evil to that of the ritual specialist in the erection of the *khoofi*: *yiphati mum-mvuma, yingaanga muluteti* or *yiphati mummvuma, yingaanga mumbaamba,* "the ritual specialization lies in the proper usage of the *m-mvuma, luteti,* and *mbaamba* plants." The *mbaamba* rachis moreover expresses the desire that the participants may prolong the line of descent: *sina dyambaamba dihwa mbaambaku, mutwapfiinga kahwa dikaandaku,* "just as the rachis constantly grows from the base of the palm tree, every group of people survives in its progeny."

(d) A branch of the *yiseleti,* a small tree of the savanna, and that of a tree with a mottled trunk to be found in the secondary forest, *n-siki,* help to place many ritual practices under the control of the *khoofi. Yiseleti* is believed to be a formidable plant because a concentrated decoction made from it can cause great pain or even lead to heavy hemorrhages if administered as an anal douche. Since its wood is used to make many ritual statuettes, which are employed as ritual weapons, *yiseleti* is also known as *ngwan-ti,* "mother plant." Such usage, which can conceal evil intents 'of the night' behind apparently well-intentioned applications 'of the day' presents an ambiguity which the *n-siki,* thanks to its mottled trunk, is able to thwart.

(e) *N-kungwayiteki,* a bush from the secondary forest, is also found in the *khoofi.* Its presence strengthens the sense of arresting the evil, which popular commentaries translate by the homonymic verb *-kuungama.* By homonymy, exegesis says: *n-kungwayiteki wakuunga biteki byoosu,* "the *n-kungwayiteki* tree brings together all the ritual statuettes." These statuettes may also be carved out of its wood.

(f) According to exegesis, the *m-booti* and *n-heeti* bushes of the savanna, whose ability it is to survive the annual burning, serve both to bestow bad luck upon the disorder and to bestow upon the afflicted that same resistance which will enable them to overcome the trial.

8. Many ritual activities aim at *-kaya,* namely trapping the agent of evil, that is, by sabotaging the evil action and reversing it against its author.

9. The small bags placed under the *khoofi* normally contain a variety of objects:

(a) *Mbakunumbakunu* is a collection of the young shoots of different species of plants from various levels in the forest and savanna; it is referred to as *-kaya n-kaanda,* "trapping all the plants." By placing it under the *khoofi,* the specialists aim at thwarting in advance all the evil practices of which each of these plants could be the medium.

(b) The addition of a few hairs of crafty and aggressive animals *(mbisi zakhemena)* (cf. 2.3.1) serves as a challenge to the sorcerers whose disguises and meddling are forthrightly exposed.

(c) Elements of normal household refuse to be found in the *khoofi* include pits of the edible fruit of the *m-bidi,* a tree found in the forest, and nuts of the oil palm, referred to respectively as *n-kanyambidi* and *n-kanyangasi,* and a dried corncob, called *n-suuswakaphiinda,* swept up and blackened in the fire. These are "objects trampled by everybody" *(yimadyaatu badyaata baatu);* this tells the evil, no matter what form it takes or where it comes from, that it will not be able to reappear.

(d) These satchels also contain *loombi,* a deadly ingredient of the ritual weapons, which neutralizes any evil use which might be made of them to the detriment of the therapeutic group. In addition to centipedes and spiders, *loombi* contains cinders obtained by burning small pieces of the dung beetle *(kokotu).* This insect, which inters human feces and can burrow its way into the earth as deep as a buried body, represents the sorcerer who "restores man to the earth." Two reptiles, again evoking the sorcerer, are also to be found in the bags: the chameleon *(lungweenya)* because of its ability to change its color to suit its background, and the long grey lizard *(kalanga)* with mottled lips which can disappear at a blink *(-vuulumuna,* a term also denoting the way in which the sorcerer can move without being seen); this lizard can be replaced by the blue-headed agame lizard *(yihala).* Because of their toxic nature, various other animals or substances may represent the malevolent act: poisonous snakes, the *kapfiinda* (a large centipede), the *dikhookwa difuula mun-zaanga* (a kind of large, deadly lizard, dead and dried), and finally the bark of the *phutu* tree which in the past was used in the poison ordeal. To increase the deadly effect of these substances, glass splinters *(biteenga byambwaata)* or a viper's tooth are also added.

10. The planting of the life tree in a healing cult differs little from the erection of the *n-saanda koongu* ancestral tree. The latter is set up within the homestead of the patri-

arch of the lineage segment which boasts the oldest ascendency in a given clan, dating back to its most distant and prestigious ancestor. The *n-saanda koongu* typifies the link between the group and its distant agnatic ascendency.

11. The *ndzaku* drug expresses initiatory filiation and somehow transmits generative life force from master to pupil. Ritual specialists, in particular healers, eat of this drug before exercising their function, when they address their master on his tomb; they scatter it over the earth before offering an item of ancestral worship. The drug is made from a variety of plant substances. One is a grass with round hollow stems known as *tsaku-tsaku*. Some commentaries accord this grass the virtue of "reminding the specialist of all that he has been taught" *(bwasakumuka bungaanga bwaphaabula)*. Another is the white yam, *toondi*. Because the tuber is found under the ground, it emphasizes that the line of life transmission between the deceased master and his pupil continues. Witness to this is found in the practice in which the successor to a specialist in matters of virile fertility places such a yam between his master's legs when he is buried. Peanuts, *nguba*, are another component of the *ndzaku* drug and represent, it is said, both fertility and the impossibility of doing anything when one is alone, just as it is impossible to shell them using only one finger. The red-brown *khidi* fruit, from the tree of the same name, signifies that the cure indeed puts an end to the disorder, since it results in the pupil's initiation. The motto *khidi twakidika, n-diingi twaniingita,* means: "The *khidi* fruit signals the end of the disorder, just as the *n-diingi* fruit means the assuaging of the illness." *Kaasu* (pounded cola nut), *n-diingi* (a tonic white fruit), and *nduungu* (pepper), also components of *ndzaku,* all signify regained strength.

12. The *khoofi* shrine summons shades to support the healing. The small bags that participants apply to the vital parts of the body when the *khoofi* is being planted contain ingredients that are reminders of an intense sharing in life which has its origins in the ancestors. According to Yaka exegesis, nut kernels contained in these small bags are reminders of the *m-fu: bafu bakhulu baatu mbidi,* "the shades of the dead, those who remain as they were." In the popular imagination the term *m-fu* represents, among other things, those hard and durable things which, in consequence, denote the world of the dead. Among the objects bearing this signification are old nut kernels, certain stones which have been worn away to resemble human forms, snail shells filled with earth found at the back of a cave, some giant forest trees, as well as the termite hills found at their feet.

13. The *kuti* or *yisiimbi* is erected in the same way as the *n-saanda* tree, namely within a white circle and accompanied by the appropriate invocation. *Kitu dyan-situ* is a succulent with speckled leaves and a white root found in the forest. A variety of *kitu* with a red rhizome that grows in the savanna is called *kitu dyatseki*. Any variety may be used in the rite. Authorities state that the plant represents the vigilance of the ancestors—represented by the root of the plant and success in the hunt—who are ready to awaken *(-kituka)* when the sorcerers, represented by the speckles, enter their metamorphosis *(-kituka)* and leave the forest or the subsoil to attack a member of the therapeutic group. In other cases, and with the same signification, they half bury a small black termite hill, *yisiimbi,* brought from the forest. It is charged with guarding the ritual area day and night, and for this the specialist carves out two holes to serve as eyes around which he applies white and red clay *(pheemba* and *muundu)*.

14. The initiands can only rise once the family patriarch has bought *(-kuula)* this

right by offering the healer approximately a day's wage. After his wife has finished swinging from the trunk of the parasol tree, the husband has to pay the same amount to the ritual specialist in order to purchase the right for her to descend. The healer seems hereby to reassert his hold over healing.

15. *-Fuundila,* "to spurt forth because of fermentation" is a homonym of *-fuundila* (the relative form of *-fuunda,* "to accuse, condemn in the cathartic trance." Whereas the majority of commentaries accept this idea of accusation, such exegesis would appear to conceal—and therefore preserve from any semantic impoverishment—the metaphor of froth intertwining the opposing forces and processes of decay and fermentation, that is, of death and life-giving in the patient's body and the life-world.

The equivalent expression, *lutswa lwaphoongu,* literally, "the winged termite of the cult," which also refers to this condemnation and reversal of the origins of a disorder, is more difficult to interpret than the expression *-fuundila fula. Lutswa* is used to describe the adult winged termite which abandons the large conical termitary *(luundu);* it can also serve as a synonym of *fula.* I should point out that oral lore emphasizes the tremendous fertility of the termite queen *(pfumwaluundu* or *yifiika)* and the fact that a termitary is believed to emerge spontaneously on the spot where the master specialist of male fertility *(yisidika)* is buried or where a *kambaandzya* mask has been burned (Devisch 1972:162). Is the termitary a cosmological metaphor of the androgynous capacity of autogeneration that the patient acquires in the cathartic trance leading to *-fuundila fula,* "to denounce/to froth or spurt sap"?

16. When a child born after the *khita* cure dies prior to weaning, it, like all infants, is buried close to the back wall of the conjugal home. Its mother's *n-noongu* is placed on its tomb, "so that the infant will soon return to the maternal womb."

Chapter Seven

1. The ritual house closely resembles a large bundle, suspended from a thick beam and bound by a creeper called *n-phemba,* which is also used to transport items. It is therefore compared to the coffin-bundle known as *n-kuundzu:* the dead body, swaddled in funeral sheets and enveloped in a linen cloth, looks like a bundle suspended from a pole to be transported to the cemetery. Perhaps this phase of seclusion could be seen as a period in which the body prepares itself for rebirth.

2. The fibrous scales *(mbuundyambati)* taken from the bottom of palms are used to wrap up the various plants and the *khawa* and attach them to the vines.

3. The bouquet placed against the wall of the ritual house is in part composed of certain plants *(m-mvuma, mbaaamba, n-heeti, mbati,* and *masamuna)* found in the *khoofi,* but of others as well:

(a) A climbing plant, *n-phemba,* reaches up to the ridgepole and comes back down to the foot of the opposite wall. Another crawls along the roof tree from one side to the other and, hanging on to the bushes of the *khoofi,* may even extend beyond the ridgepole for several meters outside the house itself. Still another is attached horizontally half way up each wall. This climbing forest plant signifies the evil turning against itself. Mottled and about two fingers thick, it can serve as a binding, at least if it has just been cut; once dried it breaks easily. When it is used to transport the shrouded body to the cemetery, this plant is referred to as *n-kaanga mbvuumbi,* "corpse binder."

(b) A forest creeper, *yinwaani*, to a certain extent plays the same role as the *n-phemba* vine as it rises up to the ridgepole and extends along it to the outside. Turning to the homonymic verb *-nwaana*, "to combat," exegesis stresses the defensive function of the refuge made of this creeper and the large *lunwaani* leaves in the following way: *wunwaana wusi kuna kuna bun-nwaanisi*, "if anyone enters into the ritual house to attack the patient, let a dispute break out."

(c) In the bouquet we also find a branch of the *n-kwaati* savanna tree, whose wood is considered as hard as iron. Commentators, finding a certain homonymy with *-kwaata*, "to catch, to capture," state: *kukwaati wutabukaku*, "if it catches you it is impossible to break away."

(d) *Mbuundzya*, a bush of the savanna which is used in a large number of medicines and which is nicknamed *m-buundzyabukoondi*, "the *m-buundzya* bush is like a net."

4. The ritual weapon *(teenda*, pl. *mateenda*, or *buta*, pl. *mata*, "gun"; or *yinwaanunu*, "something with which to fight") is wrapped in *lunwaani* leaves, evocative of *-nwaana*, "struggle." It acts as a booby-trap. This weapon is attached to the centre of the ridgepole of the seclusion house at the point where several *n-phemba* creepers cross. The ritual weapon adds to the ritual house's significance as a place of combat between deadly ensorcellment and life-giving forces, as expressed in a formula found in many incantations against an aggressor: *ndzwaandi yaamba, n-singaandi n-phemba*, "may his house be transformed into a mortuary and may this *n-phemba* creeper serve to bind his corpse" (for transportation to the cemetery). The *n-phemba* creeper, at whose end a snake's tooth is sometimes attached, also calls down the inescapable death of the sorcerer who attacked the patient.

The usual components of a ritual weapon are the following: (a) Residues of the client's nails, hair or spit which, according to specialists, can conceal his "shadows or double," thus preserving them from the attack of sorcerers whose first aim is to seize hold of their victim's shadow. (b) An assortment of plants *(mbakunumbakunu)*. (c) The deadly ingredient *loombi* (see ch. 6, n. 9 [d]). (d) An aggressive or explosive ingredient known as *khawa*, consisting of fragments taken from animals, plants, or other substances whose powers of attack or of protection are obvious. These components are all wrapped up in a small cylindrical packet similar to a cartridge. In preparing the *khawa*, the ritual specialist avoids touching the ingredients with his hands, for fear that his own commensals may become exposed to the sorcerers' plots against his client. No doubt it is for the same reason that he calls upon a "prepubescent child who has never worn clothes" to place the ingredients in the packet with the aid of a knife: the specialist himself closes the packet using a cork sealed with resin. This operation of filling and sealing the packet is known as *-soma buta*, "loading the gun." In addition to the pieces of bone and hair, and of skin from snakes (sometimes bought in Kinshasa), hair from animals, and plumes from birds of prey, the *khawa* also contains the toxic bark of the *phutu* tree; in the past this bark was used in the poison ordeal. Further ingredients include: *thuya tsaandzi*, gunpowder; *thuya mboombi*, an explosive to be found in cartridges; *kafofolu*, a match serving as a detonator; and *ndzasi*, lightning, in the shape of sand which has been vitrified by lightning or of resin which has flowed from a vitrified tree. All ritual arms experts do their best to add a most terrifying and unpredictable 'death-trap' to the *khawa*, for example, an arrow which has killed someone, or a piece of vine with which someone has hanged himself.

5. The hiltless knife is an agricultural and household implement used exclusively by women, and such a knife is never used to kill game or spill blood. When a machete is shortened and has lost its wooden hilt through the many uses a man has made of it, it only then is regarded suitable for women's use of it. It has lost its male sexual connotations: *bibiindi* refers both to the hilt of the man's machete or cutlass, as well as to a purse hanging from a stick that a man carries on his shoulder and that contains a few of his belongings. A woman's machete is a complement to the hoe, and like the latter it carries genital connotations. Used in the entrance to the ritual house, it is not accompanied by any accessories nor is it the subject of any incantation.

6. The only food forbidden to the initiand is a dish *(-dya)* consisting of meat (principally *mbisi* or *phuku* and fowl) and cassava paste; this is the only meal which restores commensality. On the other hand, the initiand may eat fresh or boiled corn, peanuts, bananas, or yams. Unlike the food served at meals, these vegetables can be prepared and, as it is said, "nibbled" *(-tafwala)* at any time of the day, even while walking through or outside the village.

7. In the context of *khita,* the *mangangatsaanga* plant is used to envelop the bottom of the *tsaanga khita,* a gourd whose neck has been removed which contains a medicine intended to lessen the pains of pregnancy or of menses. This plant is also used to wrap up the initiate's *n-noongu.* It is moreover placed in the large gourd that serves as a coffin for a twin who has died at an early age and whose rebirth is awaited.

8. If sorcery is compared to a nocturnal hunt, anti-sorcery activities and those aiming to combat evil also use the idiom of the hunt. Thus the collection of plants to be used both for protection and for trapping, as well as for medicinal cures, constitute the "ensnarement" of the evil. The ritual specialist harvests these plants by cutting the shoots at the cyme or the low branches of bushes and trees, always using a crook-like stick known as a *yikho.* This is the same term used for the hook serving as a trigger in a spring trap. The use of the *yikho* to collect these plants, even if they are well within reach, no doubt denotes the plants' capacity to entrap *(-kaya).* In order to detach a piece of the bark from a tree trunk, the ritual specialist knocks it off *(-teembula)* by hitting it with a large stick known as a *yikhookolu.* This word, which shares the same root as *yikho,* also refers to the club used to kill game caught in a trap or in nets. Finally, *yikhookolu* is also the name for the stick which the sorcerers would use to kill their victim. By rubbing off the bark of the tree-trunk with this stick, the specialist thus deals a mortal blow to the agent of evil, also hinted at by the hitting of the tree.

9. Some of the cold infusions which the *khita* recluse imbibes as a purge contain the grated root of *n-hoondasala,* a savanna vine containing white latex which also serves as a home for the *tsona* caterpillar. The homonymic verb *-sala n-hoonda,* "to kill [the illness]," specifies the use of this plant. This infusion is employed as an enema against stomach pains, vomiting, and intestinal worms. It is also used to prepare a steam bath for the treatment of eye infections. By applying the latex of this plant to wounds it is possible to create tattoos. The infusion prescribed for the *khita* recluse also involves the leaves of the savanna bushes *n-heeti, m-booti,* and *n-lolu.* Considered to be the bearers of misfortune *(n-tyambeembi)* (cf. ch. 2, n. 9), they aim at reversing the evil.

Certain warm infusions used as purgative douches consist of several plants that aim at "ensnaring" the disorder; for example, the *m-mvuma* bush found in the secondary forest augurs the arrest *(-vuma)* of the evil, and the *phaanda* tree from the forest should conduce to its capture *(-phaanda).* Taken in strong doses, an infusion of the bark and the gratings of the roots of the *phaanda* tree can cause a hemorrhage. Sometimes a red ant, *kambala,* is added, again "to inaugurate the capture of the disorder" *(kakambalala yibeefu).* In order to ensure that the curative effects spread to all parts of the body, strong smelling plants are added to the infusion. Thus, the bark of the *kubi* tree, found in forest glades, is employed because of its strong garlic-like smell. The root of the *n-nkheneti* bush, a toxic plant found in the savanna, is removed from the soil without cutting it and is then grated and boiled. This concoction has a very penetrating odor, and is administered "so that this odor may cause the illness to flee" *(muna fiimbu dyeeni yibeefu kitiinini).* In areas where palm trees are found, fragments taken from the base (known as *leembwa* or *n-sokwa mbati*) from where the palms sprout are added to the infusion so that life may become prolific again. *Yimbandzya kyahata,* "the little weed that grows all over the village" is added both to associate the coresidents to this process of renewal, while linking it to the survival of the village community: *yimbandzya n-kulwa hata,* "the little weed that is here ever since there was a village," and, commentaries add, "it has been witness to all the village disputes and their resolution."

10. The lukewarm enema used to rinse the vagina is prepared from the forest climber *n-phemba;* this is an implicit reference to conception. Exegesis accepts a homonymy between *n-phemba* and *pheemba* (white kaolin clay), stating that *n-phemba kaseemasa yivumu,* "the *n-phemba* plant makes the womb completely clear"—implying that white clay stands for the uterine life source as appropriated by men.

11. In addition to the ingredients of the purgative douche (mentioned in note 9), the cold infusion used in the *ndzaba zapheelaka* also contains *n-hoondasala, n-lolu,* and *n-heeti,* as well as the gratings of the lignified stump of the *kaloombi,* which is administered to ensure that "the internal wounds turn black *(phuta zaphiindidi).* Exegesis points to a homonymy between *kaloombi* and *loombi,* "black ashes," as well as a scar which turns black *(-phiinda)* as it heals.

12. The lukewarm infusion consists of the leaves of the parasol tree, of *mangangatsaanga,* a climbing plant found in humid regions, and of *mazeledi,* a fern from humid areas which, in ritual use, may replace this climbing plant. Also added are dried leaves taken from a spider's web, *tungyatungya,* and red wood paste *(khula)* to symbolize trouble-free gestation.

13. The infusion prepared for the gynecological patient consists of the tendrils *(maziingu)* or parts of several species of climbers destined to thwart the "binding" effect of the disorder: the *lufuundu* vine which produces fruit used as gourds (symbolizing the womb); the *yisakaamba,* whose fruit is toxic; and the thorns *(makoongi)* of the *yikayakaya* creeper, whose name recalls the homonymic term *-kaya,* used to describe ritual entrapment or reversal. Again, in order to demonstrate that healing is something very normal, the foliage of the oil palm *(leembwa)* taken from the base of the foliate crown and the village weed (cf. note 9) are also added to the infusion. Other ingredients consist of the inflorescence, *yizeendi,* of the *m-fwangulusu* plant (cf. ch. 6, n. 5) and above all the slightly toxic root of the *n-tsatsa* tree, which is considered to be an aphrodisiac. Other traditions state that this tree grows at the foot of a termite hill which appeared on the grave of the *yisidika,* the master specialist of the rite of virile fertility (cf. ch. 6, n. 15).

14. The food taboos imposed on the recluse involve: (a) All foods containing a viscous juice *(leendzi)* that, as commentaries have it, signifies the inability "to retain sperm." Those vegetables which lose their water when "cut with a knife" *(bisaka bya-*

khela mbeedi) are also forbidden; examples are the leaves of the manioc plant or of the forest plants *m-boondi* and *ndiimbula* used as vegetables; are also prohibited the "gombo" fruit *(yingoombu)* of the subligneous plant, and the fruit, *diimbulu,* of the small suffrutescent savanna plants. (b) Hen's eggs, because they symbolize a closed womb. (c) All kinds of mushrooms, because their whitish color reminds one of anemia or an albino. And (d) fish caught with a hook *(n-tsuka ndobu)* and a few small mammals, symbols of abortion.

15. This term *ngooongu* is also used to designate the envelope of leaves that is placed above the pot in which a ritual medicine simmers, and that is bound in the loincloth between the legs of a sterile woman.

16. This interpretation is based on the similarity, in form and function, between the *kamwaadi* branch and the branches placed in the *n-koongwa* of the hunt. The *n-koongwa,* literally, "hunter," is an altar erected, for example, at the point where the path to the cemetery crosses another. It is composed of a log of wood placed horizontally between four forked stakes; a longer pole extends beyond the log and rests in a fork at the ground level. This *n-koongwa,* which to some extent resembles a turtle or a swing trap, would appear to have a cosmological meaning, that of the primordial union between the sexes. In other ritual contexts, *kamwaadi* is associated with the *lwuila* termite hill and with sculpted objects placed in the earth, such as *kambandzya* and *kakuungu.* Although little information is available concerning these last objects, they refer to primordial ancestors preceding lineage society (cf. Devisch 1972: 156, 162).

17. Medication prepared from plants and intended or recommended for another person is usually the outcome of a cultic tradition acquired through initiation of some form or another. The Yaka make no distinction between the *ngangan-kisi,* elsewhere referred to as a specialist of charms *(n-kisi)* or magician, and the *ngangabuka,* in other words, the "medicine man," the herbalist. These neologisms were introduced by the missionaries to guide the behavior of those Yaka who converted to Christianity and are not used by the healers themselves.

18. Since initiation in the *khita* cult, unlike in other cults, does not invest the initiate with the art of healing, the initiate is not given the *yihalu,* namely the pharmacopoeia needed to exercise the art; instead she receives a *phaandzi* bundle of medicinal plants.

19. In order to thwart any disorder or to prevent the malevolent use of these powerful plants, the *khita* contains, among other ingredients, fragments of the bark of giant forest trees, some of which are toxic:

(a) *M-mwayi* is a forest tree with a toxic bark. It is claimed that the area immediately around this tree becomes sterile. This characteristic is transferred to the healer's art invoked to overcome the disorder; this is the meaning of the expression *m-mwayi mbuta n-ti kamwaanga bungaanga,* "just as the *m-mwayi* is a tree which dominates, thus the therapeutic art must assert itself."

(b) With regard to the *n-honu* tree, which is found in the forest glades and which is one of the components of the *yihalu* and the *phaandzi,* commentaries see a homonymy with the term *-honuka,* used to describe a goat struggling to "loosen" itself, and offer the following explanation: *mbeefu kahonuka yibeefu kyan-tabula,* "the sick person fights so that the illness may release him."

(c) *N-haandzi* is a large forest tree producing curled ligneous pods. A concentrated decoction prepared from the gratings of the roots or the bark of the trunk and administered by anal douche can cause a painful headache—"you feel that the bones of the skull are tightening" *(mboondzu kazikidi)*. This tree is included in the *yihalu* or *phaandzi* specifically to "prevent any pain which might split the patient's head" *(wunhaandziku, wun-yatiku)*.

(d) *N-kukubuundu* is a forest tree with a toxic bark which, when it falls, takes a great many other trees with it. It is also said of it that *n-kukubuundu, n-ti wudya makasa mbuumba wasimasana,* "the *n-kukubuundu* tree is poison to the squirrel and a danger to the wild cat." By placing the bark of this tree in the pharmacopoeia, the initiate assumes the power of the tree and uses it to therapeutic ends.

(e) The toxic bark of the forest tree, *phutu,* was in the past employed in the poison ordeal. Because of this use, the tree is also known as *yibala khasa n-ti wudya baloki; yibala khasa,* "the tree which kills sorcerers."

(f) Because of its straight, slippery trunk, the forest *yikuumba* tree is described in the following way: *yikuumbi, n-ti ndelumuka, n-tya phaambala kyatolwala bimati,* "*yikuumbi* is a large slippery tree, those who try to climb it risk a fracture." Ritual specialists use the bark of this tree to neutralize the sorcerer's aggression.

(g) Included in the pharmacopoeia are a number of curled plants symbolizing the "entwining" effect of the disorder and whose thwarting effect is to be reversed by the ingredients' own twisting action, *m-bindusi,* the ends of tangled creepers, and *maziingu malufuundu,* tendrils of a climbing plant whose fruit can be used as gourds.

(h) The pharmacopoeia also contains auspicious tokens of the legitimacy of the therapeutic art: a bone from each animal whose kill in the hunt or in a sacrifice was "an augury of a prosperous outcome" *(-sakwasa),* for example, of the seclusion, the family reunification, or the conjugal reunion. The pharmacopoeia is kept in a skin (of a civet, weasel, Gambian rat, or squirrel) presented when the services of the specialist are hired. The skins of these animals are used in an effort to thwart the abnormality which the *khita* therapy is intended to heal, in particular abortion. These small mammals, both because of their striped skins and in virtue of their way of concealing themselves, symbolize these abnormalities. The name of the ring, *lukata,* at the bottom of the pharmacopoeia signifies not so much a support but rather something being turned against itself: indeed, *lukata* can be a synonym of *kuundzi,* the name for the elbow-shaped branch placed in the *khita khoofi.*

20. *Tsaanga khita* consists of a series of ingredients intended to booby-trap the many routes the evil might take and to convert the obstacle to fertility into an element of fertility. Among them we find: (a) ingredients taken at random from the *yihalu* of the healer; (b) crushed bark to be used in the initiate's *phaandzi;* (c) an assortment of plants *(mbakunumbakunu);* (d) cinders from the fire lit close to the seclusion house; and finally, (e) agricultural products (peanuts and maize, for example) symbolising great fertility. These are all mixed with *khula* red wood paste and *muundu,* red clay, denoting fetal blood.

21. The therapist sometimes kneels at the crossing of the paths, close to a tuft of grass. Plucking several blades, he twines cords from them which he binds together while chanting:

1   Tutuudidi haphaambwa ndzila,
2   tukabula haphaambwa ndzilaku.
3   Phaambwandzila, n-dyakyeendzi.

1   Having reached the crossing of the paths,
2   we should not go back.
3   The crossing of the paths reabsorbs that which impairs one's gait.

According to the commentaries, this intercession indicates that the ritual specialist, by making the initiate cross the intersection of the paths, authorizes her to leave the seclusion house with impunity and to abandon the chameleon-like gait.

22. Various objects are attached above and on top of the front part of the headdress worn by the *khita* initiate to entrap the disorder and guarantee good health. A vaginal-shaped cowrie *(luziimbu lwaphasi),* whose crevice has been filled with *khawa* (the explosive ingredient used in ritual weapons), serves as "a watchful eye" to take evil-doers by surprise. A small bag contains gratings from the bushes of misfortune, *n-heeti* and *m-booti,* and a piece of the black mushroom which grows on rotten wood, whose name, *yidiiya,* also means "oblivion." Attached to the headdress are *phatulu* (two small sticks of *m-mvuma* and *n-kungwa yiteki* wood in the shape of a hook), dovetailed into each other, and *siimba dyangeembu* (bat's nails), expressing how much the initiation, and the initiate as well, is a connecting medium, a bond of union. The fine weave of grass to be found at the water's edge, *mangangatsaanga*—evocative of the placenta—that is attached to the headdress and around the skull adds to the significance of rebirth.

23. Apart from the little Maleeka guardian, the coinitiates—who do not share in the recluse's fetal condition—leave the seclusion house after three or four days' stay. At dawn on the day of their return to the village, they are taken to the stream to wash; they undergo no transitory rite. Their faces are colored like those of the patient and of the Maleeka. The head of their family leads them from the seclusion house in the presence of the ritual specialist. The group proceeds through the village collecting small presents *(n-seendu),* but they have no ritual objects. Their exit from the ritual house lifts all the ordinances laid upon them during this phase.

24. Before returning to his conjugal home, the therapist must ensure that those bonds in which he has so intimately become involved in the cure do not constitute an intrusion into his own family and conjugal space. He is careful to set the ritual objects which he brought with him on a pile of refuse at the outskirts of his homestead. They will remain there for at least one night, a transitional and regenerative period that ritual vocabulary characterizes as *yitatu,* "three days." They are sprinkled with *n-zoondza,* a substance prepared from animal excrement, in order to wash off the impurities *(mbviindu).* Prior to entering the marital home, the ritual specialist offers his first wife the *khokwa tuululu,* the hen which the head of the afflicted couple's family had given him, the day the *khoofi* was set up, as a sign of goodwill or, according to the fuller expression, *khoku katuula kundzo,* "the hen signifying that nothing will prevent him from entering under the marital roof." To properly benefit from the gift of this hen, the co-spouses rub their heels with a feather.

25. When Maleeka prepares to attend the marriage, there occur a number of ritual practices whose effect is to extend to her marriage the fertility conveyed to her by the initiation. At her marriage, the groom, the head of her parental homestead, and her uncle each present her with chickens as a tonic and symbol of transition. Moreover, her uncle, and eventually the ritual specialist who presided over the seclusion, will prescribe medicines made of savanna plants *(yifutu)* for the Maleeka.

References

Ademuwagun, Z., et al., eds. 1979. *African therapeutic systems.* Walthan, Mass.: Crossroads Press.
Akerele, O. 1984. WHO's traditional medicine program: Progress and perspectives. *WHO Chronicle* 38(2):76–81.
Anderson, E. 1958. *Messianic movements in the Lower Congo.* Uppsala: Studia Ethnographica Upsaliensia.
Anzieu, D. 1981. *Le groupe de l'inconscient. L'imaginaire groupal.* Paris: Dunod.
———. 1985. *Le Moi-peau.* Paris: Dunod.
Aryee, A. 1983. The coexistence of traditional and modern medicine in Nigeria: An example of transitional behavior in the developing world. Ph.D. diss., Boston University.
Bailleul, H. 1959. Les Bayaka: Aperçu de l'évolution politique et économique de leur pays jusqu'en 1958. *Zaïre* 12(8):823–41.
Balandier, G. 1965. *La vie quotidienne au Royaume de Kongo du XVIe au XVIIIe siècle.* Paris: Hachette.
Bannerman, R., et al. 1983. *Traditional medicine and health care.* Geneva: WHO.
Beck, B. 1978. The metaphor as a mediator between semantic and analogic modes of thought. *Current Anthropology* 19(1):83–97.
Beidelman, T. 1966. Swazi royal ritual. *Africa* 36:313–45.
Bibeau, G. 1979. The World Health Organization in encounter with African traditional medicine. In *African therapeutic systems,* ed. Z. Ademuwagun, et al., 182–86. Walthan, Mass.: Crossroads Press.
———. 1981. Préalables à une épidémiologie anthropologique de la dépression. *Psychopathologie Africaine* 17(1–3):96–112.
———. 1984. Authenticité et ambiguïté d'une implication dans un Institut africain de recherche. *Anthropologie et Sociétés* 8(3):95–115.
Bibeau, G., et al. 1979. *La médecine traditionnelle au Zaïre.* Ottawa: CRDI.
Biebuyck, D. 1985. *The Arts of Zaire.* Volume 1, *Southwestern Zaire.* Berkeley: University of California Press.
Bittremieux, L. 1936. *La société secrète des Bakhimba au Mayombe.* Bruxelles: Institut Royal Colonial Belge.
Boddy, J. 1989. *Wombs and alien spirits: Women, men, and the Zar cult in Northern Sudan.* Madison: University of Wisconsin Press.
Bonnafé, P. 1969. Un aspect religieux de l'idéologie lignagère: Le nkira des Kukuya du Congo-Brazzaville. *Cahiers des Religions Africaines* 3(6):209–97.

Bourdieu, P. 1979. *La distinction: Critique sociale du jugement.* Paris: Les Editions de Minuit.
———. 1980. *Le sens pratique.* Paris: Les Editions de Minuit.
Bourgeois, A. 1978–79. Mbwoolu sculpture of the Yaka. *African Arts* 12(3):58–61, 96.
———. 1984. *Art of the Yaka and Suku.* Meudon: A. & Fr. Chaffin.
———. 1985. *The Yaka and Suku.* Leiden: Brill.
Buakasa, Tulu kia Mpansu. 1973. *L'impensé du discours: Kindoki et nkisi en pays kongo du Zaïre.* Kinshasa: Presses Universitaires du Zaïre.
Buschkens, W. 1990. *Community health in the developing world: The case of Somalia.* Assen: Van Gorcum.
Castoriadis, C. 1975. *L'institution imaginaire de la société.* Paris: Seuil.
Castoriadis-Aulagnier, P. 1975. *La Violence de l'interprétation. Du pictogramme à l'énoncé.* Paris: Presses Universitaires de France.
Chavunduka, G. 1978. *Traditional healers and the Shona patient.* Gweru: Mambo.
Comaroff, J. 1985a. *Body of power, spirit of resistance: The culture and history of a South African people.* Chicago: University of Chicago Press.
———. 1985b. Bodily reform as historical practice: The semantics of resistance in modern South Africa. *International Journal of Psychology.* 20:541–68.
Corbey, R. 1989. *Wildheid en beheersing: De Europese verbeelding van Afrika.* Baarn: Ambo.
Corin, E. 1979. A possession psychotherapy in an urban setting: Zebola in Kinshasa. *Social Science and Medicine* 13(B):327–38.
Corin, E., and G. Bibeau. 1975. De la forme culturelle au vécu des troubles psychiques en Afrique: Propositions méthodologiques pour une étude interculturelle du champ des maladies mentales. *Africa* 45:280–315.
Crapanzano, V. 1990. Afterword. In *Modernist anthropology: From fieldwork to text,* ed. M.Manganaro, 300–308. Princeton: Princeton University Press.
Cros M. 1990. *Anthropologie du sang en Afrique: Essai d'hématologie symbolique chez les Lobi du Burkina Faso et de Côte-d'Ivoire.* Paris: L'Harmattan.
Csikszentmihalyi, M. 1977. *Beyond boredom and anxiety.* San Francisco: Jossey-Bass.
Csordas, T.J. 1980. Embodiment as a paradigm for anthropology. *Ethos* 18:5–47.
De Beir, L. 1975a. *Religion et magie des Bayaka.* St. Augustin bei Bonn: Anthropos.
———. 1975b. *Les Bayaka de M'Nene Ntoombo Lenge-Lenge.* St. Augustin bei Bonn: Anthropos.
De Boeck, F. 1991a. From knot to web: Fertility, life-transmission, health, and well-being among the Aluund of Southwest Zaire. Ph.D. diss., Catholic University of Leuven, Centre for Anthropology.
———. 1991b. Therapeutic efficacy and consensus among the Aluund of Southwest Zaire. *Africa* 61(3):159–85.
———. 1991c. Of bushbucks without horns: Male and female initiation among the Aluund of Southwest Zaire. *Journal des Africanistes* 61(1):37–72.
De Decker, H. 1968. *L'apostolat paroissial dans le diocèse de Popokabaka.* Kinshasa: Privately published.
Deflem, M. 1991. Ritual, anti-structure, and religion: A discussion of Victor Turner's processual symbolic analysis. *Journal for the Scientific Study of Religion* 30(1):1–25.
de Maximy, R. 1984. *Kinshasa, ville en suspens. Dynamique de la croissance et pro-*

blèmes d'urbanisme: approche socio-politique. Paris: Editions de l'Office de la Recherche Scientifique et Technique d'Outre-Mer.

de Saint-Moulin, L. 1976. *Atlas des collectivités du Zaïre.* Kinshasa: Presses Universitaires du Zaïre.

———. 1977. Perspectives de la croissance urbaine au Zaïre. *Zaïre-Afrique* no. 111:35–52.

———. 1987. Essai d'histoire de la population du Zaïre. *Zaïre-Afrique* no. 217:389–409.

Denis, J. 1964. *Les Yaka du Kwango: Contribution à une étude ethno-démographique.* Tervuren: Musée Royal de l'Afrique Centrale.

Devereux, G. 1970. *Essais d'ethnopsychiatrie générale.* Paris: Gallimard.

Devisch, R. 1972. Signification socio-culturelle des masques chez les Yaka. *Boletim do Instituto de Investigação cientifica de Angola* 9(2):151–76. Luanda.

———. 1979. Les Rites funéraires chez les Yaka. In *Mort, deuil et compensations mortuaires chez les Komo et les Yaka du Nord du Zaïre,* ed. R. Devisch and W. de Mahieu, 69–112. Tervuren: Musée royal de l'Afrique centrale.

———. 1981. Analyse sémantique d'une malédiction dans la société yaka. In *Combats pour un christianisme africain,* ed. A. Ngindu Mushete, 201–10. Kinshasa: Bibliothèque du CERA.

———. 1985a. Approaches to symbol and symptom in bodily space-time. *The International Journal of Psychology* 20:389–418.

———. 1985b. Perspectives on divination in contemporary sub-Saharan Africa. In *Theoretical explorations in African religion,* ed. W. Van Binsbergen and M. Schoffeleers, 50–83. London: Routledge & Kegan Paul.

———. 1986. Marge, marginalisation et liminalité: Le sorcier et le devin dans la culture Yaka du Zaïre. *Anthropologie et Sociétés* 10:117–37.

———. 1987. Le symbolisme du corps entre l'indicible et le sacré dans la culture Yaka: Quelques axes de recherche. *Cahiers des Religions Africaines* 20–21 (39–42): 145–65.

———. 1988. From equal to better: Investing the chief among the Northern Yaka of Zaire. *Africa* 58(3):261–90.

———. 1990a. The therapist and the source of healing among the Yaka of Zaire. *Culture, Medicine and Psychiatry* 14(2):213–36.

———. 1990b. The human body as a vehicle of emotions among the Yaka of Zaire. In *Personhood and agency: The experience of self and other in African cultures,* ed. M. Jackson and I. Karp, 115–33. Stockholm: Almqvist & Wiksell; Washington: Smithsonian Institution Press.

———. 1991a. Mediumistic divination among the Northern Yaka of Zaire. In *African divination systems,* ed. M. Peek, 104–23. Bloomington: Indiana University Press.

———. 1991b. The Mbwoolu cosmogony and healing cult among the Northern Yaka of Zaire. In *The creative communion: African folk models of fertility and the regeneration of life,* ed. A. Jacobson-Widding and W. van Beek, 111–28. Stockholm: Almqvist & Wiksell.

———. 1991c. Symbol and symptom among the Yaka of Zaire. In *Body and space: Symbolic models of unity and division in African cosmology and experience,* ed. A. Jacobson-Widding, 283–302. Stockholm: Almqvist & Wiksell.

———. 1991d. The symbolic and the physiological: Epigastric complaints in family medicine in Flanders. In Anthropologies of medicine: A colloquium on West European and North American perspectives, ed. B. Pfleiderer and G. Bibeau. Special issue of *Curare* 7:69–86.

Devisch, R., and B. Vervaeck. 1985. Auto-production, production et reproduction: Divination et politique chez les Yaka du Zaïre. *Social Compass* 32:111–31.

Devred, R., C. Sys, and J. M. Berce. 1958. *Notice explicative de la carte des sols et de la végétation: Cartes des sols et de la végétation du Congo Belge et du Ruanda-Urundi,* 10: *Kwango A et B.* Brussels: INEAC.

Dougherty, J., and J. Fernandez. 1981. Introduction to special issue: Symbolism and cognition. *American Ethnologist* 8:413–21.

Dozon, J. 1987. Ce que valoriser la médecine traditionnelle veut dire. *Politique Africaine* 28:9–20. Paris.

Dumon, D., and R. Devisch. 1991. *The oracle of Maama Tseembu: Divination and healing among the Yaka of Southwestern Zaire.* 50 min. color film. BRTN/VAR (Belgian Radio and Television, Science Division, Brussels). Video in Dutch, English, French, and German versions.

Dupré, M. 1975. Le système des forces *nkisi* chez les Kongo, d'après le troisième volume de K. Laman. *Africa* 41:12–28.

Durham, D., and J. Fernandez. 1991. Tropical dominions: The figurative struggle over domains of belonging and apartness in Africa. In *Beyond metaphor: The theory of tropes in anthropology,* ed. J. Fernandez, 190–210. Stanford: Stanford University Press.

Fanon, Fr. 1952. *Peau noire masques blancs.* Paris: Seuil.

Fassin, D. 1992. *Pouvoir et maladie en Afrique.* Paris: Presses Universitaires de France.

Feierman, S. 1981. Therapy as a system-in-action in northeastern Tanzania. *Social Science and Medicine* 15(B):353–60.

———. 1985. Struggles for control: The social roots of health and healing in Modern Africa. *African Studies Review* 28:73–147.

Fernandez, J. 1974. The mission of metaphor in expressive culture. *Current Anthropology* 15:119–45.

Flax, J. 1990. Postmodernism and gender relations in feminist theory. In *Feminism and postmodernism,* ed. L. J. Nicholson, 39–62. New York: Routledge.

Foster, G. 1982. Applied anthropology and international health: Retrospect and prospect. *Human Organization* 41(3):189–97.

Frankenberg, R. 1988. Gramsci, culture and medical anthropology: Kundry and Parsifall? Or rat's tail to sea serpent? *Medical Anthropology Quarterly* 2:324–37.

Good, B. 1979. The Heart of What's The Matter: The Semantics of Illness in Iran. *Culture, Medicine and Psychiatry* 1(1):25–58.

Good, B., and M. Del Vecchio Good. 1981. The meaning of symptoms: A cultural hermeneutic model for clinical practice. In *The relevance of social science for medicine,* ed. L. Eisenberg and A. Kleinman, 165–95. Dordrecht: Reidel.

Good, C. 1987. *Ethnomedical Systems in Africa: Patterns of Traditional Medicine in Rural and Urban Kenya.* New York: The Guilford Press.

Hoover, J. 1978. The seduction of Ruwej: Reconstructing Ruund history (The Nuclear Lunda: Zaire, Angola, Zambia). Ph.D. diss., Yale University.

Houyoux, J., Kinavwuidi Niwembo, and Okita Oniya. 1986. *Budgets des ménages*. Kinshasa: BEAU.
Huber, H. 1956. Magical statuettes and their accessories among the Eastern Bayaka and their neighbors. *Anthropos* 51:265–90.
Jackson, M. 1989. *Paths toward a clearing: Radical empiricism and ethnographic inquiry*. Bloomington: Indiana University Press.
Janzen, J. 1978. *The quest for therapy: Medical pluralism in Lower Zaire*. Berkeley: University of California Press.
———. 1982. *Lemba, 1650–1930: A Drum of affliction in Africa and the New World*. New York: Garland.
———. 1989. Health, religion and medicine in Central and Southern African traditions. In *Healing and restoring: Health and medicine in the world's religious traditions*, ed. L. Sullivan, 225–54. New York: Macmillan.
———. 1991. Doing *Ngoma*: A dominant trope in African religion and healing. *Journal of Religion in Africa* 21:291–308.
Janzen, J., and G. Prins, eds. 1979. Causality and classification in African medicine and health. Special issue of *Social Science and Medicine* 15B(3):169–437.
Jewsiewicki, B. 1991. Painting in Zaire: From the invention of the West to the representation of the social self. In *Africa explores: Twentieth century African art*, ed. S. Vogel and I. Ebong, 130–51. New York: The Centre for African Art; Munich: Prestel.
Kaba, S. 1981. The place of the African traditional pharmacopoeia in health services deliveries at community level and in training of health personnel. In *Afro Technical Papers*, vol. 17: *Biomedical Lectures*. Brazzaville: WHO.
Kalambay, E. 1986–87. La ville est la désillusion: L'exemple de Kinshasa (Zaïre). *Le Mois en Afrique* 22:157–62.
Kapferer, B. 1983. *A celebration of demons: Exorcism and the aesthetics of healing in Sri Lanka*. Washington: Smithsonian Institution Press.
Kirmayer, L. 1984. Culture, affect, somatization. *Transcultural Psychiatric Research Review* 21:159–88, 237–62.
Kopytoff, I. 1980. Revitalization and the genesis of cults in pragmatic religion: The Kita rite of passage among the Suku. In *Explorations in African systems of thought*, ed. I. Karp and C. Bird, 183–212. Bloomington: Indiana University Press.
Kristéva, J. 1969. *Semiotica, recherches pour une sémanalyse*. Paris: Seuil.
Lacan, J. 1949. Le Stade miroir comme formateur de la fonction du je. *Revue Française de Psychanalyse* 13:449–53.
Lamal, F. 1965. *Basuku et Bayaka des districts Kwango et Kwilu au Congo*. Tervuren: Musée Royal de l'Afrique Centrale.
Laman, K. E. 1936. *Dictionnaire kikongo-français*. Bruxelles: Mémoires Institut Royal Colonial Belge.
Lapika, Dimomfu. 1980. Pour une médecine éco-développementale au Zaïre. Ph.D. diss., Université Catholique de Louvain.
Last, M., and G. Chavunduka, eds. 1986. *The professionalisation of African medicine*. Manchester: Manchester University Press and International African Institute.
Leclerc, A. 1976. *Epousailles*. Paris: Grasset.
Levin, D. M. 1988. *The opening of vision: Nihilism and the postmodern situation*. New York: Routledge.

Lévi-Strauss, Cl. 1958. *Anthropologie structurale*. Paris: Plon.
———. 1962. *La pensée sauvage*. Paris: Plon.
Lima, M. 1971. *Fonctions sociologiques des figurines de culte Hamba dans la société et dans la culture Tshokwe (Angola)*. Luanda: Instituto de Investigação Cientifica de Angola.
Lock, M., and N. Sheper-Hughes. 1987. The mindful body: A prolegomenon to future work in medical anthropology. *Medical Anthropology* 1:6–41.
Lock, M., and D. Gordon, eds. 1988. *Biomedicine examined*. Dordrecht: Kluwer.
Lyon, M. L. 1990. Order and healing: The concept of order and its importance in the conceptualization of healing. *Medical Anthropology* 12:249–68.
Lyotard, J.-Fr. 1979. *La condition postmoderne: Rapport sur le savoir*. Paris: Les Editions de Minuit.
M'Bokolo, Elikia. 1984. Histoire des maladies, histoire et maladie. In *Le sens du mal: Anthropologie, histoire, sociologie de la maladie*, ed. M. Augé and C. Herzlich, 155–86. Paris: Editions des Archives Contemporaines.
MacGaffey, W. 1983. *Modern Kongo prophets: Religion in a plural society*. Bloomington: Indiana University Press.
———. 1986. *Religion and society in Central Africa: The Bakongo of Lower Zaire*. Chicago: University of Chicago Press.
MacLean, U., and C. Fyfe, eds. 1986. *African medicine in the modern world*. Edinburgh University: Centre of African Studies.
Mahaniah, Kimpianga. 1982. *La maladie et la guérison en milieu kongo*. Kinshasa: Centre de Vulgarisation Agricole.
Martin, E. 1987. *The women in the body: A cultural analysis of reproduction*. Boston: Beacon Press.
Memmi, A. 1957. *Portrait du colonisé précédé du portrait du colonisateur*. Paris: Ed. Buchet/Chastel-Corrêa.
McCormack, C. 1988. Health and the social power of women. *Social Science and Medicine* 26:677–84.
Merleau-Ponty, M. 1945. *Phénoménologie de la perception*. Paris: Gallimard.
———. 1964. *Le visible et l'invisible*. Paris: Gallimard.
Middleton, J. 1989. Emotional style: The cultural ordering of emotions. *Ethos* 17:187–201.
Miller, Ch. 1985. *Black darkness Africanist discourse in French*. Chicago: University of Chicago Press.
Morley, D. 1976. Paediatric priorities in evolving community programmes for developing countries. *Lancet* (Nov. 6), 1012–14.
Mudimbe, V. 1988. *The invention of Africa: Gnosis, philosophy, and the order of knowledge*. Bloomington: Indiana University Press.
Nederveen Pieterse, J. 1990. *Wit over zwart: Beelden van Afrika en Zwarten in de Westerse populaire cultuur*. Amsterdam: Koninklijk Instituut voor de Tropen.
Ngondo a Pitshadenge, 1982. *De la nuptialité et fécondité des polygames: Le cas des Yaka de Popokabaka (Zaïre)*. Tervuren: Musée royal de l'Afrique centrale.
Piazza, C. 1978. I Bayaka del Kwango e la politica coloniale Belga (1880–1960). *Africa* 33:187–215, 405–418. Rome.

References

———. 1982. Fonti Italiane per la storia dei Bayaka del Kwango (1885–1908). *Africa* 37:436–458. Rome.

Pillsbury, B. 1982. Policy and evaluation perspectives on traditional health practitioners in national health care systems. *Social Science and Medicine* 16:1825–34.

Plancquaert, M. 1971. *Les Yaka: Essai d'histoire*. Tervuren: Musée Royal de l'Afrique Centrale.

Prins, G. 1979. Disease at the crossroads: Towards a history of therapeutics in Bulozi. *Social Science and Medicine* 13(B):285–315.

———. 1989. But what was the disease? The present state of health and healing in African studies. *Past and Present* 124:159–79.

Reefe, T. 1981. *The rainbow and the kings: A history of the Luba empire to 1891*. Berkeley: University of California Press.

Remotti, F. 1987. Catégories sémantiques de l'éros chez les Wanande du Zaïre. *L'Homme* 27, no. 103:73–92.

Ricoeur, P. 1975. *La métaphore vive*. Paris: Seuil.

Roosens, E. 1963. Monde Yaka et développement économique communautaire. *Cahiers Économiques et Sociaux* 1(5–6):5–23. Léopoldville.

———. 1971. *Socio-culturele verandering in Midden-Afrika: De Yaka van Kwaango*. Antwerpen: Standaard wetenschappelijke uitgeverij.

Rose, D. 1990. *Living the ethnographic life*. Newbury Park: Sage.

Rosolato, G. 1978. *La relation d'inconnu*. Paris: Gallimard.

Ruttenberg, P., L. Van den Steen, M. Buysse, et al. 1967. *Jalons de l'évangélisation au Kwango*. Heverlee: Ed. Privée de l'IRKO.

Sandor, A. 1986. Metaphor and belief. *Journal of Anthropological Research* 42:101–22.

Smith, P. 1978. Aspects de l'organisation des rites. In *La Fonction symbolique*, ed. M. Izard and P. Smith, 139–70. Paris: Gallimard.

Sofuluwe, G., and F. Bennett. 1985. *Principles and practice of community health in Africa*. Ibadan: University Press Limited.

Stoller, P. 1989. *Fusion of the worlds: An ethnography of possession among the Songhay of Niger*. Chicago: University of Chicago Press.

Thiel, J. 1977. *Ahnen, Geister, Höchste Wesen: Religionsethnologische Untersuchungen im Zaïre-Kasai-Gebiet*. St. Augustin bei Bonn: Anthropos.

Tshonga-Onyumbe 1982. *Nkisi, nganga* et *ngangankisi* dans la musique zaïroise moderne de 1960 à 1980. *Zaïre-Afrique* 22, no. 169: 555–66.

Turner, T. S. 1980. The social skin. In *Not Work Alone*, ed. J. Cherfas and R. Lewis, 112–40. London: Temple Smith.

Turner, V. 1957. *Schism and continuity in an African society: A study of Ndembu village life*. Manchester: Manchester University Press.

———. 1967. *The forest of symbols: Aspects of Ndembu ritual*. Ithaca: Cornell University Press.

———. 1968. *The Drums of affliction: A study of religious processes among the Ndembu*. Oxford: Clarendon Press.

———. 1969. *The ritual process: Structure and anti-structure*. London: Routledge and Kegan Paul.

———. 1974. *Dramas, fields and metaphors*. Ithaca: Cornell University Press.

———. 1975. *Revelation and divination in Ndembu ritual.* Ithaca: Cornell University Press.
———. 1977. Symbols in African ritual. In *Symbolic anthropology: A reader in the study of symbols and meaning,* ed. J. L. Dolgin, D. S. Kemnitzer, and D. M. Schneider, 183–94. New York: Columbia University Press.
———. 1980a. Social dramas and stories about them. *Critical Analysis* 7:141–68.
———. 1980b. Encounter with Freud: The making of a comparative symbologist. In *The making of psychological anthropology,* ed. G. D. Spindler, 558–83. Berkeley: University of California Press.
———. 1982. *From ritual to theatre.* New York: Performing Arts Journal Publications.
———. 1985. *On the edge of the bush: Anthropology as experience.* Ed. E. L. Turner. Tucson: University of Arizona Press.
Turner, E., and Fr. Turner. 1985. Victor Turner as we remember him. *Anthropologica* 27(1–2):11–6.
Van der Beken, A. 1978. *Proverbes et vie yaka.* St. Augustin bei Bonn: Anthropos.
Van der Geest, S., and S. Reynolds-Whyte, eds. 1988. *The context of medicines in developing countries: Studies in pharmaceutical anthropology.* Dordrecht: Assen.
Van Roy, H. 1988. *Les Byaambvu du Moyen-Kwango: Histoire du Royaume Luwa-Yaka.* Berlin: Reimer.
Van Wing, J. 1920. *De geheime sekte van 't kimpasi.* Brussel: Goemaere.
Vansina, J. 1965. *Les anciens royaumes de la savane.* Léopoldville: IRES.
———. 1966. *Introduction à l'ethnographie du Congo.* Kinshasa and Bruxelles: Editions Universitaires du Congo/CRISP.
———. 1973. *The Tio kingdom of the Middle Congo, 1880–1892.* London: Oxford University Press for the I.A.I.
———. 1990. *Paths in the rainforest: Towards a history of political tradition in Equatorial Africa.* London: James Currey.
Vaughan, M. 1991. *Curing their ills: Colonial power and African illness.* Oxford: Polity Press.
Vorbichler, A. 1957. Fetischmus und Hexerei. *Kongo-Overzee* 23(1–2):35–57.
Vuyck, T. 1991. *Children of one womb: Descent, marriage, and gender in Central African societies.* Leiden: Centre of Non-Western Studies of Leiden University.
Warren, D., et al. 1982. Ghanaian national polity towards indigenous healers. *Social Science and Medicine* 21:1873–81.
Werbner, R. 1984. The Manchester School in South-Central Africa. *Annual Review of Anthropology* 13:157–85.
———. 1988. *Ritual passage, sacred journey.* Washington: Smithsonian Institution Press.
WHO. 1976. *Traditional medicine and its role in the development of health services in Africa.* WHO Regional Committee for Africa. 26th Session. Kampala, 8–15 Sept.
———. 1978. *The promotion and development of traditional medicine.* Technical Report Series, no. 622. Geneva.
Willame, J. 1966. Traditional structures and political change: A case study of the Yaka of Kwango Province. *Cahiers Économiques et Sociaux* 4(4):449–59. Léopoldville.
———. 1973. Patriarchal structures and factional politics: Toward an understanding of the dualist society. *Cahiers d'Études Africaines* 13, cahier 50:326–55.

Winnicot, D. 1971. *Playing and reality.* London: Tavistock.
Yelengi, Nkasa Tekilazaya. 1986. Une aristocratie locale parmi les conquérants: Les Tulumba chez les Yaka. *Africa* 41:429–39. Rome.
Yoder, S. 1981. Knowledge of illness and medicine among the Cokwe of Zaire. *Social Science and Medicine* 15B:237–45.
Zenoni, L. 1976. Métaphore et métonymie dans la théorie de Lacan. *Cahiers Internationaux de Symbolisme* 31/32:187–98.

Index

Abortion, 303n.8
Adultery. *See* Extramarital sex
Agnatic descent, 14, 115–22; communal sodalities associated with, 148, 154–60; and life transmission, 161; and residential kin groups, 115–19; sorcery in, 127; and therapeutic initiation, 228; and the uterine line, 67, 92. See also *Ngolu*
Aluund, 156. *See also* Luunda
ANAZA (Association Nationale des Tradipraticiens du Zaïre), 299n.6
Ancestor, 13, 115, 180–82
Androgyneity of the healer, 163, 186; of the initiate, 66, 204–6, 213, 221, 264, 266, 267
Animals, 74–86; aquatic animals, 78; bats, 203–4, 221–22; big game animals, 74–76; birds, 78–79; blending of habitats, 84–86; in blood sacrifice, 236, 270; chameleons, 232, 235, 306n.9; civet cats, 223, 230; cocks, 63–65, 151–52, 204, 236; dogs, 129, 131, 135–36; eels, 78; elephants, 157, 304n.5; fish, 78, 220, 231–32; gazelles, 87, 114; genets, 77, 222–23; goats, 129, 131, 166; hens, 63–65, 123–24, 151–52, 184, 185, 191, 196, 214, 220–21, 225, 236–37, 243, 270; hyenas, 131; insects, 78, 85, 306n.9; Kivu shrews, 76, 77; *mbisi*, 75–76, 77, 300n.5; *n-kwaati* caterpillar, 300n.1; *phuku*, 77, 301n.8; pigs, 131; rainbow snakes, 73–74; small mammals, 77, 220; snakes, 73–74, 78; water shrews, 44, 77, 210; worms, 78
Aquatic animals, 78
ATKIN (Association of Traditional Practitioners), 300n.6

Balandier, Georges, 180
Banana plants, 64

Bantu civilization: cults of affliction, 23–24; and Yaka healing cults, 7
Bats, 203–4, 221–22
Belly, the, 138–39; in dance, 260, 261; and *ndzaambi* cult, 153
Bilesi, 229–30
Biomedicine, 29–33, 299n.5
Birds, 78–79
Birth-giving, 100, 119, 134, 301n.1
Blacksmith, 156
Blood, 138; blood sacrifice, 236, 270. *See also* Menstruation
Body, 132–60; afflictions of, 146–47; as analogic operator, 49; the belly, 138–39, 153, 260, 261; blood, 138; bodily emissions, 137; bodily orifices, 132, 133, 265, 271, 276; the body's vectors, 276; bowel movements, 138; breasts, 102, 138; excretion, 138; and gender arrangements, 92–93; and group in Yaka healing cults, 37–38; the head, 138, 271; and healing, 255–81; heart, 140–41, 271; high versus low parts, 271; the hips, 260, 261; the liver, 141; physical and sensorial contact, 133–38; the relational body, 139–46; reorigination in *khita* cure, 213–45; in ritual action, 50–51, 246, 247, 248, 252; role in *khita* healing, 49–50; saliva, 272; skin, 220, 265, 270, 276; as source and agent of healing, 46–48, 264–67, 268; symbolic turning inside out in *khita* cure, 270; and symbols, 280; twofold function of, 133
Bourdieu, Pierre, 48, 276, 279
Bowel movements, 138
Breast-feeding, 110, 113
Breasts, 102, 138
Bridewealth, 101, 104–6, 165, 166, 302n.4

Calendar, 81–83
Cash crops, 83
Chameleons, 232, 235, 306n.9
Chants: and healing, 259, 260, 261, 262, 272; in *khita* cure, 196–201, 203, 208–10, 223, 226–30, 238, 240
Charcoal, 68, 126, 164
Chavunduka, G., 30, 31
Chief, the: anointing with red clay, 300n.6; and communal cults, 157, 158; and diviners, 14, 154; and hunting, 87–88; and the *Lukhaanga* cult, 155–56; and marriage, 103, 106; and *ngoongu,* 87, 156; sacred house for, 88
Children: breast-feeding and weaning, 110, 113; eating of small mammals, 77; games, 113; and grandparents, 98, 118, 139, 142; in the homestead, 94, 95; listening and speaking, 139, 140; music learning, 261; name-giving, 111–13, 164, 211; treatments for, 160
Christianity, 19, 154, 158
Circumcision: symbolic association with menstruation, 82; and the *yikubu* cult, 156–57
Circumcision ceremonies, 113–15; color symbolism, 65; *kataku* position, 64, 300n.5; and masking, 114, 135; *khita* initiates excluded from, 273; *kholuka* mask, 135; and *m-fwangulusu,* 304n.5; songs for, 72, 101; in urban context, 158
Civet cats, 223, 230
Closure, 146, 172, 177
Clothing, 111, 137
Cock crowing at dawn, 63–65, 151–52, 236; cock standing on one leg and the parasol tree, 204
Coitus. *See* Sexual intercourse
Colonialism, 5–6, 15
Color symbolism, 65–69; and the rainbow snake, 73–74
Coming-out ordeal, 231–36
Communal sodalities, 147–60; and agnatic descent, 148, 154–60; and chiefs, 157, 158; cults of affliction compared to, 1, 148, 158; and socialization, 246
Contraception, 303n.8
Cooking, 90–91, 100; as a metaphor of gestation, 61–63, 217–24
Council of elders: and bridewealth, 105; and divinatory etiology, 162–63; drumming and salvo in, 143; for infertility, 165, 168; meeting place, 116; and men's symbolic reproduction, 4; oratory in, 144
Cowives, 96, 102, 302n.5
Cowrie shells, 163, 314n.22
Csikszentmihalyi, Mihaly, 36
Cults of affliction, 1–4, 23–24, 147–60; approach to illness, 17–18; attacks on, 158; communal cults compared to, 1, 148, 158; culture as setting the scene for, 48; and divination, 149, 150, 169–73; and gendered relations, 93; interweaving of body and group, 37–38; and political control, 148; rejection by the young, 19; resistance to capitalism and bureaucracy, 30–31; and socialization, 246; social management of illness, 51–52; and sorcery, 149; symbolism of the hen and the cock, 63–65; transformative drama developed by, 38–46; transitional objects used in, 273; untamed forces counteracted by, 86–87; and the uterine line, 148, 149–54. *See also Khita* healing cult; Traditional medicine
Culture: the body as a deposit of, 255–67; as a fabric of regeneration, 4, 46–48, 254–59, 279–80; healing as work of, 48–49; and the sensorium, 48–52
Curses: on male fertility, 180; reversal of in *khita* healing, 184–85; in the uterine line, 149, 170, 171, 174–76

Dance: in healing, 259–64; in *khita* cure, 196, 197; at transitions of group and seasonal calendar, 72; weaving compared to, 72–73; and women, 71–73
De Beir, Léon, 22, 181
De Decker, Henri, 299n.1
Defilement, 97. *See also* Intrusion
Denis, Jacques, 299n.1
Destiny, 301n.3
Disrobing, 137
Diviners: attacks on, 158; and chiefs, 14, 154; clairvoyance of, 146; and cults of affliction, 149, 150, 169–73; divination associated with the uterine line, 148; divinatory etiology, 162–63, 169–78; divinatory hunt in *khita* cure, 195–96, 232; the hunter compared to, 164; initiatory seclusion of, 163;

in *ngoombu* cult, 44, 151–53, 169; on sorcerers, 126; symbolism of palm and parasol trees, 64; therapeutic approach of, 176; in towns, 28; trances, 163
Divorce, 110, 125, 142, 167, 245
Dogs, 129, 131, 135–36, 146
Douches: for infertility, 168; ingredients of, 159, 218, 219, 310n.9; plants excluded from, 227; during pregnancy, 303n.7; as purgative, 138
Dreams, 75, 98
Drumming, 143, 259, 260, 261, 262
Dung beetles, 306n.9

Earthen jars, 60, 62–63, 100
Eating, 94–95, 220
Eels, 78
Effusion, 146, 172, 173, 177, 276
Elders: assertive speech of, 144; attainment of great age, 139; piercing gaze of, 145, 273; role in marriage, 119; status of, 118. *See also* Council of elders
Elephants, 157, 304n.5
Emetics, 159
Enemas: and health, 138; ingredients of, 226, 311n.10; for inversion of the body order, 271; in *khita* cure, 218, 219, 220; method of administration, 159, 168
Etiology: divinatory, 150, 162–63, 169–78; as indication of therapy, 173–78; popular etiology of infertility, 167–69
Excretion, 138
Exogamy, 102, 129
Extramarital sex: avoidance of allusions to, 96; consequences of, 110–11; and difficult pregnancy, 109; and gynecological disorders, 169, 172; and the hunt, 126; indicated by ordeal of the live fish, 232; occurrence on the edges of fields, 59; and tobacco, 135

Fermentation: and assertive speech, 144, 163; of game, 136; as a partial death of the genitor, 136; as transformative metaphor, 40, 206, 210, 278
Fertility rituals, 245–54
Fish, 78, 220, 231–32
Fishing, 78, 231–32
Forest: forest forces in *khita* cure, 224–44; as resource for renewal, 195; and sorcery, 88–89; transitional zone between village and forest, 58–60; village contrasted with, 56–57
Fula: as origin of illness, 210, 230; ritual therapy for, 211, 212, 225, 226; and trance, 207. *See also* Fermentation; *Mooyi*

Games, 113
Gazelles, 87, 114
Gender: the body and gender arrangements, 92–93; cosmological portrayal of, 60–74; cosmology of gender arrangements, 53–91; and seniority, 142
Genets, 77, 222–23
Giving birth. *See* Birth-giving
Gluckman, Max, 249
Goats, 129, 131; goat for the prohibition, 166
Grandparents, 98, 118, 139, 142
Group, the, 132–60; and the body in Yaka healing cults, 37–38, 267; reorigination in *khita* cure, 213–45
Gynecological disorders: causes of, 171; divinatory etiology of, 169–78; and divorce, 167; and extramarital sex, 169, 172; healing process for, 268; redressive intervention in *khita* cult, 179–212; social origins of, 161; and sorcery, 169, 170, 172, 173; therapy for, 173–78; and uterine affiliation, 169–71, 174, 175, 177. *See also* Infertility
Gyn-eco-logy, 2, 213, 253

Haamba cult, 157, 158
Hamlets, 116
Head, the, 138, 271
Healers: entrusting the patient to the healer, 185–96; as former patients, 150; hunters compared to, 86–87; hunter-trapper role assumed by, 190, 192; *khita* healer's challenge to sorcery, 188–89; maternal uncle's role taken by, 186, 277; professional autonomy of, 154; qualifications of, 185; and the ruling class, 148; traditional healers as herbalists, 28; traditional healers in towns, 18, 25–33; tricksters compared to, 282; voicing the patient's needs, 263
Healing, 255–81; cultural inducers of, 268–76; etiology as indication of therapy, 173–78; healing ritual, 4, 252–53, 255–56,

Healing (*continued*)
276; homeopathy, 188, 189, 212, 267–76, 277; and *mooyi*, 258; music and dance in, 259–64, 272; and *ngoongu*, 280; and the orificial and sensory body, 268; as a productive process, 256–57; self-healing, 276–81; source of, 264–67; starting point of, 255; and weaving, 257, 258, 259, 264, 278–79. *See also* Cults of affliction; Healers; Herbal medicine; Traditional medicine
Healing cults. *See* Cults of affliction
Health, 31, 274, 275
"Health for All" program, 28, 300n.6
Heart, the, 140–41, 271
Hens: hen about to lay, 63–65, 151–52, 220–21, 236; hen for the hire of services, 191; hen for the hunt, 123–24; hen of the pact, 237; in *khita* cure, 184, 185, 196, 225, 243; symbolized by seclusion house, 214, 236, 270
Herbal medicine: and cyclic time, 272; in healing cults, 158; herbarium, 293–95; and traditional healing, 28–29
Hita, 99, 179
Homeopathy, 188, 189, 212, 267–76, 277
Homestead, the, 93–100, 117, 126, 130, 138
Hunting: anti-sorcery activities compared to, 310n.8; big game animals, 74–76; the chief as hunter, 87–88; and communal cults, 157; in different seasons, 82; divinatory hunt in *khita* cure, 195–96, 232; the diviner compared to the hunter, 164; and domestic kin relations, 122–31; the healer compared to the hunter, 86–87; hen for the hunt, 123–24; the hunt and extramarital sex, 126; hunter-trapper role assumed by *khita* healer, 190, 192; *kataku* position in, 300n.5; and life transmission, 122–23, 141; as men's work, 83, 90–91; the *n-koongwa*, 312n.16; seclusion compared to the hunt, 222; social life reflected in, 123–26; the sorcerer compared to the hunter, 88–90, 123, 130; and untamed forces, 86–91; and virility, 141; wife's rights and responsibilities regarding the hunt, 123–26
Hyenas, 131

Ihembi, 249, 250
Illness: and health as polarities, 274, 275; leprosy, 136; relapse of, 244–45; social aspects of, 51–52, 132, 161–62; sorcery as source of, 18; as upsetting of the body's vectors, 276; Yaka view of, 17–18, 30, 31, 146–47. *See also* Gynecological disorders
Imaginary realm, 4–6, 18–20, 38, 57, 128–31; definition of, 299n.1; and the hunter and sorcerer, 88–91; and ritual, 43–44, 246, 256–59, 273
Impotence, 304n.1
Incest, 129, 136
Infertility, 164–69; adultery as cause of, 172; case study of, 285–92; and *nyoka khawa*, 303n.2; popular etiology of, 167–69; and uterine affiliation, 174
Initiation, therapeutic, 224–31
Insects, 78, 85; dung beetle, 306n.9; *n-kwaati* caterpillar, 300n.1
Insemination, 134, 210–12
Intrusion, or infringement upon the domestic and conjugal boundaries, 93, 96–98, 125, 146–47, 165, 173
Isangoma, 24

Janzen, John, 25, 225

Kamwaadi, 224
Kaolin, 67–68; applied to ancestor's grave, 116; color symbolism, 69; in *khita* cure, 184, 185, 190, 271; and the maternal uncle, 67, 122; senior female as guardian of, 142; and sorcery, 127
Kataku position, 64, 195, 300n.5
Khiimbi cult, 158
Khita healing cult, 2, 153; as Bantu cult of affliction, 23; the body in, 49–50; chants in *khita* cure, 196–201, 203, 208–10, 223, 226–30, 238, 240; as corporeal praxis, 46–47; as cult with a demonstrative trance, 149; dance in *khita* cure, 196, 197; the decay and cooking of generative forces, 196–212; divinatory hunt in *khita* cure, 195–96, 232; early references to, 304n.2; enemas in *khita* cure, 218, 219, 220; fertility problems and congenital deformities related to, 171; forest forces in, 224–44; fragrant essences used in, 135; homeopathic principle of, 188, 189, 212; initiate emancipating herself from the therapeutic relationship, 241–44; kaolin in *khita* cure, 184, 185, 190, 271; leading the initiate back into society,

238–41; maternal uncles' role in, 183–85; medical preparations used in, 159; and *nyoka khawa*, 303n.2; paradox and transgression in, 267–76; parasol tree's significance for, 62, 202, 204–5, 206, 210, 211, 220; putting the ailment to death, 201; redressive aspect of *khita* cure, 179–212; reintegration of patient into the family circle, 236–38; reversal of curses in, 184–85; reversing the persecution into bonds of life transmission, 183–96; seclusion period, 183, 196, 211, 213–45, 266, 273, 310n.6, 311n.14; similar cults, 180–83; status of *khita* initiates, 213–14; the taboo of sight, 273; territaries in *khita* cure, 193, 221, 222, 224; therapeutic approach of, 177–78; therapeutic initiation in, 224–31; trance in *khita* cure, 187, 197, 206, 207, 210, 211–12, 225
Kholuka mask, 135
Khoofi shrine, 192; erection of, 193–95; objects to counteract evil agencies, 305n.7; sachets placed under, 306n.9; and seclusion hut, 215; summoning of ancestral shades, 307n.12
Khosi cult, 157
Khula paste, 217, 219, 230, 270, 271
Kimpasi, 180
Kinshasa: fieldwork map, 296; health care facilities, 27; marriage customs of city dwellers, 102–3; status of communal cults in, 158; traditional healers in, 28–29; Yaka divination and healing in, 18; Yaka migration to, 15–16; Yaka population in, 299n.2
Kinship relations: and gynecological disorders, 161; hunting versus sorcery and, 122–31; lineage groups, 115–19. *See also* Agnatic descent; Uterine filiation
Kitu, 237, 307n.13
Koola, 12
Koongo, 11, 155, 180, 181, 297
Kopytoff, Igor, 181
Kuyu, 181
Kwaango, 11, 15, 182, 298, 299n.1; fieldwork map, 297
Kyaambvu, 12
Kyeesi, 214, 284

Lacan, Jacques, 299n.1
Lamal, François, 181
Last, Murray, 30, 31

Leembi cult, 157
Lemba cult, 155
Leprosy, 136
Lianas, 80–81, 215
Life flow. See *Mooyi*
Life force. See *Ngolu*
Life transmission: agnatic and uterine lines allied in, 161; cosmology of, 53–91; hunting compared to, 122–23, 141; impediments to, 161–78; patriarchal views of, 164; as principal reason for marriage, 173; reversing the persecution into uterine bonds of, 183–96; social formation of, 92–131; uterine life transmission and maternal uncles, 121–22, 206; and wedding ceremonies, 101
Life-world, 132–60; and the body and the group in Yaka healing cults, 37–38; reorigination in *khita* cure, 213–45; transformation in ritual healing, 276
Lineage groups, 115–19
Listening, 139–40
Liver, the, 141
Loombi, 306n.9
Loonga, 301n.2
Lubongu lwataangu, 302n.6
Lukhaanga cult, 155–56; priests, 13
Lungundzyala, 63
Luteti, 194, 215, 305n.7
Luunda, 11–13, 15, 55, 62, 157, 297
Lwuila, 224

Maawa cult, 149, 153
Maleeka, 183; as house servant to initiate, 217; marriage of, 314; and *phaandzi* pharmacopoeia, 230; reintegration of initiate into the home, 236; reintegration of initiate into society, 239; sharing enemas and ointments with initiate, 219, 220; and *tsaanga khita*, 231; visit to therapist after seclusion, 242; in water ordeal of transition, 232, 233, 234, 235
Malemu cult, 158
Manchester School in South-Central Africa, 249
Mandongu cult, 158
Mangangatsaanga, 218, 231, 240, 310n.7, 311n.12, 314n.22
Manioc, 83, 100, 192, 194
Marriage, 101–6; ages at, 102; bridewealth, 101, 104–6, 165, 166, 302n.4; and chiefs,

Marriage (*continued*)
103, 106; consummation of, 106; cowives, 96, 102, 302n.5; customs of city dwellers, 102–3; divorce, 110, 125, 142, 167, 245; elders' role in, 119; exogamy, 102, 129; fertility's importance in, 164, 173; as link between various homesteads, 92; married life, 106–11; significance in Yaka society, 16; wife beating, 142
Martin, E., 303
Mataamba cult, 158
Maternal ancestral malefactor, 208
Maternal uncles, 120–22, 303n.9; and curses on a niece, 170, 172–73; the healer taking on the role of, 186, 277; and kaolin, 67, 122; in *khita* healing, 183–85; and *ngoongu*, 17; and sorcery, 127; and uterine life transmission, 121–22, 206
Mbaamba, 194, 305n.7
Mbaambi cult, 157
Mbakunumbakunu, 234, 235, 306n.9
Mbata, 182
Mbiimbya n-khanda cult. See *Yikubu* cult
Mbisi, 75–76, 77, 300n.5
Mbuundwaphoongu, 221
Mbwoolu cult, 149, 153
Men: access to forest and savanna, 57, 58; access to the *yikoolu*, 59; authoritative speech in, 143; the body and personhood in, 132, 134; curses on male fertility, 180; domestic role, 93–100; enemas and douches used by, 159; extrusive behavior in, 147; fascination with cooking outdoors, 90–91; fascination with untamed forces, 86–87; fertility in, 179–80; fishing, 78; food preferences, 136; health viewed by, 162; hunting, 74–76, 82, 83, 90–91, 141; impotence, 304n.1; marriage, 101–6; married life, 106–11; and the maternal uncle, 121–22; men's work, 81–84, 100–101; in *nkula* cult, 248; palm tree as symbol of authority of, 62; and seniority, 142; wife beating, 142. *See also* Maternal uncles
Menstruation: and bodily limits, 138; savanna associated with, 82; as source of bad luck, 301n.9; suffrutex used as sanitary towel, 209; village outskirts associated with, 58
Metaphor: ritual metaphor, 42–44; Turner on, 35–37
Metonymy, 42–43, 45

M-fwangulusu, 304n.5
M-mvuma tree, 194, 305n.7, 310n.9
M-mwayi tree, 312n.19
Months, 81–83
Moon: color symbolism, 67; crescent moon, 70, 71; full moon, 71; lunar cycles and female cycles, 70–73; new moon, 70
Mooyi: affected by illness, 146; channeled through the mother and uterine line, 14, 67, 69, 93, 109, 120, 258; and cults of affliction, 149–54; color symbolism, 69; as goal of *khita* healing, 193, 194, 195; impediments, 169–73; in life transmission, 161; in man and environment, 71–73; olfaction and sexual desire as manifestations of, 135; as source of healing, 258; tapped by sorcerers, 127. *See also* Dance; Kaolin; Maternal uncles; Moon; Sorcery
Mortuary rituals, 122
Motherhood, 94, 100, 106, 119–21
Mushrooms, 82, 300n.1
Music, 259–64. *See also* Chants; Dance; Drumming; Rhythm
Mwaadi, 143
Mwani kabwanga cult, 156
Mwani phutu cult, 157
Mwiingoony cult, 156

Name-giving, 111–13, 164, 211
Nasal instillations, 227–28
Ndembu, 33–34, 35, 36, 245–51, 297
Ndzaambi cult, 153–54, 188
Ndzaku, 307n.11
Ndzuundu cult, 158
Ngola cult, 158
Ngolu: affected by illness, 146; in the agnatic line, 13, 69, 100, 127, 275; color symbolism, 69; in life transmission, 161; in man and environment, 13, 90, 123, 225; in public male cults, 155; represented in the *ndzo makhulu*, 13; and virility, 92. *See also* Sorcery
Ngoma, 24, 72, 259
Ngoombu cult, 150–53; as cult with a demonstrative trance, 149; digging in the ground by initiates, 210; diviners in, 44, 151–53, 169
Ngoongu, 17, 278; and the chief, 87, 156; and dancing, 73; and healing, 280; released in *khita* cure, 206, 213; as the sacred, 277; and

seclusion, 223–24; symbolized by the seclusion house, 152, 217–18
N-haandzi tree, 312n.19
N-hoondasala, 310n.9
N-hwaadi cult, 157
Night of misrule, 99
N-kaanda, 158
N-kaanga, 305n.6
Nkalaany, 157
N-kanda cult, 154
Nkang'a puberty ritual, 246, 248–49
N-khanda cult. See *Yikubu* cult
Nkira, 181
Nkita cult, 180, 181
N-koolu, 190–91
N-koongwa, 312n.16
N-kuba mbadi cult, 158
N-kukubuundu tree, 313n.19
Nkula cult, 246, 247–48
N-kungwayiteki, 306n.7
N-kwaati caterpillar, 300n.1
N-kwaati tree, 300n.1
N-laangu cult, 158
N-luwa cult, 157, 158
N-ngoongi cult, 156
N-noongu. See Weaving-hook
Northern Yaka, 11, 115, 119
N-phemba, 308n.3, 309n.4, 311n.10
N-saanda tree, 193, 194–95
N-seenga, 211
N-tyabungaanga, 159
Nyoka khawa, 303n.2

Oil palms, 60
Oneiromancy, 75
Ordeal and augury of the live fish, 231–32
Orifices, bodily, 132, 133, 265, 271, 276

Palm nuts, 210, 217
Palm trees, 60–62; in *khita* healing, 210; *mbaamba,* 194, 305n.7; oil palm, 60; parasol tree compared to, 204–5; palm nuts, 210, 217; symbolized by the cock, 73. *See also* Raffia palm
Palm wine: cooking and feeding associated with, 90; and *khita* initiates, 214; in the marriage process, 103; and men's status, 62; preparation of, 60; and speaking, 143, 145; and weaving, 278–79
Paradox, 267–76

Parasol tree: crowing cock as symbol of, 64; in *khita* cure, 202, 204–5, 206, 210, 211, 220; symbolism of, 62; use in infusions, 311n.12
Parturition. *See* Birth-giving
Peanuts, 81, 83
Period of seclusion. *See* Seclusion period
Personhood, 132, 133
Pfumwaphoongu, 183
Phaambwandzila, 59–60
Phaandzi pharmacopoeia, 229, 230, 238, 312nn. 18, 19
Phoongu, 149–50. *See also* Cults of affliction
Phuku, 77, 301n.9
Pigs, 131
Plants, 74–86; in anti-sorcery activities, 310n.8; banana plants, 64; blending of habitats, 84–86; and cyclic time, 272; in enemas and douches, 227; in *khita* cure, 192, 194, 218; *kitu,* 237, 307n.13; lianas, 80–81, 215; ligneous plants, 79, 301n.10; *luteti,* 194, 215, 305n.7; *mangangatsaanga,* 218, 231, 240, 310n.7, 311n.12, 314n.22; manioc, 83, 100, 192, 194; *mbakunumbakunu,* 306n.9; *m-fwangulusu,* 304n.5; *n-kungwayiteki,* 306n.7; *n-phemba,* 308n.3, 309n.4, 311n.10; peanuts, 81, 83; in the seclusion house, 159, 215–16, 229, 308n.3; suffrutex, 81, 209, 222; tobacco, 135; vines, 80–81, 215, 310n.9; white yam, 307n.11; *yiludi,* 84. *See also* Herbal medicine; Trees
Praxiology. *See* Semantic-praxiological method
Pregnancy: abortion, 303n.8; customs on announcement of, 66, 108–9; difficult pregnancy and extramarital sex, 109; douches during, 303n.7; food prohibitions, 220; premarital, 103; sexual intercourse during, 303n.7
Primary and Preventive Health Care Programs, 25
Puberty rituals, 245–46, 248–49

Raffia palm: cloth used in *khita* healing, 191; in curtains, 216; fibers, 300n.4; in loincloths, 145; symbolism of, 60; weaving of, 72–73, 145, 211, 278–79
Rainbow, 61, 73–74, 88
Rainbow snake, 73–74
Relapse of illness, 244–45

Reproduction: abdomen as seat of, 138; men's symbolic reproduction, 4; negated by sorcery, 123; the reproductive cell, 106–15
Rhythm, 259, 260, 261, 263, 272
Ritual: autogenerative dimension of, 46; the body in ritual action, 50–51, 246, 247, 248, 252; of family unity, 99; fertility rituals, 245–54; healing ritual, 4, 252–53, 255–56, 266; knowledge in, 50; mortuary rituals, 122; puberty rituals, 245–46, 248–49; redressive effect of, 249; ritual drama, 4, 250–51, 253, 257, 266; ritual metaphor, 42–44; ritual praxis, 46–48; the ritual specialist, 251; ritual weapons, 85, 216, 309n.4; semantic-praxiological analysis of, 39–46; Turner on, 35, 36–37

Sacred house, 88
Sacrifice, 236, 270
Saliva, 272
Savanna: burning of, 82, 83; in circumcision songs, 101; and marriage, 101; menstruation associated with, 82; as transitional zone, 59; as women's milieu, 58, 59
Seasons, 81–83
Seclusion house: for circumcision, 157; hen symbolized by, 214, 236, 270; in *khita* healing, 201, 214–17; in *ngoombu* cult, 151, 152; *n-phemba* vine on, 308n.3; as outer skin of the patient, 270; plant bouquet used in, 159, 215–16, 229, 308n.3; resemblance to coffin-bundle, 308n.1; as symbol of *ngoongu*, 152, 217–18; the uninitiated and men prohibited from, 273
Seclusion period, 196, 213–45; coming-out ordeal, 231–36; end of, 211, 225, 236, 238, 273; food taboos, 220, 310n.6, 311n.14; and healing, 266; the hunt compared to seclusion, 222; and *ngoongu*, 223–24; the therapeutic group, 183
Semantic-praxiological method, 5, 40
Sexual desire, 135, 138, 168, 220
Sexual intercourse: and bodily limits, 138; celebrated in *khita* cure, 202; contraception, 303n.8; defloration, 202; incest, 129, 136; insemination, 134; and love, 142; in marriage, 110; positions of men and women, 134; during pregnancy, 303n.7; restrictions on, 96, 98; sense of smell in, 135. *See also* Extramarital sex
Shaba, 157
Shrines: contents and function of, 158; and *kataku,* 300n.5; *khoofi* shrine, 192, 193–95, 215; *yisuungu* shrine, 63
Siblings, 119
Skin, 220, 265, 270, 276
Slaves, 117
Slit gong, 163
Smell, 90, 135–36, 146, 220
Smith, Pierre, 48
Smithery, 69, 157, 158; the blacksmith, 156
Snakes, 78; rainbow snake, 73–74
Sorcery: in the agnatic line, 127; cannibal feasts and promiscuity, 91, 99, 128; color symbolism, 68; and cults of affliction, 149; and domestic kin relations, 122–31; and the forest, 88–89; and giving birth, 301n.1; and gynecological disorders, 169, 170, 172, 173; the hunter compared to the sorcerer, 88–90, 123, 130; inverting the body order, 271; *khita* healer's challenge to, 188–89; as negation of sociality and reproduction, 123; protective measures against, 130; and social disruption, 126–31; sorcerers as forest dwellers, 57, 126; as source of illness, 18; symbolism of cock crowing, 64; unmasked by a diviner, 164; and untamed forces, 86–91; in the uterine line, 126–27
Space: and bodily position, 134; cardinal points, 54–56; horizontal and vertical, 54–60; and the rainbow snake, 73–74; Yaka conception of, 53
Speaking, 140; authoritative speech, 143, 144; and palm wine, 143, 145
Suffrutex, 81, 209, 222
Suku, 181
Sun: color symbolism, 65, 66, 67; migration and settlement associated with, 119; palm tree as icon of, 61; and the rainbow snake, 73
Sun-skirt, 159
Symbols, 34–37, 250, 251, 280

Taanda, 12–13, 21, 181
Taanda N-leengi, 20, 21
Teke, 181
Termitaries: and fertility, 308n.15; in *khita*

cure, 193, 221, 222, 224; termite mounds, 60, 73–74, 307n.13
Therapeutic initiation, 224–31; and agnatic filiation, 228
Therapy. *See* Healing
Thiel, Jozef, 181
Time, 119, 134, 272; calendar, 81–83
Tio, 181
Tobacco, 135
Touch, 136
Traditional medicine, 25–33; biomedicine compared to, 29–33; defined, 23–24; and herbal medicine, 28–29; Turner on, 33–37. *See also* Cults of affliction
Trances: cults with a demonstrative trance, 149; in diviners, 163; in *khita* cure, 187, 197, 206, 207, 210, 211–12, 225; in *khosi* and *n-hwaadi* cults, 157; in *ngoombu* cult, 151, 152; paradoxical aspects of, 269; and the voice, 262–63
Transgression, 267–76
Transitional object, 273–74
Trapping, 75, 214
Trees, 79–80, 120; *m-mvuma* tree, 194, 305n.7, 310n.9; *m-mwayi* tree, 312n.19; *n-haandzi* tree, 312n.19; *n-kukubuundu* tree, 313n.19; *n-kwaati* tree, 300n.1; *n-saanda* tree, 193, 194–95; *yikuumba* tree, 313n.19; *yiseleti* tree, 194, 305n.7. *See also* Palm trees; Parasol tree
Tsaanga khita, 231, 310n.7, 313n.20
Tsiku, 169
Tsootso, 182
Tsuumbwa, 224
Turner, Victor, 7, 9, 33–37, 245–53

Untamed forces, 86–91
Uterine filiation, 14, 69, 92, 115–19; cults of affliction associated with, 148, 149–54; curses on the uterine line, 149, 170, 171, 174–76; divination associated with, 148; and gynecological disorders, 169–71, 174, 175, 177; and the individual's health and uniqueness, 119–22; and infertility, 174; and life transmission, 161; and sorcery, 126–27. See also *Mooyi*

Vansina, Jan, 180
Van Wing, Joseph, 180

Village, 116–17; forest contrasted with, 56–57; outskirts of, 58; significance to the Yaka, 16; transitional zone between village and forest, 58–60
Vines, 80–81; lianas, 80–81, 215; n-hoondasala, 310n.9
Vision, 145–46
Voice, the, 262–63

Water ordeal of transition, 232–36
Water shrew, 44, 77, 210
Weaning, 110
Weaving: dancing compared to, 72–73; and healing, 257, 258, 259, 264, 278–79; of the life force, 211; of raffia palm, 72–73, 145, 211, 278–79
Weaving-hook: collected foodstuffs attached to, 239; mock battle for, 206, 211, 225, 226; and name of the initiate's child, 241, 281; and the *phaandzi* pharmacopoeia, 230; placed under marital bed, 231; for weaving raffia fibers, 72
Werbner, Richard, 48, 249
White yam, 307n.11
Wife beating, 142
Wilson, Monica, 35
Women: abortion, 303n.8; the body and personhood in, 132; breast–feeding, 110, 113; breasts, 102, 138; confinement of, 91; and dance, 71–73; domestic role, 93–101; douches and enemas used by, 159, 168; eating of small mammals, 77; fertility and infertility in, 164–69, 179; fishing, 78; giving birth, 100, 119, 134, 301n.1; lunar cycles and female cycles, 70–73; marriage, 101–6; married life, 106–11; in masculinist fantasies, 91; menstruation, 58, 82, 138, 209, 301n.9; motherhood, 94, 100, 106, 119–21; movement patterns, 260–61; as *mwaadi,* 143; pottery making by, 63; pregnancy, 66, 103, 108–9, 220, 303n.7; puberty rituals, 245–46, 248–49; savanna activities of, 58, 59; and seniority, 142; speaking in council, 143; status of *khita* initiates, 213–14; and traditional healers, 29; wife beating, 142; wife's rights and responsibilities regarding the hunt, 123–26; women's associations, 33; women's work, 81–84, 100–101; and the *yikoolu,* 59

Index

World Health Organization (WHO), 26
Worms, 78

Yaka people, 11–20; agnatic descent in, 14, 115–22; and animals and plants, 74–86; on the body, the group, and the life-world, 132–60; colonial rule, 15; cosmology of gender arrangements and life transmission, 53–91; cults of affliction and communal sodalities, 1–4, 147–60; divination and healing in the city, 18; and economic development, 22–23; healing ritual, 253; illness viewed by, 17–18, 30, 31, 146–47; the individual viewed by, 48; Koongo, 11; location in Zaire, 297; marriage, 16, 101–6; migration to Kinshasa, 15–16; Ndembu compared to, 33–34; Northern Yaka, 11, 115, 119; population, 11, 299nn. 1, 2; social arrangements and cultural practices, 11–15; social formation of life transmission, 92–131; social identity of, 17; space conceived by, 53; uterine filiation in, 14, 115–22; view of reality, 46; the village's significance to, 16
Yibati, 96, 194

Yibwaati, 298
Yidyaata. See Intrusion
Yifiika, 115
Yifutu, 159, 218, 219
Yihalu, 187, 233, 312nn. 18, 19
Yikho gesture, 185, 186, 310n.8
Yikhookolu, 310n.8
Yikhuumba tree, 313n.19
Yikoolu, 58–59, 101
Yikubu cult, 156–57, 179
Yikula, 125
Yiludi, 84
Yimbala cult, 154
Yimbeela, 21
Yimenga, 236
Yindongu cult, 157
Yipfudila cult, 157
Yiphasi, 179
Yiseleti, 305n.7
Yisuungu shrine, 63
Yitaanda, 13, 21, 298
Yitoolu, 197

Zempléni, Andras, 265
Zoombo, 182